Life Course Research and Social Policies

Volume 12

Life course research has been developing quickly these last decades for good reasons. Life course approaches focus on essential questions about individuals' trajectories, longitudinal analyses, cross-fertilization across disciplines like life-span psychology, developmental social psychology, sociology of the life course, social demography, socio-economics, social history. Life course is also at the crossroads of several fields of specialization like family and social relationships, migration, education, professional training and employment, and health. This Series invites academic scholars to present theoretical, methodological, and empirical advances in the analysis of the life course, and to elaborate on possible implications for society and social policies applications. Topics appropriate for the series include among others: Longitudinal analyses and methods Educational and employment trajectories Occupational careers Migration Social networks and family configurations Health trajectories Non-normative events Social and individual vulnerabilities Stress over the life course Resources Accumulation of (dis) advantages and social inequalities Social mobility Personality and identity development Agency within social structures Work-family balance Social policies Volumes in this series are of interest for researchers, professionals, policy makers, and students in social sciences and related fields. Ideas and proposals for additional contributions to the Series should be sent to Laura Bernardi, Jean-Michel Bonvin, and Dario Spini, Series Editors,, Switzerland. E-mail: laura.bernardi@unil.ch. or to the publisher: Evelien Bakker, Springer Science+Business Media, P.O. Box 17, 3300 AA Dordrecht, The Netherlands. Email: Evelien.Bakker@springer.com

More information about this series at http://www.springer.com/series/10158

Michaela Kreyenfeld • Heike Trappe
Editors

Parental Life Courses after Separation and Divorce in Europe

Springer Open

Editors
Michaela Kreyenfeld
Hertie School
Berlin, Berlin, Germany

Heike Trappe
Institut für Soziologie und Demographie
Universität Rostock
Rostock, Mecklenburg-Vorpommern, Germany

ISSN 2211-7776 ISSN 2211-7784 (electronic)
Life Course Research and Social Policies
ISBN 978-3-030-44574-4 ISBN 978-3-030-44575-1 (eBook)
https://doi.org/10.1007/978-3-030-44575-1

This Springer imprint is published by the registered company Springer Nature Switzerland AG
The registered company address is: Gewerbestrasse 11, 6330 Cham, Switzerland

Preface

This book is the result of an international workshop, held in Berlin on 3–4 May 2018, on the topic of "Parental Life Courses after Separation and Divorce". The workshop brought together scholars from several European countries to present and discuss their research findings on the consequences of separation and divorce for parents' life courses. Publishing a book is never the work of the editors alone. There are many people who encouraged, helped, and supported us. Thanks go to the German Science Foundation (under Grant Number 266395921) for financing the abovementioned workshop and to the Hertie School of Governance for hosting and promoting the workshop. It was Bernadette Deelen-Mans from Springer Nature who pushed the idea of bringing the contributions of the workshop together in an edited volume. Thanks also go to Alexander James from Springer Nature who supported us in the process of producing this book. This book is made available as an open-access publication. We thank the University of Rostock and the Hertie School for their financial support of the open-access costs. Before the final book was passed to Springer Nature, a lot of hard work went into formatting and editing the texts, figures, references, and tables. We thank Annika Krömer who greatly supported us in this work. Particular thanks go to Miriam Hils who has worked with us many times before. Again, she has been a great support in the language editing and proofreading of the book. Last but not least, we thank the dedicated and disciplined authors of this volume. Without their excellent time management and responsiveness, this book would have never been finalised so quickly while still meeting high-quality standards.

Berlin, Germany
Rostock, Germany
August 2019

Michaela Kreyenfeld
Heike Trappe

Contents

Contributors

Stefanie Amberg Ludwig-Maximilians-University (LMU), Munich, Germany

Kim Bastaits PXL University of Applied Sciences and Arts, Hasselt, Belgium

Daniel Brüggmann Hertie School, Berlin, Germany

Sharon L. Christ Purdue University, West Lafayette, IN, USA

Ann-Zofie Duvander Stockholm University, Stockholm, Sweden

Tina Haux University of Kent, Kent, UK

Katya Ivanova Department of Sociology, Tilburg University, Tilburg, The Netherlands

Matthijs Kalmijn Netherlands Interdisciplinary Demographic Institute, Den Haag, The Netherlands

Katja Köppen University of Rostock, Rostock, Germany

Nicklas Korsell Swedish Social Insurance Inspectorate, Stockholm, Sweden

Michaela Kreyenfeld Hertie School, Berlin, Germany

Aušra Maslauskaitė Vytautas Magnus University, Kaunas, Lithuania

Elena Moore University of Cape Town, Cape Town, South Africa

Dimitri Mortelmans University of Antwerp, Antwerp, Belgium

Anna-Karin Nylin Stockholm University, Stockholm, Sweden

Inge Pasteels PXL University of Applied Sciences and Arts, Hasselt, Belgium

Lucinda Platt London School of Economics and Political Science, London, UK

Anke Radenacker Hertie School, Berlin, Germany

Anja Steinbach Ludwig-Maximilians-University, Duisburg, Germany

Gert Thielemans University of Antwerp, Antwerp, Belgium

Carolin Thönnissen Ludwig-Maximilians-University (LMU), Munich, Germany

Heike Trappe Institut für Soziologie und Demographie, Universität Rostock, Rostock, Mecklenburg-Vorpommern, Germany

Layla Van den Berg University of Antwerp, Antwerp, Belgium

Sabine Walper German Youth Institute and Ludwig-Maximilians-University (LMU), Munich, Germany

Part I
Economic Conditions of Divorce and Separation

Chapter 1
Introduction: Parental Life Courses After Separation and Divorce in Europe

Michaela Kreyenfeld and Heike Trappe

Introduction

Divorce rates are stagnating at high levels in most European countries. We lack fine-grained data from official sources that map divorce and, in particular, the separation rates of couples with children over time. Nevertheless, the survey data tell us that a large fraction of children experience the divorce or separation of their parents before they reach adulthood (Andersson et al. 2017). Union disruption is always a distressing event, and it is most consequential for couples with minor children. Even after their union ends, the ex-partners have to stay in contact to coordinate and negotiate their parental responsibilities. In most cases, separation and divorce mean that the family splits into separate households. While women usually continue to reside with their children, men may find it increasingly difficult to maintain close contact with their children. Little is known about how parents organise childcare responsibilities after separation and divorce, or about the conditions under which fathers remain involved in the lives of their children (Albertini and Garriga 2011; Kalmijn 2015). In addition, divorce and separation often lead to economic hardship and distress. Parents may adopt different strategies to overcome the adverse consequences of divorce and separation. "Re-partnering" and "re-employment" can be viewed as competing strategies that women may use to ameliorate the economic consequences of divorce and separation (see also Mortelmans in this volume). While this framework can be criticised for providing a simplistic view of mothers' partnership and employment choices, it nevertheless highlights the importance of employment and

M. Kreyenfeld (✉)
Hertie School, Berlin, Germany
e-mail: kreyenfeld@hertie-school.org

H. Trappe
Institut für Soziologie und Demographie, Universität Rostock,
Rostock, Mecklenburg-Vorpommern, Germany

M. Kreyenfeld, H. Trappe (eds.), *Parental Life Courses after Separation and Divorce in Europe*, Life Course Research and Social Policies 12,
https://doi.org/10.1007/978-3-030-44575-1_1

partnership transitions for parental well-being after the breakdown of a union (Jansen et al. 2009). Prior research has shown that there are gender differences in re-partnering patterns after separation and divorce (Gałęzewska et al. 2017; Ivanova et al. 2013). In addition, gender differences in the economic consequences of divorce have been examined for several countries and compared across time (Andreß et al. 2006; Popova and Navicke 2019; Raeymaeckers et al. 2008). However, most of these prior studies did not focus on parents, but instead examined all couples, regardless of whether they had minor children at the time of divorce or separation. As a consequence, we still know relatively little about the life courses of divorced and separated couples with children, at least for European countries (for the US, see, however, Cancian et al. 2014; Meyer and Carlson 2014; Musick and Michelmore 2018). The question of how the life course and gender role behaviour prior to divorce and separation affect the behaviour and well-being of mothers and fathers after the breakdown of a union also merits further investigation. Moreover, how the economic situation of parents is affected by child and spousal support payments, and whether social policies can effectively alleviate some of the economic consequences of divorce and separation, are issues that have yet to be fully addressed.

This volume seeks to close part of this research gap. The European context is an ideal laboratory for studying how political and cultural factors influence post-separation behaviour. The widely varying social policies and legal regulations that exist across European countries enable researchers to contextualise and gain a better understanding of how social policy regulations affect behaviour and parental and child well-being after divorce and separation. In this monograph, we assemble studies from a range of European countries that explore four major and interconnected themes of family life after divorce and separation. We address (a) economic conditions, (b) parent-child relationships, (c) parent and child well-being, and (d) the health-related consequences of divorce and separation. All of the studies included in this volume take a longitudinal perspective and situate post-separation behaviour and well-being in the life course. The longitudinal perspective opens up new avenues for research that seeks to understand how individuals' behaviour and conditions prior to or at the time of a divorce or separation affect their later behaviour and well-being. Before we provide an overview of the contributions of this volume, we summarise the broad trends in divorce and separation, as well as in attitudes towards divorce, in Europe. This overview must remain very general. Due to the lack of comparable data, we do not address the specific situations of unmarried couples and couples with children. Instead, we provide a broad picture of overall divorce trends.

Divorce and Separation in Europe

Divorce in Europe: A Trend Reversal or an Artefact of a Demographic Measure?

Apart from Vatican City, married couples are now legally allowed to divorce in all European countries (for an overview, see Spijker and Solsona 2012). The first European country to liberalise its divorce laws was Iceland, where divorce has been permitted since the sixteenth century. Divorce was legalised in 1791 in France and in 1794 in Luxembourg. Other European countries followed suit in the nineteenth century. Among the laggards in this trend were the southern European countries and Ireland. Divorce was not legally permitted until 1970 in Italy, until 1975 in Portugal, and until 1981 in Spain (although divorce was briefly permitted in 1934–1936 during the Second Spanish Republic). Ireland did not liberalise its divorce laws until 1995 (see chapter by Moore in this volume).[1] Although divorce is now legally permitted, the social policy context in which divorce and separation occur continues to differ strongly across European countries. A few countries still allow fault divorce, such as France and Poland. Others, such as Italy and Germany, used to mandate long separation periods before a divorce was granted. Overall, the trend towards reduced state control over marriage and divorce has changed the divorce process and the dynamics of marriages. Unilateral divorce laws shifted the balance of power towards the spouse who is more willing to exit the union. Furthermore, the shortening of the legal process as well as the abolition of fault divorce have helped to make getting divorced a faster and less conflict-ridden process than it was in the past (Härkönen 2014: 4). Changes in gender roles and in the work behaviour of women have resulted in separated parents sharing childcare duties more equally after divorce and separation. Shared physical custody is increasingly being implemented into the legal framework of some countries, while in other countries it is still the norm for one parent to be granted sole physical custody (Claessens and Mortelmans 2018).

How do divorce law and divorce behaviour relate to each other? Has the liberalisation of divorce laws resulted in higher divorce rates? Or are "high divorce countries" simply more open to enacting liberal divorce laws and gender-equal custody regulations? Efforts to compare divorce and separation behaviour across countries have, unfortunately, been greatly limited by a lack of comparable and suitable data. The only indicator that is available for (almost) all European countries for a longer time period is the crude divorce rate (CDR). The CDR divides the number of divorces in a country by its population size (multiplied by 1000). Figure 1.1 maps this measure for the years 1990, 2000, 2010, and 2017. Looking at the figure, we

[1] Most western European countries, such as Austria, Germany, Belgium, Denmark, Sweden, the Netherlands, and England and Wales, liberalised their divorce laws in the course of the nineteenth century. An exception is Scotland, which did not liberalise its divorce laws until 1976. Malta is another outlier that did not allow divorce until 2011.

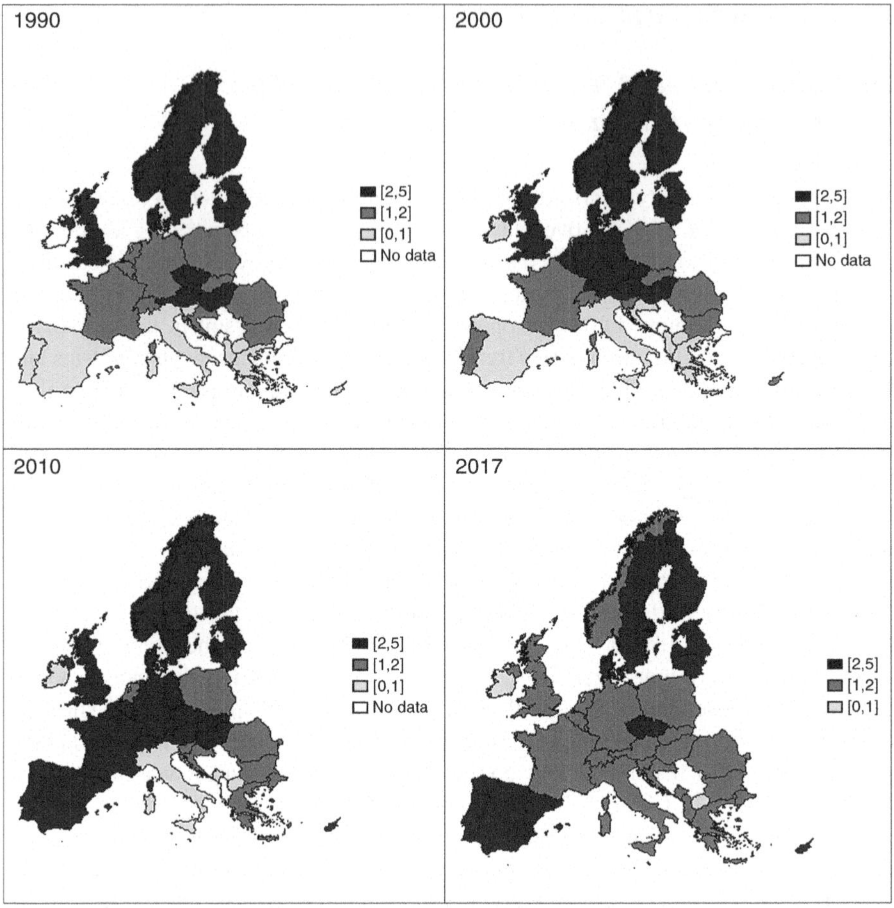

Fig. 1.1 Crude divorce rate in Europe 1990, 2000, 2010, 2017
Source: Eurostat (2019), own representation (based on the "spmap-ado" of STATA)
Notes: Only countries with valid information for 2017 are displayed. For Italy and Latvia, data for 2017 were imputed based on data from 2016. Data for Ireland for 2017 were imputed based on data from 2015

can see that in 1990, there was a regional divide characterised by high divorce rates in the Nordic countries and much lower divorce rates in southern Europe. Divorce rates were at intermediate levels in western and central and eastern European countries, except in Austria, the Czech Republic, and Hungary which had elevated CDRs. The figure also shows that by 2010, these patterns had changed, as higher divorce rates seem to have spread from northern to western Europe. This shift has been described in detail by proponents of the Second Demographic Transition Theory (SDT) who cited an increase in divorce as an "early sign" of a shift towards a more secularised society with more liberal family attitudes and family behaviour (Lesthaeghe 1983, 2010). The most recent data available from Eurostat are for 2017.

The figure indicates that by this year, cross-country differences in divorce rates seem to have narrowed. Most importantly, however, the figure shows that in many former "high divorce countries", the CDR has declined. When more refined measures such as the total divorce rate (TDR) are applied, we still find a decline or a recent levelling off in divorce intensities in certain countries, such as Denmark, Finland, Germany, the Netherlands, Norway, Portugal, Sweden, and the UK. There is considerable debate about how this decline in divorce rates should be interpreted. As fewer people marry or delay marriage until later in life, fewer people are divorcing. In addition, as those individuals who marry appear to be a selective population with more traditional views, their unions are likely to be more stable (Cohen 2019). In order to study the changes in union stability, we would need information on the duration of all unions, regardless of whether the couples are married. Unfortunately, most countries do not collect such information. Furthermore, we lack comparable information on the question of whether unions with children have become more stable over time.

Some information on the stability of unions with children is available from social science surveys. Andersson et al. (2017) used data from the Generations and Gender Survey (and related surveys) to estimate the probability of children under age 15 being affected by the dissolution of their parents' union. They found that in countries such as France, Belgium, Sweden, Austria, Estonia, Lithuania, the Czech Republic, and Hungary, about one-third of children have experienced the break-up of their parents' union. The study also reported very high parental separation probabilities of 40% for the US and Russia, and relatively low probabilities in southern European countries (such as Spain and Italy) and in Germany, where "only" around 10–20% of children have been affected by the dissolution of their parents' union. The findings of social science surveys also suggest that the relationship between education and marital stability has reversed its sign in recent years. While divorce had been more prevalent among the highly educated, the differences in divorce rates between educational groups have levelled off in recent years (Härkönen 2014). In many countries, such as Belgium, the UK, the Netherlands, and the Nordic countries, separation is now more common among the less educated than the highly educated (Matysiak et al. 2014; Van Bavel et al. 2018). There is also solid evidence that non-marital unions are less stable than marital unions, and that, in most countries, education is negatively correlated with having children in a non-marital relationship (Bennett 2017; Schnor 2014). The negative correlation between education and non-marital childbearing has sparked a debate about the effects of family change on the well-being of children. In a landmark article entitled "Diverging destinies: How children are faring under the Second Demographic Transition", McLanahan (2004) argued that the Second Demographic Transition theory (see above) had glorified the shift towards liberal attitudes, while disregarding the negative consequences that increasing rates of divorce and separation may have on the social and economic well-being of children and parents. However, comparative research has shown that social, cultural, political, and economic developments moderate the negative effects of union dissolution on parents and children (Perelli-Harris and Lyons-Amos 2016).

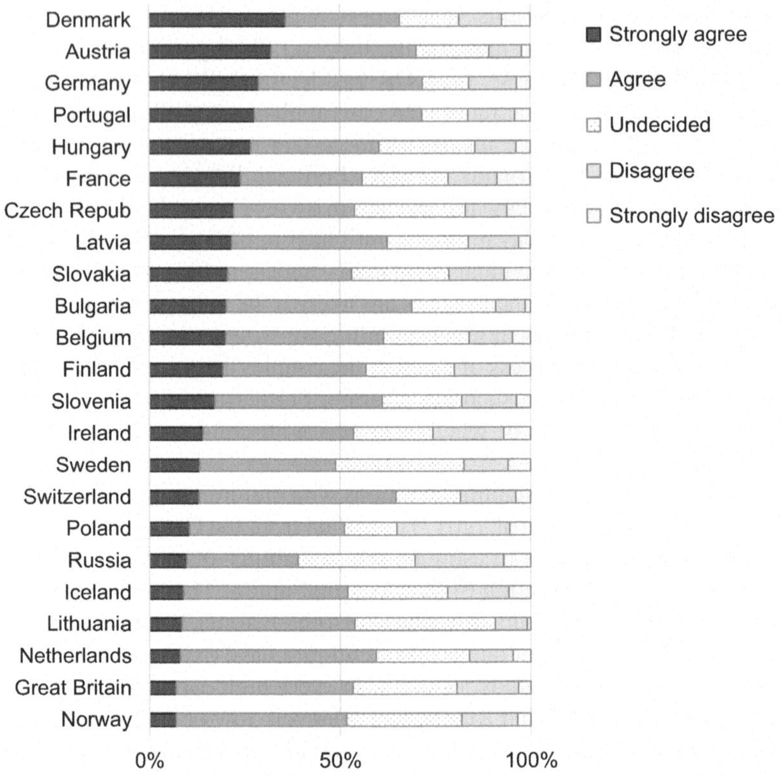

Fig. 1.2 Probability of agreeing with the statement: "*Divorce is usually the best solution when a couple can't seem to work out their marriage problems*". 2012
Source: Data come from the ISSP 2012 (ISSP Research Group, 2016)

Attitudes Towards Divorce: A Comparison of Data from 1994, 2002, and 2012

There is no longer a clear regional pattern in divorce rates, as measured by the CDR. This may be because of the many limitations of this indicator. But can we discern a clearer pattern in attitudes towards divorce across Europe? To answer this question, we employed data from the International Social Science Survey (ISSP), which collected information on family-related issues in 1994, 2002, and 2012 (ISSP Research Group 1997, 2013, 2016).[2] Figure 1.2 displays the results for the year

[2] The sample includes respondents aged 20–79 with valid information on the key variable of interest (divorce attitudes): "*Divorce is usually the best solution when a couple can't seem to work out their marriage problems*". Agreement was measured on a five-point Likert-scale with "strongly agree", "agree", "neither agree nor disagree", and "disagree strongly" as the response options. "Strongly agree" and "agree" were grouped into one category. Undecided and missing values were eliminated (except in Figure 1.2). For Spain in 2012, only a four-point scale was used; i.e., "neither agree nor disagree" was not included.

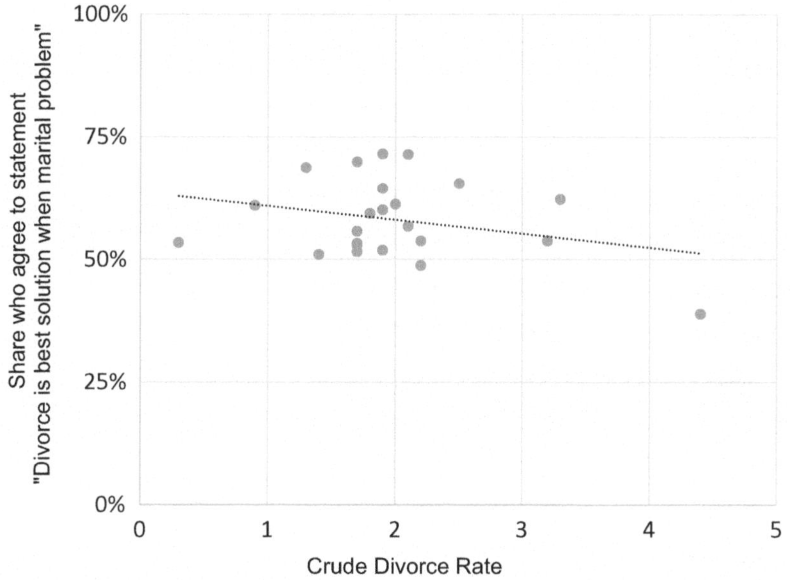

Fig. 1.3 Scatterplot of the crude divorce rate in 2012 and the share of people who agreed with the statement: "*Divorce is usually the best solution when a couple can't seem to work out their marriage problems*". 2012
Source: ISSP 2012 (weighted estimates) and Eurostat (2019)
Notes: The CDR for Russia for 2012 was imputed based on data from 2011

2012 for the item "*Divorce is usually the best solution when a couple can't seem to work out their marriage problems*". In most countries, about 50% of the population agreed or strongly agreed with that statement. However, the figure also shows that there is no clear regional pattern in responses to this question. It appears that countries that are commonly assumed to be rather traditional in their family values, such as Austria and Germany, are very open to divorce. In Sweden, the vanguard of a de-familiarised society, acceptance of divorce seems to be low. It is possible that this pattern can be attributed to differences in how the question is translated into the native language. Moreover, differences in the country-specific response patterns might have affected this comparison (Weziak-Bialowolska 2015). It is also possible that as levels of divorce have increased, public awareness of its adverse consequences is growing as well. However, the findings displayed in Fig. 1.3, in which the crude divorce rate and the attitudes towards divorce in a country are correlated, provide only slight support for this claim. The figure shows that as divorce rates increase, the share of people who agree with the statement that divorce is the best solution for a couple facing marital problems declines. However, this relationship is very much driven by Russia, where both divorce and opposition to divorce are high. Overall, attitudes towards divorce do not seem to be highly correlated with the CDR. This finding is in line with the results of a previous analysis by Rijken and

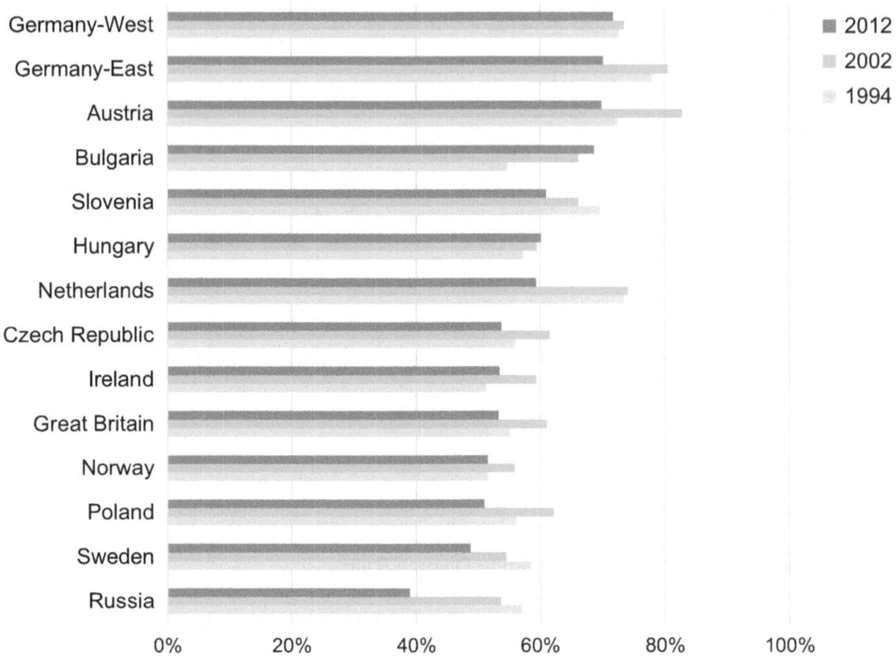

Fig. 1.4 Share of people who agree or strongly agree with the statement: "*Divorce is usually the best solution when a couple can't seem to work out their marriage problem*". 1994, 2002, 2016
Source: Data come from the ISSP 1994, 2002, 2012 (ISSP Research Group, 1997, 2013, 2016), weighted estimates. Data for Great Britain without Northern Ireland are used for 1994 and 2002

Liefbroer (2012), who correlated the CDR with attitudes towards divorce based on data from the third wave of the European Social Survey conducted in 2006/07.

To gain a better understanding of how attitudes have changed across time, we pooled the data for all available years (1994, 2002, 2012). The results for the countries that are included in all three survey years are displayed in Fig. 1.4. A comparison of the responses in the years 1994 and 2002 suggests that there was an initial liberalisation of attitudes towards divorce. However, we also see evidence of a strong backlash, with attitudes towards divorce becoming more conservative in almost all countries from 2002 to 2012. This backlash was especially pronounced in the Netherlands and Russia. Of the countries included in this comparison, West Germany, Hungary, and Bulgaria are the only countries where no major decline in acceptance of divorce occurred between 2002 and 2012. These results, which suggest that there has been a "re-traditionalisation" of divorce attitudes across Europe, are partially at odds with the conclusions of prior investigations. Halman and van Ingen (2015), who examined data from the European Value Survey 1981–2008, found that attitudes towards divorce have become more liberal in western Europe, and have not changed over time in eastern Europe. The findings of our investigations do not support the existence of an East-West divide. They neither indicate that values have become more liberal in western European countries in recent years. The differences between the outcomes of our analysis and those of the study by Halman and van Ingen (2015) may be attributable to differences in the observation periods used; i.e., our data go up to 2012, while their data only go up to 2008. Furthermore, the investigation by Halman and van Ingen (2015) modelled the linear effects of calendar time in a regression framework. Our investigation is more descriptive, but shows that there has been a non-linear development. It thus appears that although attitudes towards divorce had become more liberal by the turn of the century, there has been a backlash in recent years. These findings stand in stark contrast to widely held predictions, in particular of the Second Demographic Transition, that there would be a steady liberalisation of family values in advanced economies.

Summary of the Contributions in this Volume

This book is structured to enable us to focus on four main areas: namely, economic conditions, parent-child relationships, parental and child well-being, and health. *Dimitri Mortelmans* (University of Antwerp, Belgium) introduces the section on the economic consequences of divorce and separation (Part I) with a review of the prior findings. His overview discusses the different "coping strategies" that parents adopt to overcome the adverse economic effects of divorce and separation. It is an established finding that after union dissolution, a woman's equalised household income is likely to decline more sharply than a man's. While many women leave the labour market or reduce their working hours after having a child, undergoing a separation or divorce may prompt them to expand their labour supply. Re-partnering is often seen as an alternative strategy for improving the economic well-being of the household. Mortelmans points out that returning to the parental home is yet another potential reaction to the dissolution of a union, but notes that we currently know little about the "boomeranging" of parents who return to their own parent's household after a union dissolution. Another gap in the literature pertains to the role of social policies in ameliorating the economic consequences of divorce and separation. Mortelmans explains that the gendered consequences of divorce vary radically depending on the welfare state arrangements, particularly with regard to childcare availability and women's options for working. He emphasises, however, that we currently know relatively little about how the different policy instruments (ex-spousal maintenance, child alimony, social benefits, etc.) affect parents' coping strategies after a union dissolution, or the economic well-being of families.

Anna-Karin Nylin (Stockholm University, Sweden) uses rich Swedish register data to focus on employment as a strategy for coping with the decline in equalised income after divorce and separation. She makes the argument that divorce and separation may be beneficial for the development of earnings. As partnered women frequently reduce their working hours or withdraw from the labour market after having a child, their human capital can decay. Conversely, separated women are often pushed into the labour market. If these women remain attached to the labour market, they could have more stable and positive earnings trajectories over the long term. While the argument is compelling, Nylin refutes this hypothesis based on her data. She reports that the earnings developments of separated and partnered women with children are very similar, and that 8 years after a separation, the earnings of separated mothers even lag behind those of partnered women with children. Her findings further indicate that this pattern is particularly pronounced among women in the lowest earning brackets. Nylin concludes her investigation with a discussion of the direction of Swedish family policies. Swedish family policies are often regarded as a template for other countries, as they rigorously adhere to the ideal of gender equality in the labour market. Promoting full-time employment is seen as the most effective policy for shielding families from poverty. Her investigation suggests that this strategy may be successful for the majority of the population, but that there are subgroups in the lower earnings brackets who may have difficulties establishing themselves in the labour market. She warns that separation and divorce may represent an additional risk factor for this particular group.

Anke Radenacker (Hertie School, Germany) also draws on rich administrative data to examine mothers' earnings trajectories after divorce. Her data include divorced women in western Germany. Unlike Sweden, (West) Germany has until very recently been classified as a conservative welfare state. While rates of part-time employment have been rising, women's options for full-time employment have been greatly constrained by the restricted opening hours of day care centres as well as by the traditional view that the mother should be solely responsible for caring for her children in the first years of life. Many married women withdraw completely from the labour market after childbirth or work in marginal or part-time positions. She shows that maternal employment rates have been increasing among recent divorce cohorts, and especially among those cohorts who were affected by the change in the maintenance law in 2008, which scaled back ex-spousal maintenance payments. She also observes that a woman's employment and earnings trajectories during her marriage tend to determine her employment and earnings after her divorce. Radenacker emphasises, however, that these results must be contextualised. Unlike in Sweden, there is considerable potential for women in Germany to increase their working hours after a divorce given their low employment rates during marriage. She also reports that even though divorce pushes women towards economic independence, women's earnings lag far behind those of men: i.e., on average, women in Germany earn only 40% of men's earnings after a divorce. These findings stand in stark contrast to the Swedish results outlined above.

While Nylin and Radenacker examine how parents use increased employment and earnings to deal with the adverse effects of divorce and separation, the next paper highlights a different coping mode. *Dimitri Mortelmans, Layla Van den Berg, and Gert Thielemans* (all University of Antwerp, Belgium) focus on the return to the parental home as a strategy parents use to ameliorate the adverse effects of divorce and separation. Like the studies mentioned above, the investigation relies on large-scale register data. The main result of this investigation is that these patterns are highly gendered, with fathers being more likely than mothers to return to the parental home after union dissolution. A potential explanation for this finding is that women are more likely than men to be living with their children after separation, which makes moving into their parents' home a more complex proposition. They also find that parents on welfare are less likely to use this coping strategy, possibly because they may no longer qualify for means-tested benefits if they move in with their own parents. The authors also look at differences in these patterns by migration background. They find that while there are hardly any differences between individuals with Moroccan and Belgian citizenship, Turkish nationals stand out as having a high probability of returning to the parental home. Overall, the paper demonstrates that in order to understand these patterns, welfare state incentives and cultural factors must be taken into account.

The section on parent-child relationships (Part II) starts with a contribution by *Ann-Zofie Duvander* (Stockholm University, Sweden) and *Nicklas Korsell* (Swedish Inspectorate of the Social Insurance, Sweden). Based on Swedish register data, the authors examine the question of whether separating can lead couples to share their parental leave more equally. Sweden has adopted a very flexible parental leave system that allows parents to take leave from work to care for their children until the children reach age eight. As some couples split up before their children have reached that age, it is possible to analyse how separation affects the use of leave by parents. The authors assume that separation could lead to a more gender-equal sharing of parental leave. The results of the investigation do not, however, support this hypothesis. The most important finding is that separation causes both fathers and mothers to take less leave. This is probably because economic constraints and career considerations make it less likely that separated parents will claim all of their leave benefits. The authors therefore conclude that the children of separated parents are at a disadvantage, as they are less likely than other children to enjoy spending time with both of their parents.

Elena Moore (University of Cape Town, South Africa) contributes a qualitative case study on Ireland, one of the last countries in Europe to legalise divorce. She notes that although divorce is now legal in Ireland, couples still face onerous legal restrictions, such as a required separation period of 4 years preceding the divorce. Moore draws on qualitative longitudinal interview data from separated and divorced parents and examines how the emotional experience of divorce is shaped by the particular social context. Her study reveals how feelings of fear can arise in response to structural inequalities that are rooted in a legal system that creates uncertainties for both parents. While fathers fear a loss of access to their children during the prolonged separation period, mothers fear a loss of power in making parenting decisions. Moore shows how parents "manage" their fears by working with their ex-spouse to develop new ways of parenting.

The chapter by *Tina Haux* (University of Kent, UK) and *Lucinda Platt* (London School of Economics and Political Science, UK) addresses the particular role of mothers after union dissolution by investigating whether they report feeling less confident in their parenting efficacy, and, if so, how long this perception lasts. Haux and Platt analyse prospectively collected data on more than 10,000 mothers from the Millennium Cohort Study, a large representative study of children born in the UK in 2000–2001. Each of these mothers was living with the child's father when the child was around 9 months old, and was followed until the child was around 7 years old. While the authors observe no initial difference in levels of parenting competence, they find that among the 17% of mothers who ever separated, their confidence in their parenting declines more than that of non-separated mothers. Even though parenting confidence increases in both groups as the children grow older, separated mothers' perceived parenting competence remains lower than that of coupled mothers. The greater involvement of non-resident fathers does not seem to change this pattern. These findings suggest that the impact of separation on mothers' parenting confidence is long-lasting, given that at least in the current societal context of the UK, a mother who separates has to re-conceive her role as that of a sole parent, and has to deal with widespread negative social perceptions of single mothers.

The last chapter in the section on parent-child relations focuses on the co-parenting of ex-partners and its influence on non-resident fathers' contact with their children. *Sabine Walper* (German Youth Institute and Ludwig-Maximilians-University of Munich, Germany), *Stefanie Amberg, Carolin Thönnissen* (both Ludwig-Maximilians-University of Munich, Germany), and *Sharol L. Christ* (German Youth Institute, Germany and Purdue University, USA) investigate different features of maternal gatekeeping after union dissolution, addressing its predictors as well as its effects on father-child contact in Germany. The authors assume that co-parenting problems are an important mediator in the reduction in father-child contact that is often observed after a separation. They test their analytic model based on two different datasets: an intervention study that targets a broad range of separated parents (KiB), and the German Family Panel (pairfam). Overall, their findings paint a more nuanced picture of maternal gatekeeping than the image that is often found in the literature. They show that for mothers in particular, having a negative view of the other parent is linked to higher levels of co-parenting conflict, more child-related worries, and the father having less frequent contact with their children. The authors thus conclude that when the mother has an unfavourable view of the father, she is often less willing to facilitate father-child contact. For other features of maternal gatekeeping, such as protective gatekeeping, the analysis finds only limited support. Noting that only a small amount of the variance in father-child contact can be explained by the indicators measuring the quality of co-parenting, the authors suggest that other factors might be more powerful in shaping the frequency of father-child contact.

The book's next section is devoted to the well-being of parents and children after union dissolution. It starts with a chapter by *Inge Pasteels and Kim Bastaits* (both PXL University of Applied Sciences and Arts, Belgium) that takes the children's perspective into account. Based on data of the multi-actor study Divorce in Flanders (conducted in 2009–2010), the authors investigate feelings of loneliness in relation to different residential arrangements among children between the ages of 10 and 17. Given that in Belgium joint physical custody after a divorce has been the rule rather than the exception since 2006, the authors are able to compare the emotional well-being of children in joint physical custody and in other living arrangements. Their empirical evidence suggests that children's feelings of loneliness are not strongly associated with their living arrangements, but also that children report greater feelings of loneliness if their father has multiple post-divorce relationships or if their mother has a new co-residing partner. Overall, the results underline the importance of distinguishing conceptually between different indicators of emotional well-being, such as feelings of loneliness, self-esteem, life satisfaction, and depression.

Aušra Maslauskaitė (Vytautas Magnus University, Lithuania) and *Anja Steinbach* (University of Duisburg-Essen, Germany) focus in their chapter on fathers' well-being after union dissolution. Using data from the cross-sectional survey Fathering after Union Dissolution, which was conducted in Lithuania in 2016, they study the extent to which fathers' involvement with their non-resident minor children and the quality of the co-parenting relationship are associated with fathers' psychological well-being. They find that the self-assessed quality of the father's relationship with his child is the most important factor contributing to paternal well-being: i.e., the better the perceived quality of the father-child relationship is, the lower the level of depressive feelings and the higher the level of general life satisfaction the father reports. In addition, they show that while re-partnering has a strong positive impact on fathers' emotional well-being, the frequency of father-child contact and the quality of the co-parenting relationship does not. The authors conclude by observing that the relationship between paternal involvement and well-being is complex.

Katja Köppen (University of Rostock, Germany), *Michaela Kreyenfeld* (Hertie School, Germany), and *Heike Trappe* (University of Rostock, Germany) scrutinise the "gendered realities" argument, which asserts that after separation, the well-being of mothers and fathers is shaped in different ways. While mothers tend to suffer from a loss of income, fathers often face reduced contact with their children. Using 10 years of panel data from the German Family Panel (pairfam), the authors confirm previous findings indicating that following a separation, satisfaction with family life declines more among fathers than among mothers, and that mothers tend to report a greater reduction in their satisfaction with their household's financial situation than fathers. They also show that, contrary to expectations, physical custody arrangements are only weakly associated with parental well-being. Whether parents practise shared parenting is not shown to positively or negatively influence their well-being. Instead, being employed is found to be the decisive factor in parents' satisfaction with their household's financial situation. Again, it emerges that re-partnering has a large positive impact not only on the father's but also on the mother's well-being. The authors discuss the lack of a clear concept of shared parenting in the social sciences and its consequences for operational definitions, which might, in turn, influence the empirical results.

The concluding section of the book deals with the health-related implications of divorce and separation. *Katya Ivanova* (Tilburg University, the Netherlands) and *Matthijs Kalmijn* (University of Amsterdam, the Netherlands) turn their attention to young Dutch adults between 25 and 35 years of age. Based on data from the OKiN survey (Parents and Children in the Netherlands), they focus on self-reported depressive feelings by young adults, and examine whether these feelings are associated with family instability experienced during childhood. In particular, the authors investigate whether having experienced a parental separation or having lived with a stepparent in childhood are related to mental health later on. In addition, they look at whether parental union dissolution and living in a stepfamily are only detrimental in cases of conflict, either between the respondent's separated parents or between the respondent and the stepparent. In line with previous research, they find that parental union dissolution has long-term effects on the children involved, as it increases their level of depressive symptoms. Furthermore, their findings clearly underline the role conflict plays in the association between family turmoil during childhood and maladjustment in adulthood, providing support for the "good divorce" and the "good stepparent" hypotheses. The authors conclude that having experienced parental separation is associated with an increase in depressive symptoms only for those young women and men who were exposed to heightened post-separation conflict between their parents, and that having lived with a stepparent is only detrimental in cases of high levels of stepparent-child conflict.

Daniel Brüggmann (Hertie School, Germany) uses rich linked administrative data from the statutory German pension system to study the relationship between divorce and work disability in West Germany, and thus also focuses on long-term health issues. He compares women and men over a period of 7 years before and 4 years after a divorce. To isolate the impact of divorce on the uptake of work disability, the divorcees are matched with a comparable control group of individuals who did not undergo divorce. In Germany, work disability is defined as sick leave that is taken after 6 weeks of illness. Thus, individuals on work disability leave are unable to fully participate in the labour market and often lack access to secure income. The empirical evidence shows that the health of divorcees declines considerably around the time of separation, and that their risk of claiming work disability is strongly elevated even 4 years after a divorce. On average, women's post-divorce health status is found to recover more quickly than that of men. The chapter also points to the importance of selection and reversed causality. The health status of the divorcees had been lower than that of the control group in the period preceding the divorce. Thus, poor health may be not just a consequence, but a cause of increased divorce risk.

Conclusions and Possible Avenues for Future Research

This volume focused on the effects of union dissolution on parents. Union dissolution is a major "life course risk" (Vandecasteele 2011: 249) that affects parents' economic and social well-being, employment and earnings, health, and parenting behaviour. However, context matters. Social policies can buffer families against some of the adverse consequences of union dissolution (Diewald 2016; DiPrete 2002). Prior work has emphasised the role of work-family policies in the economic well-being of separated parents. More recently, scholars have stressed that the legal frameworks and the corresponding policies that regulate physical custody arrangements for children are increasingly affecting parents' economic and social well-being. Despite some modest efforts by the European Union to provide guidelines for harmonised regulations, post-separation policies still vary widely across European countries. On the one hand, Europe seems to be an ideal laboratory for researchers who are interested in investigating the effects of post-separation policies. On the other hand, we still lack a comparable and comprehensive European database that maps post-separation policies. Indeed, there is not even a common definition of shared physical custody across countries. Thus, it would be beyond the scope of such a volume to claim that the European experience can be used to distinguish clear-cut policy effects. The contribution of this volume is more modest. It brings together novel research on how separation and divorce influence different life course domains of parents in selected European countries, allowing us to contextualise the findings. There is ample evidence that within societies, the life course implications of a union dissolution depend strongly on an individual's social position with respect to, for instance, gender, education, and social class; and can therefore lead to cumulative disadvantages for particularly vulnerable groups (Leopold 2018; Popova and Navicke 2019; Vandecasteele 2011). This volume also sheds light on how social, cultural, and legal conditions within societies shape parental life courses after family dissolution, and highlights the potential ramifications of these patterns for social stratification.

We have included only a few countries in this study: namely, Belgium, Germany, Ireland, Lithuania, the Netherlands, Sweden, and the UK. Yet the contributions on even this small number of countries demonstrate the variety of policy regulations, parenting practices, and living arrangements that exist among divorced and separated parents across Europe. The studies also illustrate that divorce and separation "operate" in context-specific ways. For example, divorce seems to push women in Germany into the labour market, facilitating their economic independence and long-term labour market integration (see the chapter by Radenacker in this volume). In Sweden, by contrast, female employment rates are generally high. Thus, divorce and separation do not affect women's employment decisions to the same extent in Sweden as they do in Germany. Nylin (in this volume) even finds that the earnings trajectories of separated mothers in Sweden are not as steep as those of partnered mothers. Although the earnings of separated mothers are, overall, more favourable in Sweden than in Germany, there are particular groups of mothers in Sweden who have a low earnings potential, and for whom a separation represents a severe life course risk.

Shared parenting is another area that seems highly context-specific. This arrangement is now widespread in several European countries, including Sweden and Belgium. But in other countries where shared parenting is not yet common, such as Germany and Ireland, co-parenting after divorce and separation can place significant pressure on parents (see the chapters by Köppen et al.; Moore; Walper et al. in this volume). Cherlin (1978) once characterised the stepfamily as an "incomplete institution" due to the lack of normative prescriptions about how such families should act. The same can be said of co-parenting today. Several countries lack a legal framework that regulates co-parenting, and, above all, these countries lack a culture that fosters positive communication between ex-partners. The role of fathers has been changing in recent years, and fathers increasingly want to stay involved in their children's lives beyond separation. However, negotiating parental and care responsibilities after separation and divorce can be burdensome and challenging for ex-partners, especially in countries where shared parenting is still uncommon (see also Steinbach 2019).

Almost all of the contributions in this volume emphasise that in order to understand post-separation behaviour, it is important to consider the life course, and, thus, the role of path dependency. While we have some insight into how early life conditions affect health and well-being after divorce and separation (e.g., chapters by Brüggmann; Ivanova and Kalmijn in this volume), some related questions have yet to be examined. For example, does a father's level of involvement in childcare prior to separation correspond to his level of engagement in his children's lives after the break-up? Is a father who had previously taken parental leave more likely than other fathers to ask for joint physical custody? Or is the likelihood of seeking joint physical custody unrelated to a father's level of involvement before the break-up? While it is important for family counsellors, family law professionals, and policy-makers to be able to provide reliable information about these issues and to answer questions of this kind, the comprehensive life course data that would be needed to do so are rarely available (for an exception, see, e.g., Poortman 2018).

The contributions that are assembled in this volume use high-quality data drawn from small and large surveys, administrative data, and in-depth interviews to depict how parents and children fare after divorce and separation in a broad range of European countries. Unfortunately, a direct comparison across countries was often not possible because the population included in the different types of datasets differed. A particular problem was that some datasets cover only divorcees, while others also cover ex-partners who had not been married. Landmark studies like "Divorce in Flanders" include only divorcees (e.g., Pasteels and Bastaits in this volume). Nordic register data enable researchers to identify the dissolution of a non-marital union (e.g., Nylin in this volume), but register data for Germany and Belgium cover only divorcees (e.g., Mortelmans et al.; Radenacker in this volume). As marriage rates decline and ratios of non-marital childbearing rise, investigations that focus on divorcees only are becoming increasingly selected. Thus, there appears to be a consensus that future research should focus on union instability instead of divorce. This premise is reflected in recent family surveys that are designed to collect complete union histories (e.g., Ivanova and Kalmijn in this volume). However, the terminology surrounding union dissolution seems to be more "sticky". The main network of European research in this area is the "Divorce Network", which hosts an annual "Divorce Conference". Most of the studies conducted under the heading of "divorce research" are on the causes and consequences of union (in)stability. Thus, it seems high time to reflect that reality through a change in terminology.

Acknowledgments We thank the German Science Foundation under the Grant Agreement (under Grant Number 266395921) for supporting our research.

References

Albertini, M., & Garriga, A. (2011). The effect of divorce on parent-child contacts: Evidence on two declining effect hypotheses. *European Societies, 13*(2), 257–278. https://doi.org/10.1080/14616696.2010.483002.

Andersson, G., Thomson, E., & Duntava, A. (2017). Life-table representations of family dynamics in the 21st century. *Demographic Research, 37*(35), 1081–1230. https://doi.org/10.4054/DemRes.2017.37.35.

Andreß, H.-J., Borgloh, B., Brockel, M., Giesselmann, M., & Hummelsheim, D. (2006). The economic consequences of partnership dissolution: A comparative analysis of panel studies from Belgium, Germany, Great Britain, Italy, and Sweden. *European Sociological Review, 22*(5), 533–560. https://doi.org/10.1093/esr/jcl012.

Bennett, N. G. (2017). A reflection on the changing dynamics of union formation and dissolution. *Demographic Research, 36*(12), 371–390. https://doi.org/10.4054/DemRes.2017.36.12.

Cancian, M., Meyer, D. R., Brown, P. R., & Cook, S. T. (2014). Who gets custody now? Dramatic changes in children's living arrangements after divorce. *Demography, 51*(4), 1381–1396. https://doi.org/10.1007/s13524-014-0307-8.

Cherlin, A. J. (1978). Remarriage as an incomplete institution. *American Journal of Sociology, 84*(3), 634–650. https://doi.org/10.1086/226830.

Claessens, E., & Mortelmans, D. (2018). Challenges for child support schemes: Accounting for shared care and complex families. *Journal of European Social Policy, 28*(3), 211–223. https://doi.org/10.1177/0958928717753592.

Cohen, P. N. (2019). The coming divorce decline. *Socius: Sociological Research for a Dynamic World, 5*. https://doi.org/10.1177/2378023119873497.

Diewald, M. (2016). Life course risks and welfare states' risk management. In M. J. Shanahan, J. T. Mortimer, & M. Kirkpatrick Johnson (Eds.), *Handbook of the life course* (pp. 677–687). Cham: Springer.

DiPrete, T. A. (2002). Life course risks, mobility regimes, and mobility consequences: A comparison of Sweden, Germany, and the United States. *American Journal of Sociology, 108*(2), 267–309. https://www.jstor.org/stable/10.1086/344811.

Eurostat. (2019). Divorce indicators [demo_ndivind]. https://ec.europa.eu/eurostat/data/database.

Gałęzewska, P., Perelli-Harris, B., & Berrington, A. (2017). Cross-national differences in women's repartnering behaviour in Europe: The role of individual demographic characteristics. *Demographic Research, 37*(8), 189–228. https://doi.org/10.4054/DemRes.2017.37.8.

Halman, L., & van Ingen, E. (2015). Secularization and changing moral views: European trends in church attendance and views on homosexuality, divorce, abortion, and euthanasia. *European Sociological Review, 31*(5), 616–627. https://doi.org/10.1093/esr/jcv064.

Härkönen, J. (2014). Solomonic choices: Parental separation, child well-being and family policies in Europe. *European Policy Brief 1*. http://www.familiesandsocieties.eu/wp-content/uploads/2014/12/EuropeanPolicyBrief1_FamiliesAndSocieties.pdf

ISSP Research Group. (1997). *International social survey programme: Family and changing gender roles II – ISSP 1994. GESIS Data Archive, Cologne. ZA2620 Data file Version 1.0.0.* https://doi.org/10.4232/1.2620.

ISSP Research Group. (2013). *International social survey programme: Family and changing gender roles III – ISSP 2002. GESIS Data Archive, Cologne. ZA3880 Data file Version 1.1.0.* https://doi.org/10.4232/1.11564.

ISSP Research Group. (2016). *International social survey programme: Family and changing gender roles IV. ISSP 2012. GESIS Data Archive, Cologne. ZA5900 Data file Version 4.0.0.* doi:https://doi.org/10.4232/1.12661.

Ivanova, K., Kalmijn, M., & Uunk, W. (2013). The effect of children on men's and women's chances of re-partnering in a European context. *European Journal of Population, 49*(4), 417–444. https://doi.org/10.1007/s10680-013-9294-5.

Jansen, M., Mortelmans, D., & Snoeckx, L. (2009). Repartnering and (re)employment: Strategies to cope with the economic consequences of partnership dissolution. *Journal of Marriage and Family, 71*(5), 1271–1293. https://doi.org/10.1111/j.1741-3737.2009.00668.x.

Kalmijn, M. (2015). Father-child relations after divorce in four European countries: Patterns and determinants. *Comparative Population Studies – Zeitschrift für Bevölkerungsforschung, 40*(3), 251–276. https://doi.org/10.12765/CPoS-2015-10en.

Leopold, T. (2018). Gender differences in the consequences of divorce: A study of multiple outcomes. *Demography, 55*(3), 769–797. https://doi.org/10.1007/s13524-018-0667-6.

Lesthaeghe, R. (1983). A century of demographic and cultural change in Western Europe: An exploration of underlying dimensions. *Population and Development Review, 9*(3), 411–435.

Lesthaeghe, R. (2010). The unfolding story of the second demographic transition. *Population and Development Review, 36*(2), 211–251. https://doi.org/10.1111/j.1728-4457.2010.00328.x.

Matysiak, A., Styrc, M., & Vignoli, D. (2014). The educational gradient in marital disruption: A meta-analysis of European research findings. *Population Studies, 68*(2), 197–215. https://doi.org/10.1080/00324728.2013.856459.

McLanahan, S. (2004). Diverging destinies: How children are faring under the second demographic transition. *Demography, 41*(4), 607–627. https://doi.org/10.1353/dem.2004.0033.

Meyer, D. R., & Carlson, M. J. (2014). Family complexity: Implications for policy and research. *The Annals of the American Academy of Political and Social Science, 654*(1), 259–276. https://doi.org/10.1177/0002716214531385.

Musick, K., & Michelmore, K. (2018). Cross-national comparisons of union stability in cohabiting and married families with children. *Demography, 55*(4), 1389–1421. https://doi.org/10.1007/s13524-018-0683-6.

Perelli-Harris, B., & Lyons-Amos, M. (2016). Partnership patterns in the United States and across Europe: The role of education and country context. *Social Forces, 95*(1), 251–282. https://doi.org/10.1093/sf/sow054.

Poortman, A.-R. (2018). Postdivorce parent-child contact and child well-being: The importance of predivorce parental involvement. *Journal of Marriage and Family, 80*(3), 671–683. https://doi.org/10.1111/jomf.12474.

Popova, D., & Navicke, J. (2019). The probability of poverty for mothers after childbirth and divorce in Europe: The role of social stratification and tax-benefit policies. *Social Science Research, 78*(1), 57–70. https://doi.org/10.1016/j.ssresearch.2018.10.007.

Raeymaeckers, P., Dewilde, C., Snoeckx, L., & Mortelmans, D. (2008). Childcare strategies of divorced mothers in Europe: A comparative analysis. *European Sociological Review, 24*(1), 115–131. https://doi.org/10.1093/esr/jcm040.

Rijken, A., & Liefbroer, A. (2012). European views of divorce among parents of young children: Understanding cross-national variation. *Demographic Research, 27*(2), 25–52. https://doi.org/10.4054/DemRes.2012.27.2.

Schnor, C. (2014). *The contexts of partnership and childbearing as determinants of union stability: A quantitative analysis on western and eastern German partnerships with data from the German Family Panel*. Rostock: Max Planck Institute for Demographic Research: https://www.demogr.mpg.de/en/projects_publications/publications_1904/dissertations/the_contexts_of_partnership_and_childbearing_as_determinants_of_union_stability_a_quantitative_5344.htm. Accessed 19 Aug 2019.

Spijker, J., & Solsona, M. (2012). *Atlas of divorce and post-divorce indicators in Europe* (Papers de Demografia 412). Universitat Autònoma de Barcelona (Spain): https://docs.google.com/file/d/0B5AdSqP9auWvTmg4RnJTMGRtMUE/edit. Accessed 20 July 2019.

Steinbach, A. (2019). Children's and parents' well-being in joint physical custody: A literature review. *Family Process, 58*(2), 353–369. https://doi.org/10.1111/famp.12372.

Van Bavel, J., Schwartz, C. R., & Esteve, A. (2018). The reversal of the gender gap in education and its consequences for family life. *Annual Review of Sociology, 44*, 341–360. https://doi.org/10.1146/annurev-soc-073117-041215.

Vandecasteele, L. (2011). Life course risks or cumulative disadvantage? The structuring effect of social stratification determinants and life course events on poverty transitions in Europe. *European Sociological Review, 27*(2), 246–263. https://doi.org/10.1093/esr/jcq005.

Weziak-Bialowolska, D. (2015). Differences in gender norms between countries: Are they valid? The issue of measurement invariance. *European Journal of Population, 31*(1), 51–76. https://doi.org/10.1007/s10680-014-9329-6.

Chapter 2
Economic Consequences of Divorce: A Review

Dimitri Mortelmans

Introduction

In the social sciences, empirical results are often inconclusive or contradictory, as different studies may, for example, use different concepts, measurements that are more or less sophisticated, or data that are not completely comparable. In this chapter, we look at an exception to this prevailing pattern. This review article tells the story of the financial consequences of relationship break-ups. As will become clear throughout the chapter, one central finding dominates the research on this topic: namely, that in financial terms, women suffer more than men from a break-up. There are, of course, many nuances to this general finding. For example, as McManus and DiPrete (2001) have pointed out, it is a myth to think that men never lose financially from a divorce.

Previous research on the consequences of divorce has primarily focused on how children are affected by marital dissolution and partnership breakdown. In their review article, Amato and Keith (1991) identified no less than 15 different areas of life in which children are affected by divorce (e.g., conduct, academic achievement, parent-child relationships, social adjustment). For adults, similar domains, such as social networks, loneliness, or health, have also been studied (Mortelmans 2019). The economic situation of an individual after a divorce is key, because it affects other domains of the person's life course, and particularly his/her health and wellbeing. Financial difficulties following the end of a relationship are attributable not only to a loss of economies of scale. Indeed, money problems in the wake of a break-up may be caused by many other challenges in the personal lives of the ex-partners, and of their family members and friends.

D. Mortelmans (✉)
University of Antwerp, Antwerp, Belgium
e-mail: dimitri.mortelmans@uantwerpen.be

M. Kreyenfeld, H. Trappe (eds.), *Parental Life Courses after Separation and Divorce in Europe*, Life Course Research and Social Policies 12,
https://doi.org/10.1007/978-3-030-44575-1_2

In this chapter, we first examine the magnitude of the financial consequences of divorce. Many authors have produced estimates of the decrease in income after relationship dissolution. Despite the overall gendered conclusions in all of these studies, we will map the difficulties that can arise when investigating these income trajectories. Next, we will focus on coping strategies. When confronted with financial losses, it is unrealistic to assume that people will react passively. Instead, people tend to develop strategies for coping with these losses in an effort to regain their pre-break-up income levels. Finally, we will look at the financial consequences of lone parenthood. Even though divorcees with and without children face financial losses, most studies have found that the presence of children places additional financial burdens on the ex-partners, and particularly on the mother, who usually continues to live with the children.

It's the Measurement, Stupid!

Although all of the results on the financial consequences of union dissolution point in the same direction, the findings regarding the magnitude of the financial drawbacks of divorce for women (and for men) differ substantially. Studies have found differences both between and within countries, and across time. To gain more insight into the financial consequences of relationship dissolution, we need to take these differences into account. Thus, before we can tackle the actual percentages of income lost (or gained) presented in these results, we must address some methodological issues.

The first issue that we need to clear up is what kind of *event* are we looking at. Most studies simply consider the functional end of the relationship – i.e., the point at which the partners are no longer living together – as the event to be studied (for an overview, see: Andreß et al. 2006; McKeever and Wolfinger 2001). For marriages, we found no study that took the actual legal divorce as the turning point when studying the financial consequences of the break-up, as legal procedures can take a long time in many countries. For this reason, the actual split of the household is considered a more realistic and common point of reference. A similar approach is used in studies that include cohabitations. From the earliest study onwards (Avellar and Smock 2005), the split of a cohabiting relationship has been understood to represent the end of the relationship. Even when couples are legally cohabiting (in those countries where this is possible), the same conceptualisation is used as the point of divorce. Thus, when we use the term divorce in this chapter, we are actually referring to the split of the household (i.e., the point at which the two partners stop living together), and never to the legal reality that accompanies this process. As a side note, most studies that rely on longitudinal data use a yearly measurement of the household composition, which implies that splitting up in January or in December is considered as the same event.

A second issue that must be addressed is the way in which income is measured. Most studies use data on household income, rather than on individual income. The reasoning behind this approach is that it makes more sense to get an estimate of disposable income, rather than of earnings from labour (van Damme et al. 2009). The household income is composed of all financial contributions from all household members both before and after the break-up. Generally included are income from labour, assets, and public and private transfers (including child and spousal support); while taxes and payable maintenance expenses are deducted (Andreß et al. 2006; Bayaz-Ozturk et al. 2018). In some cases, split analyses are done on income components derived from public transfers (e.g., welfare support), and from private sources such as labour (de Vaus et al. 2017). When register data are used, the measurement of household income usually relies on more restricted information, as child maintenance transfers or assets are often not available in administrative data. In this case, household income is usually defined as the sum of social security-based income sources, such as labour income and welfare benefits (de Regt et al. 2012; Tamborini et al. 2015).

There are clear financial benefits for couples who live together, as certain expenses can be shared (housing, food, etc.). Additionally, the added cost of living for an extra person in the household is lower than the original cost. These economies of scale are lost after a break-up, and need to be taken into account when looking at the income trajectories before and after the dissolution. This is why most studies do not simply use household income, but instead use equivalized household income to measure the income levels of ex-partners. In this measurement approach, the total household income is equivalised based on the composition of the household (Atkinson et al. 1995). Two types of equivalence scales are commonly found in the literature. The first is the OECD modified equivalence scale (Förster 2007), which uses a unity weight for the first adult and a weight of 0.5 for each additional adult. Children are weighted with a value of 0.3. This scale was created by Hagenaars et al. (1994), and was adopted by the OECD and Eurostat. The second is the Square Root Scale, which simply divides the household income by the square root of household size. The difference between these scales is expressed as "equivalence elasticity" (Förster 2007) ranging from zero (unadjusted household income) to one (per capita household income). The OECD modified equivalence scale has an elasticity of 0.53, and the square root scale reaches a similar elasticity value of 0.50.

Financial Losses After Divorce

Following these methodological clarifications, we look at the actual decline in the ex-partners' financial resources after a break-up. Most studies report the percentage decrease in income from the year before the break-up to one year after the break-up. In addition to differences in the methodological choices made and in the data used, two dimensions seem to determine the differences in the sizes of the economic consequences reported in the literature: time and geography. We illustrate these different approaches by providing an overview of studies on this topic across time for the US (from 1960 until today), and then for the European context (from the 1990s until today). As we mentioned above, the results are always compared by gender, as the consequences of divorce for women tend to differ substantially from those for men.

Divorces

The oldest results from the US were reviewed by Smock (1993), who reported that financial losses for women were found in studies from the 1970s and 1980s. Conversely, in this same period, increases in equivalent household income were observed for men. In her own study, which used longitudinal panel data from the US to compare divorce cohorts from the 1960s and the 1980s, Smock observed financial losses for white women of between 46% (oldest cohort) and 43% (1980s cohort), and for black women of between 51% and 45%. She also found that financial losses for white men shifted from −7% in the oldest cohort to +7% in the younger cohort; and that for black men, financial losses increased over time from 13% to 29%. Around the same time, Burkhauser et al. (1991) found a loss in income of 39% among women and of 7% among men. In their analysis of the financial losses associated with divorce in the US in the late 1990s, DiPrete and McManus (2000) reported that the adjusted household income loss was 15% for men, compared to 26% for women. The most recent results also show a substantial decline in income among women. For women in the US, Hauser et al. (2018) reported a decrease of 25%, while de Vaus et al. (2017) reported a decrease of 30%. These results are comparable to those found in the 1990s and 2000s. Some studies that took only individual household income into account showed a divergence of income between US women and US men. Investigating *labour earnings,* Tamborini et al. (2015) reported that women's earnings increased over time during the post-divorce period, and that the financial losses they suffered after divorce subsequently decreased. Unfortunately, this study did not take the household income into account, which makes it difficult to compare these findings to those of other studies.

The results for Europe are somewhat comparable to those for the US, as they show that women tend to lose financially while men display a more diverse pattern of gains and losses (Andreß et al. 2006). Results across time are available for Germany (often in comparison with the US) and the UK. In the oldest studies, German women were found to have income losses of 44% (Burkhauser et al. 1991), 32% (Andreß et al. 2006), and 25% (Uunk 2004). This trend seems to be relatively stable over time, as more recent findings show a drop in income for women of 26% (Hauser et al. 2016) and 35% (de Vaus et al. 2017). German men, on average, have been shown to lose much less in terms of equalized household income: i.e., they were found to have income losses of 7% (Burkhauser et al. 1991), 2% (Andreß et al. 2006), and 23% (DiPrete and McManus 2000). The most recent findings indicate that German men may even gain financially after divorce, albeit modestly (<5%) (de Vaus et al. 2017; Hauser et al. 2016). For the UK, the oldest results point to a substantial decline in income for women, ranging from 26% (Uunk 2004) and 27% (Dewilde 2003) to 18% (Jarvis and Jenkins 1999). Shifts over time were again found to be fairly limited, as de Vaus et al. (2017) found a 25% decrease in women's equivalent household income based on the most recent available panel data. The results for other European countries are comparable, displaying the same pattern of substantial losses among women and small losses or gains among men (Andreß et al. 2006; Uunk 2004).

Cohabitations

With regard to the dissolution of cohabiting unions, we expect to find that the financial losses are more modest. First, compared to married couples, cohabiters tend to have a more equal division of paid work (Snoeckx et al. 2008). Thus, married women are more likely than cohabitating women to be financially dependent on their partner. Second, cohabiters are less likely to have children, and they tend to be younger when ending a relationship (Batalova and Cohen 2002; Brines and Joyner 1999; Hamplova 2002; Rindfuss and Vandenheuvel 1990; Wu and Schimmele 2007). As we will discuss in more detail later in this chapter, having dependent children is disadvantageous for income trajectories after a break-up. Furthermore, a number of important (indirect) costs are involved with childrearing that can indirectly affect a woman's financial status (e.g., staying home to care for her children instead of being active on the labour market).

While most studies consider previously married partners, far fewer results on post-dissolution income trajectories are available for previously cohabiting partners. The oldest study on the economic consequences of the dissolution of cohabitating relationships was conducted in the US by Avellar and Smock (2005). They found that previously married men gained in equalized household income (+11%), while formerly cohabitating men lost a small percentage of their income (−1.8%). The losses of previously cohabiting women were shown to be more limited (−24%) than those of previously married women (−48%). For the Netherlands, Manting and Bouman (2006) found that the post-relationship decline in economic well-being was greater for divorced women (−23%) than for formerly cohabitating women (−14%). The economic consequences of relationship dissolution were shown to be more severe for formerly cohabitating men (−4%) than for divorced men (+7%). Using Belgian register data, de Regt et al. (2012) also found a more substantial drop in income for divorced women (−33%) than for cohabiting women (−22%). Over time, there have been fewer studies on this issue that allow us to compare and observe trends. However, for the US, Tach and Eads (2015) observed a diminishing gap in income losses between divorced and formerly cohabiting ex-partners. They argued that for US women, the consequences of divorce have become more positive, but the consequences of the break-up of a cohabiting relationship have become more negative. They explained this surprising finding by pointing to the changing composition of both married and cohabiting couples in terms of economic background. In the US, married households have become economically stronger and are more likely to have two earners, while cohabiting households tend to be situated at the lower end of the income distribution. Furthermore, the repartnering market has changed significantly, with more disadvantaged divorcees tending to cohabit instead of remarrying.

Individual and Institutional Differentials in Consequences

The most important divide in the financial consequences of relationship dissolution is clearly between women and men. There is, therefore, a large body of research on the factors that might explain these gendered income trajectories. At the individual level, labour market participation appears to be the main explanatory factor. Married women have lower levels of labour market attachment, as many of them are not working or are working part-time. In a classic male breadwinner model, the husband works and the wife cares (more) for the children (Becker 1981), which leads to a specialised division of labour in the (former) couple. When the relationship ends, the woman often has less human capital than the man, especially if her labour market skills have depreciated while she stayed home to do the housework and care for the children. A second important explanatory factor is the presence of (young) children in the household. Having children not only limits a woman's opportunities to participate in the labour market (see further), it also limits a woman's time resources, and makes it more difficult for her to divide her time between child care, housework, and paid labour. In addition, if the mother has physical custody of the children, her household may have greater economic needs (Raeymaeckers et al. 2008a).

When we look at the relative declines in equalized household income for men and women at the individual level, we see marked differences between countries. Institutional factors have a clear and substantial additional impact on the financial consequences of union dissolution. For both women and men, the economic consequences of divorce differ not only over time, but by country and geographic region. Some studies have compared pairs of countries, and have focused on the specific differences between them (e.g., Burkhauser et al. 1991; Dewilde 2006). Others have performed large-scale comparisons of multiple countries (Andreß et al. 2006; de Vaus et al. 2017; Uunk 2004). In such broad comparisons, country differences are often explained using welfare state typologies (e.g., Esping-Andersen 1990; Ferragina and Seeleib-Kaiser 2011). A first general conclusion we can draw from these comparative studies is that there are institutional influences that go beyond the compositional differences between countries (Uunk 2004). While household size and labour market attachment patterns differ between countries, the institutional context also has an impact on the financial consequences of divorce for women (for men, hardly any study has considered institutional factors). In terms of the decline in income, a clear north-south gradient is observed throughout Europe, with a break-up having a smaller average effect on income in the Scandinavian countries than in the Southern Europe. In most studies, the impact of three different institutional policies is reviewed: income-related welfare provisions (e.g., social welfare), employment-related policies, and family policies (e.g., child care provisions). Both Uunk (2004) and de Vaus et al. (2017) concluded that social welfare (direct income-related measures) has the largest impact on the post-divorce income trajectories of women. The provision of child care can also help women remain active in the labour market, which could, in turn, raise their income. Nevertheless, multivariate analyses have shown that the effect of direct income support outweighs that of child care payments. This finding is consistent over time. Receiving income support might have negative consequences for the life course of a divorced woman, as it may create a "welfare trap" that discourages her from participating in the labour market. This lack of labour market attachment could also negatively affect the woman's income position later in life, as her pension rights will be substantially reduced.

Coping Strategies (for Women)

A second way of approaching the economic consequences of a break-up is to look not at the loss in resources, but at the subsequent recovery. When we apply a life course framework, we can see that people's lives do not halt after a break-up. The sociology of the life course stresses that there are temporal shifts in people's lives (Mortelmans et al. 2016). This implies that life goes on after divorce, and that people take action when confronted with adversity. Looking at the post-break-up strategies of former partners inevitably brings us to the concept of coping strategies. A coping strategy is defined as "a behavioural pattern of an actor to deal with problems, referring to the usual and institutionalized ways of feeling, thinking and acting in such situations" (Boeije and Nievaard 1995: 350). When examining the financial coping behaviour of ex-partners after a divorce, we can discern two main coping mechanisms: finding a new partner and changing one's labour market behaviour. Both strategies are known to positively influence the financial well-being of an ex-spouse. A third potential strategy that is sometimes considered is returning to the parental home, also termed the "boomerang effect" or the "boomerang move" (Albertini et al. 2018).

Repartnering

The first coping strategy might be somewhat controversial. Coping as a concept entails an intentional behavioural component. Unlike (re-)employment, repartnering cannot be seen exclusively as an intentional strategy to alleviate the financial drawbacks of a break-up. A new relationship might offer not just financial security, but the fulfilment of the need for friendship, affection, and love. Nevertheless, as this pathway can be seen as a mechanism for alleviating financial pressures after the break-up, it can be considered a coping strategy.

In the literature, we find three arguments that can help us understand the likelihood of finding a new partner after a break-up: needs, opportunities, and attractiveness (de Graaf and Kalmijn 2003). These three components cannot be seen as independent of each other, and have been jointly taken into account in studies that map repartnering processes. The *need* argument refers to the financial, emotional, and social needs people are seeking to meet by entering a new relationship. The *opportunities* argument is based on the observation that people need to be able to meet new partners in order to form a new bond. The greater the opportunities people have to meet partners, the higher their likelihood of finding a match, and the higher their odds of repartnering. The "first marriage market" is generally comprised of schools and leisure locations where (young) people meet before they enter a long-term relationship (de Graaf and Kalmijn 2003; Kalmijn 1998). After the break-up of a long-term relationship, people enter the "second marriage market", where the opportunities to meet a new partner are more limited. The third argument concerns the *attractiveness* of people on the repartnering market. This term does not refer exclusively to "physical attractiveness". Especially on the second marriage market, characteristics such as the presence of children from a prior relationship or the nature of the break-up itself are very relevant, as these factors can make people more or less attractive to others (de Graaf and Kalmijn 2003).

The determinants of repartnering, such as the presence of children, sex, educational level, income situation, and age, can be interpreted in multiple and opposing ways depending on which argument is applied to the repartnering process. Studies that take repartnering into account as a coping strategy have observed different patterns by gender, with men, on average, repartnering faster and more frequently than women (Coleman et al. 2000; Lampard and Peggs 1999; Schmiege et al. 2001; South 1991). While having (young) children may intensify a divorcee's economic pressures, it can also lower the individual's repartnering chances because she has decreased meeting opportunities and is considered less attractive. Conversely, having a good job tends to improve a divorcee's attractiveness and opportunities to meet a partner, while also increasing the individual's repartnering needs from a specialisation logic point of view (Becker 1981; Becker et al. 1977). From a Beckerian point of view, this dynamic only applies to men. For a woman, having a job reduces her need to repartner for financial reasons, and makes her less attractive (from the classic Becker (1981) point of view), as she is less available to form a specialized household with a single earner. Older divorcees tend to experience more difficulties than their younger counterparts in finding a new partner (de Graaf and Kalmijn 2003). This dynamic is also gendered in the sense that older women have lower repartnering chances than older men, partly due to the tendency of men to marry younger women (Schmiege et al. 2001). As we mentioned above, resident children have a consistently negative effect on the likelihood of repartnering (Di Nallo 2019; Pasteels and Mortelmans 2015; Sweeney 1997). Socio-economic factors influence the repartnering behaviours of both men and women, albeit in opposite directions. For women, a non-significant or a negative educational gradient has been found, which appears to be related to an independence effect among higher educated women (Ozawo and Yoon 2002). For men, it has been shown that their chances of repartnering increase as their educational level rises. Finally, with respect to individual earnings and labour market attachment, the results show evidence of a two-tiered family system (Furstenberg 2016), whereby higher labour market activity levels and higher earnings are associated with a higher probability of entering a new partnership (Dewilde and Uunk 2008; Pasteels and Mortelmans 2017). In summary, we can state that the effects of human resource determinants are more straightforward for men than for women. All of the arguments concerning needs, meeting opportunities, and attractiveness move in the same direction for men, which is not the case for women.

(Re-)employment

A second strategy described in the literature is working more or entering the labour market (Joshi 1998; Poortman 2000). When a divorcee increases his/her labour market activity in response to the breakdown of the relationship, his/her income position is increased and his/her risk of poverty is reduced (Dewilde 2006). Not surprisingly, women face more barriers to increasing their labour market activity because their care burden often makes it difficult for them to work more (Stier et al. 2001; van der Lippe and van Dijk 2002). Also, the pre-break gender role patterns – with women being more likely than men to have cared for their children at the cost of their career – influence the ex-partners' ability to return to the labour market later on. There are few detailed studies on the employment patterns of divorced men, as most men were already working full-time before their relationship ended, and continued to do so thereafter (Thielemans and Mortelmans 2018). As Gornick et al. (1998) put it, the majority of men do not suffer from the "child-penalty".

In addition to this gender difference, the success of the (re-)employment coping strategy has been shown to be dependent on various socio-economic and demographic determinants. Education is a logical differentiator, as the higher educated are more likely than the less educated to have substantial work experience. In particular, higher educated women tend to work more than their less educated counterparts while married or in a long-term cohabitating relationship (Vanderheyden and Mortelmans 2013). Age is also negatively related to this strategy, as human capital depreciates with the length of time people (mainly women) are absent from the labour market (van Damme et al. 2009). Another factor that can make it difficult for women to increase their labour market participation is having to care for (young) children. The more children there are in the household, and the younger the ages of the children, the lower the probability that the mother will successfully (re-)enter the labour market. Although women face the prospect of greater financial losses after a break-up (see above), and will therefore use this coping strategy more extensively, it is not completely absent in the lives of men, as men may also experience labour market setbacks (unemployment, periods of sickness) that lead them to develop other labour market strategies (Kalmijn 2005; McManus and DiPrete

2001). Nevertheless, the sizes of these effects tend to be more limited for men than for women.

The coping strategy of working does not operate independently of the strategy of repartnering. Research has shown that when women combine the two strategies, the benefits of (re-)entering full-time employment outweigh the benefits of repartnering. Surprisingly, this effect was not found to be mitigated by education. Although the higher educated tend to have a different pre-divorce position and are likely to find it easier to change their labour market position compared to their counterparts with medium or lower educational levels, the labour market strategy was found to have only a small effect and the repartnering strategy was found to have no effect. It seems that repartnering, at least for women, has an equal effect on their post-divorce income trajectories. For men, repartnering tends to improve their financial circumstances – but again, this coping strategy does not appear to be as effective as entering either full-time or part-time employment (Jansen et al. 2009).

Returning to the Parental Home

Compared to the repartnering and labour market strategies, the boomerang effect of returning to the parental home has received far less attention in the literature as a coping strategy for alleviating the financial consequences of a break-up. This is because the boomerang effect predominantly applies to young adults who return to the parental home after taking an unsuccessful step towards independence (South and Lei 2015). The interest in boomerang effects has grown in recent years, as the global economic crisis led to dramatic changes in the housing trajectories of young adults (Stone et al. 2014). Following the emergence of this new interest in the literature, researchers started turning their attention to boomerang effects later in the life course.

Two life course events are closely related to boomeranging: namely, becoming unemployed and experiencing the break-up of a relationship. Nevertheless, as most studies that have examined these effects have focused on young adults, they have mainly taken only short or middle-long relationships into account. However, returning to the parental home can also be used as a coping strategy to manage financial setbacks after a long-term relationship ends. Far fewer studies have examined such cases (Albertini et al. 2018; Guzzo 2016). Our knowledge about this coping strategy is therefore still limited, especially compared to our knowledge about the two previously described strategies. Again, the gender differences in the strategies used for coping with financial challenges also apply to the return to the parental home, with men having a higher probability of boomeranging. This may seem counterintuitive given the evidence that daughters receive more help from their parents than sons in difficult times (Fingerman et al. 2009). This finding may be explained by results showing that a larger share of women (and especially mothers) than men stay in the couple's home after the break-up (Ongaro et al. 2008; Stone et al. 2014; Sullivan 2007). An individual's labour market status and income position are also closely connected to this coping strategy: if an individual's financial challenges are less severe (because the person has a higher income or is in full-time employment), the chances are greater that s/he will remain independent (Guzzo 2016; Kleinepier et al. 2017). Moreover, whether a divorcee uses returning to the parental home as a coping strategy depends not only on the characteristics of the former partner, but on the characteristics of the parental home itself (Stone et al. 2014). It is, of course, the case that the financial resources of the parents and the availability of a room in the parental home determine whether it is possible for the divorcee to return home (Goldscheider and Goldscheider 1998). However, studies have also shown that cultural factors, such as shared values or strong social and emotional ties in the family, increase the likelihood of returning (South and Lei 2015).

Lone Parenthood and Poverty After Divorce

As we have explained above, a woman's economic well-being after a relationship fails may be negatively affected if she has primary responsibility for her children (and is thus in a classic mother-centred custodial arrangement) (Poortman 2000). First, the presence of children increases the economic needs of the family (as measured in equivalence scales in statistical models). Second, having children affects a woman's labour market options (Drobnic 2000; Raeymaeckers et al. 2008b; Thielemans and Mortelmans 2018) and her attractiveness in the remarriage market (Buckle et al. 1996; Coleman et al. 2000). As this book focuses on parental trajectories after union dissolution, we have added an exploration of this issue to our review. While we cannot provide a comprehensive overview of the difficulties lone parent families experience,[1] we can offer some general insights into the financial situations of lone parents. The issue of poverty is thus a leading theme in this section.

All of the studies that have examined the financial consequences of relationship dissolution have found that the income declines are greater and the recovery periods are more difficult and more protracted among parents (especially mothers) than among childless individuals (e.g., Jarvis and Jenkins 1999; Mortelmans and Jansen 2010). Therefore, the focus of the research on the financial consequences of divorce for parents moves to the issue of poverty[2] for the partner who takes care of the couple's children after the break-up (in most cases, the mother). It has been

[1] For a more comprehensive overview of lone parenthood, see Bernardi and Mortelmans (2018) and Nieuwenhuis and Maldonado (2018).

[2] *Poverty* in these studies is defined as a percentage (usually 60%) of the median net household equivalised income of the population. When the income drops below this threshold, the subject is considered to be poor (Aassve et al. 2007). The EU has reformulated this 60% threshold as "at-risk-of-poverty" (AROP), as more definitions of poverty have become available. This term is now used in all recent studies, whereas the older studies used the term "poverty" to refer to this 60% median income threshold (Hübgen 2018).

consistently shown that these lone parents have a substantially higher poverty risk than the general population, and – in line with the overall story told in this chapter – that this risk is greatest for lone mothers. Early research on the economic consequences of union dissolution for lone mothers was conducted in the US in 2004 (Fitzgerald and Ribar 2004; Martin 2006), and was later replicated in other countries (Harkness 2018; Jenkins 2008; Treanor 2018). The highest at-risk-of-poverty rates among lone mothers were reported in US studies: i.e., of 63% (without transfer payments) and of 51% (with transfer payments) (Casey and Maldonado 2012). Conversely, in European studies, the at-risk-of-poverty rates of lone mothers have generally been found to be lower, ranging from 7% in Poland to 37% in Latvia. Low at-risk-of-poverty rates for lone parents have also been reported for Sweden (15%), Norway (16%), and the Netherlands (16%). The highest at-risk-of-poverty rates in the European context have been reported for Eastern European countries like Lithuania (32%) and Hungary (31%), and for Ireland (29%), Spain (27%), and Italy (27%) (Hübgen 2018; OECD 2011).

Research on the determinants of these poverty risks falls within the larger field of poverty studies, with individual factors like relationship break-ups, age, and educational level being identified as risk factors (Brady and Burroway 2012; Misra et al. 2007). In addition to applying this individual risk model, researchers are increasingly taking into account the institutional factors that contribute to the at-risk-of-poverty rates among lone mothers. As the number of lone mothers has increased significantly in recent decades (Bernardi et al. 2018a), policies directed at alleviating poverty among lone parents have received substantial attention in the research community (Aassve et al. 2007). A central theme in these welfare state studies has been the debate about the universal provision of social rights versus the use of targeted support. Universalism is a perspective that calls for social policies that are directed at all citizens, and that seek to reduce economic inequality in general. Targeted policies are directed at particular groups, such as lone parents (Zagel and Hübgen 2018). An example of the first approach is a policy that provides universal access to the health care system for all residents of a country. Some examples of the latter approach are the welfare benefits and the specific tax reductions lone parents receive in some countries. In a broad comparison of OECD countries, Bradshaw et al. (2018) found that the incomes of most lone parents are supplemented by benefits. In countries like Ireland, the UK, Denmark, Sweden, and Australia, these benefits can amount to 40% of the household's total income. Most countries provide lone parent families with income-tested family benefits together with non-income-tested cash benefits for children.

With regard to lone parents, two main goals of social policy measures can be discerned. First, direct poverty measures are designed to ensure that lone parent families remain above the poverty threshold. The aforementioned tax reductions and enhanced family allowances clearly have this income-based objective in mind. A second goal is to help lone parents become or stay active on the labour market, and to balance working with managing their care burden. In a large comparative study of policy measures and their effects on poverty among lone parents in OECD countries, Bradshaw et al. (2018) found that cash transfers are highly effective in reducing poverty and keeping people in the labour market. However, the broader policy mix in each country must be taken into account. There are, for example, countries that provide cash benefits, but that also reduce the housing subsidies of the families who receive these benefits (Bernardi et al. 2018b).

Conclusion

In this review, we took an unorthodox path by starting with the overall conclusion: namely, that women fare worse economically after a break-up than men. Throughout the literature, this simple yet far-reaching conclusion is replicated again and again, regardless of the time period, geographic focus, or methodology used. A surprising finding of this review was that most studies found that these losses declined only slightly over time, regardless of whether the couples were previously married or cohabiting. Although the gender income gap is shrinking due to the growth in dual-earner households and the increases in women's earnings, the overall conclusion that women are disadvantaged relative to men remains intact after almost five decades (Tamborini et al. 2015).

We have provided some additional nuance to this general conclusion by reviewing the many studies that have been conducted on this topic. Countries can alleviate this gap by actively supporting divorcees, and lone parents in particular. The welfare state is an important source of (social) support – although the case could also be made that the existence of the welfare state has made breaking up much more feasible than it was in the past. Moreover, from a legal point of view, divorcing or leaving one's partner (and children) has never been easier.

The focus on economic consequences might give the impression that divorce is detrimental only for women, and that only men gain from a break-up. This is, of course, not the case. For example, the more intense contact between women and their children through classic custodial arrangements tends to enhance the level of contact and care exchanged later in life (Cooney and Uhlenberg 1990; Pezzin and Schone 1999). For these reasons, it could be argued that over the long term, women pay the greater financial price following a break-up, while men pay the greater social price.

What will the future bring? Given the recurring findings on this topic, we can realistically assume that the economic consequences of divorce will continue to harm women more than men. While there are some indications that the dual-earner family system is helping to reduce this gender gap, differences in earnings are likely to remain. However, a new development that researchers will need to take into account is the shift in custody arrangements. Increasingly, countries are abandoning the idea that children should grow up with their mother after their parents' break-up. Joint physical custody legislation has been passed in a number of countries, and continued joint parenthood arrangements for women and men are gaining ground (Bastaits and Mortelmans 2016). Joint physical custody changes not only the child support system (Claessens and Mortelmans 2018), but fathers' responsibilities to their children. When children are living a substantial amount of time with their father under a joint physical custody arrangement, the father is obliged not only to take on parenting responsibilities, but to shoulder financial obligations. This shared responsibility also opens up labour market opportunities for the mother, and may therefore limit her financial disadvantages. As the minds of legislators and judges are slow to change, it may take some time before we see the equalizing effects of joint custody in our data and models. Yet it appears that the sharing of parental responsibilities has the potential to reduce the gendered results we have presented in this chapter. We hope that in 10 years' time we will be able to start a new review with the words: "There was a time when only women suffered financially from a relationship break-up". Until then, we look to the welfare state to support families in the wake of a break-up, and to take action to reduce the huge poverty risks women and their children face today.

References

Aassve, A., Betti, G., Mazzuco, S., & Mencarini, L. (2007). Marital disruption and economic well-being: A comparative analysis. *Journal of the Royal Statistical Society: Series A (Statistics in Society), 170*(3), 781–799. https://doi.org/10.1111/j.1467-985X.2007.00483.x.

Albertini, M., Gähler, M., & Härkönen, J. (2018). Moving back to "mamma"? Divorce, intergenerational coresidence, and latent family solidarity in Sweden. *Population, Space and Place, 24*(6). https://doi.org/10.1002/psp.2142.

Amato, P. R., & Keith, B. (1991). Parental divorce and the well-being of children: A meta-analysis. *Psychological Bulletin, 110*(1), 26–36. https://doi.org/10.1037/0033-2909.110.1.26.

Andreß, H.-J., Borgloh, B., Bröckel, M., Giesselmann, M., & Hummelsheim, D. (2006). The economic consequences of partnership dissolution: A comparative analysis of panel studies from Belgium, Germany, Great Britain, Italy, and Sweden. *European Sociological Review, 22*(5), 533–560. https://doi.org/10.1093/esr/jcl012.

Atkinson, A. B., Rainwater, L., & Smeeding, T. (1995). *Income distribution in OECD Countries* (OECD Social Policy Studies, 18). Paris: OECD.

Avellar, S., & Smock, P. J. (2005). The economic consequences of the dissolution of cohabiting unions. *Journal of Marriage and Family, 67*(2), 315–327. https://doi.org/10.1111/j.0022-2445.2005.00118.x.

Bastaits, K., & Mortelmans, D. (2016). Parenting as mediator between post-divorce family structure and children's well-being. *Journal of Child and Family Studies, 25*(7), 2178–2188. https://doi.org/10.1007/s10826-016-0395-8.

Batalova, J. A., & Cohen, P. N. (2002). Premarital cohabitation and housework: Couples in cross-national perspective. *Journal of Marriage and the Family, 64*(3), 743–755. https://doi.org/10.1111/j.1741-3737.2002.00743.x.

Bayaz-Ozturk, G., Burkhauser, R. V., Couch, K. A., & Hauser, R. (2018). The effects of union dissolution on the economic resources of men and women: A comparative analysis of Germany and the United States, 1985–2013. *The Annals of the American Academy of Political and Social Science, 680*(1), 235–258. https://doi.org/10.1177/0002716218793608.

Becker, G. S. (1981). *A treatise on the family*. Cambridge: Harvard University Press.

Becker, G. S., Landes, E. M., & Michael, R. T. (1977). An economic analysis of marital instability. *Journal of Political Economy, 85*(6), 1141–1187. https://doi.org/10.1086/260631.

Bernardi, L., & Mortelmans, D. (2018). *Lone parenthood in the life course*. Cham: Springer.

Bernardi, L., Mortelmans, D., & Larenza, O. (2018a). Changing lone parents, changing life courses. In L. Bernardi & D. Mortelmans (Eds.), *Lone parenthood in a life course perspective* (pp. 1–28). Cham: Springer.

Bernardi, L., Mortelmans, D., & Vono de Vilhena, D. (2018b). Supporting lone parents and their children in Europe: Insights from a dialogue between researchers and policy makers. *Population & Policy Compact: Policy Briefs, 15*, 1–4.

Boeije, H. R., & Nievaard, A. C. (1995). Strategieën en perspectieven van verzorgenden in het verpleeghuis. *Tijdschrift voor Sociologie, 16*(4), 345–361.

Bradshaw, J., Keung, A., & Chzhen, Y. (2018). Cash benefits and poverty in single-parent families. In R. Nieuwenhuis & L. C. Maldonado (Eds.), *The triple bind of single-parent families* (pp. 31–50). Bristol: Policy Press.

Brady, D., & Burroway, R. (2012). Targeting, universalism, and single-mother poverty: A multilevel analysis across 18 affluent democracies. *Demography, 49*(2), 719–746. https://doi.org/10.1007/s13524-012-0094-z.

Brines, J., & Joyner, K. (1999). The ties that bind: Principles of cohesion in cohabitation and marriage. *American Sociological Review, 64*(3), 333–355. https://doi.org/10.2307/2657490.

Buckle, L., Gallup, G. G., & Rodd, Z. A. (1996). Marriage as a reproductive contract: Patterns of marriage, divorce, and remarriage. *Ethology and Sociobiology, 17*(6), 363–377. https://doi.org/10.1016/S0162-3095(96)00075-1.

Burkhauser, R. V., Duncan, G. J., Hauser, R., & Berntsen, R. (1991). Wife or Frau, women do worse: A comparison of men and women in the United States and Germany after marital dissolution. *Demography, 28*(3), 353–360. https://doi.org/10.2307/2061461.

Casey, T., & Maldonado, L. C. (2012). *Worst off: Single-parent families in the United States. A cross-national comparison of single parenthood in the US and sixteen other high-income countries*. New York: Legal Momentum.

Claessens, E., & Mortelmans, D. (2018). Challenges for child support schemes: Accounting for shared care and complex families. *Journal of European Social Policy, 28*(3), 211–223. https://doi.org/10.1177/0958928717753592.

Coleman, M., Ganong, L., & Fine, M. A. (2000). Reinvestigating remarriage: Another decade of progress. *Journal of Marriage and Family, 62*(4), 1288–1307. https://doi.org/10.1111/j.1741-3737.2000.01288.x.

Cooney, T. M., & Uhlenberg, P. (1990). The role of divorce in men's relations with their adult children after mid-life. *Journal of Marriage and Family, 52*(3), 677–688. https://doi.org/10.2307/352933.

de Graaf, P. M., & Kalmijn, M. (2003). Alternative routes in the remarriage market: Competing-risk analyses of union formation after divorce. *Social Forces, 81*(4), 1459–1498. https://doi.org/10.1353/sof.2003.0052.

de Regt, S., Mortelmans, D., & Marynissen, T. (2012). Financial consequences of relationship dissolution: A longitudinal comparison of formerly married and unmarried cohabiting men and women. *Sociology, 47*(1), 90–108. https://doi.org/10.1177/0038038512453793.

de Vaus, D. A., Gray, M., Qu, L., & Stanton, D. (2017). The economic consequences of divorce in six OECD countries. *Australian Journal of Social Issues, 52*(2), 180–199. https://doi.org/10.1002/ajs4.13.

Dewilde, C. (2003). The financial consequences of relationship dissolution for women in western Europe. In E. Ruspini & A. Dale (Eds.), *The gender dimension of social change: The contribution of dynamic research to the study of women's life courses* (pp. 81–110). Bristol: The Policy Press.

Dewilde, C. (2006). Becoming poor in Belgium and Britain: The impact of demographic and labour market events. *Sociological Research Online, 11*(1), 87–103. https://doi.org/10.5153/sro.1206.

Dewilde, C., & Uunk, W. (2008). Remarriage as a way to overcome the financial consequences of divorce: A test of the economic need hypothesis for European women. *European Sociological Review, 24*(3), 393–407. https://doi.org/10.1093/esr/jcn025.

Di Nallo, A. (2019). Gender gap in repartnering: The role of parental status and custodial arrangements. *Journal of Marriage and Family, 81*(1), 59–78. https://doi.org/10.1111/jomf.12527.
DiPrete, T. A., & McManus, P. A. (2000). Family change, employment transitions, and the welfare state: Household income dynamics in the United States and Germany. *American Sociological Review, 65*(3), 343–370. https://doi.org/10.2307/2657461.
Drobnic, S. (2000). The effects of children on married and lone mothers' employment in the United States and (West) Germany. *European Sociological Review, 16*(2), 137–157. https://doi.org/10.1093/esr/16.2.137.
Esping-Andersen, G. (1990). *The three worlds of welfare capitalism*. Princeton: Princeton University Press.
Ferragina, E., & Seeleib-Kaiser, M. (2011). Welfare regime debate: past, present, future? *Policy & Politics, 39*(4), 583–611. https://doi.org/10.1332/030557311X603592.
Fingerman, K., Miller, L., Birditt, K., & Zarit, S. (2009). Giving to the good and the needy: Parental support of grown children. *Journal of Marriage and Family, 71*(5), 1220–1233. https://doi.org/10.1111/j.1741-3737.2009.00665.x.
Fitzgerald, J. M., & Ribar, D. C. (2004). Welfare reform and female headship. *Demography, 41*(2), 189–212. https://doi.org/10.1353/dem.2004.0014.
Förster, M. F. (2007). *What are equivalence scales?* http://www.oecd.org/eco/growth/OECD-Note-EquivalenceScales.pdf. Accessed 25 June 2019.
Furstenberg, F. F. (2016). The changing American family: An overview from 1965 to 2015. In D. Mortelmans, K. Matthijs, E. Alofs, & B. Segaert (Eds.), *Changing family dynamics and demographic evolution: The family kaleidoscope* (pp. 13–25). Cheltenham: Edward Elgar.
Goldscheider, F. K., & Goldscheider, C. (1998). The effects of childhood family structure on leaving and returning home. *Journal of Marriage and Family, 60*(3), 745–756. https://doi.org/10.2307/353543.
Gornick, J. C., Meyers, M. K., & Ross, K. E. (1998). Public policies and the employment of mothers: A cross-national study. *Social Science Quarterly, 79*(1), 35–54.
Guzzo, K. B. (2016). Do young mothers and fathers differ in the likelihood of returning home? *Journal of Marriage and Family, 78*(5), 1332–1351. https://doi.org/10.1111/jomf.12347.
Hagenaars, A., De Vos, K., & Zaïdi, M. A. (1994). *Poverty statistics in the late 1980s: Research based on micro data*. Luxembourg: Office for official publications of the European Communities.
Hamplova, D. (2002). Marriage and cohabitation: Qualitative differences in partnership arrangements. *Czech Sociological Review, 38*(6), 771–788. https://nbn-resolving.org/urn:nbn:de:0168-ssoar-56280.
Harkness, S. (2018). The economic consequences of becoming a lone mother. In L. Bernardi & D. Mortelmans (Eds.), *Lone parenthood in a life course perspective* (pp. 213–234). Cham: Springer.
Hauser, R., Burkhauser, R. V., Couch, K. A., & Bayaz-Ozturk, G. (2016). *Wife or Frau, women still do worse: A comparison of men and women in the United States and Germany after union dissolutions in the 1990s and 2000s*. Working papers, 2016/39.
Hauser, R., Burkhauser, R. V., Couch, K. A., & Bayaz-Ozturk, G. (2018). Wife or Frau, women still do worse: A comparison of men and women in the United States and Germany after union dissolutions in the 1990s and 2000s. In M. Erlingagen, K. Hank, & M. Kreyenfeld (Eds.), *Innovation und Wissenstransfer in der empirischen Sozial- und Verhaltensforschung* (pp. 167–188). Frankfurt/Main, New York: Campus.
Hübgen, S. (2018). Only a husband away from poverty? Lone mothers' poverty risks in a European Comparison. In L. Bernardi & D. Mortelmans (Eds.), *Lone parenthood in a life course perspective* (pp. 167–190). Cham: Springer.
Jansen, M., Mortelmans, D., & Snoeckx, L. (2009). Repartnering and (Re)employment: Strategies to cope with the economic consequences of partnership dissolution. *Journal of Marriage and Family, 71*(5), 1271–1293. https://doi.org/10.1111/j.1741-3737.2009.00668.x.

Jarvis, S., & Jenkins, S. P. (1999). Marital splits and income changes: Evidence from the British household panel survey. *Population Studies, 53*(2), 237–254. https://doi.org/10.1080/00324720308077.

Jenkins, S. P. (2008). *Marital splits and income changes over the longer term*. Institute for Social and Economic Research Working Paper (2008–07).

Joshi, H. (1998). The opportunity costs of childbearing: More than mother's business. *Journal of Population Economics, 11*(2), 161–183. https://doi.org/10.1007/s001480050063.

Kalmijn, M. (1998). Intermarriage and homogamy: Causes, patterns, trends. *Annual Review of Sociology, 24*, 395–421. https://doi.org/10.1146/annurev.soc.24.1.395.

Kalmijn, M. (2005). The effects of divorce on men's employment and social security histories. *European Journal of Population, 21*(4), 347–366. https://doi.org/10.1007/s10680-005-0200-7.

Kleinepier, T., Berrington, A., & Stoeldraijer, L. (2017). Ethnic differences in returning home: Explanations from a life course perspective. *Journal of Marriage and Family, 79*(4), 1023–1040. https://doi.org/10.1111/jomf.12399.

Lampard, R., & Peggs, K. (1999). Repartnering: The relevance of parenthood and gender to cohabitation and remarriage among the formerly married. *British Journal of Sociology, 50*(3), 443–465. https://doi.org/10.1111/j.1468-4446.1999.00443.x.

Manting, D., & Bouman, A. M. (2006). Short- and long-term economic consequences of the dissolution of marital and consensual unions: The example of the Netherlands. *European Sociological Review, 22*(4), 413–429. https://doi.org/10.1093/esr/jcl005.

Martin, M. A. (2006). Family structure and income inequality in families with children, 1976 to 2000. *Demography, 43*(3), 421–445. https://doi.org/10.1353/dem.2006.0025.

McKeever, M., & Wolfinger, N. H. (2001). Reexamining the economic costs of marital disruption for women. *Social Science Quarterly, 82*(1), 202–217. https://doi.org/10.1111/0038-4941.00018.

McManus, P. A., & DiPrete, T. A. (2001). Losers and winners: The financial consequences of separation and divorce for men. *American Sociological Review, 66*(2), 246–268. https://doi.org/10.2307/2657417.

Misra, J., Moller, S., & Budig, M. J. (2007). Work family policies and poverty for partnered and single women in Europe and North America. *Gender & Society, 21*(6), 804–827. https://doi.org/10.1177/0891243207308445.

Mortelmans, D. (2019). Divorce in Europe. In *New insights in trends, causes and consequences of relation break-ups*. Basel: Springer International Publishing.

Mortelmans, D., & Jansen, M. (2010). Income dynamics after divorce: A latent growth model of income change on the European community household panel. *Cahiers économiques de Bruxelles Université libre de Bruxelles, 53*(1), 85–107.

Mortelmans, D., Matthijs, K., Alofs, E., & Segaert, B. (2016). *Changing family dynamics and demographic evolution: The family kaleidoscope*. Cheltenham: Edward Elgar.

Nieuwenhuis, R., & Maldonado, L. C. (2018). *The triple bind of single-parent families*. Bristol: Policy Press.

OECD. (2011). *Doing better for families*. Paris: OECD Publishing.

Ongaro, F., Mazzuco, S., & Meggiolaro, S. (2008). Economic consequences of union dissolution in Italy: Findings from the European community household panel. *European Journal of Population, 25*(1), 45–65. https://doi.org/10.1007/s10680-008-9157-7.

Ozawo, M., & Yoon, H. (2002). The economic benefit of remarriage: Gender and income class. *Journal of Divorce and Remarriage, 36*(3–4), 21–39. https://doi.org/10.1300/J087v36n03_02.

Pasteels, I., & Mortelmans, D. (2015). Dyadic analysis of repartnering after divorce: Do children matter? *Journal of Family Research, Special Issue, 10*, 143–164.

Pasteels, I., & Mortelmans, D. (2017). The socioeconomic determinants of repartnering after divorce or separation in Belgium. *Demographic Research, 36*, 1785–1812. https://doi.org/10.4054/DemRes.2017.36.58.

Pezzin, L. E., & Schone, B. S. (1999). Parental marital disruption and intergenerational transfers: An analysis of lone elderly parents and their children. *Demography, 36*(3), 287–297. https://doi.org/10.2307/2648053.

Poortman, A.-R. (2000). Sex differences in the economic consequences of separation. A panel study of the Netherlands. *European Sociological Review, 16*(4), 367–383. https://doi.org/10.1093/esr/16.4.367.

Raeymaeckers, P., Dewilde, C., Snoeckx, L., & Mortelmans, D. (2008a). Childcare strategies of divorced mothers in Europe: A comparative analysis. *European Sociological Review, 24*(1), 115–131. https://doi.org/10.1093/esr/jcm04.

Raeymaeckers, P., Dewilde, C., Snoeckx, L., & Mortelmans, D. (2008b). The influence of formal and informal support systems on the labour supply of divorced mothers. *European Societies, 10*(3), 453–477. https://doi.org/10.1080/14616690701833480.

Rindfuss, R. R., & Vandenheuvel, A. (1990). Cohabitation: Precursor to marriage or an alternative to being single? *Population and Development Review, 16*(4), 703–726. https://doi.org/10.2307/1972963.

Schmiege, C. J., Richards, L. N., & Zvonkovic, A. M. (2001). Remarriage: For love or money? *Journal of Divorce and Remarriage, 36*(1–2), 123–140. https://doi.org/10.1300/J087v36n01_07.

Smock, P. J. (1993). The economic costs of marital disruption for young women over the past two decades. *Demography, 30*(3), 353–371. https://doi.org/10.2307/2061645.

Snoeckx, L., Dehertogh, B., & Mortelmans, D. (2008). The distribution of household tasks in first-marriage families and stepfamilies across Europe. In J. Pryor (Ed.), *The international handbook of stepfamilies: Policy and practice in legal, research, and clinical environments* (pp. 277–298). Hoboken: Wiley.

South, S. J. (1991). Sociodemographic differentials in mate selection preferences. *Journal of Marriage and Family, 53*(4), 928–940. https://doi.org/10.2307/352998.

South, S. J., & Lei, L. (2015). Failures-to-launch and boomerang kids: Contemporary determinants of leaving and returning to the parental home. *Social Forces, 94*(2), 863–890. https://doi.org/10.1093/sf/sov064.

Stier, H., Lewin-Epstein, N., & Braun, M. (2001). Welfare regimes, family-supportive policies, and women's employment along the life-course. *American Journal of Sociology, 106*(6), 1731–1760. https://doi.org/10.1086/321302.

Stone, J., Berrington, A., & Falkingham, J. (2014). Gender, turning points, and boomerangs: Returning home in young adulthood in Great Britain. *Demography, 51*(1), 257–276. https://doi.org/10.1007/s13524-013-0247-8.

Sullivan, O. (2007). Housing movements of the divorced and separated. *Housing Studies, 1*(1), 35–48. https://doi.org/10.1080/02673038608720561.

Sweeney, M. (1997). Remarriage of women and men after divorce: The role of socioeconomic prospects. *Journal of Family Issues, 18*(5), 479–502. https://doi.org/10.1177/019251397018005002.

Tach, L. M., & Eads, A. (2015). Trends in the economic consequences of marital and cohabitation dissolution in the United States. *Demography, 52*(2), 401–432. https://doi.org/10.1007/s13524-015-0374-5.

Tamborini, C. R., Couch, K. A., & Reznik, G. L. (2015). Long-term impact of divorce on women's earnings across multiple divorce windows: A life course perspective. *Advances in Life Course Research, 26*, 44–59. https://doi.org/10.1016/j.alcr.2015.06.001.

Thielemans, G., & Mortelmans, D. (2018). Female labour force participation after divorce: How employment histories matter. *Journal of Family and Economic Issues Online First, 40*(2), 180–193. https://doi.org/10.1007/s10834-018-9600-9.

Treanor, M. C. (2018). Income poverty, material deprivation, and lone parenthood. In R. Nieuwenhuis & L. C. Maldonado (Eds.), *The triple bind of single-parent families* (pp. 81–100). Bristol: Policy Press.

Uunk, W. (2004). The economic consequences of divorce for women in the European Union: The impact of welfare state arrangements. *European Journal of Population, 20*(3), 251–285. https://doi.org/10.1007/s10680-004-1694-0.

van Damme, M., Kalmijn, M., & Uunk, W. (2009). The employment of separated women: The impact of individual and institutional factors. *European Sociological Review, 25*(2), 183–197. https://doi.org/10.1093/esr/jcn042.
van der Lippe, T., & van Dijk, L. (2002). Comparative research on women's employment. *Annual Review of Sociology, 28*, 221–241. https://doi.org/10.1146/annurev.soc.28.110601.140833.
Vanderheyden, G., & Mortelmans, D. (2013). Arbeidstrajecten van vrouwen in de periode rond hun (echt)scheiding. In M. Corijn & C. Van Peer (Eds.), *Gezinstransities in Vlaanderen* (pp. 137–156). Brussel: Studiedienst van de Vlaamse Regering.
Wu, Z., & Schimmele, C. M. (2007). Uncoupling in late life. *Generations, 31*(3), 41–46.
Zagel, H., & Hübgen, S. (2018). A life-course approach to single mothers' economic wellbeing in different welfare states. In R. Nieuwenhuis & L. C. Maldonado (Eds.), *The triple bind of single-parent families* (pp. 171–194). Bristol: Policy Press.

Chapter 3
Earnings Trajectories Following Parental Separation Among First-Time Parents in Sweden

Anna-Karin Nylin

Introduction

A large body of research has focused on various aspects of the transition to parenthood and the transition to becoming a single parent; two life events with long-lasting and highly gendered economic consequences. When couples enter parenthood, gender inequalities are often reproduced and reinforced, as women tend to increase the time they spend in care work while decreasing the time they spend in paid work (Evertsson and Boye 2016). This pattern causes the earnings gap between women and men to widen (Musick et al. 2017), even in Sweden, a country known for having high maternal labour force participation rates, a long history of family policy investment, and strong norms of gender equality (Angelov et al. 2016; Nylin et al. 2019). Most of today's single-parent families are the result of a separation of a married or cohabiting couple (Heuveline et al. 2003). In light of these trends, researchers have turned their attention to a wide range of effects that parents as well as children face following a parental separation, including the economic ramifications of separation. Early research on this topic has shown that women experience large declines in household income after divorce and separation, which is generally attributed to a gendered division of labour that existed before the separation (see the review by Holden and Smock 1991). However, later research on this issue has found that men also suffer economically from separation and divorce, which may be due to a drop in earnings related to health impairments following the separation (Brüggmann in this volume). But it appears that some men experience a decrease in household income after a separation because they had interrupted employment after the birth of their first child, or because their female partner was the prime earner in the family (Andreß et al. 2006; McManus and DiPrete 2001).

A.-K. Nylin (✉)
Stockholm University, Stockholm, Sweden
e-mail: anna-karin.nylin@sociology.su.se

M. Kreyenfeld, H. Trappe (eds.), *Parental Life Courses after Separation and Divorce in Europe*, Life Course Research and Social Policies 12,
https://doi.org/10.1007/978-3-030-44575-1_3

This chapter contributes to the large body of literature that has examined gender differences in the economic consequences following parental separation. I focus on the effects of separation on the individual earnings of fathers and mothers. In particular, I investigate the question of how the gendered division of work before separation affects the subsequent earning trajectories of the ex-partners. The data come from a large-scale Swedish register dataset covering the total population. I have chosen to study Sweden in part because it represents a setting in which parental separation is rather common and is less stigmatised than it is in many other countries. Moreover, it is common in Sweden for mothers to participate in the labour force and for fathers to retain a large degree of responsibility for their children post-separation. In addition, Swedish registers cover the whole population, and therefore provide a sample size that is large enough to allow me to longitudinally explore the economic development of coupled women and men as they enter parenthood, and after they separate. These register data thus offer me a unique opportunity to follow family members across households in order to understand subgroup variation. By contrast, panel survey data either do not follow both partners after separation, or follow them with relatively low participation rates.

The analytical sample contains women and men who had their first child between 2002 and 2004, and who were living together at the time of the birth. The earning trajectories of fathers and mothers are investigated up to 8 years after the first birth. I compare men and women who remained partnered with women and men who separated until their first child reached age eight. The latter group is further distinguished by whether separation occurred one, three, or 5 years after the first birth. Earnings are measured in terms of annual earnings in Swedish Krona (SEK). In order to operationalise the gendered division of work before separation, I include a measure for the earnings position 2 years before becoming a parent, measured in earnings quartiles. A caveat of the analysis is that the data do not contain working hours. Another caveat is that re-partnering and its effects on earnings are not examined.

The Swedish Context

Parental Separation of Married and Cohabiting Couples

Declining rates of marriage combined with increasing rates of cohabitation and separation have long distinguished Sweden as a forerunner in demographic change. During the 1970s and 1980s, the non-marital childbearing ratio increased, and cohabitation, even among parents, became a common living arrangement in Sweden (Ohlsson-Wijk et al. 2018). It was also during the 1970s that the requirement that spouses mutually agree to divorce was removed, and divorce rates started to increase (Hoem 1997). Even though divorce risks had levelled off at the turn of the last century (Andersson and Kolk 2016), divorce remains a common transition among Swedish parents. Moreover, like divorce rates among married couples, separation rates among cohabiting couples have been increasing. Today in Sweden, separation rates among cohabiting parents are only slightly higher than divorce rates among married parents (Thomson 2005). Under Swedish law, the differences between divorcing and dissolving a cohabiting union are small. Thus, the two types of couples have similar social security benefits, legal rights, and economic benefits (Perelli-Harris and Sánchez Gassen 2012); and their child custody rights are the same (Schiratzki 2008).

The Role of the Welfare System

In Sweden, the female employment rate has long been high, and is currently almost the same as the male employment rate, even among parents (Statistics Sweden [SCB] 2016). This near parity in employment levels is usually ascribed to the Swedish welfare system. Individual taxation promotes female employment (Selin 2014), and women have the legal right to return to their previous employer and position after taking parental leave (Föräldraledighetslag 1995: 584, The Parental Leave Act 1995: 584). The availability of affordable, high-quality public childcare allows mothers and fathers to stay in paid work after having children, and is used by most parents (Swedish National Agency for Education 2018). This comprehensive welfare system has been found to provide parents with more reliable protection against poverty than other welfare systems that do not encourage parental employment to the same extent (Ferrarini 2006). Hence, if women in Sweden separate, they are less economically vulnerable than their counterparts in many other countries, who may be forced to give up paid employment when they enter motherhood. However, even though single mothers in Sweden are less economically vulnerable than single mothers in other countries, their situations have worsened over time (Nieuwenhuis and Maldonado 2018), as their equalized disposable household income levels have been lagging further and further behind those of coupled mothers (SCB, Household's finances 2014). There is evidence that in Sweden, the financial situations of single parents deteriorated more and did not recover as quickly as the financial situations of the rest of the population during the economic crisis in the 1990s. It has also been shown that reductions in social benefits and the enactment of stricter rules for obtaining means-tested benefits affected single parents more than coupled parents. Although the household earnings of single parents improved during the 2000s, the lower means-tested benefit levels have prevented the incomes of single parents from catching up with those of parents in unions (Swedish Social Insurance Agency 2009).

Prior Research and Hypotheses

Economic Consequences of Parenthood

Parenthood has been found to have a negative impact on women's wages (Gangl and Ziefle 2009), even in Sweden (Angelov et al. 2016; Nylin et al. 2019), where policies supporting the dual earner-carer model have been implemented (Gornick and Meyers 2003). When women take time off from work to care for children, their future earnings are often negatively affected, in part because the breaks they take tend to be considerably longer than those taken by men (Duvander and Viklund 2014). In addition, women decrease their paid work hours by almost 10%, on average, after they have children (Kennerberg 2007). Among parents of children between three and 5 years old, one-third of the mothers, but just 10% of the fathers, are working part time (SCB 2016). Spells of part-time employment can have long-term consequences for an individual's career development and future earnings (Duvander et al. 2015). Using Swedish register data, several studies have shown that there are large gender gaps in income and wages up to 15 years after childbirth, and that women with low educational attainment and earnings are hit harder than other groups (Angelov et al. 2016; Duvander et al. 2015).

The economic approach suggests that parenthood can have a negative impact on wages through various channels. It is, for example, possible that parents are perceived as being less productive (Becker 1993; Budig and England 2001; Mincer and Polacheck 1974). Parents may also be less able than workers without children to invest in on-the-job training (Evertsson 2004). This is especially likely to be the case for women, as they are mainly responsible for childbearing. Thus, in the workplace, women often fall behind men in terms of their experience and compensation levels. While motherhood penalties tend to be smaller in the Nordic countries than they are elsewhere (Sigle-Rushton and Waldfogel 2007), statistical discrimination against all women of childbearing age may explain a portion of the gender differences in wages (Mandel and Semyonov 2005; Ruhm 1998). A tendency for women to take mother-friendly jobs has also been observed in some countries, with women trading higher wages for flexibility (Gangl and Ziefle 2009). By contrast, men have been found to be rewarded with earning premiums after entering parenthood (Cooke 2014; Hodges and Budig 2010; Petersen et al. 2014). There is, however, evidence that when men take even short periods of parental leave, they experience negative wage effects (Albrecht et al. 2015; Evertsson 2016). Signalling theory suggests that employers perceive men who take leave as less committed to their jobs, and penalize them with lower wages (Albrecht et al. 1999; Evertsson 2016). Wage losses after taking time away from work appear to be greatest for the most highly educated women and men (Albrecht et al. 1999; England et al. 2016; Evertsson 2016; Glauber 2018).

Economic Consequences of Union Dissolution

A large body of literature has examined the economic consequences of divorce and separation based on longitudinal data. These studies have shown that after a divorce, women tend to suffer economically as their household income declines and their dependency burden grows (see review by Holden and Smock 1991); and that women with children suffer the most (Mortelmans and Defever 2018; Page and Stevens 2004). Later studies have also found that as the female labour market participation rate increases and the gender wage gap decreases, men are also likely to suffer economically following a divorce. Yet on average, the household income levels of men still decline less than those of women following union dissolution (McManus and DiPrete 2001).

To mitigate the negative economic consequences of a separation, parents tend to use a range of personal strategies, called "coping mechanisms" (see Mortelmans in this volume). One of the main strategies parents use to deal with the cost of union dissolution is increasing their own labour earnings (Duncan and Hoffman 1985; McManus and DiPrete 2001; Weiss 1984). The use of this strategy is the core focus of this study. Especially for a single parent with a higher income level, his/her own labour income is usually the most important component of the household's income (McManus and DiPrete 2001; Weiss 1984).

De Vaus et al. (2017) used data from the United States, the UK, Switzerland, Korea, Germany, and Australia to examine the economic consequences of divorce. They showed that the cross-country differences in these consequences can be explained in large part by differences in women's labour earnings. In the countries where women's labour market participation rates tend to be high while married, women's income levels are more likely to recuperate after they separate (de Vaus et al. 2017). However, when mothers work full-time while married or cohabiting, like they often do in Sweden, there is little scope to further increase their employment after they separate. If women have secure working conditions and high earnings, they may instead choose to reduce their work hours or change to a more flexible job in order to better reconcile work and family life (Alsarve et al. 2017). Thus, women might trade higher earnings for having more time with their family.

Another important strategy parents use to mitigate the economic consequences of separation is re-partnering (DiPrete and McManus 2000; Duncan and Hoffman 1985; Holden and Smock 1991). It has been found that for women, re-partnering is a more effective way to increase their economic well-being than expanding their employment activities (Jansen et al. 2009). Other studies have shown that re-partnering has a smaller impact on women's economic well-being (McKeever and Wolfinger 2001; Ozawa and Yoon 2002). Unfortunately, there is no possibility to control for re-partnering in this study.

Shared parenting arrangements and child alimony can also mitigate economic consequences of divorce and separation. Currently in Sweden, 35% of children with separated parents are in shared physical custody arrangements (SCB 2014). This share is considerably higher than it is in many other countries (Wadsby et al. 2014).

When Swedish mothers instead collect child alimony, they often only receive the minimum level of 1250 SEK[1] per month, regardless of the father's income.

In addition to alimony payments, various forms of governmental support can mitigate the economic consequences of separation. Single parents may receive targeted cash benefits or more general types of support. The most common form of state support in Sweden is institutional childcare, which ensures that parents have access to the labour market. This type of support has been shown to benefit parents more than targeted income-related benefits (Bradshaw and Finch 2002; Maldonado and Nieuwenhuis 2015; Uunk 2004).

Hypotheses

In this study, changes in parents' earnings following the birth of their first child are analysed by comparing couples who separated with couples who stayed together for at least 8 years. From earlier research, we know that parents, and especially mothers, tend to suffer economically following a separation. To deal with the negative economic consequences of a separation, parents may seek to increase their labour earnings by, for example, moving to a better-paying job, increasing their working hours, or shortening their parental leave period. If parents who separate invest more in paid work in order to increase their earnings, it is likely that their human capital will also increase relative to that of coupled parents. If this is the case, it may be assumed that compared to coupled parents, separated parents experience more earnings growth, not just immediately after the separation, but over the long term.

If parents want to increase their labour earnings by increasing their working hours, their ability to do so depends on how much they were working before the separation. Having a child affects the working hours of parents in a highly gendered way, with men spending more time than women in paid work. Thus, men might have less room than women to improve their labour market earnings. However, having substantial childcare obligations could prevent women from expanding their paid work activities in order to increase their earnings. Hence, it is possible that separation has only small effects on the earnings trajectories of both mothers and fathers.

The economic impact of separation may differ depending on when the separation took place. As the mother often takes the initial period of parental leave, leaving the father to take parental leave later in the child's life (Eriksson 2018), women who separate in the year immediately after giving birth may face greater difficulties in adjusting their labour earnings in response to the separation than women who separate when their child is older. As fathers generally use considerably less parental leave than mothers, the timing of the separation might be less relevant for men than it is for women.

As individuals have different economic positions before they become parents, their options for adjusting their earnings in response to a separation are also likely

[1]This is the same amount that the government pays to parents with sole custody of the children when the other parent refuses to provide economic support (Statistics Sweden 2014).

to differ. Parents with high labour earnings pre-birth may have been working longer hours, and might therefore have little room to further increase their hours post-separation. At the same time, however, parents with high pre-birth labour earnings may be in a better position than their counterparts with lower earnings to reduce their working hours. They might also have better chances of moving to a more parent-friendly job, or of trading higher earnings for more flexibility in order to improve their work-family balance post-separation. Yet parents who use this strategy risk having lower earnings growth in the long term due to human capital depreciation. Conversely, parents with low pre-birth labour earnings may have been in part-time work, and might thus have room for upward adjustments in earnings after a separation. Low-earning parents are also likely to need to increase their work earnings, as separation can be costly. Parents who pursue this strategy have lower chances of suffering from human capital depreciation, and higher chances of experiencing positive earnings growth in the long run. However, as having low labour earnings pre-birth is also associated with poorer job mobility and socio-economic circumstances, the ability of these parents to improve their labour earnings might be limited, leaving them especially vulnerable to the negative economic consequences of parental separation.

Data, Variables, and Method

Method

Earlier research on post-separation changes in earnings trajectories has not always compared women and men who separated with couples who stayed together. However, a study that focuses only on changes in earnings among those who separated risks overstating earnings losses. Hence, it is important to compare mothers and fathers who did and did not separate (Bayaz-Ozturk et al. 2018); especially given that couples who remain together also experience earnings changes in relation to childbirth. To estimate the earnings trajectories of parents in relation to their entry into parenthood and to the event of separation, and to identify possible differences between women and men who did and did not separate, I rely on fixed-effects models. Fixed-effects models control not only for observable variables, but for unobservable variables that are stable over time (Allison 2009). Nonetheless, time-varying unobservable differences between intact couples and separated couples can still result in selection effects.

The outcome variable is annual pre-tax earnings in SEK, not including work-related transfers like parental leave benefits. While the transformation of earnings to a logged scale is often used, I do not use it here because my interest in this study lies in investigating within-person changes from 2 years before the birth, rather than in assessing proportionality between groups. The analysis is done separately for women and men in different labour earnings quartiles (see below). I estimate how women's and men's predicted earnings trajectories change across subgroups of couples who stayed together and couples who separated one, three, and 5 years after the first birth by modelling two-way interactions between time to/from birth and subgroups. The model can be summarised by the following equation:

$$Y_{it} = \sum_{s=-2}^{s=8} \eta_s D_i S_i + \gamma X_{it} + \alpha_i + \mu_{it}$$

where Y measures labour earnings for individual i in year t, D is a set of $s = 11$ dummies for each year two before and up to eight after the first birth (reference is 2 years before the birth), and S represents dummies for subgroups of women and men who stayed together and women and men who separated. The X is a vector of controls that vary across individuals and years. α_i is a couple-level fixed effect, and μ_{it} is the error term. The control vectors consist of the time-varying events of having a second child and getting married, as well as the individual's own level of education, the other parent's level of education, and the other parent's annual labour earnings. Ideally, I would also control for re-partnering and hours worked, but the data used here do not allow me to do so.

Data

Having access to information on the total population from Swedish administrative registers allows me to perform a fine-grained analysis in which potential subgroup variation in earnings trajectories among first-time parents following separation is explored. I follow women and men who became parents for the first time between 2002 and 2004 using a panel dataset in which earnings trajectories are analysed separately in different earnings quartiles. The study population is restricted to women and men who had positive earnings 2 years before the birth, and who did not earn more than one million SEK during a given year (based on 2012 values). This restriction led to 7% of the original sample of couples being dropped in the analysis of women, and 10% being dropped in the analysis of men. The majority of the excluded cases were due to women or men lacking labour income 2 years before birth. Censoring was carried out if a parent emigrated or died during the observation window or before the union dissolution. In the study, 67,429 women and 70,330 men are followed from 2 years before the first birth. Due to censoring, around 2% of these women and men cannot be followed for a full 8 years after the first birth.

Independent Variables

To explore subgroup variation in earnings adjustments among women and men, the population is divided into earnings quartiles based on their labour earnings 2 years before the first birth. Table 3.1 reports the numbers of women and men who stayed together compared to the numbers who separated within 8 years of the first birth.

Table 3.1a Number of women in labour earnings quartiles 2 years before the first birth

			of which separated		
	Coupled	Separation within 8 years after birth	Separation when child was age one	Separation when child was age three	Separation when child was age five
1st quartile	14,300	4499	44%	39%	35%
2nd quartile	15,584	3208	24%	27%	27%
3rd quartile	16,307	2481	18%	20%	20%
4th quartile	16,704	2082	15%	14%	18%
Total	62,895	12,270	1369	1552	1613

Table 3.1b Number of men in labour earnings quartiles 2 years before the first birth

			of which separated		
	Coupled	Separation within 8 years after birth	Separation when child was age one	Separation when child was age three	Separation when child was age five
1st quartile	14,613	5155	45%	40%	35%
2nd quartile	16,088	3671	24%	26%	28%
3rd quartile	16,822	2949	17%	20%	19%
4th quartile	17,506	2250	14%	14%	17%
Total	65,029	14,025	1632	1844	1825

The findings displayed in the table show that separation is associated with lower earnings, as nearly 40% of the women and men who separated, compared to just over 20% of the women and men who stayed together, are in the lowest earnings quartile. The results also indicate that the women and men who separated 1 year after the first birth are overrepresented in the lowest earnings quartile compared to the women and men who separated later (see shares in Tables 3.1a and b).

Education is measured as the educational attainment for both the index person and the other parent. This indicator is allowed to vary over years, as it is common for women and men in Sweden to increase their levels of education later in life, even after becoming parents (Thalberg 2013). Like the dependent variable, the labour earnings of the other parent are measured annually as pre-tax earnings in SEK, not including work-related transfers like parental leave benefits. The event of a second birth or of a marriage is controlled for yearly as a binary variable.

Results

Descriptive Results

Tables 3.2a and b report the average labour earnings 2 years before the first birth among women and men. We can see that men tended to have higher earnings than women before the birth. This observation is partly attributable to men being somewhat older than their partners when they become parents, but it is also due to gender differences on the labour market. The earnings differences 2 years before the first birth are small between the women and men who stayed coupled for at least 8 years and the women and men who separated.

The general earnings trajectories are illustrated in Fig. 3.1, and show that both women's and men's earnings decreased following childbirth. However, women's earnings decreased more because they generally took a longer parental leave. A second earnings dip is also visible among women 3 years after the first birth. This is due to the birth of a second child. At 8 years after the first birth, women's earnings had returned to their pre-birth earnings level, while men's earnings had surpassed that level. This is found to be the case for all parents, regardless of when they separated (not shown in Fig. 3.1).

Regression Results

The results from the fixed-effects models are presented in terms of average predicted probabilities (average marginal effects). Figure 3.2 visualises women's earnings trajectories from 2 years before the first birth to 8 years after. Due to the width

Table 3.2a Average labour earnings 2 years before the first birth in thousands of SEK, women

	Coupled	Separation when child was age one	Separation when child was age three	Separation when child was age five
1st quartile	143	139	140	141
2nd quartile	218	216	216	215
3rd quartile	265	264	265	264
4th quartile	378	382	372	369

Table 3.2b Average labour earnings 2 years before the first birth in thousands of SEK, men

	Coupled	Separation when child was age one	Separation when child was age three	Separation when child was age five
1st quartile	177	168	172	173
2nd quartile	264	262	263	263
3rd quartile	321	320	318	320
4th quartile	457	461	443	462

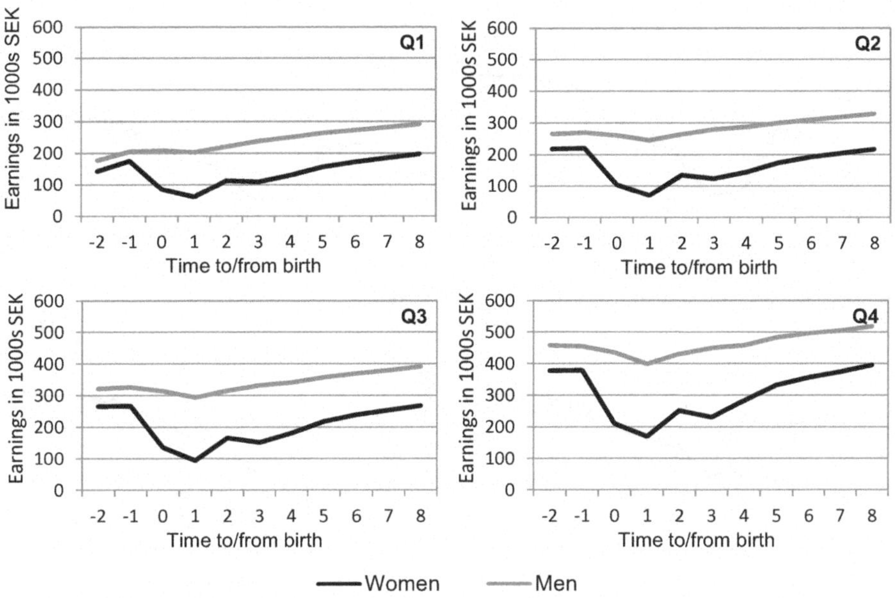

Fig. 3.1 Average labour earnings by time to/from the first birth in earnings quartiles 2 years before the first birth

of the scale, the differences between women who separated and women who stayed coupled can be hard to discern in the figure. Therefore, Table 3.3 also shows the differences in percentage points between separated and coupled women. The full set of marginal effects, including confidence intervals, are found in Tables 3.5-3.12 in the appendix.

Women who separated, with the exception of those in the two highest earnings quartiles, are shown to have more positive earnings trajectories in the year of separation than women who stayed coupled. This finding indicates that these women increased their labour supply, and thus increased their labour earnings after separating. However, these differences are small and often statistically insignificant. Hence, it appears that the development of earnings among women prior to separation and a few years after separation was similar to the development among women who stayed coupled. But by 8 years after the first birth, the earnings trajectories of separated and coupled women had diverged, leaving separated women with poorer earnings trajectories. This lagged effect of separation is most evident among women who separated one or 3 years after the first birth. However, it is possible that the gap between coupled women and women who separated 5 years after the first birth will increase as time goes by. The largest discrepancies in changes in earnings are found between coupled women and separated women in the lowest earnings quartile. Between these women, a gap of up to 40 percentage points in earnings growth can be seen 8 years after the first birth.

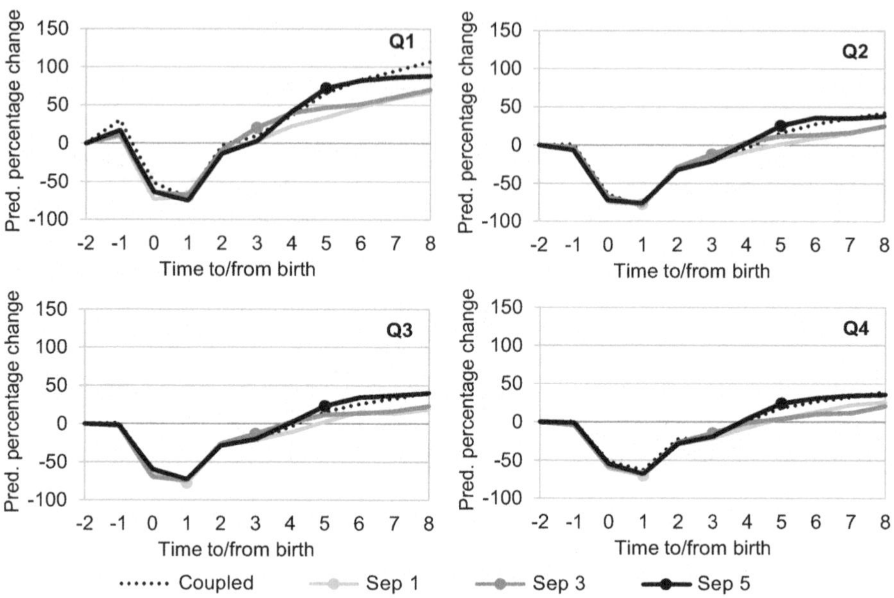

Fig. 3.2 Predicted percentage change from 2 years before the first birth among women by subgroups and earnings quartiles

Notes: Results from fixed-effects model with annual earnings as a dependent variable. Control variables are: annual labour earnings of the other parent, own educational level and educational level of the other parent, event of marriage, and event of the second birth

Table 3.3 Percentage point distance from coupled women's predicted changes in labour earnings at the year of separation and at 8 years after the first birth

	Year of separation			Eight years after birth		
	Separation when child was age one	Separation when child was age three	Separation when child was age five	Separation when child was age one	Separation when child was age three	Separation when child was age five
1st quartile	1	10	6	−40	−37	−19
2nd quartile	3	10	9	−17	−18	−4
3rd quartile	−2	9	8	−21	−17	0
4th quartile	−8	4	6	−14	−19	−4

Notes: see Fig. 3.2

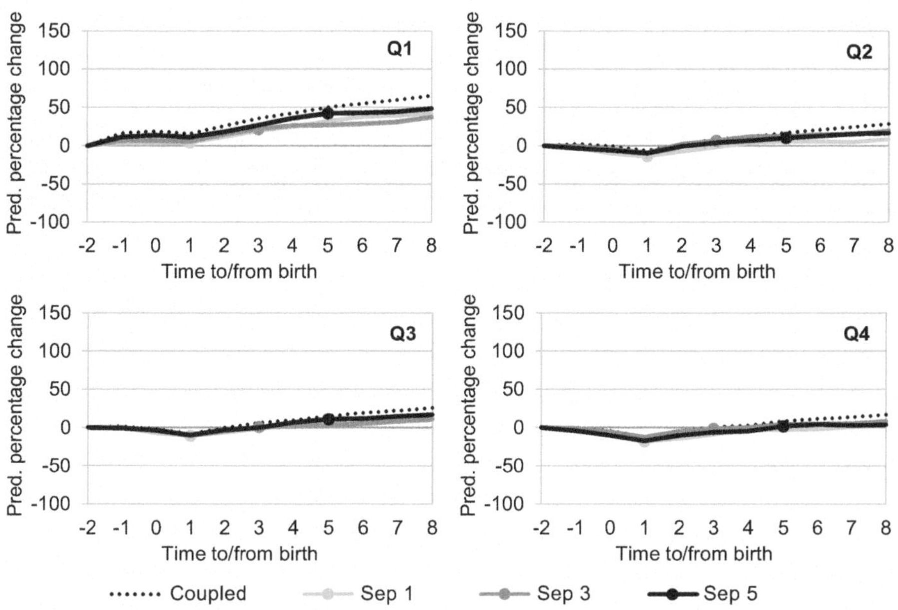

Fig. 3.3 Predicted percentage change from 2 years before the first birth among men by subgroups and earnings quartiles

Notes: Results from fixed-effects model with annual earnings as a dependent variable. Control variables are: annual labour earnings of the other parent, own educational level and educational level of the other parent, event of marriage, and event of second birth.

Figure 3.3 shows the predicted changes in earnings between men who separated and men who stayed coupled. As above, the differences in earnings changes between the study groups are also given in numbers in Table 3.4. Unlike among women, the results show that men who separated had poorer earnings growth directly after separating than men who stayed coupled. These poorer earnings developments intensified with time. Thus, like among women, we find a lagged separation effect on men's earnings trajectories 8 years after the first birth. The discrepancies in earnings growth between separated and coupled men observed at 8 years after the first birth were often close to the magnitude of the differences found among women in earnings quartiles two to four. The discrepancies between men are found to be largest in the lowest earnings quartile, but still considerably smaller than those detected among women in the lowest earnings quartile. However, earnings growth at 8 years after the first birth are shown to be lower among men who separated 5 years after the first birth than among men who stayed coupled, and this difference appears to be greater than it is among women. Moreover, earnings developments among men in the lowest earnings quartile stand out compared to those among men in the higher earnings quartiles, as coupled men displayed stronger earnings growth than separated men even before they separated. This result could be due to selection effects that the statistical methods cannot account for.

Table 3.4 Percentage point distance from coupled men's predicted changes in work income at year of separation and at 8 years after birth

	Year of separation			Eight years after birth		
	Separation when child was age one	Separation when child was age three	Separation when child was age five	Separation when child was age one	Separation when child was age three	Separation when child was age five
1st quartile	−12	−14	−8	−23	−28	−17
2nd quartile	−7	−2	−7	−20	−9	−12
3rd quartile	−3	−6	−4	−13	−15	−9
4th quartile	−6	−2	−7	−15	−9	−13

Notes: see Fig. 3.3

Discussion

Prior research has shown that divorce and separation have negative economic consequences for both women and men. Typically, the disposable incomes of the ex-partners decline because they move into separate households and no longer benefit from the economies of scale that exist when resources are pooled in one household unit. Moreover, women often experience a rapid decrease in their equivalent household income, both because they continue to reside with their children, and because they may not have worked full-time prior to the union dissolution. Thus, in most cases, women and men need to increase their labour supply and their own labour earnings following a separation. A positive side effect of this pressure is that the ex-partners' human capital accumulation should increase as well, which should result in separated parents having better earnings trajectories than coupled mothers and fathers. However, the findings from this study do not support this assumption. Instead, a lagged separation effect is detected, whereby separated parents were on a lower earnings trajectory than coupled parents 8 years after the separation. A gendered effect is found to exist, as the gaps between the earnings developments of separated and coupled women were considerably larger than they were among men. It appears that the timing of separation had little effect on the results, with the possible exception for those parents who separated 5 years after the first birth. Separated women and men in the lowest pre-birth earnings quartile suffered from the poorest earnings growth compared to coupled parents.

The finding that the earnings adjustments directly following separation were small is in line with cross-national findings on changes in household income after separation. Andreß et al. (2006) found that the negative economic consequences of separation were smaller and more gender-equal in Sweden than they were in Belgium, Germany, Great Britain, and Italy. They attributed this pattern to Sweden's high employment rate among mothers, which they argued acts as a safeguard against economic difficulties. As most women and men in Sweden tend to be in full time paid work, their opportunities to increase their working hours in order to improve their earnings are small. Even when on parental leave, their earnings are secured. Thus, the extent to which women and men in Sweden need to improve their economic situations after separating might be lower than it is elsewhere. This could also be a reason why in this study the timing of separation is shown to have a rather small effect on earnings developments.

However, even though the negative consequences of separation appear to be more modest in Sweden than in other countries, Andreß et al. (2006) also found that women and men have to deal with more long-run negative consequences in Sweden than they do in other countries. This observation matches this study's finding of a lagged separation effect on labour earnings. This result raises the question of what the causes of such a lagged separation effect might be. It is possible that single parents reduce their labour supply in the long run. As time elapses, parents might feel the need to decrease their work hours in order to balance their total workload at the expense of higher earnings. An argument that speaks against this interpretation is that over time, children are becoming increasingly independent. The chances of a new partner joining the family also rise, balancing out the increased workload the parent faces while single. This should make room for parents who are separated to once again focus on paid work to a similar degree as coupled parents, which should, in turn, result in improved earnings trajectories. As no evidence of such a pattern is found in this study, other factors might be at play. It is possible that employer discrimination against single parents has an impact. Earlier research has shown that both women and men are punished with wage losses (Aisenbrey et al. 2009; Albrecht et al. 2015; Evertsson 2016; Gangl and Ziefle 2009), possibly due to reductions in human capital accumulation when they become parents (Becker 1993; Mincer and Polacheck 1974). Although these wage penalties are small in Nordic countries (Sigle-Rushton and Waldfogel 2007), they may have a greater impact on separated parents if employers perceive them as having more difficulties committing themselves to paid work than parents in intact couples. An important task for future research is to isolate the effects that stem from employer behaviour from the effects that are related to lone parents' deliberate choices to reduce their labour market engagement.

The assumption that parents with differing initial resources tackle separation differently is confirmed to some extent. The results show that women in the highest earnings quartile who separated 1 year after the first birth saw a decrease in their earnings (compared to coupled women in the same earnings bracket). This finding could be due to these women taking more unpaid parental leave days than others (see Duvander and Korsell in this volume). The strategy of trading earnings for family time is most often used by those with economic flexibility to do so (Alsarve et al. 2017). It appears, however, that the use of this strategy did not result in poorer earnings growth in the long term for the women in this group, as theories on human capital depreciation suggest. Instead, the lagged separation effect is found to be strongest among parents with the lowest pre-birth labour earnings. This finding indicates that these parents are especially vulnerable to the economic consequences of separation. While the belief that employment is the best strategy to shield parents from poverty is strongly anchored in Swedish policy-making, it may be difficult for some groups of low-income parents in this country to increase their earnings. As labour markets have become more unequal and employment more precarious, the economic well-being of single parents is under threat. In line with Nieuwenhuis and Maldonado (2018), it can be argued that social benefits, social assistance, and child support payments are important instruments for improving the economic well-being of single parents.

Acknowledgments This work was supported by the Swedish Research Council for Health, Working Life and Welfare [2015-01139] and the Swedish Research Council [2015-013191].

Appendix (Tables 3.5, 3.6, 3.7, 3.8, 3.9, 3.10, 3.11 and 3.12)

Table 3.5 Predicted marginal effect on labour earnings from 2 years before the first birth among women in earnings quartile 1, by time to/from the first birth

	Coupled		Sep. 1		Sep. 3		Sep. 5	
−2	110,353	± 1367	110,353	± 1367	110,353	± 1367	110,353	± 1367
−1	143,791	± 1435	120,047	± 8220	122,559	± 8142	128,731	± 8408
0	53,308	± 1419	29,410	± 8207	39,492	± 8130	40,314	± 8405
1	32,039	± 1380	33,467	± 8202	35,581	± 8120	27,469	± 8397
2	107,686	± 1261	97,238	± 8200	100,725	± 8108	95,906	± 8375
3	121,328	± 1281	114,164	± 8195	132,827	± 8106	113,625	± 8372
4	151,079	± 1335	135,217	± 8195	153,981	± 8115	156,500	± 8374
5	182,688	± 1373	147,915	± 8216	161,647	± 8126	189,859	± 8377
6	201,895	± 1401	162,373	± 8225	166,301	± 8141	200,993	± 8385
7	215,192	± 1421	175,592	± 8236	176,830	± 8144	205,482	± 8396
8	228,284	± 1442	184,171	± 8260	187,993	± 8155	207,629	± 8401

Table 3.6 Predicted marginal effect on labour earnings from 2 years before the first birth among women in earnings quartile 2, by time to/from the first birth

	Coupled		Sep. 1		Sep. 3		Sep. 5	
−2	176,894	± 1244	176,894	± 1244	176,894	± 1244	176,894	± 1244
−1	178,867	± 1275	170,275	± 10,409	172,397	± 9068	165,875	± 8903
0	63,561	± 1260	43,954	± 10,404	56,685	± 9066	48,479	± 8896
1	33,390	± 1227	39,047	± 10,402	36,141	± 9062	41,822	± 8889
2	125,580	± 1108	121,273	± 10,431	125,286	± 9052	119,810	± 8876
3	137,971	± 1124	140,872	± 10,467	155,212	± 9053	140,333	± 8876
4	169,727	± 1173	162,104	± 10,466	183,281	± 9075	181,364	± 8877
5	204,954	± 1208	178,862	± 10,466	197,404	± 9098	221,336	± 8879
6	225,378	± 1233	192,442	± 10,467	199,947	± 9110	239,992	± 8885
7	239,391	± 1251	203,392	± 10,487	205,400	± 9137	238,789	± 8891
8	251,535	± 1269	221,234	± 10,498	220,158	± 9144	243,618	± 8903

Table 3.7 Predicted marginal effect on labour earnings from 2 years before the first birth among women in earnings quartile 3, by time to/from the first birth

	Coupled		Sep. 1		Sep. 3		Sep. 5	
−2	218,437	1400	218,437	1400	218,437	1400	218,437	1400
−1	220,089	1400	211,909	13,520	211,934	11,817	214,870	11,815
0	89,526	1382	76,649	13,519	65,411	11,814	88,338	11,812
1	53,633	1342	48,182	13,518	55,780	11,810	58,937	11,807
2	157,494	1198	156,123	13,510	161,198	11,789	155,939	11,791
3	169,758	1228	171,224	13,557	188,713	11,790	174,349	11,783
4	210,113	1283	193,873	13,588	221,573	11,817	221,262	11,777
5	251,844	1316	223,629	13,654	243,641	11,816	268,676	11,780
6	275,045	1338	251,395	13,706	247,786	11,835	293,229	11,790
7	290,825	1354	246,767	13,720	253,774	11,845	299,049	11,812
8	306,114	1369	259,253	13,721	268,212	11,866	305,962	11,810

Table 3.8 Predicted marginal effect on labour earnings from 2 years before the first birth among women in earnings quartile 4, by time to/from the first birth

	Coupled		Sep. 1		Sep. 3		Sep. 5	
−2	317,109	2052	317,109	2052	317,109	2052	317,109	2052
−1	318,813	2023	313,845	21,386	303,211	20,893	314,164	17,668
0	152,012	1996	123,569	21,385	131,328	20,892	143,645	17,661
1	119,176	1935	93,309	21,382	100,368	20,843	100,468	17,653
2	245,105	1713	224,883	21,401	232,360	20,826	227,314	17,633
3	256,269	1775	249,313	21,406	269,896	20,827	257,538	17,637
4	321,291	1854	293,852	21,436	313,802	20,833	331,022	17,639
5	375,349	1894	331,550	21,436	329,272	20,861	394,474	17,645
6	401,531	1919	358,759	21,437	349,369	20,944	414,676	17,661
7	420,116	1937	386,408	21,499	353,877	20,932	425,679	17,678
8	443,067	1954	399,021	21,498	382,451	20,959	429,356	17,679

Table 3.9 Predicted marginal effect on labour earnings from 2 years before the first birth among men in earnings quartile 1, by time to/from the first birth

	Coupled		Sep. 1		Sep. 3		Sep. 5	
−2	178,136	± 1491	178,136	± 1491	178,136	± 1491	178,136	± 1491
−1	206,797	± 1583	183,360	± 8390	189,147	± 8255	198,241	± 8811
0	212,103	± 1629	184,131	± 8375	189,832	± 8253	202,260	± 8822
1	206,012	± 1620	185,010	± 8369	187,991	± 8244	197,770	± 8815
2	224,095	± 1415	198,808	± 8362	203,965	± 8221	210,156	± 8780
3	241,757	± 1434	212,433	± 8356	216,424	± 8219	226,142	± 8778
4	253,506	± 1486	222,698	± 8373	224,891	± 8232	241,873	± 8778
5	267,011	± 1539	234,757	± 8381	225,768	± 8242	253,059	± 8786
6	276,143	± 1583	244,805	± 8389	228,899	± 8253	254,391	± 8797
7	284,513	± 1617	248,145	± 8405	233,115	± 8268	256,991	± 8811
8	294,145	± 1650	252,649	± 8418	244,278	± 8284	264,223	± 8815

Table 3.10 Predicted marginal effect on labour earnings from 2 years before the first birth among men in earnings quartile 2, by time to/from the first birth

	Coupled		Sep. 1		Sep. 3		Sep. 5	
−2	259,956	± 1237	259,956	± 1237	259,956	± 1237	259,956	± 1237
−1	265,662	± 1275	252,377	± 9761	256,988	± 8644	250,494	± 8385
0	257,868	± 1332	232,455	± 9768	247,685	± 8647	244,542	± 8385
1	242,912	± 1333	224,422	± 9766	235,123	± 8642	234,341	± 8373
2	263,803	± 1127	239,976	± 9757	265,149	± 8616	258,390	± 8349
3	281,859	± 1138	255,192	± 9765	276,603	± 8618	270,518	± 8345
4	289,763	± 1183	270,428	± 9772	290,788	± 8624	277,707	± 8348
5	303,788	± 1229	274,638	± 9794	291,687	± 8645	286,360	± 8354
6	313,847	± 1266	273,519	± 9811	297,008	± 8653	293,031	± 8376
7	322,965	± 1294	272,997	± 9823	297,648	± 8655	300,745	± 8379
8	333,414	± 1322	281,807	± 9833	309,860	± 8659	302,633	± 8388

Table 3.11 Predicted marginal effect on labour earnings from 2 years before the first birth among men in earnings quartile 3, by time to/from the first birth

	Coupled		Sep. 1		Sep. 3		Sep. 5	
−2	315,239	± 1358	315,239	± 1358	315,239	± 1358	315,239	± 13,580
−1	320,041	± 1368	312,681	± 12,578	315,175	± 11,065	312,700	± 11,090
0	309,163	± 1428	291,200	± 12,573	301,610	± 11,057	304,030	± 11,097
1	289,400	± 1433	280,214	± 12,552	282,646	± 11,046	284,972	± 11,093
2	314,409	± 1193	295,564	± 12,584	300,157	± 11,027	306,172	± 11,070
3	334,611	± 1210	310,563	± 12,594	316,940	± 11,020	314,754	± 11,070
4	345,081	± 1260	326,833	± 12,621	319,917	± 11,035	336,215	± 11,073
5	361,946	± 1307	328,349	± 12,621	323,483	± 11,037	349,561	± 11,080
6	375,043	± 1348	334,741	± 12,649	331,156	± 11,031	351,552	± 11,089
7	384,600	± 1376	344,007	± 12,663	340,810	± 11,049	361,460	± 11,100
8	397,124	± 1405	356,506	± 12,666	348,610	± 11,076	368,177	± 11,100

Table 3.12 Predicted marginal effect on labour earnings from 2 years before the first birth among men in earnings quartile 4, by time to/from the first birth

	Coupled		Sep. 1		Sep. 3		Sep. 5	
−2	450,096	± 1883	450,096	± 18,830	450,096	± 1883	450,096	± 18,830
−1	447,523	± 1862	449,187	± 18,964	444,217	± 18,201	431,135	± 16,616
0	429,525	± 1918	409,080	± 18,953	424,267	± 18,157	404,226	± 16,610
1	394,625	± 1914	368,411	± 18,953	393,079	± 18,157	372,149	± 16,609
2	430,255	± 1607	385,110	± 18,957	426,984	± 18,132	405,129	± 16,564
3	452,691	± 1651	408,401	± 19,051	442,426	± 18,132	423,204	± 16,554
4	462,265	± 1716	434,737	± 19,048	450,684	± 18,181	429,901	± 16,544
5	487,682	± 1776	435,958	± 19,074	468,419	± 18,203	458,209	± 16,552
6	501,709	± 1819	439,876	± 19,077	471,031	± 18,263	470,144	± 16,569
7	511,708	± 1852	453,599	± 19,102	473,319	± 18,302	463,457	± 16,572
8	525,738	± 1890	458,882	± 19,129	486,733	± 18,324	467,187	± 16,573

References

Aisenbrey, S., Evertsson, M., & Grunow, D. (2009). Is there a career penalty for mothers' time out? A comparison of Germany, Sweden and the United States. *Social Forces, 88*(2), 573–606. https://doi.org/10.1353/sof.0.0252.

Albrecht, J. M., Edin, P.-A., Sundström, M., & Vroman, S. B. (1999). Career interruptions and subsequent earnings: A reexamination using Swedish data. *The Journal of Human Resources, 34*(2), 294–311. https://doi.org/10.2307/146347.

Albrecht, J., Thoursie, P., & Vroman, S. (2015). *Parental leave and the glass ceiling in Sweden* (Working paper 2015: 14). Uppsala: IFAU, Institutet för arbetsmarknadspolitisk utvärdering.

Allison, P. D. (2009). *Fixed effects regression models* (Quantitative applications in the social sciences, Vol. 160). London: SAGE Publications.

Alsarve, J., Lundqvist, Å., & Roman, C. (2017). *Ensamma mammor: Dilemman, resurser, strategier*. Malmö: Gleerups.

Andersson, G., & Kolk, M. (2016). Trends in childbearing, marriage and divorce in Sweden: An update with data up to 2012. *Finnish Yearbook of Population Research, 50*(2015), 21–30.

Andreß, H. J., Borgloh, B., Bröckel, M., Giesselmann, M., & Hummelsheim, D. (2006). The economic consequences of partnership dissolution: A comparative analysis of panel studies from Belgium, Germany, Great Britain, Italy, and Sweden. *European Sociological Review, 22*(5), 533–560. https://doi.org/10.1093/esr/jcl012.

Angelov, N., Johansson, P., & Lindahl, E. (2016). Parenthood and the gender gap in pay. *Journal of Labor Economics, 34*(3), 545–579. https://doi.org/10.1086/684851.

Bayaz-Ozturk, G., Burkhauser, R. V., Couch, K. A., & Hauser, R. (2018). The effects of union dissolution on the economic resources of men and women: A comparative analysis of Germany and the United States, 1985–2013. *The Annals of the American Academy of Political and Social Science, 680*(1), 235–258. https://doi.org/10.1177/0002716218793608.

Becker, G. S. (1993). *Human capital: A theoretical and empirical analysis, with special reference to education*. Chicago: University of Chicago Press.

Bradshaw, J., & Finch, N. (2002). *A comparison of child benefit packages in 22 countries* (Research report no 174). Leeds: Department for Work and Pensions.

Budig, J. M., & England, P. (2001). The wage penalty for motherhood. *American Sociological Review, 66*(2), 204–225. https://doi.org/10.2307/2657415.

Cooke, L. P. (2014). Gendered parenthood penalties and premiums across the earnings distribution in Australia, the United Kingdom, and the United States. *European Sociological Review, 30*(3), 360–372. https://doi.org/10.1093/esr/jcu044.

de Vaus, D., Gray, M., Qu, L., & Stanton, D. (2017). The economic consequences of divorce in six OECD countries. *Australian Social Policy Association, 52*(2), 180–199. https://doi.org/10.1002/ajs4.13.

DiPrete, T. A., & McManus, P. A. (2000). Family change, employment transitions, and the welfare state: Household income dynamics in the United States and Germany. *American Sociological Review, 65*(3), 343–370. https://doi.org/10.2307/2657461.

Duncan, G. J., & Hoffman, S. D. (1985). A reconsideration of the economic consequences of marital dissolution. *Demography, 22*(4), 485–497. https://doi.org/10.2307/2061584.

Duvander, A. -Z., & Viklund, I. (2014). Kvinnors och mäns föräldraledighet. In SOU 2014:28 (Ed.), *Lönsamt arbete? Familjeansvarets fördelning och konsekvenser* [Profitable work? Distribution and consequences of family responsibility] (Governmental report for the delegation for gender equality in working life, pp. 23–61). Stockholm: Fritzes.

Duvander, A.-Z., Ferrarini, T., & Johansson, M. (2015). *Familjepolitik för alla? En ESO-rapport om föräldrapenning och jämställdhet* [Family policy for everyone? An ESO report on parental benefit and gender equality] (Rapport till Expertgruppen för studier i offentlig ekonomi 2015: 5). Stockholm: Elanders Sverige AB.

England, P., Bearak, J., Budig, M. J., & Hodges, M. J. (2016). Do highly paid, highly skilled women experience the largest motherhood penalty? *American Sociological Review, 81*(6), 1161–1189. https://doi.org/10.1177/0003122416673598.

Eriksson, H. (2018). Taking turns or having it all: Care trajectories of dual-caring couples. *European Journal of Population, 35*(1), 191–219. https://doi.org/10.1007/s10680-018-9473-5.

Evertsson, M. (2004). Formal on-the-job training: A gender-typed experience and wage-related advantage? *European Sociological Review, 20*(1), 79–94. https://doi.org/10.1093/esr/20.1.79.

Evertsson, M. (2016). Parental leave and careers: Women's and men's wages after parental leave in Sweden. *Advances in Life Course Research, 29*, 26–40. https://doi.org/10.1016/j.alcr.2016.02.002.

Evertsson, M., & Boye, K. (2016). The gendered transition to parenthood: Lasting inequalities in the home and in the labor market. In R. A. Scott & M. C. Buchmann (Eds.), *Emerging trends in the social and behavioral sciences: An interdisciplinary, searchable, and linkable resource* (pp. 1–16). Wiley Online Library.

Ferrarini, T. (2006). *Parental leave institutions in eighteen post-war welfare States*. Doctoral Dissertation, Stockholm University, Swedish Institute for Social Research.

Föräldraledighetslag. [Parental Leave Act]. (1995). Government Offices of Sweden. SFS 1995: 584. https://www.riksdagen.se/sv/dokument-lagar/dokument/svensk-forfattningssamling/foraldraledighetslag-1995584_sfs-1995-584. Accessed 20 July 2019.

Gangl, M., & Ziefle, A. (2009). Motherhood, labor force behavior, and women's careers: An empirical assessment of the wage penalty for motherhood in Britain, Germany, and the United States. *Demography, 46*(2), 341–369. https://doi.org/10.1353/dem.0.0056.

Glauber, R. (2018). Trends in the motherhood wage penalty and fatherhood wage premium for low, middle, and high earners. *Demography, 55*(5), 1663–1680. https://doi.org/10.1007/s13524-018-0712-5.

Gornick, J., & Meyers, M. (2003). *Families that work: Policies for reconciling parenthood and employment*. New York: Russell Sage Foundation.

Heuveline, P., Timberlake, J. M., & Furstenberg, F. F. (2003). Shifting childrearing to single mothers: Results from 17 western countries. *Population and Development Review, 29*(1), 47–71. https://doi.org/10.1111/j.1728-4457.2003.00047.x.

Hodges, M. J., & Budig, M. J. (2010). Who gets the daddy bonus? Organizational hegemonic masculinity and the impact of fatherhood on earnings. *Gender & Society, 24*(6), 717–745. https://doi.org/10.1177/0891243210386729.

Hoem, J. M. (1997). Educational gradients in divorce risks in Sweden in recent decades. *Population Studies, 51*(1), 19–27. https://doi.org/10.1080/0032472031000149696.

Holden, K. C., & Smock, P. J. (1991). The economic costs of marital dissolution: Why do women bear a disproportionate cost? *Annual Review of Sociology, 17*(1), 51–78. https://doi.org/10.1146/annurev.so.17.080191.000411.

Jansen, M., Mortelmans, D., & Snoeckx, L. (2009). Repartnering and (re)employment: Strategies to cope with the economic consequences of partnership dissolution. *Journal of Marriage and Family, 71*(5), 1271–1293. https://doi.org/10.1111/j.1741-3737.2009.00668.x.

Kennerberg, L. (2007). *Hur förändras kvinnors och mäns arbetssituation när de får barn?* [How do women's and men's work situations change when they have children?] (Rapport 2007:9). Uppsala: IFAU – Institutet för arbetsmarknadspolitisk utvärdering.

Maldonado, L. C., & Nieuwenhuis, R. (2015). Family policies and single parent poverty in 18 OECD countries, 1978–2008. *Community, Work & Family, 18*(4), 395–415. https://doi.org/10.1080/13668803.2015.1080661.

Mandel, H., & Semyonov, M. (2005). Family policies, wage structures, and gender gaps: Source of earnings inequality in 20 countries. *American Sociological Review, 70*(6), 949–967. https://doi.org/10.1177/000312240507000604.

McKeever, M., & Wolfinger, N. H. (2001). Reexamining the economic costs of marital disruption for women. *Social Science Quarterly, 82*(1), 202–217. https://doi.org/10.1111/0038-4941.00018.

McManus, P. A., & DiPrete, T. A. (2001). Losers and winners: The financial consequences of separation and divorce for men. *American Sociological Review, 66*(2), 246–268. https://doi.org/10.2307/2657417.

Mincer, J., & Polacheck, S. (1974). Family investments in human capital: Earnings of women. *Journal of Political Economy, 82*(2), 76–108. https://doi.org/10.1086/260293.

Mortelmans, D., & Defever, C. (2018). Income trajectories of lone parents after divorce: A view with Belgian register data. In L. Bernardi & D. Mortelmans (Eds.), *Lone parenthood in the life course* (pp. 191–211). Cham: Springer. https://doi.org/10.1007/978-3-319-63295-7.

Musick, K., Bea, M. D., & Gonalons-Pons, P. (2017). *Cross-national comparisons of his and her work and earnings following parenthood.* Paper presented at the female-breadwinner families workshop, December 12–13, London.

Nieuwenhuis, R., & Maldonado, L. C. (2018). *The triple bind of single-parent families. Resources, employment and policies to improve well-being.* Bristol: Policy Press.

Nylin, A.-K., Musick, K., Billingsley, S., Duvander, A.-Z., & Evertsson, M. (2019). *Trends over time in his and her earnings following parenthood in Sweden.* Stockholm Research Reports in Demography 2019:03.

Ohlsson-Wijk, S., Brandén, M., & Duvander, A.-Z. (2018). Committing to marriage? The role of marriage attitudes and gender equality among young cohabiters in Sweden. *Stockholm research reports in demography 2018–11.*

Ozawa, M. N., & Yoon, H.-S. (2002). The economic benefit of remarriage: Gender and income class. *Journal of Divorce and Remarriage, 36*(3), 21–39. https://doi.org/10.1300/J087v36n03_02.

Page, M. E., & Stevens, A. H. (2004). The economic consequences of absent parents. *Journal of Human Resources, 39*(1), 80–107. https://doi.org/10.2307/3559006.

Perelli-Harris, B., & Sánchez Gassen, N. (2012). How similar are cohabitation and marriage? Legal approaches to cohabitation across Western Europe. *Population and Development Review, 38*(3), 435–467. https://doi.org/10.1111/j.1728-4457.2012.00511.x.

Petersen, T., Penner, A. M., & Høgsnes, G. (2014). From motherhood penalties to husband premia: The new challenge for gender equality and family policy, lessons from Norway. *American Journal of Sociology, 119*(5), 1434–1472. https://doi.org/10.1086/674571.

Ruhm, C. R. (1998). The economic consequences of parental leave mandates: Lessons from Europe. *The Quarterly Journal of Economics, 113*(1), 285–317. https://doi.org/10.1162/003355398555586.

Schiratzki, J. (2008). *Mamma och Pappa inför Rätta. [Mom and dad in court].* Stockholm: Iustus.

Selin, H. (2014). The rise in female employment and the role of tax incentives: An empirical analysis of the Swedish individual tax reform of 1971. *International Tax and Public Finance, 21*(5), 894–922. https://doi.org/10.1007/s10797-013-9283-y.

Sigle-Rushton, W., & Waldfogel, J. (2007). Motherhood and women's earnings in Anglo-American, continental European, and Nordic countries. *Feminist Economics, 13*(2), 55–91. https://doi.org/10.1080/13545700601184849.

Statistics Sweden. (2014). *Olika familjer lever på olika sätt – om barns boende och försörjning efter en separation* [Different families live in different ways - about children's living and livelihood after a separation]. Demografiska rapporter, 2014: 1. Örebro: Statistics Sweden.

Statistics Sweden. (2016). *Women and men in Sweden 2016: Facts and figures.* Örebro: Statistics Sweden.

Statistics Sweden, Household's finances. (2014). *Disposable income by type of household, 2011–2017.* Median value in SEK thousands, 2017 prices. Statistics Sweden. http://www.scb.se/he0110-en. Accessed 31 May 2019.

Swedish National Agency for Education. (2018). *Tabell 2B. Inskrivna barn 2007–2018. Andel av alla barn i befolkningen* [Table 2B. Children registered in pre-school. Share of all children]. National Agency for Education. https://www.skolverket.se/skolutveckling/statistik. Accessed 31 May 2019.

Swedish Social Insurance Agency. (2009). Ensamstående föräldrars ekonomiska situation [Single parents' economic situation]. *Social Insurance Report, 2009*(4).

Thalberg, S. (2013). *Students and family formation. Studies on educational enrolment and child-bearing in Sweden.* Doctoral dissertation, Stockholm University, Department of Sociology.

Thomson, E. (2005). Partnerships & parenthood: A comparative view of cohabitation, marriage, and childbearing. In A. Booth & A.-C. Crouter (Eds.), *The new population problem: Why families in developed countries are shrinking and what it means* (pp. 129–150). Mahwah: Taylor & Francis.

Uunk, W. (2004). The economic consequences of divorce for women in the European Union: The impact of welfare state arrangements. *European Journal of Population, 20*(3), 251–285. https://doi.org/10.1007/s10680-004-1694-0.

Wadsby, M., Priebe, G., & Svedin, C. G. (2014). Adolescents with alternating residence after parental divorce: A comparison with adolescents living with both parents or with a single parent. *Journal of Child Custody, 11*(3), 202–215. https://doi.org/10.1080/15379418.2014.943448

Weiss, R. S. (1984). The impact of marital dissolution on income and consumption in single-parent households. *Journal of Marriage and the Family, 46*(1), 115–127. https://doi.org/10.2307/351870.

Chapter 4
Changes in Mothers' Earnings Around the Time of Divorce

Anke Radenacker

Introduction

Germany has seen a rapid increase in women's employment rates in the last decade (Eurostat 2019). Most of this growth can be attributed to an expansion of marginal and part-time employment, and, in recent years, to some increases in full-time employment among women (Geisler et al. 2016). However, the comparatively high female employment rate in Germany hides the fact that the earned income of the average woman is only a fraction of her total household earnings, because she is unlikely to be working full-time (OECD 2017). When a couple separates, the female partner's precarious income situation often becomes apparent, especially if she is a mother. Thus, in Germany, the risk of poverty for lone mothers is four times higher than it is for partnered mothers (Hübgen 2018). In addition, women's employment discontinuities and low earnings during marriage can have long-lasting effects on their financial well-being, not only around the time of divorce, but over the long term, as their statutory pension benefits are based on their current earnings (Hammerschmid and Rowold 2019; Madero-Cabib and Fasang 2016).

Previous research on the economic consequences of divorce mainly focused on equivalent household income. These studies found moderate changes in income for men, but sharp declines in income for women around the time of divorce and separation (Andreß et al. 2003; Andreß and Bröckel 2007; Burkhauser et al. 1991; Duncan and Hoffman 1985; Finnie 1993; Hauser et al. 2016; Jarvis and Jenkins 1999; Leopold 2018; Poortman 2000).[1] A comparison of these consequences across

[1] This list includes only studies in which both women and men were included.

A. Radenacker (✉)
Hertie School, Berlin, Germany
e-mail: radenacker@hertie-school.org

M. Kreyenfeld, H. Trappe (eds.), *Parental Life Courses after Separation and Divorce in Europe*, Life Course Research and Social Policies 12,
https://doi.org/10.1007/978-3-030-44575-1_4

time revealed that the economic situations of divorced women have improved little in recent decades. Bröckel and Andreß (2015), who tracked women's equivalent income after divorce in Germany from the mid-1980s until the late 2000s reported that there were no substantial changes. This result was unexpected, given that women's labour force participation has increased significantly over time.

Cross-national studies have suggested that women expand their employment activities after divorce or separation (Van Damme et al. 2009; Van Damme and Kalmijn 2014). Furthermore, there is some evidence that women's earnings increase after divorce or separation. Several US studies reported earnings increases among divorced women (e.g., Bradbury and Katz 2002; Smock 1994); Tamborini et al. 2015). Moreover, Raz-Yurovich (2013) and Herbst and Kaplan (2016) found for Israel that the earnings of divorced women increased. Nylin (in this volume) showed for Sweden that the earnings development of separated mothers was more negative in the long run than for coupled mothers. This is in line with Raz-Yurovich (2013) who finds a reduction in the salary growth rates of women following divorce. While some research on this topic has been conducted in the German context, these studies did not cover more recent developments. In our study, we seek to close this research gap by drawing on recent data for Germany to investigate how mothers' earnings change around the time of divorce.

Our analysis uses register data of the German statutory pension insurance, which includes monthly data on women's earnings over the whole life course, as well as monthly fertility biographies and marital histories of divorcees. The size of the dataset allows us to provide a detailed description of subgroups of women, which has previously not been possible because of the small sample sizes of the national panel surveys that were used to study this issue in the past. Our main interest lies in examining changes in earnings around the time of divorce across time; that is, across the divorce cohorts of 1992–1999, 2000–2007, and 2008–2013. On the basis of these data, we explore the relationship between individual earnings and relevant family-related covariates. The method we employ in our analysis is pooled OLS-regression.

Institutional Context

In comparative studies, Germany serves as the prime example of a country where the male breadwinner model remains dominant (Andreß 2003; Andreß et al. 2006; Lewis 1992; Lewis and Ostner 1994). Thus, family and social policies in Germany have long supported family arrangements in which the male partner is the primary earner. Since the female employment rate in Germany has increased substantially over the last several decades (Eurostat 2019), it has recently been argued that the dominant family arrangement in the country is now the *modern* male breadwinner model, in which the wife works part-time; and that the dual earner model is gaining strength (Trappe et al. 2015). However, in Germany, relative to other European countries, the share of part-time work among employed women is high, the average hours worked in part-time jobs are low, and the resulting relative contribution of women to household earnings is likewise low (OECD 2017). The employment of mothers in Germany has long been impeded by the insufficient availability of child care, especially for children under age three. In 2017, about 93% of 3–5-year-olds and around 33% of children under age three were in child care. Only 10 years previously, the share of children under age three in child care was just 16% (Federal Statistical Office 2018: 66ff.). The shares of children in day care who are under age three and are in full-time care vary strongly by region. Moreover, the employment behaviour of mothers differs by region, with eastern German women being more likely than western German women to enrol their children in day care, and to be in full-time employment. The expansion of child care in Germany was accompanied by the legal entitlement to access to institutional child care. Parents have been entitled to a child care place after their child turns 3 years old since 1996, and after their child turns 1 year old since 2013.[2]

Overall in Germany, women's opportunities to combine work and family life have improved significantly. At the same time, however, the individual responsibilities of divorced mothers have increased. This shift is most evident in a change in the maintenance law enacted in 2008. Prior to 2008, a mother who divorced was not expected to work, and was entitled to receive rather generous ex-spousal maintenance until her youngest child reached age eight. After that point, the mother was expected to work part-time. Moreover, if the mother did not work full-time, the support she received from her ex-spouse did not end until the youngest child turned 15 years old. Until that point, the care-giving parent generally received ex-spousal maintenance as well as child alimony from the non-resident parent. The legal context changed abruptly as a result of a decision of the German Federal Constitutional Court that requested to abolish the unequal treatment of children born to unmarried mothers, who previously had shorter maintenance claims than children of married mothers (BVerfG, Beschluss des Ersten Senats vom 28. Februar 2007, 1 BvL 9/04, Rn. (1-78)). The reform meant a drastic cut in ex-spousal maintenance claims to the level of those for unmarried mothers. Since 2008, separated and divorced mothers receive maintenance payments only until their youngest child turns 3 years old. After this point, the mother is expected to take up employment or extend her working hours. Child alimony payments were not affected by this reform. While these entitlements apply equally to lone fathers, the share of single parents in Germany who are mothers was 88% in 2017 (Federal Statistical Office 2018: 55).

[2] Another step towards promoting a dual earner model was taken in 2007, with the enactment of a parental leave reform. Since the reform, paid leave has been limited to a maximum of 12 months, with a replacement rate of 65% for those with middle income levels, and up to 100% for those with low income levels. Unpaid leave can be taken for an additional 2 years. Two months of paid leave for the partner that expire if not used were also added. This led to a significant increase in the share of fathers taking leave, from 3% before the reform in 2006 to 36% in 2015 (BMFSFJ 2018: 16). While this reform was an important turning point in German family policies, it is of no major relevance for this investigation, as only a few of the women in our sample had their first child after the reform.

The recent changes in the institutional context in Germany that have incentivised single mothers to take more individual responsibility, and to combine work and family life to a greater extent than in the past, would suggest that divorced women in Germany have been expanding their employment activities (and their earnings) over time. In view of our analyses of earnings changes around divorce across time, we expect to find that mothers' earnings tend to increase during the divorce process, and across time.

Literature Review

Divorce and Household Income

The divorce literature has unanimously found that women who separate or divorce face adverse economic consequences, and that they generally suffer far greater losses than men (Andreß et al. 2003; Andreß and Bröckel 2007; Burkhauser et al. 1991; Duncan and Hoffman 1985; Finnie 1993; Hauser et al. 2016; Jarvis and Jenkins 1999; Leopold 2018; Poortman 2000). According to these studies, women's economic losses range from 24% to 44% of household income (adjusted for the composition of the household), whereas the changes in men's income levels range from losses of 7% to gains of 6%. It appears that the adverse effects divorced women face are not primarily attributable to the loss of economies of scale when a two-adult household splits into two single-person households. Instead, the main reason women suffer more than men in divorce is that the economically weaker party loses access to the pooled household income of the couple, which, on average, results in high relative and absolute income losses for the female partner. Average income losses following divorce vary considerably across countries, as they depend on the level of inequality in market income between the partners, and the opportunities of the lower-income partner to remain or become active on the labour market around the time of the divorce. The main explanations for the gender gap in the economic outcomes of the partners following union dissolution are women's lower labour force attachment levels before separation and divorce, and women's greater likelihood of being the main carer for the children after union dissolution.

In addition to individual characteristics, the institutional context plays an important role in mitigating adverse effects. Uunk (2004) showed in a comparison of 14 European countries that income-related policy measures mitigate the negative consequences more than employment-related measures. However, institutional conditions play a decisive role not only in alleviating adverse outcomes, but in providing policies that support the autonomy of women, and especially of mothers, by encouraging them to participate in the labour market while married (Andreß et al. 2006).

While the options for combining market work and family obligations have improved somewhat in Germany during the last two to three decades, recent research on the changing economic consequences of divorce for women in Germany has found that divorced women's income situations have not improved since the 1990s, but have instead either stagnated or even deteriorated (Bröckel and Andreß 2015; Hauser et al. 2016); and that gender differences in divorce outcomes remain substantial (Leopold 2018: Table S1). This pattern stability in divorce outcomes has also been found for Switzerland (Kessler 2018).

Divorce and Women's Earnings

While the majority of studies on the economic consequences of divorce for women focused on household income, fewer studies have examined the employment rates and individual earnings of divorced women. Cross-national studies that included Germany reported that women's employment levels increased after divorce or separation (Van Damme et al. 2009; Van Damme and Kalmijn 2014). Women in Germany are among those with the largest increases in employment, primarily because their pre-divorce employment rates tend to be low (Van Damme et al. 2009). In addition, there are a few existing studies on the employment behaviour of single mothers, including mothers who were previously cohabiting as well as mothers who were married. The findings of these studies suggest that institutional factors, such as the availability of child care, affect the employment behaviour of single mothers in Germany more than individual factors, such as low education or early motherhood (Hancioglu and Hartmann 2014). Zagel (2014, 2015) pointed out that the importance of these factors for single mothers in Germany differs depending on whether they are lower or middle class.

Studies that examine the impact of divorce on individual earnings have been rare. Research conducted in the US has found persistent increases in women's earnings after divorce, especially for women who did not remarry (Tamborini et al. 2015; Couch et al. 2013). Raz-Yurovich (2013) reported that divorced salaried women in Israel had increased employment stability and a higher number of jobs, but that their earnings increases were not significant. But Herbst and Kaplan (2016) found, also for Israel, that salaried mothers' earnings increased significantly up to 3 years after divorce.

The advantage of using household income to measure the economic outcomes of women is that it provides a more complete picture of the income situation of a household. However, this approach is also based on the assumption that each of the married spouses has equal access to this income. The question of whether married couples actually share the household income equally has been raised (Findlay and Wright 1996). Moreover, an increase in the household income following a divorce might be caused by the presence of a new partner in the household. By using individual earnings, we can better estimate in our study the amount of income the women had at their disposal before and after divorce.

Data and Method

Data & Sample Selection

The dataset we draw upon is a scientific use file of a sample of insurance accounts (VSKT2015) of the German statutory pension insurance (Himmelreicher and Stegmann 2008). It contains monthly data on women's earnings during their whole life course starting at age 14, as well as monthly fertility biographies of women (Kreyenfeld and Mika 2006). It was combined with information from a register of pension splitting procedures. These data include monthly marital histories for women who divorced. This combined dataset (SUF-VSKT-VA 2015) is newly available as a scientific use file from the Research Data Centre of the German Statutory Pension Fund, and provides the basis for this investigation.[3] There are many advantages to using this dataset. Unlike the data that have typically been used to address similar research questions, such as data from the German Socio-Economic Panel (GSOEP), these data do not suffer from attrition or non-response bias. The insured individuals have a vested interest in disclosing their earnings and fertility details, as their pension calculations are based on the correctness and the completeness of their data. Furthermore, the dataset includes a much larger number of divorcees than most social science surveys. This large sample size allows us to perform analyses of subgroups of the divorced population that previous studies were not able to undertake. However, there are also some disadvantages associated with using this dataset. First, the data are not a representative sample of the resident German population. Certain groups, such as civil servants and farmers, are not covered. Furthermore, not all divorces are included in the data, as only divorces that involved a "pension splitting procedure" are registered. Pension splitting means that the pension entitlements that were accrued during the marriage by both partners are added up and then divided equally between the spouses. While this is the default process for dividing retirement benefits in German divorce law, couples can agree to exclude pension splitting from the divorce proceedings. Little is known about the characteristics of the couples who do not use pension splitting, but it is likely that most are couples with short marriages or marriages during which the partners had more or less equal earnings (Keck et al. 2019).

The SUF-VSKT-VA 2015 dataset is comprised of 267,812 individuals born between 1948 and 1985. Younger cohorts are not included because insurance accounts are "cleared" for the first time at age 29, and complete information is available only after this "clearance" has occurred. Furthermore, only individuals with German citizenship who were living in Germany in 2015 are included in this data file. For the purposes of our analyses, we further restrict the sample to women who started the divorce process between 1992 and 2013, and who were between 20 and 54 years old at the time of the divorce. In addition, we have restricted the analysis to individuals in West Germany, as understanding the employment and divorce patterns of East Germans would have required a separate investigation. We have

[3] http://forschung.deutsche-rentenversicherung.de/FdzPortalWeb/

furthermore limited the sample to individuals who divorced after at least 3 years of marriage. Finally, we include first marriages only. After these selection criteria are applied, we end up with a total sample of 6850 divorced mothers.

Variables

Individual Earnings The dependent variable is individual labour earnings measured in the form of pension points. Pension points are accumulated throughout the life course, not only from employment, but from creditable periods, such as periods spent in child-rearing, education, work disability, or even unemployment. For our analyses, we only use pension points earned from employment that is subject to social security payments to mirror individual labour earnings. This includes earnings from certain forms of self-employment that are subject to social security payments, such as self-employment as a child care professional, a midwife, or a crafts person. An individual earns one pension point based on the yearly average income. The yearly average income is adjusted on an annual basis, and amounted to €35,363 for West Germany in 2015 (Appendix 1, Book VI of the German Social Welfare Code). The maximum number of pension points an individual can earn in 1 year is about two points (€72,600 in 2015, Appendix 2, Book VI of the German Social Welfare Code). Earnings above this threshold are not pensionable earnings, and thus do not increase pension entitlements. This threshold is of little significance for women, as they rarely reach it. We create a measure of yearly earnings by summing up the earnings of 12 months per calendar year. Women who were not employed are included, and thus contribute zero earnings for the months and years they were not employed. We measure earnings in 1-year intervals, starting from 2 years before the divorce until 2 years after the divorce. Thus, we end up with 4-year episodes that include five points in time around the event. We argue that the majority of the employment changes associated with divorce happen during this period.

Figure 4.1 shows the distribution of earnings in the year of divorce for mothers of the divorce cohorts 1992–1999, 2000–2007, and 2008–2013.[4] The share of mothers with zero earnings (and who thus were not employed for the whole year when the divorce was filed) decreased substantially across the cohorts. Accordingly, the share of divorced mothers with positive earnings increased across the cohorts. The increases were largest in the two lower earnings groups ($0 \leq 0.2$ earnings points and $0.2 \leq 0.4$ earnings points) and in the highest earnings group (more than 0.8 earnings points). The share of mothers with medium earnings ($0.4 \leq 0.6$ and $0.6 \leq 0.8$)

[4] As the distribution of earnings does not follow a normal distribution, we also used the natural logarithm of earnings points. To calculate the natural logarithm, we have set values of zero to a small positive amount of 0.0001. Using the log of earnings in the regressions yielded similar results in terms of the signs of the coefficients, the size of the coefficients relative to the reference group, and the significance of the results. However, as the coefficients were more difficult to interpret, we decided to report unlogged earnings.

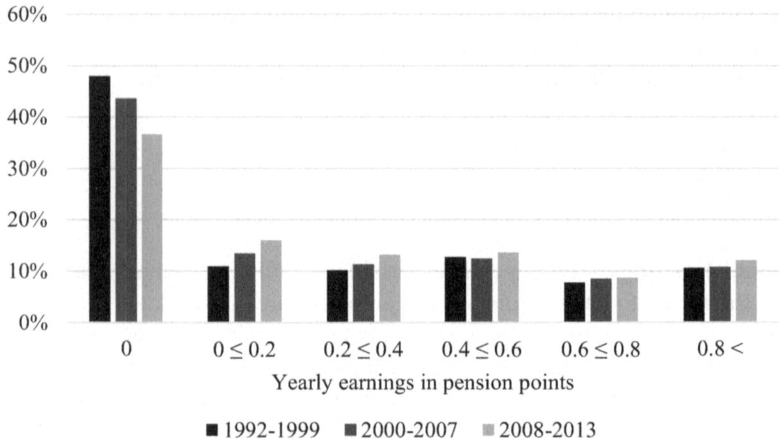

Fig. 4.1 Distribution of average yearly earning points from employment, West German mothers in the year of divorce, by divorce cohorts
Source: SUF-VSKT-VA 2015, own calculations

remained rather stable across the divorce cohorts. This changed distribution might point to a growing divide in mothers' earnings at the time of divorce.

Number of children A person is defined as a mother if she had at least one child under the age of 18 at the time of the divorce. We can assume that the birth of children is recorded very reliably, as each child increases the individual's qualifying period and total amount of pension points.

Age of youngest child This variable gives the age of the youngest minor child at the time of the divorce.

Duration of marriage The marriage duration is the time between the month of the marriage and the month of the postal delivery of the divorce petition from the family court to the defendant (see "divorce" variable below).

Maximum yearly earning points during marriage This variable reflects the highest yearly amount of earning points the woman ever earned during her marriage. It serves as a proxy for the woman's earnings potential.

Divorce The pension data do not include information on the exact timing of the separation. Instead, the end of the so-called "marriage time" is marked by the postal delivery of the divorce petition from the family court to the defendant.[5] It is this event that is referred to as divorce throughout the chapter. Due to a statutory waiting time of 1 year before a divorce can be filed in Germany, the actual separation of the couple would have taken place at least 10 months before the event that we call divorce here.

[5] Neither the date of the actual separation of the couple nor the date of the effective divorce are relevant for the calculation of pensions. Therefore, these dates are not included in the data. Only the so-called "marriage time" is relevant for the equalization of pension points, which were jointly accumulated by both spouses during their marriage.

Table 4.1 Summary statistics, divorced mothers with minor children, by divorce cohort

	1992–1999	2000–2007	2008–2013
Age at marriage	22.6	23.8	25.1
Age at first birth	23.2	24.4	25.6
Age at divorce	33.8	35.7	37.4
Duration of marriage	11.7	12.2	12.7
Number of minor children at divorce	1.75	1.76	1.75
Age of the youngest child at divorce	7.4	8.1	8.4
Maximum of yearly earning points during marriage	0.53	0.54	0.55
N (individuals)	2186	2660	2004

Source: SUF-VSKT-VA 2015, own calculations

Divorce cohort We distinguished three divorce cohorts: 1992 to 1999, 2000 to 2007, and 2008 to 2013. We use the year 1999 as a cut-point to enable us to compare our results to the findings of Bröckel and Andreß (2015), who looked at the time trends in divorce consequences before and after the turn of the millennium. We also use the year 2007 as another cut-point to account for the 2008 changes in the regulations for spousal maintenance that drastically reduced maintenance claims.

Age at marriage, age at divorce These variables are self-explanatory. We exclude them from the regression analyses due to multicollinearity, but report their means in the summary statistics in Table 4.1.

Table 4.1 shows the summary statistics of the variables that are included in the analyses. We can see that the age at marriage, the age at first birth, and the age at divorce of divorced mothers increased across the divorce cohorts. The number of children remained stable across the cohorts, but the age of the youngest child increased. It is possible that these composition changes led to changes in the labour force attachment of divorced mothers over time, as mothers' labour force attachment generally increases with the age of the youngest child. The maximum number of yearly earnings points women had during marriage increased only slightly across the divorce cohorts. This finding can be attributed to a decrease in the number of mothers with zero earnings that was accompanied by an increase in earnings, mostly at the lower end of the earnings distribution (see Fig. 4.1).

Research Design

The analysis consists of a descriptive part and a section that contains regression analysis. The descriptive part describes the evolution of women's earnings around the time of divorce by showing the mean earnings by the time since the divorce. Therefore, we created a balanced panel of five yearly observations per individual. The earliest possible divorce took place in 1992, with a corresponding observation window that lasted from 1990 to 1994; the last possible divorce took place in 2013, with an observation window that lasted from 2011 to 2015.

We first display the descriptive results; that is, mothers' earnings before and after divorce across the three divorce cohorts. Second, we examine the role of family-related determinants on earnings around the time of divorce in a regression model. This analysis relies on pooled OLS regression (Giesselmann and Windzio 2012). As we use several observations per individual, we employ cluster robust standard errors. Third, to find out whether subgroups of divorced mothers had similar changes in their earnings across time, we show interactions between relevant variables and the three divorce cohorts. A main disadvantage of our investigation is that we only have divorcees in our sample, and therefore cannot consider changes in employment and earnings behaviour in the population of married mothers.

Results

Earnings during the Divorce Process

The findings on mothers' earnings around the time of divorce point to two important developments (Fig. 4.2). First, the earnings of divorced mothers increased constantly throughout the divorce process. Second, the average earnings levels of mothers[6] around the time of divorce increased slightly across the divorce cohorts, especially in the years after the divorce. Between the earlier cohorts, the change was rather small from the 2 years before to the 2 years after divorce. However, the earnings increase started earlier in the 2000–2007 divorce cohort than in the 1992–1999 divorce cohort, which is, nevertheless, a favourable development. The somewhat more substantial earnings increases took place in the most recent cohort, 2008–2013. Both 2 years before and 2 years after divorce, the average earnings of divorced mothers in this cohort were higher than those in the two preceding cohorts. More generally, the rather low average earnings of the divorcing mothers should be pointed out. Two years before they divorced, and thus while they were still married, their earnings were between 20% and 25% of the average earnings (one earnings point corresponds to the average earnings of a given year). Four years later, after steady increases, their earnings were still less than 40% of the average earnings.[7]

Results from Pooled OLS-Regression

The main focus of the multivariate analyses is on the development of earnings across the divorce cohorts. Table 4.2 shows the results of two pooled OLS-regression models, with Model 1 being the empty model and Model 2 being the model with the

[6] As we mentioned earlier, mothers with zero earnings are included.

[7] The increase across cohorts from 0.33 (1990–1999) to 0.38 (2007–2013) earnings points 2 years after divorce corresponds to about €1770 of gross yearly income in 2015 euros.

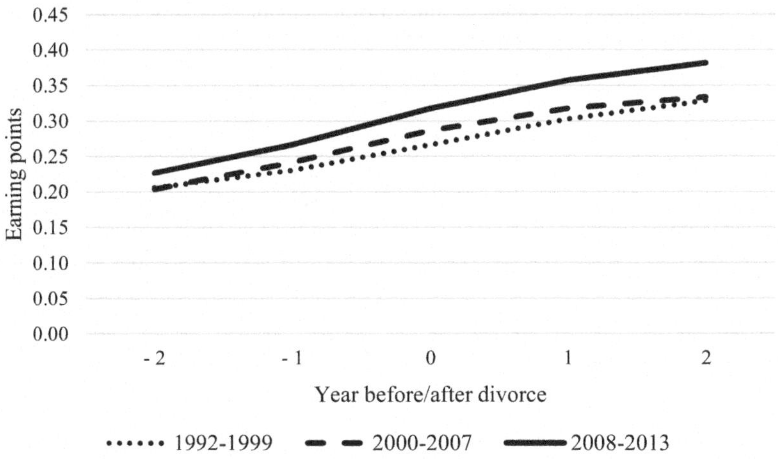

Fig. 4.2 Average yearly earning points of West German mothers with minor children during the divorce process, by divorce cohorts
Source: SUF-VSKT-VA 2015, own calculations

full set of control variables.[8] First, Model 1 confirms the descriptive finding of a positive development in earnings in the most recent divorce cohort. Mothers of the 2008–2013 divorce cohort had significantly higher earnings than mothers of the 1992–1999 divorce cohort. The change in divorced mothers' earnings between 1992–1999 and 2000–2007 was positive, but was small and insignificant.

After adding control variables, the size of the earnings increases for the 2008–2013 divorce cohort compared to the 1990s cohort is somewhat reduced (Model 2 in Table 4.2). The control variables for the number of children and the age of the youngest child reflect the known relationships. Having more children and younger children tends to inhibit the employment of mothers during marriage and after divorce, and thus decreases the earnings of divorced mothers. Interestingly, having three or more children was not more detrimental to mothers' earnings than having two children in contrast to having one child. The role of marital earnings for the earnings of divorced mothers was likewise important. We find a significant positive relationship between mothers' marital earnings and their earnings around the time of divorce.

As a last step, we show the earnings changes across divorce cohorts for groups of mothers by the age of the youngest child (Fig. 4.3) and by marital earnings (Fig. 4.4). Both figures show that the changes in earnings across the divorce cohorts were not the same for all groups of mothers. As Fig. 4.3 shows, only mothers with children under age twelve increased their earnings. The earnings increase was largest for mothers with children aged three to five and aged six to eleven. An increase for these age groups might be a consequence of the maintenance law reform of 2008,

[8] We use categorical variables of those explained in section "Variables".

Table 4.2 Determinants of individual earnings, divorced mothers in West Germany with minor children, Beta coefficients from pooled OLS-regression

	Model 1		Model 2	
Divorce cohort				
1992–1999	0		0	
2000–2007	0.009		0.002	
2008–2013	0.042	***	0.027	***
Number of children				
One			0	
Two			−0.052	***
Three or more			−0.051	***
Age of the youngest child				
0–2 years			0	
3–5 years			0.063	***
6–11 years			0.131	***
12–17 years			0.211	***
Max. yearly earning points during marriage				
Zero earnings			0	
More than 0, less than or equal to 0.5			0.078	***
More than 0.5, less than or equal to 0.9			0.267	***
More than 0.9			0.594	***
R^2	0.002		0.389	
N (person years)	34,188		34,188	

Source: SUF-VSKT-VA 2015, own calculations

Notes: * $p < 0.05$, ** $p < 0.01$, *** $p < 0.001$. Model 2 additionally includes dummies for each year before/after divorce and controls for the duration of marriage (continuous)

which increased the employment obligations for mothers with children of those ages. The earnings of mothers with children aged twelve to 17 even showed a small decrease across the divorce cohorts.[9] As a side effect, the differences between these subgroups of mothers by the age of the youngest child decreased over time.

Notes: Additionally controlling for all variables included in Model 2 of Table 4.2

Finally, in Fig. 4.4, the development of mothers' earnings by marital earnings is displayed. First, the figure shows the large earnings disparities between these subgroups, especially between the mothers with the highest marital earnings and all of the other mothers. More importantly, the positive trend of increased earnings around the time of divorce between the latest and the earliest divorce cohort took place only for the two higher income groups with marital earnings above 0.5 earnings points. For the two lower earnings groups, earnings stagnated at a very low level. This finding adds to our general observation that the economic divide within the group of divorced mothers has been growing over time.

[9] Additional analyses have shown that the finding for mothers of children aged 12–17 was mainly driven by mothers with children aged 16 and 17.

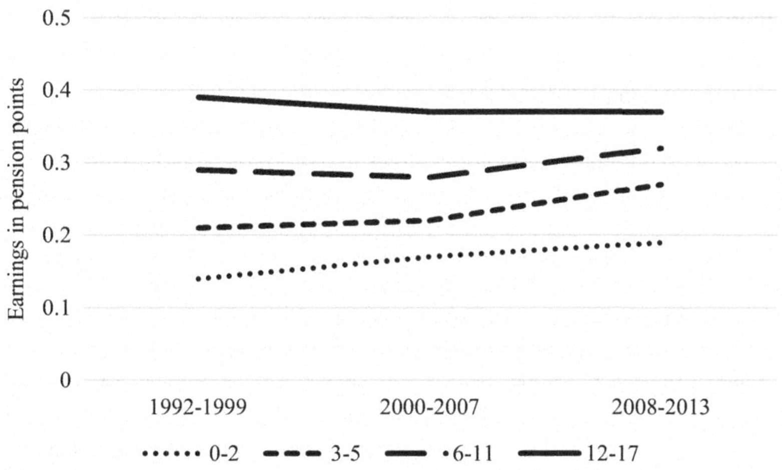

Fig. 4.3 Determinants of individual earnings, divorced mothers in West Germany with minor children, Predictive margins from pooled OLS-regression, interaction between divorce cohort and age of the youngest child
Source: SUF-VSKT-VA 2015, own calculations
Note: Additionally controlling for all variables included in Model 2 of Table 4.2

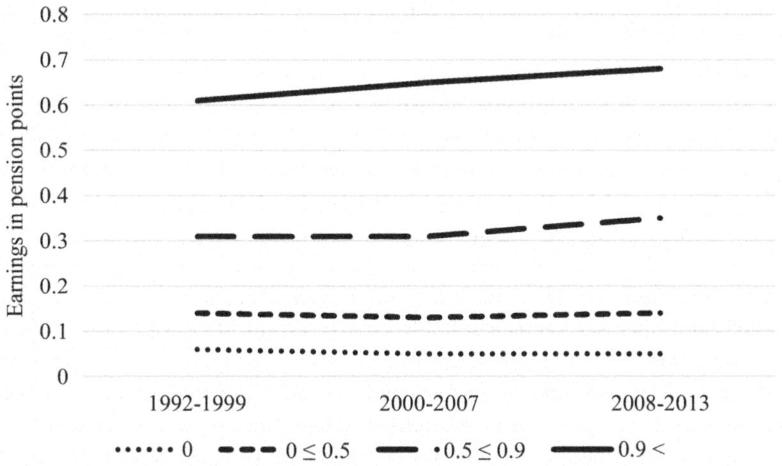

Fig. 4.4 Determinants of individual earnings, divorced mothers in West Germany with minor children, Predictive margins from pooled OLS-regression, interaction between divorce cohort and maximum amount of yearly marital earnings
Source: SUF-VSKT-VA 2015, own calculations
Note: Additionally controlling for all variables included in Model 2 of Table 4.2

Discussion

This study has capitalised on German register data to show that the earnings of divorced mothers increase considerably during the process of divorce. Furthermore, we have found that there were major changes in employment and earnings across the divorce cohorts we studied, with the most recent cohort of divorced women having the highest average earnings. However, while these developments seem positive, the overall picture was bleaker when we compared the earnings of divorced women with average earnings in Germany. The average earnings of divorced West German mothers are found to be far below the levels necessary to be financially independent, both around the time of divorce and thereafter. Another important finding from our study is that social differences among divorced mothers grew over time. On average, the earnings of divorced mothers increased across the observed divorce cohorts. However, this positive trend did not take place for all groups of mothers considered here. The mothers with zero or low marital earnings of the most recent divorce cohort of 2008–2013 fared no better than similar mothers of the 1992–1999 divorce cohort. Moreover, the results of the regression clearly show that mothers' low average earnings around the time of divorce were the result of both factors that were relevant at the time of divorce, like having young children; and factors that were relevant before the divorce, such as low marital earnings. Together, these factors inhibited mothers' employment behaviour and reduced their earnings at the time of divorce.

Our investigation contributes to the literature in many ways. First, there is a dearth of research on the question of how divorce impacts individual earnings. In previous studies on the economic consequences of divorce, mothers' earnings trajectories have usually been hidden behind measures of household income following divorce. While household income is an important measure, it is a poor indicator of the individual economic independence of women. Second, our study went beyond prior research, as the register data we used allowed us to discern differences across population subgroups.

Despite the many benefits of using these register data, it also comes with some serious caveats. The main caveat of the analyses is that we were only able to examine divorced women, because the register data include detailed marital histories only for those who were divorced. Thus, we were unable to identify the married women in the data, who could have served as a suitable control group. It is, for example, possible that the married mothers experienced similar earnings changes over a 5-year period, either because their children grew older and needed less intensive care, or because their income rose due to seniority. Moreover, when thinking about the increases we observed across the cohorts, we should consider the possibility that the improved availability of child care and the increased pressure following the maintenance reform improved the employment and earnings situations of all mothers. It should also be noted that, despite these developments, we found that the average earnings of divorcing mothers were quite low while they were still married. Their average earnings 2 years before divorce did not increase between 1992–1999 and 2000–2007. We therefore assume that part of the positive time trend can be attributed to the improved employment and earnings situations of divorced mothers. To the extent that we have overestimated the positive relationship between divorce and earnings, the adverse financial situation of divorced mothers in West Germany appears even starker.

Despite these caveats, there are major policy conclusions that can be derived from this investigation. Divorce may be seen as a trigger event that serves to reveal the imbalances in wage labour and care responsibilities between mothers and fathers. Such imbalances already exist during the years when women are married and raising children, especially in a (modern) male breadwinner context like Germany. Our findings on the impact of divorce on earnings are not primarily the consequence of divorce itself. Instead, they are mainly the result of an unequal distribution of market work and care work between the partners. Therefore, policy attempts to improve the financial situations of divorced mothers need to start focusing on the time when women are marrying and forming a family.

Acknowledgments This book chapter originates from work for the project "Divorce, separation and the economic security of women in Germany" (Az. Ia4-12141-1/20), funded by the Fördernetzwerk Interdisziplinäre Sozialpolitikforschung (FIS) of the German Federal Ministry of Labour and Social Affairs.

References

Andreß, H.-J. (2003). Die ökonomischen Risiken von Trennung und Scheidung im Ländervergleich: Ein Forschungsprogramm. [The economic risks of separation and divorce in international comparison: A research programme]. *Zeitschrift für Sozialreform, 49*(4), 620–651.

Andreß, H.-J., Borgloh, B., Güllner, M., Wilking, K. (2003). Wenn aus Liebe rote Zahlen werden. Über die wirtschaftlichen Folgen von Trennung und Scheidung. [When love turns into being in the red. About the economic consequences of separation and divorce]. Wiesbaden: Westdeutscher Verlag.

Andreß, H.-J., & Bröckel, M. (2007). Income and life satisfaction after marital disruption in Germany. *Journal of Marriage and Family, 69*(2), 500–512. https://doi.org/10.1111/j.1741-3737.2007.00379.x.

Andreß, H.-J., Borgloh, B., Bröckel, M., Giesselmann, M., & Hummelsheim, D. (2006). The economic consequences of partnership dissolution: A comparative analysis of panel studies from Belgium, Germany, Great Britain, Italy, and Sweden. *European Sociological Review, 22*(5), 533–560. https://doi.org/10.1093/esr/jcl012.

BMFSFJ. (2018). *Väterreport: Vater sein in Deutschland heute. [Fathers' report: Being a father in Germany today]*. Berlin: Bundesministerium für Familie, Senioren, Frauen und Jugend.

Bradbury, K., & Katz, J. (2002). Women's labor market involvement and family income mobility when marriages end. *New England Economic Review, 4*, 41–74.

Bröckel, M., & Andreß, H.-J. (2015). The economic consequences of divorce in Germany: What has changed since the turn of the millennium? *Comparative Population Studies, 40*(3), 277–312. https://doi.org/10.12765/CPoS-2015-04en.

Burkhauser, R. V., Duncan, G. J., Hauser, R., & Berntsen, R. (1991). Wife or frau, women do worse: A comparison of men and women in the United States and Germany after marital dissolution. *Demography, 28*(3), 353–360. https://doi.org/10.2307/2061461.

BverfG. (2007). Beschluss des Ersten Senats vom 28. Februar 2007 - 1 BvL 9/04 -, Rn. (1-78). http://www.bverfg.de/e/ls20070228_1bvl000904.html.

Couch, K. A., Tamborini, C. R., Reznik, G., & Phillips, J. W. R. (2013). Divorce, women's earnings, and retirement over the life course. In K. Couch, M. C. Daly, & J. Zissimopoulos (Eds.), *Lifecycle events and their consequences: Job loss, family change, and declines in health* (pp. 133–157). Stanford: Stanford University Press.

Duncan, G. J., & Hoffman, S. D. (1985). A reconsideration of the economic consequences of marital dissolution. *Demography, 22*(4), 485–497. https://doi.org/10.2307/2061584.

Eurostat. (2019). Employment and activity by sex and age – annual data [lfsi_emp_a]. http://appsso.eurostat.ec.europa.eu/nui/submitViewTableAction.do. Accessed 19 July 2019.

Federal Statistical Office. (2018). *Datenreport 2018. Ein Sozialbericht für die Bundesrepublik Deutschland. [Data report 2018: A social indicators report for the Federal Republic of Germany].* Federal Statistical Office (Destatis) and Wissenschaftszentrum Berlin für Sozialforschung (WZB).

Findlay, J., & Wright, R. E. (1996). Gender, poverty, and the intra-household distribution of resources. *Review of Income and Wealth, 42*(3), 335–351. https://doi.org/10.1111/j.1475-4991.1996.tb00186.x.

Finnie, R. (1993). Women, men, and the economic consequences of divorce: Evidence from Canadian longitudinal data. *Canadian Review of Sociology/Revue canadienne de sociologie, 30*(2), 205–241. https://doi.org/10.1111/j.1755-618X.1993.tb00173.x.

Geisler, E., Kreyenfeld, M., & Trappe, H. (2016). Erwerbsbeteiligung von Müttern und Vätern in Ost- und Westdeutschland: Strukturstarre oder Trendwende? [Labour force attachment of mothers and fathers in East and West Germany: Structural rigidity or trend reversal?]. *Archiv für Wissenschaft und Praxis der sozialen Arbeit, 47*(2), 4–15.

Giesselmann, M., & Windzio, M. (2012). *Regressionsmodelle zur Analyse von Paneldaten* [Regression models for ananlysing panel data]. Wiesbaden: Springer.

Hammerschmid, A., & Rowold, C. (2019). Gender Pension Gaps in Europa hängen eindeutiger mit Arbeitsmärkten als mit Rentensystemen zusammen. [Gender pension gaps depend more strongly on labor markets than on pension systems]. *DIW Wochenbericht Nr. 25/2019.* https://doi.org/10.18723/diw_wb:2019-25-1.

Hancioglu, M., & Hartmann, B. (2014). What makes single mothers expand or reduce employment? *Journal of Family and Economic Issues, 35*(1), 27–39. https://doi.org/10.1007/s10834-013-9355-2.

Hauser, R., Burkhauser, R. V., Couch, K. A., & Bayaz-Ozturk, G. (2016). Wife or Frau, women still do worse: A comparison of men and women in the United States and Germany after union dissolutions in the 1990s and 2000s. *Working Paper 2016–39*: University of Connecticut, Department of Economics.

Herbst, A., & Kaplan, A. (2016). Mothers' postdivorce earnings in the context of welfare policy change. *International Journal of Social Welfare, 25*(3), 222–234. https://doi.org/10.1111/ijsw.12205.

Himmelreicher, R. K., & Stegmann, M. (2008). New possibilities for socio-economic research through longitudinal data from the Research Data Centre of the German Federal Pension Insurance (FDZ-RV). *Journal of Contextual Economics: Schmollers Jahrbuch, 128*(4), 647–660.

Hübgen, S. (2018). Only a husband away from poverty? Lone mothers' poverty risks in a European comparison. In L. Bernardi & D. Mortelmans (Eds.), *Lone parenthood in the life course* (pp. 167–189). Cham: Springer. https://doi.org/10.1007/978-3-319-63295-7_8.

Jarvis, S., & Jenkins, S. P. (1999). Marital splits and income changes: Evidence from the British household panel survey. *Population Studies, 53*(2), 237–254. https://doi.org/10.1080/00324720308077.

Keck, W., Radenacker, A., Kreyenfeld, M., & Mika, T. (2019). FDZ-RV scientific use file: Statutory pension insurance accounts and divorce. *[Unpublished Manuscript].*

Kessler, D. (2018). The consequences of divorce for mothers and fathers: Unequal but converging? *LIVES Working Papers, 71*, 1–30. https://doi.org/10.12682/lives.2296-1658.2018.71.

Kreyenfeld, M., & Mika, T. (2006). Analysemöglichkeiten der Biografiedaten des "Scientific Use File VVL 2004" im Bereich Fertilität und Familie. [Analytical capacities of biography data of the "Scientific Use File VVL 2004" in the field of fertility and family]. *Deutsche Rentenversicherung, 9–10*, 583–608.

Leopold, T. (2018). Gender differences in the consequences of divorce: A study of multiple outcomes. *Demography, 55*(3), 769–797. https://doi.org/10.1007/s13524-018-0667-6.

Lewis, J. (1992). Gender and the development of welfare regimes. *Journal of European Social Policy, 2*(3), 159–173. https://doi.org/10.1177/095892879200200301.

Lewis, J., & Ostner, I. (1994). Gender and the evolution of European social policies. *ZeS Working Paper, 94*(4).

Madero-Cabib, I., & Fasang, A. E. (2016). Gendered work-family life courses and financial well-being in retirement. *Advances in Life Course Research, 27*, 43–60. https://doi.org/10.1016/j.alcr.2015.11.003.

OECD. (2017). *Dare to Share – Deutschlands Weg zur Partnerschaftlichkeit in Familie und Beruf. [Dare to share – Germany's experience promoting equal partnership in families]*. Paris: OECD Publishing. https://doi.org/10.1787/9789264263420-de.

Poortman, A.-R. (2000). Sex differences in the economic consequences of separation: A panel study of the Netherlands. *European Sociological Review, 16*(4), 367–383. https://doi.org/10.1093/esr/16.4.367.

Raz-Yurovich, L. (2013). Divorce penalty or divorce premium? A longitudinal analysis of the consequences of divorce for men's and women's economic activity. *European Sociological Review, 29*(2), 373–385. https://doi.org/10.1093/esr/jcr073.

Smock, P. J. (1994). Gender and the Short-Run Economic Consequences of Marital Disruption. *Social Forces, 73*(1), 243–262. https://doi.org/10.1093/sf/73.1.243.

Tamborini, C. R., Couch, K. A., & Reznik, G. L. (2015). Long-term impact of divorce on women's earnings across multiple divorce windows: A life course perspective. *Advances in Life Course Research, 26*, 44–59. https://doi.org/10.1016/j.alcr.2015.06.001.

Trappe, H., Pollmann-Schult, M., & Schmitt, C. (2015). The rise and decline of the male breadwinner model: Institutional underpinnings and future expectations. *European Sociological Review, 31*(2), 230–242. https://doi.org/10.1093/esr/jcv015.

Uunk, W. (2004). The economic consequences of divorce for women in Europe: The impact of welfare state arrangements. *European Journal of Population, 20*(3), 251–285. https://doi.org/10.1007/s10680-004-1694-0.

Van Damme, M., & Kalmijn, M. (2014). The dynamic relationships between union dissolution and women's employment: A life-history analysis of 16 countries. *Social Science Research, 48*, 261–278. https://doi.org/10.1016/j.ssresearch.2014.06.009.

Van Damme, M., Kalmijn, M., & Uunk, W. (2009). The employment of separated women in Europe: Individual and institutional determinants. *European Sociological Review, 25*(2), 183–197. https://doi.org/10.1093/esr/jcn042.

Zagel, H. (2014). Are all single mothers the same? Evidence from British and West German women's employment trajectories. *European Sociological Review, 30*(1), 49–63. https://doi.org/10.1093/esr/jct021.

Zagel, H. (2015). Understanding differences in labour market attachment of single mothers in Great Britain and West Germany. In J. Goebel, M. Kroh, C. Schröder, & J. Schupp (Eds.), *SOEP papers on multidisciplinary panel data research*. Berlin: Deutsches Institut für Wirtschaftsforschung.

Chapter 5
Parents Returning to Parents: Does Migration Background Have an Influence on the "Boomerang Effect" Among Parents After Divorce?

Dimitri Mortelmans, Gert Thielemans, and Layla Van den Berg

Introduction

Life course studies have often investigated the questions of why, and, if so, to what extent adult children return to the parental home. The economic recession of 2008 has sparked a renewed interest in understanding how socio-economic conditions and welfare state policies influence this so-called "boomerang effect" (Arundel and Lennartz 2017). In addition to job loss, divorce or relationship dissolution is generally considered to be one of the major life events that can cause adults to return to their parents' home. Surprisingly, most existing studies on this topic have focused on young adults. Thus, the boomerang effect is placed in a context of young adults returning soon after leaving the parental home to gain independence from their parents or in response parent-child conflicts. Only a few studies (e.g., Albertini et al. 2018) have examined the boomerang effect among adults who are somewhat older, and who use returning to the parental home as a post-divorce housing strategy. Moreover, even fewer studies have taken parenthood among divorcees into account when investigating the return to the parental home after a break-up (Guzzo 2016).

A second gap in the existing literature on the boomerang effect is that most studies do not consider population heterogeneity in migration status and origin group. It is, however, important to take this heterogeneity into account given the increasing diversity in most societies, and the differences between migrant and native-born populations in terms of family patterns, socio-economic position, and family attitudes. Research has also shown that acceptance of union dissolution – and of divorce in particular – is much lower in certain minority groups than it is the majority population (Koelet et al. 2009a). In addition, there is evidence that in Europe, some migrant groups have more universalistic family values than native populations, who

D. Mortelmans (✉) · G. Thielemans · L. Van den Berg
University of Antwerp, Antwerp, Belgium
e-mail: dimitri.mortelmans@uantwerpen.be

M. Kreyenfeld, H. Trappe (eds.), *Parental Life Courses after Separation and Divorce in Europe*, Life Course Research and Social Policies 12,
https://doi.org/10.1007/978-3-030-44575-1_5

tend to display more individualistic value patterns (Merz et al. 2009; Phalet and Schönpflug 2001). It has, for example, been shown that if an individual has to leave the marital home due to divorce, his/her ethnic background will greatly affect his/her likelihood of returning to the parental home (Kleinepier et al. 2017). Whether this effect differs depending on the individual's characteristics prior to the union dissolution and the characteristics of the parental household remains to be investigated.

While taking migrant populations into account, this chapter poses two main research questions. First, we investigate whether having a migrant background influences the likelihood among mothers and fathers of returning to the parental home after a relationship break-up (marriage or cohabitation). We look at how the boomerang effect plays out differently in the lives of fathers and mothers of Belgian, Turkish, and Moroccan origin, and take the migration background of the ex-partner into account. Second, we investigate whether economic and family differentials within these origin groups influence the likelihood of returning to the parental home (Mortelmans et al. 2019).

To answer these research questions, we use data from the Crossroads Bank of Social Security. These register data contain three "dissolving cohorts" (separation in 2007, 2008, or 2009). In the following, we provide an overview of the literature on the boomerang effect in the context of divorce and separation, and then present hypotheses that address our central research questions.

Prior Research and Hypotheses

In general, men are more likely than women to return to the parental home after a divorce or the end of a cohabiting partnership. Among the potential explanations for this gender difference are that the presence of children increases the likelihood that women will stay in the previously shared home after the relationship ends (Ongaro et al. 2008; Stone et al. 2014; Sullivan 2007). It has, conversely, also been argued that women are more likely than men to turn to their parents for help, and that daughters are more likely than sons to receive assistance from their parents, especially in times of need (Guzzo 2016). Additionally, there is evidence that adult children with children of their own receive more support from their parents than childless adults (Fingerman et al. 2009). As women are more likely than men to be living with their children after leaving a relationship, it may be expected that women would have higher odds of returning to the parental home (Guzzo 2016). However, most empirical studies have provided support for the hypothesis that men have a greater tendency than women to return home. Stone et al. (2014) found that in the UK, mothers were significantly less likely than fathers to return to the parental home after relationship dissolution. Meanwhile, Guzzo (2016) found evidence that led them to reject their hypothesis that mothers have an increased likelihood of moving back in with their parents. Based on these empirical findings, we formulate the following hypothesis:

Hypothesis 1: Net of socio-demographic and economic characteristics, fathers are more likely than mothers to return to their parents' home after relationship dissolution, regardless of whether they have a migrant background.

Although research on the consequences of divorce among couples with a migrant background is limited, the existing studies on this topic have shown that the likelihood of returning to the parental home after divorce may differ by migrant background. Whereas adult children having autonomy and being independent of their parents are norms in Western societies (Billari et al. 2001), these norms appear to be less prevalent among minority groups with a non-Western background (Merz et al. 2009; Phalet and Schönpflug 2001). Family relationships, community ties, and intergenerational support are often emphasised among these groups. In addition, both first- and second-generation migrants tend to lean on support from informal networks in all domains of life, such as in finding a job, organising informal childcare, and finding a suitable partner. Receiving informal support is particularly important for subpopulations who have limited educational and labour market opportunities, such as individuals with a Turkish or a Moroccan background living in Belgium. Men and women who are first- or second-generation Turkish or Moroccan migrants often find themselves in a precarious socio-economic position because they tend to have limited opportunities, while also facing relatively high levels of discrimination on the labour and housing markets (Baert et al. 2015; Zick et al. 2008). A qualitative study by Koelet et al. (2009a) conducted among divorced men and women who were second-generation Turkish or Moroccan migrants showed that even though their parents often disapproved of divorce as a solution for relationship problems, their parents continued to support them. The results also showed that divorcees of Turkish or Moroccan origin often returned to the parental home as a strategy for coping with financial difficulties. Moreover, the study found that receiving informal support, mainly from the divorcees' immediate family, was often a stepping stone to receiving formal support. An analysis of quantitative data from the Belgian National Register showed that the odds of returning to the parental home were highest among Turkish men (Koelet et al. 2009a). Our hypothesis is, therefore, as follows:

Hypothesis 2: The probability of returning to the parental home after divorce or separation is higher for Turks and Moroccans than it is for Belgians.

In addition, the likelihood of returning home might differ not just between men and women or between people with different migrant backgrounds, but between men and women within these communities. Koelet et al. (2009b) found that although the Turkish and the Moroccan communities are generally more disapproving of divorce than the Belgian community, the stigma is more severe for women than for men. As maintaining marital satisfaction is often seen as the wife's responsibility, women are more likely than men to be blamed by the community for the failure of a marriage. Hence, parent-child conflict is expected to arise more frequently for women than for men with a Turkish or a Moroccan background. Based on these assumptions, our hypothesis is a follows:

Hypothesis 3: Mothers with a Moroccan or a Turkish background are less likely to return home after divorce or separation than fathers with the same background.

In addition to differences by gender, there are several other explanations for why some types of parents are more likely than others to move back in with their parents after a divorce. Access to financial resources is an important factor in whether adult children return to the parental home (Goldscheider and Goldscheider 1998; Whittington and Peters 1996). Paying not just for housing, but for utilities, food, and other basics of daily living can be difficult for single individuals (Furstenberg et al. 2005). Thus, economic necessity may drive these newly single people back into their parents' home. This observation leads us to formulate the following hypothesis:

Hypothesis 4: Individual income is negatively associated with the probability of returning to the parental home after divorce or separation, regardless of the person's gender or migrant background.

Unemployment and inactivity restrict people's residential independence in two ways. First, if individuals lack economic resources because they have no labour market income, they may be unable to pay rent or make mortgage payments. Moreover, people who lack steady employment and adequate income face barriers to being accepted as a tenant (Loopmans et al. 2014) or to obtaining a loan, especially since the economic recession of 2008. However, net of the income effects that are inherent in an individual's employment status, the issue of childcare arises for parents who are employed. Men and women with children who are employed full-time may benefit from the childcare that their own parents (i.e., their children's grandparents) can provide. Guzzo (2016) and Kleinepier et al. (2017) found that parents with year-round, full-time employment were the least likely to return home. These studies did not, however, specifically identify parents with different employment patterns, and they did not account for personal income. We therefore propose the following hypothesis:

Hypothesis 5: Net of income effects, employment is positively associated with the probability of parents returning to the parental home after divorce or separation, regardless of their gender or migrant background.

Although we predict that, in general, returning to the parental home has a negative association with income, there is one low-income group who might be less prone to return to the parental home: parents who receive welfare benefits. At the macro level, Arundel and Lennartz (2017) argued that the likelihood of returning home is lower in more protective welfare states such as Belgium. At the micro level, there are several explanations for why welfare dependency is negatively related to returning to the parental home. First, recipients of means-tested benefits might find that they would lose the benefits they are currently receiving if they moved in with their parents, as the combined household income would render them ineligible. Second, individuals who receive welfare benefits have better access to affordable, social, and state-provided housing than non-recipients. In addition, single parents receive more benefits than childless singles, and they are often given priority in the allocation of social housing. As women are more likely than men to be the primary carers for their children, we test the following hypotheses:

Hypothesis 6: Net of income and employment effects, welfare dependency is (a) associated with a lower likelihood of returning to the parental home after divorce or separation. This association is (b) weaker for men than it is for women.

In addition to generally assuming that returning to the parental home is more common among second-generation Moroccan and Turkish migrants than among the native population, we expect to find variation within each origin group. First, we expect to observe differences depending on the relationship type of the ex-couples. Among Moroccan and Turkish origin groups, the majority of unions are marriages, and unmarried cohabitation is less common. Qualitative research by Koelet et al. (2009b) has shown that the parents of second-generation Turkish and Moroccan migrants are less supportive of unmarried cohabitation, and generally expect a serious relationship to result in engagement and marriage. Additionally, second-generation migrants often adhere to the traditional views on union formation that are dominant in their parents' countries of origin (De Valk and Liefbroer 2007). When a man or – in particular – a woman from a migrant community opts for unmarried cohabitation instead of marriage, it is often a strong indication of the individual's independence from the influence of his/her parents, given that this choice conflicts with their community's norms on union formation. In light of the marriage norm among these migrant groups and the implications of a failure to adhere to it, we test the following hypothesis:

Hypothesis 7: The probability of returning to the parental home after divorce or separation is higher for Turks and Moroccans who were formerly married rather than cohabiting than it is for Belgians.

Second, we expect to find differences in the propensity to return to the parental home depending on the migrant status of the partner. While the number of marriage migrations has decreased considerably over the past decade (Dupont et al. 2017), substantial shares of second-generation Turks and Moroccans have married a first-generation partner from their country of origin (Huschek et al. 2012). For second-generation parents of Turkish and Moroccan origin, choosing a first-generation partner from their country and/or region of origin is often preferred to choosing a partner from the second generation or from another origin group (Koelet et al. 2009a). In addition, an individual who chooses a partner from his/her country of origin generally has strong connections with his/her migrant community in both in the country of residence and the country of origin (Lievens 1997), which can, in turn, strengthen the individual's bonds with his/her family and the broader migrant community. The decision not to follow the partner choice expectations of one's parents and community can be an indication that an individual has a greater need for independence or a greater cultural distance from his/her home country. We therefore propose the following hypothesis:

Hypothesis 8: The probability of returning to the parental home is higher for Turkish and Moroccan ex-partners whose former spouse was a first-generation migrant.

Methods

Data

In this study, we used Belgian data from the Data Warehouse on Labour Market and Social Security. This large-scale administrative dataset contains information from nearly all social security agencies in Belgium (e.g., the National Office of Social Security, the National Employment Office, and the National Institute for Health and Disability Insurance). A sample was drawn that consists of 46,050 households who had experienced the dissolution of their relationship in 2007, 2008, or 2009. In the registers, the definition of a household was based on co-residence. The sample unit was based on the relationship status of couples in a household at moment t (2007–2008–2009) compared to their status at t−1. The use of this approach allowed us to draw a sample of 21,600 divorced couples (at time t) and 24,450 separated (and formerly cohabitating) couples (at time t). To enable us to study differentials by origin group, the sample was stratified by the (non)-migrant status (Belgian, European, or non-European) and gender of at least one of the (ex-)partners. "Migrant status" is defined as being a first-, second- (parents), or third- (grandparents) generation migrant based on the country of birth of the individual and of his/her (grand) parents. If no information on the country of birth was available, we used an individual's first nationality as an alternative indicator of his/her origin. For the Belgian sample members, we added the requirement that the respondent's partner also had a non-migrant Belgian background. For couples in which one of the partners had a migrant background, no restrictions regarding the migrant background of the other partner were applied. This sampling strategy resulted in 30,000 couples with two Belgian partners, 3000 couples with a European woman, 6500 couples with a European man, 3000 couples with a non-European woman, and 3550 couples with a non-European man. As each household had to be married or cohabiting at t-1, the total number of individuals in the sample was 92,100 (each of the 46,050 sample members and his/her respective (ex-)partner). Recent migration movements are not immediately registered in the Data Warehouse. Since the most recent data in the study were from 2013 (t + 4 in the 2009-wave), we assume that migrants from the most recent wave are not included in our sample. Moreover, as illegal migration is not covered by the administrative data, undocumented migrants could not be included in the models.

The data provide yearly information on both the ex-partners and their household members after union dissolution. For this chapter, we limited the sample to mothers and fathers who were of Belgian origin or Turkish or Moroccan migrants of the second generation or later. The respondents' parental status was determined based

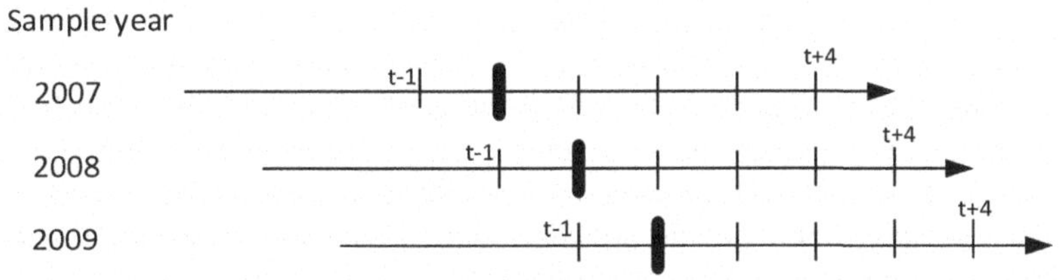

Fig. 5.1 Longitudinal data structure of the study
Source: Data Warehouse on Labour Market and Social Security

on the presence of at least one dependent child in the household at t−1. We excluded ex-partners who were first-generation immigrants. Since first-generation migrants often come to Belgium without their parents, including them would have posed a measurement problem in our models. As we have no information on a potential return to the parental home in the country of origin, we would have underestimated the return parameter. For migrants of the second or a subsequent generation, we could be certain that their parents were present in Belgium, and that data on them would be available in the registers. In addition, self-employed individuals were excluded from the analysis because the database contained no reliable information on their income. We imposed a maximum age of 44 for inclusion in the sample, as the probability of having no living parent rises with age. We assumed that setting an age limit of 44 would mean that for most couples in the sample, their parents would still be alive. We did not have any information on the status of the parents, as we only observed them in our panel when the adult children returned to the parental home. With these restrictions taken into account, we used data from 25,444 mothers, of whom 57.9% were divorced and 42.1% had been previously living with a partner without being married. We used data from 20,108 fathers, of whom 63.4% were divorced and 36.6% had experienced the dissolution of an unmarried cohabitation.

The data used for the analyses was organised as a person-file. Longitudinal information for each year from 2007–2013 was used to determine whether the parents returned to the parental home within 4 years (t + 4) of their break-up in 2007, 2008, or 2009. For the independent variables and the control variables, longitudinal information was used only from the year prior to the break-up (t−1). Since we were estimating person-level logistic regressions, no time-varying information was included in the analyses. The structure of the data is illustrated in Fig. 5.1.

Variables

The dependent variable was a dummy variable indicating that an individual had returned to the parental home after a break-up. When the administrative data indicated that the individual had registered at the same address as (at least) one of his/

her parents, the dependent variable showed unity. We did not take the timing of the return into account. Thus, whenever we observed a return, the dependent variable was coded as "return" (1). We had no information on who moved in with whom, but with the age selection set at 44, we assumed that the ex-partner joined the parental home, and not vice versa (for example, in response to care needs). Therefore, the dependent variable should be interpreted as merely referring to the ex-partner sharing a household with (at least) one parent.

All models were controlled for the migrant status of each respondent. We distinguished the fathers and mothers who were of Belgian origin from those who were of Turkish or Moroccan origin, and were second- (or later-) generation migrants. The Belgian respondents were used as a reference category in all models. In addition to controlling for the background of each respondent, we controlled for the background of the former partner. We used three dummies representing (1) the first generation, (2) the second generation of the same origin, and (3) the mixed character of the couple when the partner was of another origin.

We controlled for a number of background variables. These variables refer to differences between the formerly married or cohabiting partners, welfare dependency, age (mean-centred plus age squared), and region (Flanders, Wallonia, Brussels Capital Region). The control variable "having young children in the household" (at $t-1$) measured the presence of children younger than 3 years old. The total number of children of the ex-couple is self-explanatory. Labour market participation was measured with two dummies: employed full-time (more than 80%) or part-time (80% or less). The reference category was made up of respondents who were either not active on the labour market or unemployed. Individual income included the respondent's earnings from employment, as well as any public transfers s/he received due to the disability or career interruption of the ex-partner. Childcare transfers or partner alimony payments were not included in the income data. Since partner alimony was structurally reduced by the law of 2007, only the absence of information on childcare transfers limited our ability to assess the respondents' total income. In the Belgian context, welfare benefits are based on an individual's prior labour market experience and household size. There are no specific public subsidies aimed at separated or divorced men and women or immigrants. However, previous studies have shown that people with a migrant background tend to have a higher level of welfare dependency than their native-born counterparts (Carpentier et al. 2014). All models were also estimated separately for men and women.

Analytical Strategy

The register data allowed us to determine for each respondent whether the boomerang effect was observable 4 years after the break-up, while controlling for pre-separation characteristics. Using such a large sample had several advantages. First, the statistical power was greater, making the parameter estimates more robust. Second, it allowed us to examine the boomerang effect in more detail (e.g., including the dissolution of cohabitating unions among groups with a migrant background). As far as we know, no other study has ever combined a sample of post-dissolution trajectories of this magnitude with a focus on respondents with a migrant background.

We used binary logistic regression to model the return to the parental home within 4 years of a union dissolution (Mortelmans 2010). Given that our follow-up period was limited to 4 years and our data were yearly, rather than quarterly or monthly, performing a discrete-time event history analysis would have offered little additional insight beyond that which a regular logistic regression approach could provide.

In a first step, we studied the effects of gender (M1) and migrant status (M2) for the complete sample by estimating models for both fathers and mothers. We then examined the interaction between gender and migrant status (M3).

In a second step, we estimated four models for fathers and mothers separately. The first two models introduced the migrant background (M1) and the partner background (M2). In Model 3, we added variables related to union type and economic status (income, dependency, and work status). Model 4 included the interaction between migrant background and socio-economic variables (employment, welfare dependency, and individual income). Model 5 included the interaction between migrant background and the characteristics of the former couple (union type and partner background).

Each model included all of the control variables.

Results

Descriptive Analysis

Table 5.1 provides the descriptive statistics by migration background (Belgian, Moroccan, Turkish). Belgians made up 86.9%, Moroccan migrants represented 9.5%, and Turkish migrants accounted for 3.6% of the sample. The composition of the couples in the sample that included a Belgian (ex-) partner was mostly homogeneous. Mixed couples made up less than 20% of the sample, and in most of these couples (16%), the migrant partner was from the second generation of any other origin group. It is important to note that in most of these previously mixed couples, the migrant partner had a migration background other than Moroccan or Turkish. Therefore, the frequencies in the column of Belgian couples did not add up to the frequencies of mixed couples in which a Moroccan or a Turkish migrant had a Belgian partner. Among the individuals with a Moroccan or a Turkish background, the shares of partners who were first or second generation were about the same. Mixed couples that included a Belgian partner represented around 10% of the sample, and there were almost no mixed couples that included a partner with another migrant background. Because the share of mixed (non-Belgian) couples was small,

Table 5.1 Unweighted frequencies for main variables in year t−1, column percent

	Belgian	Moroccan	Turkish
Gender (t−1)			
Men	17752 (45%)	1752 (41%)	604 (37%)
Women	21848 (55%)	2557 (59%)	1039 (63%)
Background partner (t−1)			
Partner = 1st generation	806 (2%)	2065 (48%)	823 (50%)
Partner = 2nd generation	6227 (16%)	1749 (41%)	651 (40%)
Partner = Belgian	32567 (82%)	491 (11%)	164 (9.9%)
Partner = Other		4 (0.1%)	5 (0.3%)
Welfare state dependency (t−1)			
0%	22724 (57%)	1362 (32%)	379 (23%)
1–19%	10559 (27%)	932 (22%)	411 (25%)
20–39%	2454 (6%)	501 (12%)	233 (14%)
40–59%	973 (2%)	283 (6%)	130 (8%)
60–79%	661 (2%)	269 (6%)	87 (5%)
80–100%	2229 (6%)	962 (22%)	404 (25%)
Employment status (t−1)			
Full-time	21717 (54.8%)	1319 (30.6%)	455 (27.7%)
Part-time	13054 (33.0%)	1465 (34.0%)	572 (34.8%)
Inactive or unemployed	4829 (12.2%)	1525 (35.4%)	616 (37.5%)
Young child (<3 year) in hh. (t−1)	27562 (70%)	3419 (79%)	1120 (68%)
Number of children (t−1) (mean)	1.21	1.25	1.33
Married couple	13982 (35%)	2768 (64%)	1154 (70%)
Mean age (t−1)			
Man	30.4	29.5	28.4
Woman	29.4	27.7	27.3
Region			
Flanders	23857 (60%)	1398 (32%)	798 (48%)
Brussels capital region	2056 (5%)	1965 (46%)	406 (25%)
Wallonia	13,687 (35%)	946 (22%)	439 (27%)
Returns to the parental home			
Man	4400 (25%)	448 (26%)	214 (35%)
Woman	4467 (20%)	509 (20%)	219 (21%)
Subjects (t−1)	39600	4309	1643

Source: Belgian Crossroads Bank for Social Security, calculations by authors

we decided to include both Belgian partners and partners and other nationalities in the reference category in our multivariate models. Looking at Table 5.1, we can clearly see that the comparison mainly involved Belgian partners.

The individual characteristics of the ex-partners were generally similar. In terms of age, no major differences were found. However, the share of couples who were married was larger in the Turkish and Moroccan communities than in the Belgian sample. Although our aim was to include in the analysis equal shares of married and cohabiting couples (which we succeeded in doing in the original Belgian sample), the number of cohabitating couples among the Turks and the Moroccans was too low to allow us to include equal shares of the two relationship types. It also appears that the Moroccan ex-partners were more likely to have young children in the household than the Belgian or the Turkish ex-partners. Among the Belgian ex-partners, the regional spread was in line with that of the overall population: i.e., 60% were from the North (Flanders) and 40% were from the South or Brussels. Among the ex-partners with a migrant background, much higher percentages were from the Brussels Capital Region.

When we examined the economic backgrounds of the former couples, we observed that large shares were working full-time before the break-up. However, compared to the Belgian couples, the couples in the Moroccan and Turkish communities were more likely to be inactive or unemployed, and to be dependent on welfare state transfers. These observations confirmed our assumption that the Moroccan and Turkish households were, on average, in a weaker economic position than their Belgian counterparts.

Regression Results

In a first step of the multivariate analyses, three models were estimated on the total sample (Table 5.2). The first model showed an overall effect that women with children returned less to the parental home after a break-up than men. This finding confirmed our hypothesis 1, which stated that the boomerang effect after a break-up is a gendered process. The second model, which added the migrant background of the parent, showed a significant positive effect of having a Turkish background. The

Table 5.2 Logistic regression of returning to the parental home, (0: not returning to parental home, 1: returning to parental home), unstandardized coefficients

	M1		M2		M3	
Intercept	4.16	***	4.18	***	4.16	***
Gender (Ref. = Man)						
Woman	−0.40	***	−0.40	***	−0.36	***
Migrant background (Ref. = Belgian)						
Moroccan			0.12	*	0.47	**
Turkish			0.35	***	1.28	***
Gender × Migrant						
Woman × Moroccan					−0.24	**
Woman × Turkish					−0.59	***

Source: Belgian Crossroads Bank for Social Security, calculations by the authors
Notes: All models are also controlled for Age, Age^2, Partner origin (Ref. = Belgian+Other), Married (Ref. = Cohabiting), Working full-time & working part-time (Ref. = Inactive or unemployed), Individual income, region in Belgium, share of welfare state dependency, young child (<3 year) in the household; number of children in the household. Significance levels: * $p < .05$; ** $p < .01$; *** $p < .001$

Turks were more likely than the Belgians to return to the parental home. This was also the case for the Moroccans, but this effect was significant only after control variables were added. The effect for Moroccans was also much smaller than the effect for the Turks, and its significance was also on $p < 0.05$. Nevertheless, the model confirmed hypothesis 2, as it showed that Belgian ex-partners were significantly less likely to return to the parental home than ex-partners with a migrant background. When interacting gender and background in model 3 (hypothesis 3), we found that women in both groups were far less likely than men to return to the parental home. This was shown to be the case for both Turkish and Moroccan women; but again, the effect was found to be more pronounced in the Turkish community.

To test our hypotheses by gender, we estimated separate models for men and women, as shown in Tables 5.3 and 5.4. Table 5.3 presents the results for men. In Model 1, we observed a strong positive effect of returning to the parental home for Turkish fathers. For Moroccan fathers, the effect was weaker, although still significant. When controlling for the previous partner (M2), we found higher odds of returning to the parental home for Moroccan fathers (M3). However, in the interaction models (M4 and M5), the effect of returning again disappeared for the Moroccan fathers. A second observation from Model 2 was that the migrant background of the previous partner mattered for men. When coupled with a partner from the first generation, men were less likely to return to the parental home. When the previous partner was from the second or third generation, men were no less likely to return to the parental home than they were if their former partner was Belgian. Having been married rather than cohabiting was found to slightly increase the likelihood of returning to the parental home.

Both of the income-related components were shown to be negative. In Model 3, we learned that having a higher income reduced the odds of returning to the parental home after a break-up. In addition, the more a father depended on welfare benefits, the less likely he was to return to the parental home. However, being employed increased the probability of returning for fathers, but only if they were working full-time (as was the case for most of the fathers in the sample).

Models 4 and 5 in Table 5.3 tested the hypotheses on the interactions between migrant background and economic resources and family composition. With respect to economic resources, the findings indicated that having a high individual income had different implications for Belgians than for individuals with a migration background. Compared to their Belgian counterparts, higher-income individuals with a migration background were more likely to return to the parental home. For fathers with a Moroccan or – in particular – a Turkish background, the pattern even reversed, with the association between individual income and the likelihood of returning to the parental home turning positive. Moreover, compared to Belgian fathers, the effects of full- and part-time employment Moroccan and Turkish fathers were reversed, although these differences were not statistically significant. The effect of welfare dependency on the likelihood of returning to the parental home was found to be rather similar across all three groups. The interaction in Model 5 showed that the effect of whether a couple had been married on the likelihood of returning to the

Table 5.3 Logistic regression of returning to the parental home, 0: not returning to parental home, 1: returning to parental home, unstandardized coefficients, men

	M1		M2		M3		M4		M5	
Intercept	3.12	***	3.21	***	3.31	***	3.36	***	3.30	***
Migrant background (Ref. = Belgian)										
Moroccan	0.17	*	0.24	**	0.27	***	0.16		0.16	
Turkish	0.59	***	0.67	***	0.69	***	0.46		0.90	***
Work status (Ref = Inactive or- unemployed)										
Full-time (t−1)					0.24	**	0.28	**	0.23	**
Part-time (t−1)					0.13		0.15		0.12	
Welfare dependency (t−1)					−0.32	***	−0.33	***	−0.32	***
Individual income (t−1)					−0.14	***	−0.15	***	−0.14	***
Married (t−1) (ref. = cohabiting)			0.08	*	0.10	*	0.10	*	0.09	*
Partner background (ref. = other)										
First generation			−0.29	***	−0.26	**	−0.27	***	−0.21	*
Second generation			−0.07		−0.08		−0.08		−0.09	
Interactions with migrant background										
Moroccan × Full-time							−0.32			
Moroccan × Part-time							−0.17			
Moroccan × Welfare dependency							0.08			
Moroccan × Individual income							0.19	*		
Moroccan × Married									0.11	
Moroccan × Partner = 1st generation									−0.02	
Moroccan × Partner = 2nd generation									0.07	
Turkish × Full-time							−0.52			
Turkish × Part-time							−0.11			
Turkish × Welfare dependency							0.10			
Turkish × Individual income							0.33	*		
Turkish × Married									−0.25	
Turkish × Partner = 1st generation									−0.17	
Turkish × Partner = 2nd generation									0.05	

Source: Belgian Crossroads Bank for Social Security, calculations by the authors

Notes: All models are also controlled for Age, Age^2, region in Belgium, young child (<3 year) in the household; number of children in the household. Significance levels: *p < .05; **p < .01; ***p < .001

Table 5.4 Logistic regression of returning to the parental home, 0: not returning to parental home, 1: returning to parental home, unstandardized coefficients, women

	M1		M2		M3		M4		M5	
Intercept	2.36	***	2.40	***	3.02	***	2.99	***	3.01	***
Migrant background (Ref. = Belgian)										
Moroccan	−0.16	*	−0.10		−0.04		0.03		−0.58	**
Turkish	0.08		0.01		0.08		0.41	*	−0.07	
Work status (Ref = Inactive or- unemployed)										
Full-time (t−1)					0.47	***	0.50	***	0.48	***
Part-time (t−1)					0.29	***	0.33	***	0.30	***
Welfare dependency (t−1)					−0.26	***	−0.20	**	−0.26	***
Individual income (t−1)					−0.08	***	−0.08	**	−0.08	***
Married (t−1) (Ref. = Cohabiting)			0.02		0.04		0.04		−0.01	
Partner background (Ref. = Other)										
First generation			−0.15	*	−0.06		−0.06		−0.02	
Second generation			−0.06		−0.04		−0.04		−0.08	
Interactions with migrant background										
Moroccan × Full-time							−0.13			
Moroccan × Part-time							−0.15			
Moroccan × Welfare dependency							−0.13			
Moroccan × Individual income							0.05			
Moroccan × Married									0.38	*
Moroccan × Partner = 1st generation									0.25	
Moroccan × Partner = 2nd generation									0.40	
Turkish × Full-time							0.02			
Turkish × Part-time							−0.39			
Turkish × Welfare dependency							−0.55	*		
Turkish × Individual income							−0.02			
Turkish × Married									0.46	
Turkish × Partner = 1st generation									−0.44	
Turkish × Partner = 2nd generation									0.14	

Source: Belgian Crossroads Bank for Social Security, calculations by the authors

Notes: All models are also controlled for Age, Age^2, region in Belgium, young child (<3 year) in the household; number of children in the household. Significance levels: *p < .05; **p < .01; ***p < .001

parental home did not vary by origin group, or by the migration background of the partner (i.e., no differences were observed between Moroccan and Turkish fathers). The main effect of having a first-generation ex-partner decreased in this model, but stayed significant.

For women, the same five models were estimated (see Table 5.4). The first important result was found in Models 1 to 3: namely, that the main effects of the migration background of the woman and of her former partner on her likelihood of returning to the parental home were non-significant. We already showed in Table 5.2 that mothers were significantly less likely than fathers to return to the parental home. This overall pattern did not differ among Belgian, Moroccan, and Turkish mothers. When we looked at the effect of the woman's previous partner, we found that having a first-generation partner had a significant negative effect, but that this effect disappeared as soon as we controlled for other factors in Model 3. Again, our results indicated that the characteristics of a mother's previous partner did not play a role in her decision to return (or, rather, not to return) to the parental home. No differences in the likelihood of returning to the parental home were found between mothers depending on whether they had been married or cohabiting.

Individual economic resources played a similar role for all mothers. Among mothers, having a higher income or being dependent on welfare was associated with a lower likelihood of returning to the parental home. The effect of work status on the likelihood of returning to the parental home for mothers was similar to that for fathers. Mothers who were working full-time or part-time were more likely than those who were inactive or unemployed to return. It thus appears that the decision to return to the parental home was affected by the challenges single mothers face in combining work and family. Like for fathers, the interaction effects with migrant background (Models 4 and 5 in Table 5.4) for mothers did not differ much across the Moroccan and Turkish origin groups. The findings indicated that welfare dependency played a different role for Turkish than for Moroccan mothers, although why this was the case is unclear. The results further showed that Moroccan women who had been married were more likely than those who had been cohabiting to return to the parental home following a union dissolution.

Before turning to the discussion, we should point out the effects of some control variables (not shown in the tables). Age was found to be highly significant and negative both among men and women. The registers did not provide an indicator for home ownership or assets. However, age can be considered a proxy for this indicator, as older people are more likely than younger people to own a home and to have sizeable financial assets. Thus, it appears likely that the negative effect of age, in addition to the negative effect of income, confirmed our assumption that the accumulation of wealth gave the former partners more freedom, and enabled them to remain independent of their parents. The regional differences we observed were also striking, with the boomerang effect being more pronounced in the North (Flanders) than in the South (Wallonia) or Brussels. It is, however, possible, that this effect was conflated with the legal status of the former relationship, as marriage is still more common in Flanders than in Wallonia.

With regard to children, we saw no effects in any of the models for men. Among men, neither the presence of young children nor the total number of children appeared to played a role in the decision to return to the parental home. The findings showed that among women, both effects were highly significant, but were in opposite directions. The presence of young children made it more likely that a woman would to return to the parental home, which illustrates the importance of work-life balance for single mothers. However, effect of the total number of children was negative, which indicates that having a larger family made it more difficult for a woman to return to her parents' home.

Discussion and Conclusion

This research addressed several new issues related to the study of the "boomerang effect". We focused on the housing strategies of ex-partners with children after the end of either a marriage or a cohabiting relationship. Whereas most previous studies on adult children returning to the parental home focused on young adults, we focused on adults who had children of their own. Furthermore, we expanded our knowledge on this topic by looking at how cultural heterogeneity and gender influenced the likelihood of returning to the parental home. While the divorce rate is still lower among migrant couples with a Turkish or a Moroccan background than it is among native Belgians, it has been rising (Corijn and Lodewijckx 2009). Moreover, although the housing choices of individuals are subject to the same general mechanisms (e.g., their economic resources), regardless of their migration background, it is likely that the propensity of newly single parents to return to the home of their own parents is related to their cultural background and the societal position of their ethnic group.

Among people with a Turkish or Maghreb background – who make up 2.1% and 3.2% of the Belgian population, respectively (Noppe et al. 2018) – maintaining family and community ties and intergenerational support are often valued over asserting autonomy and independence from one's parents. However, in communities that hold on to these more traditional values, divorcees are likely to face stigma and negative attitudes, especially if they are women (Koelet et al. 2009b). Our expectation (hypothesis 3) that fathers with a Turkish or a Moroccan background would be more likely to return to the parental home than mothers of the same origin groups was only partly confirmed after controlling for relevant socio-economic and demographic factors. The initial models showed that, net of other effects, fathers were more likely than mothers to return to their parents' home (hypothesis 1), and that these associations were stronger for fathers and mothers with either a Turkish or a Moroccan background (hypothesis 2).

The separate models for men and women revealed that economic and family characteristics did not affect all of the subgroups in the same way. More specifically, when we interacted migrant background with these characteristics, we found that family and economic characteristics operated differently for men and women with migrant backgrounds. We found, for example, that for men with a Moroccan or a Turkish background, the interaction term for economic resources was both positive and larger in absolute terms than the negative base effect. In other words, while having a higher income decreased the probability of returning to the parental home for Belgian men, it increased probability for men with a migrant background. These results suggest that for these men, the cultural norm of maintaining close ties with family outweighed their desire to live independently. Another potential explanation for this finding is that these men faced discrimination in the housing market. A survey conducted by Heylen et al. (2007) found that 26% of Flemish owners of apartment buildings said they prefer to look for another tenant if an applicant has a migrant background. Heylen et al. (2007) found that although this share was lower among the private owners surveyed who rent out social housing, it was still 8.6%. These findings imply that whether it is due to actual or statistical discrimination, people with migrant backgrounds have, *ceteris paribus*, more trouble finding suitable housing than native Belgians, even when they have sufficient means to live independently.

No such associations were found for women. However, Turkish mothers who were dependent on welfare were shown to have a lower probability of returning to the parental home than other groups. This might be because these single mothers were at risk of losing (part of) their means-tested benefits if they moved into their parents' household. Another potential explanation for this finding is that because women tend to be the primary carers for their children, these women might have been eligible for social housing. Moreover, as the stigma attached to divorce is greater for women than for men in the Turkish and Moroccan communities (Koelet et al. 2009b), these women might have preferred to be independent. This would also explain why the same association was not found for men.

There are several limitations to our study. First, although it is known that children are more likely to reside with their mother than with their father after a divorce, we were not able to explicitly control for these arrangements. As a result, the associations we found might suffer from omitted variable bias. In addition, we could not control for the characteristics of the parents of the separated and divorced individuals in our sample. These characteristics are important, as they might have shown that in some of these families, returning home was not feasible economically, or that the parents' values either facilitated or hindered the return of their child after a divorce or a separation. Finally, the register data did not allow us to control for the educational attainment or the job status of either the adult children or their parents. Since these are crucial components of an individual's SES, this is a notable blind spot in our analyses. Even though the registers offer a large amount of statistical power, missing information on educational attainment or on the parents' characteristics (e.g., the size of the parents' residence) is a considerable limitation of this study. Higher levels of education are usually associated with more liberal attitudes towards marriage and divorce (Kalmijn and Kraaykamp 2007), although these effects are likely smaller for migrant populations than they are for majority populations (Kalmijn and Kraaykamp 2018).

In conclusion, this research has furthered our understanding of the tendency of parents to return to the home of their own parents after a relationship break-up by looking at differences in these patterns by gender and cultural background, and at the effects of socioeconomic and family indicators on the likelihood of returning. Research on divorce and separation has consistently shown that union dissolution is associated with financial downturns, especially for women. One of the strategies divorcees use to deal with their challenging circumstances is to return to the parental home. Especially when (young) children are living in the household, this strategy could free up parents to explore other potential coping strategies, such as increasing their labour market activities or finding a new partner. There are, however, barriers to employing these strategies, such as the welfare traps inherent to the system. Conversely, cultural norms can encourage or discourage a return to the parental home. Future research should investigate whether the decision to return to the parental home is beneficial for the financial and/or the subjective wellbeing of both the divorced parents and their children. Given that around 20% of Belgian children are living in households that are at risk of poverty (Vandenbroucke and Vinck 2015), gaining additional insight into the effectiveness of the various coping mechanisms parents turn to after a relationship ends is indispensible.

References

Albertini, M., Gähler, M., & Härkönen, J. (2018). Moving back to "mamma"? Divorce, intergenerational coresidence, and latent family solidarity in Sweden. *Population, Space and Place, 24*(6). https://doi.org/10.1002/psp.2142.

Arundel, R., & Lennartz, C. (2017). Returning to the parental home: Boomerang moves of younger adults and the welfare regime context. *Journal of European Social Policy, 27*(3), 276–294. https://doi.org/10.1177/0958928716684315.

Baert, S., Cockx, B., Gheyle, N., & Vandamme, C. (2015). Is there less discrimination in occupations where recruitment is difficult? *ILR Review, 68*(3), 467–500. https://doi.org/10.1177/0019793915570873.

Billari, F. C., Philipov, D., & Baizán, P. (2001). Leaving home in Europe: The experience of cohorts born around 1960. *International Journal of Population Geography, 7*(5), 339–356. https://doi.org/10.1002/ijpg.231.

Carpentier, S., Neels, K., & Van den Bosch, K. (2014). How do exit rates from social assistance benefit in Belgium vary with individual and local agency characteristics? In S. Carcillo, H. Immervoll, S. P. Jenkins, S. Königs, & K. Tatsiramos (Eds.), *Safety nets and benefit dependence* (pp. 151–187). Bingley: Emerald Group Publishing Limited.

Corijn, M., & Lodewijckx, E. (2009). *Echtscheiding en leefvorm na echtscheiding in het Vlaamse Gewest: verschillen naar herkomst: een analyse op basis van Rijksregistergegevens voor volwassenen en kinderen*. Statistiek Vlaanderen. Studiedienst van de Vlaamse Regering.

De Valk, H. A., & Liefbroer, A. C. (2007). Parental influence on union formation preferences among Turkish, Moroccan, and Dutch adolescents in the Netherlands. *Journal of Cross-Cultural Psychology, 38*(4), 487–505. https://doi.org/10.1177/0022022107302316.

Dupont, E., Van Pottelberge, A., Van de Putte, B., Lievens, J., & Caestecker, F. (2017). Partner choices in long established migrant communities in Belgium. *Historical Life Course Studies, 4*, 20–40.

Fingerman, K., Miller, L., Birditt, K., & Zarit, S. (2009). Giving to the good and the needy: Parental support of grown children. *Journal of Marriage and Family, 71*(5), 1220–1233. https://doi.org/10.1111/j.1741-3737.2009.00665.x.

Furstenberg, F. F., Rumbaut, R. C., & Settersten, R. A. (2005). On the frontier of adulthood: Emerging themes and new directions. In R. A. Settersten, F. F. Furstenberg, & R. G. Rumbaut (Eds.), *On the frontier of adulthood: Theory, research, and public policy* (pp. 3–25). Chicago: University of Chicago Press.

Goldscheider, F. K., & Goldscheider, C. (1998). The effects of childhood family structure on leaving and returning home. *Journal of Marriage and Family, 60*(3), 745–756. https://doi.org/10.2307/353543.

Guzzo, K. B. (2016). Do young mothers and fathers differ in the likelihood of returning home? *Journal of Marriage and Family, 78*(5), 1332–1351. https://doi.org/10.1111/jomf.12347.

Heylen, K., Le Roy, M., Vandenbroucke, P., Vandekerckhove, B., & Winters, S. (2007). *Wonen in Vlaanderen. De resultaten van de Woonsurvey 2005 en de Uitwendige Woningschouwing 2005*. Brussels: Ministerie van de Vlaamse Gemeenschap, Departement RWO – Woonbeleid.

Huschek, D., de Valk, H. A., & Liefbroer, A. C. (2012). Partner choice patterns among the descendants of Turkish immigrants in Europe. *European Journal of Population/Revue européenne de Démographie, 28*(3), 241–268. https://doi.org/10.1007/s10680-012-9265-2.

Kalmijn, M., & Kraaykamp, G. (2007). Social stratification and attitudes: A comparative analysis of the effects of class and education in Europe. *The British Journal of Sociology, 58*(4), 547–576. https://doi.org/10.1111/j.1468-4446.2007.00166.x.

Kalmijn, M., & Kraaykamp, G. (2018). Determinants of cultural assimilation in the second generation. A longitudinal analysis of values about marriage and sexuality among Moroccan and Turkish migrants. *Journal of Ethnic and Migration Studies, 44*(5), 697–717. https://doi.org/10.1080/1369183X.2017.1363644.

Kleinepier, T., Berrington, A., & Stoeldraijer, L. (2017). Ethnic differences in returning home: Explanations from a life course perspective. *Journal of Marriage and Family, 79*(4), 1023–1040. https://doi.org/10.1111/jomf.12399.

Koelet, S., Corijn, M., Lodewijckx, E., Mortelmans, D., d'Hooge, A., & Hermans, P. (2009a). *Echtscheiding bij personen van Turkse en Marokkaanse herkomst Deel 2: Kwantitatieve en kwalitatieve studie*. Antwerp: Steunpunt Gelijkansenbeleid.

Koelet, S., Hermans, P., Torfs, N., Vanvoorden, K., & Timmerman, C. (2009b). *Echtscheiding bij personen van Turkse en Marokkaanse herkomst Deel 1: Literatuurstudie*. Antwerp: Steunpunt Gelijkansenbeleid.

Lievens, J. (1997). *The third wave of immigration from Turkey and Morocco: Determinants and characteristics*. Ghent: Department of Sociology.

Loopmans, M., Minon, C., Perrin, N., & Teller, J. (2014). Onderzoek van de private huisvestingsmarkt in België in het kader van de Diversiteitsbarometer. In Interfederaal Gelijke Kansen Centrum (Ed.), *Diversiteitsbarometer Huisvesting* (pp. 136–245). Brussels: Interfederaal Gelijke Kansen Centrum.

Merz, E.-M., Özeke-Kocabas, E., Oort, F. J., & Schuengel, C. (2009). Intergenerational family solidarity: Value differences between immigrant groups and generations. *Journal of Family Psychology, 23*(3), 291–300. https://doi.org/10.1037/a0015819.

Mortelmans, D. (2010). *Logistische Regressie* (Vol. 6). Leuven: Acco.

Mortelmans, D., Van den Berg, L., & Thielemans, G. (2019). Coping strategies of migrant ex-partners: Does work, family, or a new partner help you through the dark times? In D. Mortelmans (Ed.), *Divorce in Europe*. Brussels: Springer (forthcoming).

Noppe, J., Vanweddingen, M., Doyen, G., Stuyck, K., Feys, Y., & Buysschaert, P. (2018). *Vlaamse Migratie en Integratiemonitor*. Brussels: Agentschap Binnenlands Bestuur.

Ongaro, F., Mazzuco, S., & Meggiolaro, S. (2008). Economic consequences of union dissolution in Italy: Findings from the European Community Household Panel. *European Journal of Population, 25*(1), 45–65. https://doi.org/10.1007/s10680-008-9157-7.

Phalet, K., & Schönpflug, U. (2001). Intergenerational transmission of collectivism and achievement values in two acculturation contexts the case of Turkish families in Germany and Turkish and Moroccan families in the Netherlands. *Journal of Cross-Cultural Psychology, 32*(2), 186–201. https://doi.org/10.1177/0022022101032002006.

Stone, J., Berrington, A., & Falkingham, J. (2014). Gender, turning points, and boomerangs: Returning home in young adulthood in Great Britain. *Demography, 51*(1), 257–276. https://doi.org/10.1007/s13524-013-0247-8.

Sullivan, O. (2007). Housing movements of the divorced and separated. *Housing Studies, 1*(1), 35–48. https://doi.org/10.1080/02673038608720561.

Vandenbroucke, F., & Vinck, J. (2015). Child poverty risks in Belgium, Wallonia and Flanders: Accounting for a worrying performance. *Belgisch Tijdschrift voor Sociale Zekerheid, 1*(2015), 51–98.

Whittington, L. A., & Peters, H. E. (1996). Economic incentives for financial and residential independence. *Demography, 33*(1), 82–97. https://doi.org/10.2307/2061715.

Zick, A., Pettigrew, T. F., & Wagner, U. (2008). Ethnic prejudice and discrimination in Europe. *Journal of Social Issues, 64*(2), 233–251. https://doi.org/10.1111/j.1540-4560.2008.00559.x.

Part II
Parent-Child Relationships

Chapter 6
Will Separations Lead to More or Less Gender-Equal Parenthood? Mothers' and Fathers' Parental Leave Use in Sweden

Ann-Zofie Duvander and Nicklas Korsell

Introduction

Gender equality and shared parenting are closely related in Sweden. The premise that parents should share the responsibility for their children has strong support in Sweden, and is rarely contested in either the public or the political discourse. The concept of shared parenting is supported by research pointing to the positive aspects of gender-equal parenting, and especially of the involvement of the father (Hwang and Lamb 1997; Sarkadi et al. 2007). There is also a growing interest in the use of parental leave by fathers among both policy-makers and researchers. But what does shared parenting mean if the parents are not living together? Is gender-equal parenting practised in such cases? Is sharing the responsibility for care possible after the child's parents separate? Sweden is the ideal setting for investigating these questions, not only because a substantial share of Swedish parents lives apart, but because Sweden has high levels of gender equality, not least among parents. For instance, in Sweden, nine out of ten fathers take some parental leave, and 79% of all mothers with preschool children participate in the labour force (compared to 93% of equivalent group fathers, see scb.se). The country also has strong norms and high levels of agreement about the positive aspects of gender equality, including for parenting (Valarino et al. 2018). In this study, we investigate how parental care is shared by estimating the uptake of parental leave by mothers and fathers.

In Sweden, parental leave entitlement consists of 16 months of parental benefit days that can be used at any time during a child's preschool years. It is common practice for parents to save days for use after the child's first years of life that enable

A.-Z. Duvander (✉)
Stockholm University, Stockholm, Sweden
e-mail: ann-zofie.duvander@sociology.su.se

N. Korsell
Swedish Social Insurance Inspectorate, Stockholm, Sweden

M. Kreyenfeld, H. Trappe (eds.), *Parental Life Courses after Separation and Divorce in Europe*, Life Course Research and Social Policies 12,
https://doi.org/10.1007/978-3-030-44575-1_6

them to, for example, prolong holidays or bridge days when the child's preschool is closed. Indeed, around half of the days used by fathers and about 15 percent of the days used by mothers are taken after the child's second birthday (www.forsakringskassan.se). As mothers use many more days than fathers early in the child's life, these percentages amount to about 40–50 days for both mothers and fathers. As the leave is for each individual child, each of the two parents of the child "owns" half of the days, but is permitted to transfer some of his/her days to the other parent. Swedish family policy has the explicit aim to enable and encourage the sharing of parental leave, regardless of whether the parents are living together. Our investigation of the use of parental leave by separated parents sheds light on the question of whether this policy goal is being achieved for the subgroup of separated parents. Furthermore, our study provides insight into the question of how parents negotiate their use parental leave.

The most common reason cited by parents for why they share the leave unequally is that they face economic constraints. In most cases, this means that the family cannot afford for the father to stay home for a long period. If the parents are living apart, these economic decisions are likely to be made differently. Compared to parents who live together, separated parents may, for example, face greater financial pressures, but will also have more reasons to make decisions individually. Thus, when the parents are separated, the parental leave days taken by one parent are less likely to benefit the other parent, and each parent has a stronger incentive to save his/her own days. In this study, we will compare the use of parental leave between parents who did and did not separate, and analyse how leave use differed depending on the age of the child at the time of separation. Our main question is whether having separated led parents to use parental leave differently. While we control for common confounding factors of parental separation, we will not be able to make a strict causal claim about how separation affects parental leave use. Rather, we see our findings as exploratory and descriptive. Nevertheless, we draw some conclusions for the question of whether the Swedish parental leave entitlement has been successful in reaching subgroups of parents who separated during their child's preschool years. The findings will be discussed based on the assumption that the parents' approaches to negotiating leave, and their preferences for taking leave, is likely to be affected by a separation.

Theoretical Considerations

Earnings-related parental leave provides parents with economic compensation while they are caring for their child at home, while also protecting the parents' employment contracts (Blum et al. 2018). However, even if parents are financially compensated while taking leave, they may have economic reasons for not taking it, such as the fear that being absent from work could damage their career progression and future wages (Evertsson and Duvander 2010; Rege and Solli 2013). Moreover, most parents do not receive 100% of their previous income while on leave. As a result of these economic incentives and gendered parenting norms – and because of physiological considerations like a desire to breastfeed – the mother usually takes most of the parental leave, and almost always takes the first part of the leave entitlement. When the parents live together, they often seek to optimize their household economy by having the mother take most of the parental leave and become the main carer for the child. Economic reasoning is also the most common justification given by Swedish parents for not sharing leave equally (National Social Insurance Board 2003; Swedish Social Insurance Agency 2013). In the bargaining process used by a couple in deciding which partner takes parental leave, the decision-making power often rests with the partner who has the most power over the family's economic resources (Lundberg and Pollak 1996), or a common decision is reached based on considerations of economic optimisation and specialisation (Becker 1991). The decision of how the leave will be shared might also be based on norms and gendered behaviour that are rarely questioned (Brines 1994; West and Zimmerman 1987); or even on the partners' preferences for providing child care, which may be gendered and contextual (Närvi 2012).

However, when the parents separate, these motivations for the gendered sharing of parental leave may change for several different reasons. First, because the parents live in different households after the separation, the economic gains or losses of the parent who earns the least are not shared with the other parent. If we assume that both parents prefer to be on leave, there are no economic gains associated with not using leave for the parent who earns more, and his/her bargaining position becomes stronger. As each of the parents has a separate household income, they are likely to calculate their gains and losses separately. Nonetheless, the parents still need to negotiate how they intend to share a fixed number of parental leave days. From the perspective of specialisation, neither parent gains from specialising in either care work or paid employment. Indeed, it might be very risky for a separated parent to specialise, as spending too little time on either childcare or waged work may lead to a deficit that is harmful for the child-parent relationship, or for the economic sustainability of the one-parent household.

Furthermore, the norms and preferences regarding parental leave and childcare after a separation are likely to be contextual. In a society in which traditional norms prevail, the external shock of a separation often leads parents to fall back on gendered behavioural patterns, with the mother taking the main responsibility for childcare. But in a society in which gender-equal parenting is highly valued, the separation may actually be a tipping point towards a more equal sharing of parenting responsibilities, especially given that economic considerations would tend to reinforce such an outcome. In this chapter, we will investigate whether separated parents in Sweden are indeed more likely to share parenting responsibilities than their cohabiting counterparts. It should, however, be noted that a separation is usually accompanied by economic constraints that are also likely to influence how parents share leave. Financial pressures could make it more difficult for parents to use their leave benefits, as a single parent may be unable to afford the reduction in income while on leave. It is also possible that when parents face economic constraints, they see their resources as scarce, and thus become less willing to be generous when negotiating how leave days are shared.

In sum, the sharing of parental leave after separation becomes a litmus test of whether individual concerns about economic optimisation trump gendered behavioural patterns in a context in which the level of gender equality is fairly high, such as in Sweden. Thus, if the advantages associated with specialisation are lost, or the bargaining positions of parents change after separation, these factors could become more important than normative gendered behavioural patterns, and we would expect to find that the separated fathers in our sample used more parental leave than the fathers who were partnered. If, however, normative gendered behaviour functions as a fall-back position when parents separate, we would expect to see that the separated fathers took fewer leave days than the fathers who were partnered. Moreover, we would expect to find that in response to increased economic pressure after a separation, both the separated mothers and the separated parents combined used fewer days of leave than their non-separated counterparts.

Institutional Background and Research Question

Parental Leave

The parental leave preferences of both parents – that is, whether the father and/or the mother want to stay home or participate in the labour market – are major unknown factors. Caring for a child is not just a task that is likely to be preferred to other household work; it is an investment in the parent-child relationship (Nitsche and Grunow 2018). The childcare provided by parents taking parental leave differs from other forms of childcare, as it is exchanged for labour market work. Moreover, a parent's concerns about the loss of income when taking leave may depend not only on his/her own income level, but on the loss of the other parent's potential income if the parents share a household (Sundström and Duvander 2002).

In Sweden, a mother and a father are entitled to 8 months of paid parental leave each when they have a child, or a combined total of 16 months (480 days). The length of the leave entitlement has been extended in several steps since 1974, when parents were granted a combined total of 6 months of leave. For children born before 2014, these parental benefit days can be used at any time until the child reaches age 8 (see www.forsakringskassan.se). Parental leave benefit levels are linked to earnings. While parents receive approximately 80% of their previous earnings over most of the leave period, 3 months of the leave entitlement are compensated at a low flat rate. Parents who had a low or no income prior to having a child receive a low flat rate for the whole leave period. In 1995, one month of leave was reserved for each parent. This reform, which was aimed at increasing the uptake of leave by fathers, is often referred to as the "daddy month" (or the "mummy month"). Also starting in 1995, the leave entitlement was allocated to each individual parent. This means that a parent who wants to use more than 240 days needs the other parent to sign over days to him/her. This was initially done using a paper form, but can now be done with an electronic signature. It is important to note that these regulations are the same for parents regardless of whether they are living together. A second month was reserved for each parent in 2002, and a third month was reserved for each parent in 2016. Since these months were reserved, the share of leave taken by fathers has increased substantially (Duvander and Johansson 2012). Today, nine out of ten fathers use some parental leave, and fathers use an average of slightly more than one-quarter of all of the parental benefit days taken in a year (Forsakringskassan.se).

Parental leave legislation also gives parents the flexibility to mix paid and unpaid days, and thus to choose the benefit levels and number of leave days that best fit their preferences and their economic circumstances. It is common for Swedish parents to use both paid and unpaid leave (Duvander and Viklund 2020; Eriksson 2014). However, the numbers of parental leave days taken and the levels of compensation parents receive while on leave vary considerably between families. Moreover, many parents save days for use during the child's preschool years. For example, for children born in 2007, fathers used an average of 48 days and mothers used an average of 54 days after the child's second birthday (official statistics, Swedish Social Insurance Agency, see www.forsakringskassan.se). It should also be emphasised that not all parental leave days are used; on average, parents had not used between 30 and 40 days by the time the child turned age 8, and thus forfeited these days (see www.forsakringskassan.se). In most cases, the days that would have been paid at a low flat rate were the ones that were left unused.

Previous studies have shown that in Sweden, the fathers who use the most leave and the mothers who use the least leave have higher levels of education (Swedish Social Insurance Agency 2013; Duvander and Johansson 2014). Parents who are highly educated tend to have better job situations than parents who have less education. For example, a highly educated father may be in a strong position to negotiate leave, and a highly educated mother may have an incentive to go back to work early. There is evidence that the parents with medium to relatively high income levels take the longest leave, while the parents with the highest income levels take somewhat shorter periods of leave (Duvander and Viklund 2020). The fathers who take the fewest leave days are those who have no earnings and/or no employment. As the mothers in the same situation tend to take most of their leave entitlement, it is clear that gendered norms interact with economic conditions in determining how much leave parents take. Attitudes also seem to affect the uptake of leave, as the fathers who have the most gender-equal attitudes and the mothers who are the most family-oriented tend to use the most leave (Duvander 2014).

Parental Responsibilities after Separation

In Sweden, the principle that both the mother and the father are equally responsible for their children is reinforced, regardless of whether they live together. Rates of parental separation were increasing in Sweden up to the turn of the century, and have since been stable or even slightly declining (Statistics Sweden 2013).

While parental separation is relatively frequent in Sweden, it is less common for a mother to be single from the beginning of her child's life. Only around one in 20 children in Sweden are born to a single mother, and this share does not seem to be increasing over time (Thomson and Eriksson 2013). However, around one in four children experience a parental separation during their childhood years (children aged 0–17 years, Statistics Sweden 2014), and around one in five children experience a parental separation during their preschool years (own calculations). Most Swedish parents have joint legal custody after they separate. Although the expectations for the mother and the father after they separate have been – and still are to a large extent – different, joint custody after separation has been permitted since 1976, provided the parents are in agreement (Government proposition 1975/1976: 170). Since 1998, awarding joint custody has been the default practice (Government proposition 1997/98: 7). Policy developments and legislation in Sweden may be characterised as increasingly gender-neutral and individualised. Thus, in most cases, the mother and the father are granted the same rights and responsibilities in relation to their child, regardless of whether they live together.

However, not all joint custody arrangements are the same. The legal framework that regulates the parents' economic responsibilities to their child has changed significantly over time. While current policy encourages parents to organise these payments themselves, it was still common at the beginning of the 2000s for separating parents to turn to the Swedish Social Insurance Agency for help in managing these transactions, and in determining the amounts to be paid. However, since 2016, the parents have been expected to negotiate and agree on such transactions between themselves. Thus, current family law is based on the concepts of individual responsibility, collaboration, and equal power relations between parents (Government proposition 2014/2015).

A parallel development has been the shift towards joint physical custody arrangements that enable separated parents to continue to share childcare responsibilities (Fransson et al. 2015, 2018). Under such an arrangement, the child lives half the time with the mother and half the time with the father. The popularity of joint physical custody has increased dramatically in recent years. The share of Swedish children with separated parents who live in such an arrangement has risen from just 1-2% in the mid-1980s to 35–40% in the mid-2010s (Statistics Sweden 2014). However, the most common situation for Swedish children is to live primarily with their mother after a separation: 30% live only with their mother, and in addition more than 20% live with their mother most of the time. Less than 5% of the children of separated parents live only with their father, and less than 5% live with their father most of the time (Statistics Sweden 2014). As there are no registers that track where the children of separated parents live, these statistics are based on surveys. Thus, estimates differ between sources, and have large confidence margins.

Although a majority of Swedish children are not living with both parents following a separation, the frequency of their contact with the non-residential parent seems to have increased. In Sweden, there is a strong social norm that a father should continue to be involved in his child's life after a separation. Family policy measures, such as parental leave, temporary parental leave, and child allowance, make no distinction between parents based on whether they live with their children, and are available to all parents with custody. The gender-equal sharing of parental leave is an important component of the aim to create a gender-equal society in Sweden. This overarching goal of gender equality is reflected not just in the country's family policy, but in its labour market policy and other parts of the political agenda.

The strong norm that childcare responsibilities should be shared equally by the parents regardless of gender leads us to expect that fathers will be less inclined to transfer their half of the days to the mother after a separation. Thus, parental leave may be used on a more gender-equal basis following a separation, which would indicate that parents are sharing responsibility for their children. Nevertheless, while there has been a shift towards a more gender-equal and individualised distribution of responsibilities for children, it is also important to keep in mind that even in Sweden, gendered structures still prevail. Parental leave use statistics, data from time use studies, and parents' reports of who is responsible for various childcare tasks all indicate that mothers continue to be the main care providers (Swedish Social Insurance Agency 2013; Neilson 2016). In addition, as there is still a gender pay gap, fathers' opportunity costs are higher than those of mothers when using leave. Thus, it is also possible that when parents separate, the mother takes on the bulk of the care responsibilities, and the father's use of parental leave is reduced.

Our contradictory expectations of whether separated parents in Sweden share leave more or less than cohabiting parents leads us to formulate the following research questions: Did fathers and mothers who separated use more or less parental leave individually than non-separating fathers and mothers? And, what impact did separation have on the total amount of parental leave used?

Data and Analytical Strategy

Data

Administrative register data from the Swedish Social Insurance Agency are used for the analysis. The sample covers the parents of all children born in Sweden in 2002 and 2003, and the observation period is the full 8 years during which parental leave could be used. For these two cohorts, the same parental leave regulations applied. Parents with custody had the right to 8 months of leave, but could transfer all but two of these months to the other parent. To ensure that the parental leave was not used for other children in the family, the sample is restricted to first-born children, and the models control for continued childbearing. To ensure that both parents were engaged in childrearing, we included in the sample only parents who had lived together previously, and had joint custody for the whole study period. For the sake of simplicity, parents who lived with each other again after separating were excluded. We also excluded parents who emigrated or died during the observation period, and parents of children who emigrated or died. In addition, we excluded parents of children who were born abroad, adopted, or multiple births, as special rules for parental leave apply in these cases. Finally, we excluded same-sex couples, as our interest here is in examining changes in gender equality. After applying the above criteria, the total number of parental couples in the sample was 63,040.

The data provide detailed information on childbearing, annual income, and social insurance benefits, including parental leave benefits. They also contain information on the parents' individual characteristics, such as sex, birth year, educational level, and country of birth; and on the birth order of the child. The dependent variable is the categorised number of days of parental leave used.

Our indicator of the parents' status as living together or separated was based on whether they were registered as living at the same address. We assumed that the parents of a common child who were registered at the same address were living together as a couple. If a parent moved to another address (or if both parents moved to different addresses), we assumed that the parents separated. There is a marginal risk that parents who were registered as living together were not living together as a couple if, for example, they were living in separate dwelling units at the same address (e.g., if they were living in the same building block with multiple apartments). There is also some fuzziness regarding the exact timing of separation, as the separation process can be gradual, and a change of address may come later. As the data do not include information on civil status, we were unable to tell when a potential divorce took place. In the Swedish context, the consequences of separating after cohabiting and divorcing after being married are likely to be similar for parents, as the legal differences between these types of unions are slight, and cohabitation is completely accepted.

It is obviously the case that the number of parental leave days a mother and a father can use is restricted by the number of days provided for in the legislation, and by the number of days used by the other parent. However, we found a surprising amount of variation not just in the extent to which the days the parents used were correlated, but in the total number of days they took. While it was quite common for a father to use no days in the first 2 years of his child's life, the most common pattern observed among fathers was to use exactly 60 days, which corresponds to the 2 months "reserved" for the father. Among mothers, using no leave was found to be very uncommon, but a peak was observed at 240 days; i.e., at the point at which half of all of the days had been used. It is likely that when the mother had used half of all of the days, the father started to use the other half, but spread his days out over the child's preschool years. It is also possible that in such cases, the father was not giving the mother permission to use "his" allocated days, but that he was not using them either. The most common pattern found for mothers was to use 330 days, which in most cases meant that the mother was using days with earnings-related benefits, and not days that would have been paid at a low flat rate.

Description of the Sample

In the descriptive Table 6.1, the distribution of leave use is categorised into the four categories used in the multinomial regression. The table shows in the last column how common the categories of use are by year of separation, and compared to the distribution among parents who did not separate. We see clear patterns. For example, using no leave was much more common among fathers who separated early. Still, it is worth pointing out that almost half of the fathers who separated in the first year of their child's life used more than 2 months of leave during their child's first 2 years. In an international perspective, this number can be considered high.

In Table 6.2, we see the background variables used in the regressions. While separating in the first year of the child's life was quite uncommon, the separation rates were stable thereafter, at between 2% and 3% of all couples separating every year. On average, the mother was younger and both the mother and the father had lower income levels the year before the child was born in couples who separated than in couples who stayed together. The separating couples were also more likely to have a lower educational level. Finally, separation was more common among foreign-born parents.

Analytical Strategy

We will use multinomial logistic regression analysis to investigate whether the separating parents used parental leave to a greater or lesser extent than the parents who were living together over the first 8 years of their first-born child's life. Our main focus is on the question of whether parental leave use differs between the parents who separated and those who did not. First, we analyse the mothers', the fathers', and the total number of days used in interaction with the time when the separation took place. In these analyses, we follow the parents for 8 years, and the outcome is the completed number of days. The models include background variables on each parent's age at childbirth, income the year before childbirth, educational level, and whether s/he is foreign-born. The full models can be found in the appendix. Here, we will focus on presenting the model results by the child's age at separation.

Next, to differentiate any diverging patterns of leave use before and after separation, we analyse these periods separately. We compare parental leave use before and after separation for couples who separated at different ages of the child to the parental leave use of couples who did not separate using a bivariate regression model. Specifically, we perform seven bivariate regressions, with each regression including those couples who separated when the child was k years old, and those who did not separate. In each regression, we use a bivariate outcome vector $(y_{i,<k}\ y_{i,\geq k})$ where $y_{i,<k}$ describes the i:th parents benefit days the years before year k, and $y_{i,\geq k}$ shows the days as from year k (inclusive). We control for the parent's level of education, individual income (in quintiles), and age; and for whether the parent was

Table 6.1 Use of parental leave by calendar year and gender

		Child's age at separation								No separation
		0 year	1 year	2 year	3 year	4 year	5 year	6 year	7 year	
Mother's parental leave days	<=240 days	14.12	13.64	12.92	12.78	13.19	13.6	12.65	12.45	12.14
	240–325 days	23.4	25.04	26.14	27.17	26.38	28.86	27.31	25.65	28.4
	326–335 days	7.99	7.36	7.78	8.13	6.87	8.23	6.87	8.3	6.66
	335–420	54.49	53.97	53.16	51.92	53.57	49.31	53.16	53.6	52.79
Father's parental leave days	0 days	9.13	7.69	5.87	5	4.61	4.77	3.48	3.6	2.2
	1–55	19.54	20.25	19.24	16.53	18.34	16.55	16.32	16.33	11.76
	56–65	22.4	23.22	23.05	22.7	24.12	20.02	21.17	25.92	21.91
	66–420	48.93	48.84	51.84	55.76	52.94	58.67	59.03	54.15	64.13
Total parental leave days	0–389 days	24.54	24.38	23.35	21.09	20.87	22.18	17.78	19.46	14.82
	390–419	22.68	22.98	22.91	23.68	21.59	20.8	24.47	21.77	18.92
	420–479	45.36	45.79	46.48	46.92	51.22	50.09	50.78	50.46	56.95
	480	7.42	6.86	7.27	8.31	6.32	6.93	6.97	8.3	9.32
N		701	1210	1362	1119	1107	1154	1091	1084	39,483
% of all couples		1.5	2.5	2.8	2.3	2.3	2.4	2.3	2.2	81.7

Table 6.2 Descriptive table for parents' characteristics by separation year

		Child's age at separation								
		0	1	2	3	4	5	6	7	No separation
Mother's age at childbirth	< 25 years	48.9	50.3	42.8	41	34.7	30.9	31.3	27.1	16
	25–29 years	28.7	28.4	31.6	35	35.5	37.7	38.1	42.3	42.1
	30–34 years	16.3	17.1	18.8	19.4	23.1	24.1	23.1	24.2	33.3
	35–39 years	5.3	3.8	5.7	4	5.7	6.6	6.6	5.7	7.8
	> = 40 years	0.8	0.6	1.2	0.7	1	0.8	0.9	0.8	0.9
Income quintile	Father	2.7	2.9	3	3.1	3.2	3.2	3.3	3.4	3.7
	Mother	2.3	2.2	2.4	2.4	2.6	2.6	2.7	2.7	3.1
Educational level	Both parents ≥ tertiary	17	14.4	15	13.3	19.7	21.8	20.4	24.1	34
	Mother ≥ tertiary, Father ≤ secondary	14.9	12.5	14.8	14.9	17.4	15.9	17.9	16.6	19.5
	Mother ≤ secondary, Father ≥ tertiary.	8.6	8.9	8.1	10.7	10.5	9.2	9.5	11.5	10.6
	Both parents ≤ secondary	59.5	64.2	62.1	61.1	52.5	53.2	52.3	47.9	36
Foreign born	No	85.5	88.6	90.6	89.6	91.3	89.8	93.5	90.6	92.5
	Yes	14.5	11.4	9.4	10.4	8.7	10.2	6.6	9.4	7.5
N		724	1224	1376	1140	1117	1166	1100	1097	39,952
% of all couples		1.5	2.5	2.8	2.3	2.3	2.4	2.2	2.2	81.7

foreign-born. We also control for the birth cohort of the child being 2002 or 2003, and for continued childbearing during the observation period. The covariates thus include both time-independent as well as time-dependent variables.

We use a bivariate outcome vector as an empirical strategy to control for individual variations in overall benefit use. If we were to use only the benefit days that were taken after separation, any differences found between separated and cohabiting parents may reflect overall differences in use between the two groups emanating from confounding variables; that is, variables that cause variations in both days used and separation propensity (Figs. 6.1 and 6.2).

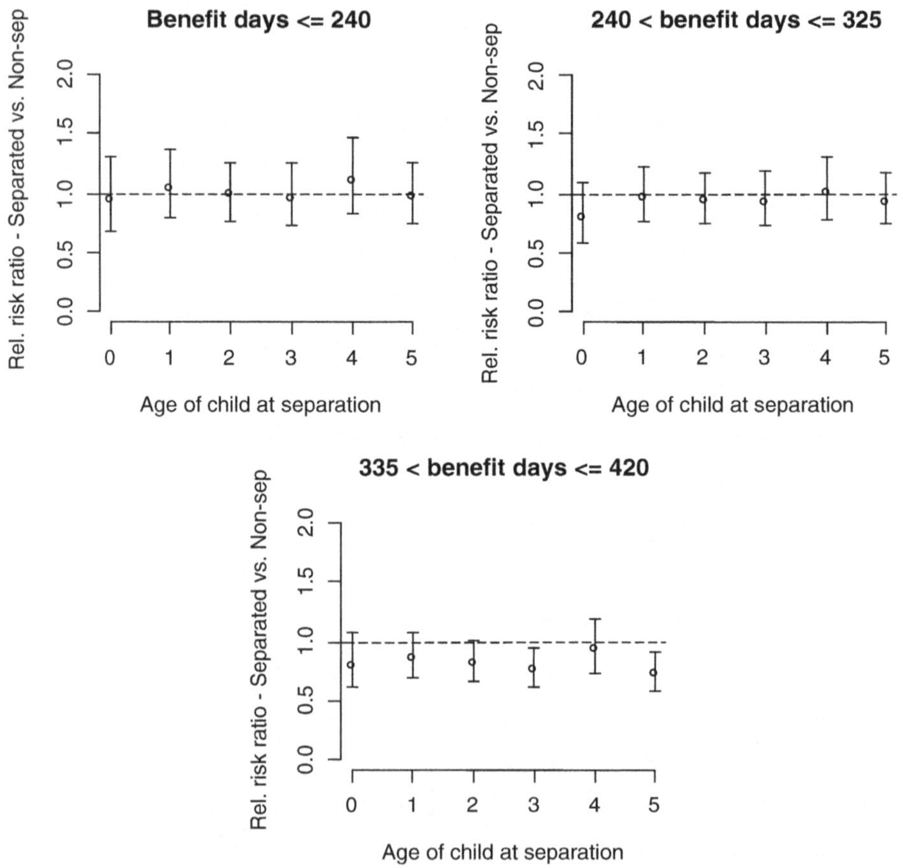

Fig. 6.1 Multinomial regression results. Mothers' use of parental leave (1) up to 240 days, (2) 241–325 days, (3) 326–335 days (reference), (4) 335–420 days. Relative risk ratios and 95% confidence interval

Note: Further controls in the model were parents' income, education, and foreign origin (see Table 6.3 in the Appendix for the full model)

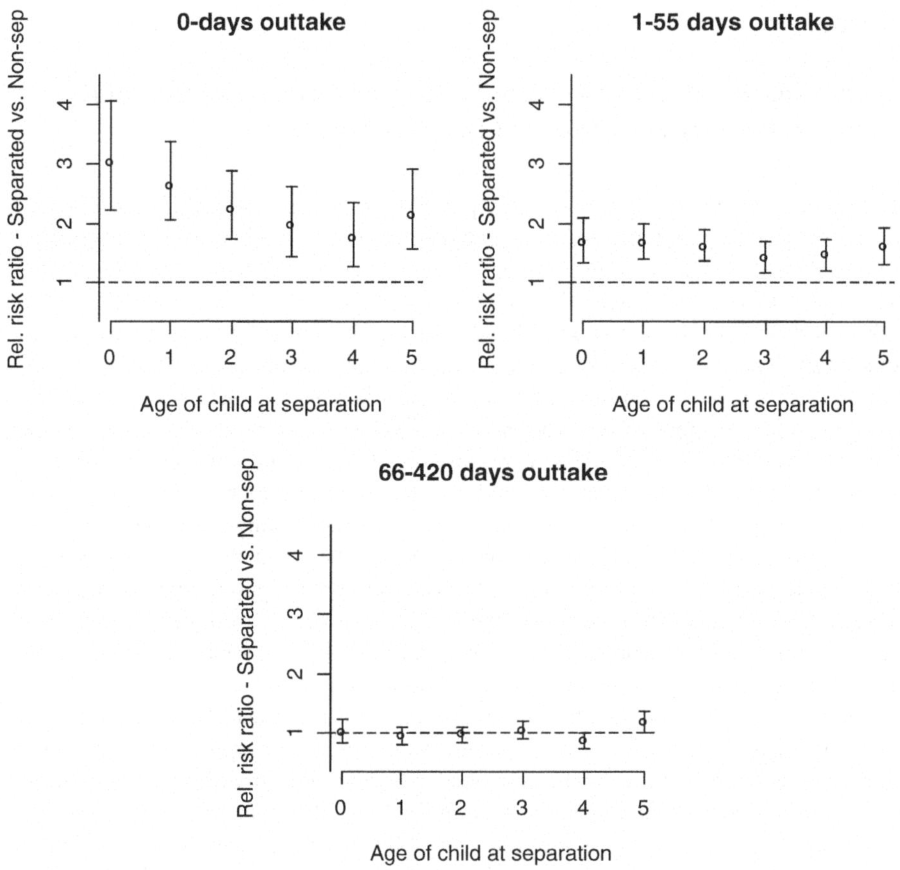

Fig. 6.2 Multinomial regression results. Fathers' use of parental leave (1) up to 240 days, (2) 241–325 days, (3) 326–335 days (reference), (4) 335–420 days. Relative risk ratios and 95% confidence interval

Note: Further controls in the model were parents' income, education, and foreign origin (see Table 6.4 in the Appendix for the full model)

One of the estimated regression results that underlies Figs. 6.4, 6.5 and 6.6 is found in appendix Table 6.6. The table shows the estimated parameters from a bivariate regression for the father's leave use among those fathers who separated when the child was 1 year old and those who did not separate during the first 8 years of the child's life. Note that we have two columns for the two outcome variables: $y_{i,<1}$ = benefit days before the child turns 1 year old, and $y_{i,\geq 1}$= benefit days from when the child turns 1 year old up to child's eighth birthday.

Results

Determinants of Using Parental Leave by Gender: Differences Between Parents Who Did and Did Not Separate

In Fig. 6.1, the relative risk ratio for separated mothers of using different numbers of days depending on when they separated compared to mothers who did not separate is presented. The reference category is using between 326 and 335 days; that is, 11 months of parental leave. The graph in the upper-left corner shows the risk of taking a short leave of up to 8 months (240 days) for mothers who separated at various times. The confidence intervals are quite large for this group, and no significantly different risk of taking such a short leave is detected for separated mothers. The graph in the upper-right corner shows the relative risk ratios for using between 8 and 11 months (240–325 days) of leave. It also indicates that the relative risk ratios are similar for the separating and non-separating mothers. In the graph at the bottom of Fig. 6.1, we can see the relative risk ratios of taking a long leave of up to 14 months (335–420 days), Again, the difference between the separated and the non-separated mothers is quite small. The mothers who separated when their child was 2, 3, or 5 years old were somewhat less likely to have used 8 to 11 months of leave, but the mothers who separated when their child was 4 years old did not differ in their leave usage from the mothers who did not separate.

Next, in Fig. 6.2, we turn to the fathers' parental leave use. Here, the reference category of use is 55–65 days, or around 2 months. The graph in the upper-right corner shows that the fathers who separated at any point during the child's preschool years had a higher probability of not using the leave. It seems that if a father separated early – and especially in the first year of his child's life – he was less likely to take any leave at all. In the graph in the upper-right corner of Fig. 6.2, we can see that the fathers who separated were also more likely to use less than 2 months of leave. There is no visible difference depending on when the father separated. In the graph at the bottom of Fig. 6.2, the relative risk ratios for using more than 2 months of leave are displayed. However, they show no difference between separating and non-separating fathers in their chances of taking such a long leave.

In Fig. 6.3, the total leave is considered; that is the combined days used by the mother and the father. The maximum length of leave is 16 months, and the reference category is having used more than 14 months of leave, but not all of the available leave days. We know from the descriptive table that all of the leave days were used for fewer than one in ten children, and that the parents used more than 14 months of leave (but not the full leave) in only about half of all cases. It thus appears that not using all of the benefits for each child was quite common. The graph in the upper-right corner indicates that among parents who separated, it was much more common with a short leave of up to 13 months. In many cases this means that the low paid flat rate days were not used, and thus forfeited. Moreover, it was also more common to use between 13 and 14 months of leave; again with quite a few days being

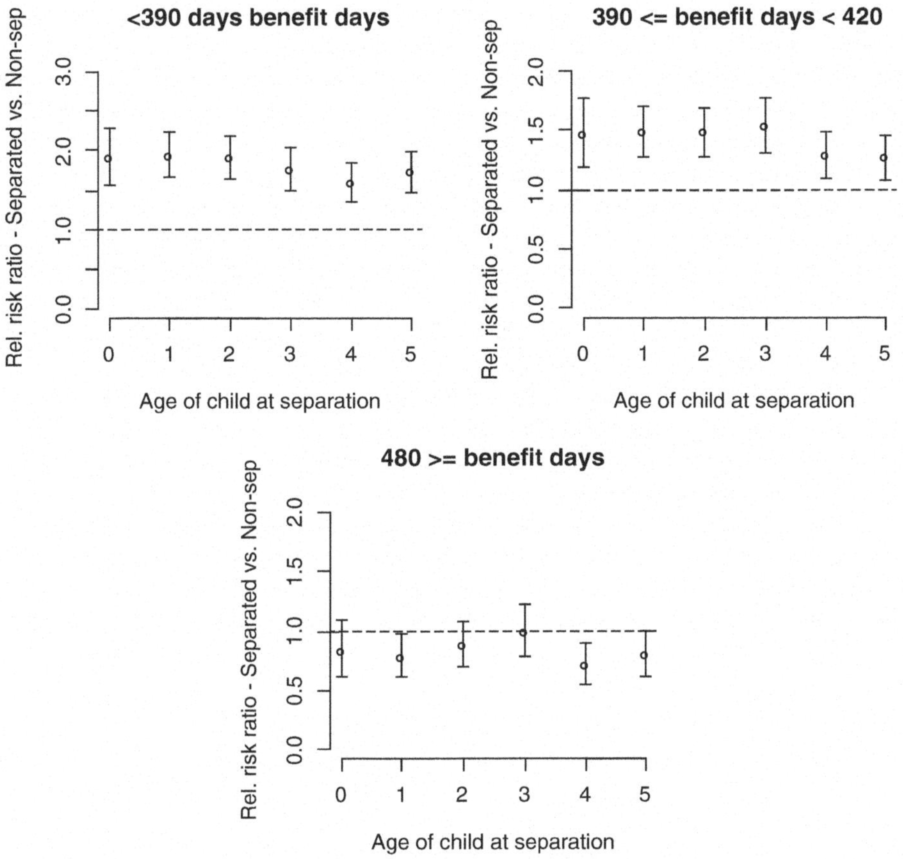

Fig. 6.3 Multinomial regression Total use in categories, (1) 480 days, (2) 479–420 days (REF), (3) 419–390 days, (4) less than 390 days
Note: Further controls in the model were parents' income and education, and the foreign origin of both parents (see Table 6.5 in the Appendix for the full model)

forfeited. In the bottom graph of Fig. 6.3, we can also see that the separating parents were less likely to have used all of the days; that is, to have maximised their leave. There are no clear differences based on the child's age at separation in these models of total leave length.

Taking Leave Before and After Separation

In the above model, we considered the completed number of days of leave depending on when the parents separated. However, the pattern of when the leave days were used can, of course, vary depending on whether we are considering the days used before or after the separation. Therefore, we also considered how many days were used before and after the separation depending on when the separation happened. These results are summarised in Fig. 6.4 for mothers, in Fig. 6.5 for fathers, and in Fig. 6.6 for total leave use. Here, the model specification is a bivariate regression model with simultaneous estimation of days before and after the separation (see Swedish social insurance inspectorare 2017).

Figure 6.4 indicates that, compared to the mothers who did not separate, the mothers who separated in the first year of the child's life used, on average, twelve more days before the separation, and 18 fewer days after the separation. For the mothers who separated later in the child's life, we see no statistically significant higher level of use before the separation, but somewhat fewer days used after the separation, especially for the mothers who separated relatively early.

In Fig. 6.5, we can see that the fathers who separated – and especially the fathers who separated early – used fewer days after the separation. For the period before the separation, we observe large variations in use (seen in the large confidence intervals), and no indication that fewer days were used.

Finally, the total number of days used before and after a separation mirror the combined number of days used by the mother and the father, as indicated in Fig. 6.6. We can see that having separated early was associated with having used more days before the separation, and fewer days after. We also find that having separated later

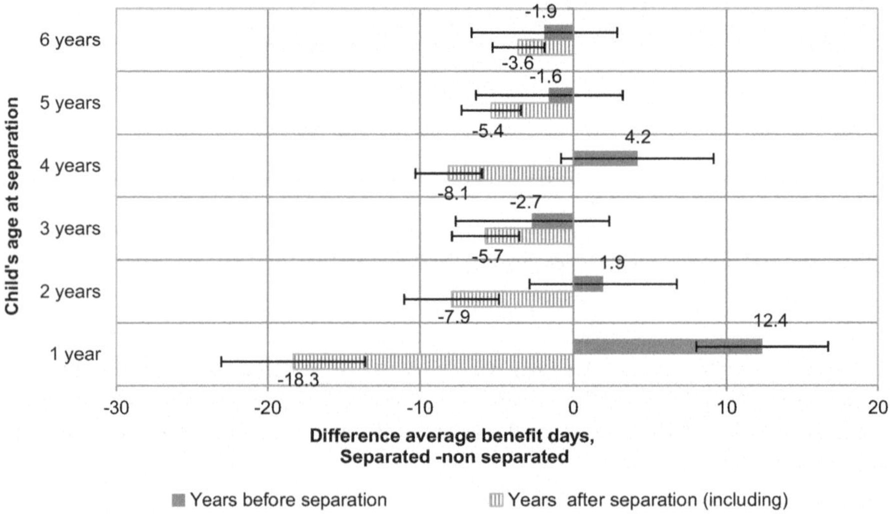

Fig. 6.4 Differences between separated and non-separated parents' benefit days before and after separation. Average number of days for mothers

Note: Further controls in the model were fathers' and mothers' age, education, birth country, and income quintiles; as well as the child's year of birth and continued childbearing. See Table 6.6 for an example of regression; all six regressions for the figure are available upon request

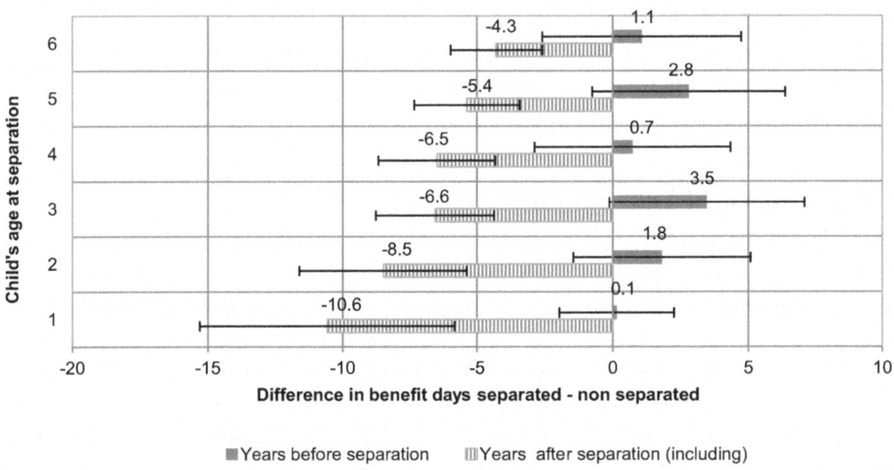

Fig. 6.5 Differences between separated and non-separated parents' benefit days before and after separation. Average number of days for fathers
Note: Further controls in the model were fathers' and mothers' age, education, birth country, and income quintiles; as well as the child's year of birth and continued childbearing. See Table 6.6 for an example of regression; all six regressions for the figure are available upon request

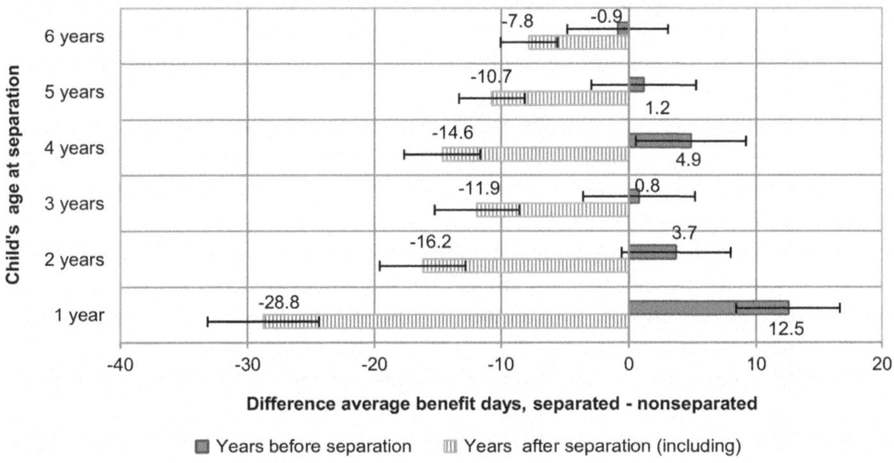

Fig. 6.6 Differences between separated and non-separated parents' benefit days before and after separation. Average number of days for the parents together
Note: Further controls in the model were fathers' and mothers' age, education, birth country, and income quintiles; as well as the child's year of birth and continued childbearing. See Table 6.6 for an example of regression; all six regressions for the figure are available upon request

was associated with having used fewer days after the separation. Thus, we can conclude that the major differences in parental leave use between the separated and the non-separated parents lie in the patterns of use after the separation.

Conclusion and Discussion

In this chapter, we investigated whether parents who separated used their parental leave differently than parents who remained together. The underlying question was whether parenting responsibilities were shared differently after a separation than they were when the parents were living together. This question is specific to the Swedish context in the beginning of the 2000s. Sweden is the ideal case for investigating this issue for a number of reasons. First, parental separation is common in Sweden, with up to 20% of all first-born children experiencing a parental separation during their preschool years. Second, as parental leave can be used during the whole preschool period, it is quite common for parents to have leave days they could share after a separation. In addition, parental leave is shared between the mother and the father in most cases, also in cases of separation. The leave is set up as an individual entitlement that is allocated to each parent, regardless of his/her living arrangements, but that can be transferred between parents. Thus, it is likely that a separation will change the conditions under which parents negotiate how the leave is shared. For an international audience, it is paramount to point out the uniqueness in Swedish family policy, which emphasises that parents have shared and gender-neutral responsibilities to their children, and which assumes parents to collaborate even after they have separated.

We had conflicting expectations about whether parental leave would turn out to be shared more or less equally after a separation, and about how many days would be used by the mother, the father, and in total. We might have expected that after a separation, the parents revert to traditional patterns of sharing, with the mother taking on the bulk of the childcare responsibilities, given that the children are still more likely live with the mother than the father, and maternal care is still characterised in many studies as forming the foundation of childrearing. However, it might also be the case that having to negotiate sharing leave renders the situation more gender-equal, as the father may be less keen to transfer his days to the mother, and more interested in using the days allocated to him. Any negotiations over leave days are likely to be framed by the economic pressures that many separated parents face, which can make it harder for them to use their leave benefits, and particularly the low flat rate days. When we considered parental leave use over the whole period that leave was available, we found that the separating mothers used about the same number of days as the non-separating mothers. However, we also found that the mothers who separated early used more days before the separation, and then fewer days after the separation than the cohabiting mothers. We believe that the more intensive use early on was related to the mothers' economic constraints. Moreover, if they were anticipating separating and were already starting to carry the costs of caring for their child on their own, the mothers would often not have had the option of being flexible and taking unpaid leave. The fathers who separated used fewer parental leave days than the fathers who did not separate. The fathers who separated were more likely to have used no days; and, if they used days, they often took a short leave only. However, most of the fathers who separated used some leave, and the probability of using a large number of days (more than 2 months) was as high for the fathers who separated as it was for the fathers who did not. Thus, we observed more variation in leave use among the separating fathers. We also observed that the differences in leave use were mainly related to lower use after a separation. In the analysis of the total leave used by the mother and the father, we found that taking a shorter leave was more common among the parents who separated. Our findings show that these parents together used fewer days after separating, but somewhat more days before separating. This pattern was linked to higher use by mothers before the separation. It is therefore possible that the mothers were taking more leave in anticipation of the coming separation.

As both the mothers and the fathers used fewer days after they separated, our most important conclusion is not about changes in gendered norms or in the strategies parents use to negotiate leave, but rather about the economic constraints that separated parents face. The separated parents did not use the leave to the same extent as the non-separated parents. Thus, it appears that parental leave is seen as less accessible by parents who separated early. In the end, it is the children of separated parents who are most affected by their parents taking shorter leave periods, as they have less access to their parents. This is an obvious policy concern that should be addressed. However, it should also be noted that both mothers and fathers use parental leave after a separation. In particular, our finding that fathers who separated took leave indicates that they continued to be engaged in childrearing after separating. In addition, we should emphasise that the data used in this study are for children born in the early 2000s, and that we would expect the patterns we observed to change over time. Moreover, we do not think that the patterns would be the same across different contexts, especially not in societies in which fathers' participation in childcare is not the norm. In terms of the state of gender-equal parenting after separation in Sweden, we leave it up to the reader to decide whether they consider the glass to be half-full or half-empty.

Appendix

Table 6.3 Multinomial regression result. Mothers' use of parental leave in categories (1) up to 240 days, (2) 241–325 days, (3) 326–335 days (Reference), (4) 335–420 days

	Parental leave days							
	0–240		241–325		326–335		336–420	
Age at sep								
Age 0	0.937		0.796		1	–	0.801	
Age 1	1.048		0.961		1	–	0.861	
Age 2	0.985		0.935		1	–	0.813	
Age 3	0.959		0.933		1	–	0.755	*
Age 4	1.104		1.015		1	–	0.934	
Age 5	0.972		0.931		1	–	0.724	**
No separation	Ref.		Ref.				Ref.	
Income quintile								
1	3.686	***	1.206	**	1	–	1.084	
2	1.376	***	0.937		1	–	0.879	*
3	Ref.		Ref.				Ref.	–
4	1.303	***	1.159	**	1	–	0.877	**
5	2.012	***	1.267	***	1	–	0.58	***
Education								
Basic	0.406	***	0.551	***	1		1.02	
Secondary	0.452	***	0.633	***	1		1.143	**
Tertiary≤2 years	0.84		0.808	**	1		0.928	
Tertiary>2 years	Ref.		Ref.				Ref.	
Migration background								
Foreign born	0.725	***	0.639	***	1		0.854	**
Swedish-born	Ref.		Ref.				Ref.	

Relative risk ratios. (see also Fig. 6.1)
Note: *** $p < 0.001$; ** $p < 0.01$; * $p < 0.05$

Table 6.4 Multinomial regression result. Fathers' use of parental leave in categories (1) up to 240 days, (2) 241–325 days, (3) 326–335 days (Reference), (4) 335–420 days

	Parental leave days							
	0–240		241–325		326–335		336–420	
Age at sep								
Age 0	3.004	***	1.66	***	1	–	0.992	
Age 1	2.628	***	1.655	***	1	–	0.93	
Age 2	2.219	***	1.588	***	1	–	0.944	
Age 3	1.94	***	1.394	***	1	–	1.028	
Age 4	1.711	***	1.44	***	1	–	0.854	*
Age 5	2.133	***	1.578	***	1	–	1.158	
No separation	Ref.		Ref.				Ref.	–
Income quintile								
1st quintile	2.876	***	1.012		1	–	0.56	***
2nd quintile	1.859	***	1.11		1	–	0.868	**
3rd quintile	Ref.		Ref.				Ref.	–
4th quintile	0.595	***	0.896	*	1	–	1.043	
5th quintile	1.555	***	1.115	*	1	–	0.913	*
Education								
Basic	1.356	**	0.929		1		0.376	***
Secondary	0.931		0.91	*	1		0.516	***
Tertiary≤2 years	1.110		1.009		1		0.706	***
Tertiary>2 years	Ref.		Ref.				Ref.	
Migration background								
Foreign born	0.756	***	1.191	**	1		2.264	***
Swedish-born	Ref.		Ref.				Ref.	

Relative risk ratios. (see also Fig. 6.2)
Note: *** $p < 0.001$; **$p < 0.01$; * $p < 0.05$

Table 6.5 Multinomial regression result. Total use of parental leave in categories (1) up to 389 days, (2) 390–419 days, (3) 420-479 days (Reference), (4) 480 and more days

	Parental leave days							
	0–389		390–419		420–479		480 and more	
Age at sep								
Age 0	1.898	***	1.456	***	1	–	0.813	
Age 1	1.919	***	1.475	***	1	–	0.767	*
Age 2	1.898	***	1.471	***	1	–	0.861	
Age 3	1.735	***	1.524	***	1	–	0.975	
Age 4	1.560	***	1.271	**	1	–	0.696	**
Age 5	1.707	***	1.254	**	1	–	0.783	*
No separation	Ref.		Ref.				Ref.	–
Income quintile mother								
1st quintile	1.695	***	1.164	***	1	–	1.722	***
2nd quintile	1.276	***	1.137	***	1	–	1.116	*
3rd quintile	Ref.		Ref.				Ref.	–
4th quintile	1.130	**	1.090	*	1	–	1.097	
5th quintile	1.806	***	1.420	***	1	–	1.034	
Income quintile father								
1st quintile	1.220	***	1.127	*	1	–	1.352	***
2nd quintile	1.194	***	1.151	**	1	–	1.180	*
3rd quintile	Ref.		Ref.				Ref.	–
4th quintile	0.858	***	0.910	*	1	–	1.105	
5th quintile	1.170	***	1.085	*	1	–	1.137	*
Education								
Both low	0,817	***	0,959		1		0,985	
Mother low, father high	0,904	*	0,928		1		1,1	
Mother high, father low	0,764	***	0,883	***	1		1023	
Both high	Ref.		Ref.				Ref.	
Migration background								
Foreign born	0,897	*	0,977		1		0,578	***
Swedish-born	Ref.		Ref.				Ref.	

Relative risk ratios. (see also Fig. 6.3)
Note: *** $p < 0.001$; **$p < 0.01$; * $p < 0.05$

Table 6.6 OLS-regression results for the fathers' benefit days before and after the child turned 1 year old

	Before $y_{i,<1}$		After $y_{i,\geq 1}$	
Separation				
Separation at child's age 1	0.1		−10.6	***
No separation				
Fathers' age	−0.3		−0.8	
<25 year	−0.1		0.3	
30–34 year	0.0		−1.0	

(continued)

Table 6.6 (continued)

	Before $y_{i,<1}$		After $y_{i,\geq 1}$	
Separation				
35–39 year	−1.0		−5.6	***
≥ 40 year	Ref.		Ref.	
Mothers age	2.5	***	−2.1	**
<25 year	−0.3		1.9	**
30–34 year	0.8		0.6	0,618
35–39 year	0.5		6.7	*
≥ 40 year	Ref.		Ref.	
Parents education				
Both parents ≥ post secondary	5.4	***	24.4	***
Mother ≥ post secondary. Father ≤secondary school.	3.3	***	11.4	***
Mother ≤secondary school. Father ≥ post secondary.	0.8		7.2	***
Both parents ≤ secondary school.(Ref)	Ref.		Ref.	
Migration background				
Parent(s) have foreign background	−7.8	***	−11.3	***
Both parents Swedish-born	Ref.		Ref.	
Income percentile father				
1st quintile	−10.3	***	−14.0	***
2nd quintile	−0.7		−4.9	***
3rd quintile	0.3		1.1	
4th quintile	−3.5	***	−7.6	***
5th quintile	Ref.		Ref.	
Income percentile mother				
1st quintile	17.6	***	7.1	***
2nd quintile	4.8	***	1.3	**
3rd quintile	0.0		6.8	***
4th quintile	2.3	***	16.5	***
5th quintile	Ref.		Ref.	
Cohort first child				
2002	0.1		−3.0	***
2003	Ref.		Ref.	
New child				
1st year	7.0	*	−16.5	**
2nd year	1.1	*	−4.4	***
3rd year	Ref.		Ref.	
4th year	0.3		0.5	
5th year	2.2	**	−0.1	
6th year	1.3		−2.0	
7th year	−0.4		−1.3	
8th year	1.2		4.0	
No new child within 8 years	3.6	***	−4.5	***

$y_{i,\geq 1}$: = benefit days before the child turns 1 year old and $y_{i,\geq 1}$= benefit days from when the child turns 1 year old up to the child's eighth birthday

Note: Only fathers who separated when the child was 1 year old and those who did not separate at all during the first 8 years of the child's life. *** $p < 0.001$; **$p < 0.01$; * $p < 0.05$

References

Becker, G. (1991). *A treatise of the family*. Cambridge: Harvard University Press.

Blum, S., Koslowski, A., Macht, A., & Moss, P. (2018). *14th international review of leave policies and research 2018*. International Network on Leave Policies & Research. https://www.leavenetwork.org. Accessed 15 June 2019.

Brines, J. (1994). Economic dependency, gender, and the division of labor at home. *American Journal of Sociology, 100*(3), 652–688. https://doi.org/10.1086/230577.

Duvander, A.-Z. (2014). How long should parental leave be? Attitudes to gender equality, family, and work as determinants of women's and men's parental leave in Sweden. *Journal of Family Issues, 35*(7), 909–926. https://doi.org/10.1177/0192513X14522242.

Duvander, A.-Z., & Johansson, M. (2012). What are the effects of reforms promoting fathers' parental leave use? *Journal of European Social Policy, 22*(3), 319–330. https://doi.org/10.1177/0958928712440201.

Duvander, A.-Z., & Johansson, M. (2014). Parental leave use for different fathers: A study of the impact of three Swedish parental leave reforms. In G. B. Eydal & T. Rostgaard (Eds.), *Fatherhood in the Nordic Welfare States: Comparing care policies and practice* (pp. 349–369). Bristol: Policy Press. https://doi.org/10.1332/policypress/9781447310471.001.0001.

Duvander, A-Z., & Viklund, I. 2020. How long is the parental leave and for whom? An analysis of methodological and policy dimensions of leave length and division in Sweden. *International Journal of Sociology and Social Policy,* https://doi.org/10.1108/IJSSP-06-2019-0108 Early cite.

Eriksson, H. (2014). Conceptualizing child care patterns in a dual-carer setting. *Stockholm Research Reports in Demography, 2014*(5).

Evertsson, M., & Duvander, A.-Z. (2010). Parental leave: Possibility or trap? Does family leave length effect Swedish women's labour market opportunities? *European Sociological Review, 27*(4), 435–450. https://doi.org/10.1093/esr/jcq018.

Fransson, E., Bergström, M., & Hjern, A. (2015). *Barn i växelvis boende – en forskningsöversikt*. Centre for Health and Equity Studies: Stockholm University.

Fransson, E., Låftman, S. B., Östberg, V., & Bergström, M. (2018). Wellbeing among children with single parents in Sweden: Focusing on shared residence. In R. Nieuwenhuis & L. Maldonado (Eds.), *The triple bind of single-parent families: Resources, employment, and policies to improve wellbeing* (pp. 145–168). Bristol: Policy Press. https://doi.org/10.2307/j.ctt2204rvq.13.

Government proposition. (1976). *Om ändring i föräldrabalken m.m. 1975/76: 170*. Regeringens proposition.

Government proposition. (1997). *Vårdnad boende umgänge 1997/98: 7*. Regeringens proposition.

Government proposition. (2015). *Ökad reglering av barns underhåll utanför underhållsstödet 2014/15: 145*. Regeringens proposition.

Hwang, P., & Lamb, M. (1997). Father involvement in Sweden: A longitudinal study of its stability and correlates. *International Journal of Behavioral Development, 21*(3), 621–632. https://doi.org/10.1080/016502597384811.

Lundberg, S., & Pollak, R. (1996). Bargaining and distribution in marriage. *Journal of Economic Perspectives, 10*(4), 139–158. https://doi.org/10.1257/jep.10.4.139.

Närvi, J. (2012). Negotiating care and career within institutional constraints – Work insecurity and gendered ideals of parenthood in Finland. *Community, Work & Family, 15*(4), 451–470. https://doi.org/10.1080/13668803.2012.724827.

National Social Insurance Board. (2003). *Time and money*. Social Insurance 2003. National Social Insurance Board.

Neilson, J. (2016). *Converging times: Parenthood, time allocation, and the gender division of labour in Sweden 1990–2010*. Lund: Printed in Sweden by Media-Tryck, Lund University.

Nitsche, N., & Grunow, D. (2018). Do economic resources play a role in bargaining childcare in couples? Parental investment in cases of matching and mismatching gender ideologies in Germany. *European Societies, 20*(5), 785–815. https://doi.org/10.1080/14616696.2018.1473626.

Rege, M., & Solli, I. (2013). The impact of paternity leave on fathers' future earnings. *Demography, 50*(6), 2255–2277. https://doi.org/10.1007/s13524-013-0233-1.

Sarkadi, A., Kristiansson, R., Oberklaid, F., & Bremberg, S. (2007). Fathers' involvement and children's development outcomes: A systematic review of longitudinal studies. *Acta Pediatrica, 97*(2), 153–158. https://doi.org/10.1111/j.1651-2227.2007.00572.x.

Statistics Sweden. (2013). Barn, Föräldrar och separation. Utvecklingen under 2000-talet. *Demografiska rapporter, 2013*, 1.

Statistics Sweden. (2014). Olika familjer lever på olika sätt: om barns boende och försörjning efter en separation. *Demografiska rapporter 2014,* 1.

Sundström, M., & Duvander, A.-Z. (2002). Gender division of childcare and the sharing of parental leave among new parents in Sweden. *European Sociological Research, 18*(4), 433–447. https://doi.org/10.1093/esr/18.4.433.

Swedish Social Insurance Inspectorate. (2017). Föräldrapenninguttag före och efter en separation. En analys av hur separerade föräldrar använde föräldrapenning i jämförelse med de som inte separerade. *Report 2017,* 11. Stockholm: Swedish Inspectorate of the Social Insurance.

Swedish Social Insurance Agency. (2013). Ojämställd arbetsbörda. Föräldraledighetens betydelse för fördelning av betalt och obetalt arbete. *Socialförsäkringsrapport 2013*, 9. Stockholm: Försäkringskassan.

Thomson, E., & Eriksson, H. (2013). Register-based estimates of parents' coresidence in Sweden, 1969–2007. *Demographic Research, 29*(42), 1153–1186. https://doi.org/10.4054/DemRes.2013.29.42.

Valarino, I., Duvander, A.-Z., Haas, L., & Neyer, G. (2018). Exploring leave policy preferences. A comparison of Austria, Sweden, Switzerland and the United States. *Social Politics: International Studies in Gender, State & Society, 25*(1), 118–147. https://doi.org/10.1093/sp/jxx020.

West, C., & Zimmerman, D. H. (1987). Doing gender. *Gender and Society, 1*(2), 125–151. https://doi.org/10.1177/0891243287001002002.

Chapter 7
Divorce, Emotions, and Legal Regulations: Shared Parenting in a Climate of Fear

Elena Moore

Introduction

Much of the research on divorce and personal relationships has overlooked the role of emotions. The limited research available on the emotional experience of divorce highlights the ways that divorcees are often denied the legitimacy and space to articulate feelings of loss, guilt, and anger, as parents are expected to focus on the best interests of the child (Sclater and Piper 1999; Sclater 1998). In essence, the law is based on the assumption that divorcing couples can side-line their emotions and behave "responsibly" and reasonably when negotiating their divorce. This chapter investigates the lived experience and social relational dimension of fear, as experienced by a sample of separated and divorced parents.

Empirical evidence indicates that the level of post-divorce parental involvement is far greater today than it was in previous decades. Most European countries have adopted a new approach to family law that focuses on both parents (EU Resolution 2079). But can two parents in a conflicted relationship share parenting? What does it take to succeed at shared parenting, and how should each parent involved in such an arrangement behave? Moreover, how do parents manage the transition to post-divorce family life when the legal certainties of rights and responsibilities do not address the uncertainties surrounding their emotional lives? This chapter unpacks how a sample of divorced mothers and fathers who engage in a joint parenting arrangement, but who have little communication with the other parent, experience and manage their feelings of fear. A special focus of this analysis is on the legal framework, and how it shapes shared parenting as well as the experience of fear. I

This chapter is based on published material in Moore (2017).

E. Moore (✉)
University of Cape Town, Cape Town, South Africa
e-mail: elena.moore@uct.ac.za

M. Kreyenfeld, H. Trappe (eds.), *Parental Life Courses after Separation and Divorce in Europe*, Life Course Research and Social Policies 12,
https://doi.org/10.1007/978-3-030-44575-1_7

argue that divorcees are subject to manifold life course uncertainties that generate fear and anxieties. The findings presented in the chapter show how a sample of divorced parents manage fear by turning to the courts to solidify their role in sustaining family life. The results also indicate that these parents tend to manage their fear by turning to other experts, such as child and family psychologists, who are expected to ascertain what is in the child's best interest. The findings further demonstrate that mothers' and fathers' experiences of fear are gendered, that fear directs change in post-separation practices of parenting.

The empirical data on which this chapter draws are from Ireland. I argue that the socio-culturally traditional and restrictive legal context of divorce in Ireland frames the level of commitment and emotion work that post-divorce family life requires of parents. While the idiosyncrasies of the Irish context are identified, my conclusions refer to more general ideas concerning emotion work and commitment that go beyond the specifics of the local context. Ireland was one of the last countries in Europe to legalise divorce. I have argued elsewhere (2017: 34) that the timing of divorce legislation in Ireland gave the legislature a unique opportunity to craft a restrictive form of divorce that upholds the sanctity of marriage, but that also addresses three major concerns raised in the international literature on divorce in the early 1990s: (1) the risk of poverty, (2) parental conflict and the impact on the child, and (3) the need to promote and encourage shared parenting and parent-child contact. In 1995, following a second referendum, Ireland opted to permit no fault-based divorce. Previously, divorce in Ireland had been tightly controlled, and the requirements for exiting a marriage were extremely restrictive (Moore 2017). The conditions or grounds for divorce under Section 5 of the Family Law (Divorce) Act 1996 were: (1) separation for four years; (2) no prospect of reconciliation; and (3) proper provision for the children and the other spouse. Moore (2016) argued that the longest periods of actual separation required for divorce are in Ireland, Malta, and Cyprus. Although mediation services have been provided by the state free of charge since 1986 (Conneely 2002: 1), the uptake of mediation among family law disputants remains low (McGowan 2018). The data on which this chapter is based reveal some of the practical effects this restrictive legislation has had on family relationships. However, in May 2019, another referendum was held on the question of whether the required waiting period should be reduced to two years. An overwhelming majority (82%) voted in favour of amending the law, and it may be hoped that the new legislation will greatly improve the lives of children and divorcees by reducing the trauma caused by protracted family law proceedings.

Theoretical Considerations: Joint Parenting and the Responsible Divorcee

Joint parenting is approached differently across countries. Some countries have adopted a case-by-case approach, and hear the views of the child in court proceedings before ordering a joint parenting arrangement. In other countries, shared parenting is the default arrangement. The two main focal points of the body of research on joint parenting are: (a) the recognition of a pro-contact culture, and (b) the quality of the relationship between the parents that is necessary to facilitate joint parenting. Scholars in the UK (Trinder et al. 2002), Australia (Rhoades 2007), and the US (Bauserman 2002) have shown that a pro-contact culture has been emerging in which children are given the right to contact with both parents. In the UK, the terms "custody" and "access" have been abolished, as they were linked to the idea of winning and losing children. According to Smart and Neale (1999: 38), the term "access" was seen as giving too much power to the parent with whom the child lived, while diminishing the role of the non-resident parent. It was hoped that awarding joint custody to both parents would encourage both the mother and the father to feel "concerned and responsible for" their children, and would help to reduce conflict. Sclater (2003) observed that lawmakers hoped that this approach would persuade fathers of the benefits of joint parenting, and encourage them to remain involved in the lives of their children after separation. Mahon and Moore (2011: 30) argued that the focus on both parents constituted a new approach to family law in most countries.

Having recognised the fragility of adult relationships in contemporary society, lawmakers shifted the focus of family law away from spouses and towards parents by affirming the paramount importance of the welfare principle in the Children's Act 1989 in the UK and the Guardianship of Infants Act (1964) in Ireland.[1] This principle states that in the event of a custody or access[2] dispute, the welfare of the child is paramount, and will form the basis of all decisions relating to his/her upbringing. The encouragement of parent-child contact post-divorce became a dominant issue in law and in policy in the UK and Ireland.

Written from the perspective of the child and not the adult, these laws state that is the right of each child "to know and be cared for by his or her parents" (UN Convention on the Rights of the Child, Article 7, paragraph 1) and to maintain a personal relationship and direct contact with both parents on a regular basis (UN Convention on the Rights of the Child, Article 9, paragraph 3).[3] Thus, the parental relationship with the child is clearly affirmed in policy and in law, even when the

[1] The Children Act 1997 section 9 introduced section 11A into the 1964 Act, which declares that a court in making an order under section 1 may, it if thinks appropriate, grant custody to the father and mother jointly.

[2] Whereas in the UK, the legislature (1989 Act) abolished the terms "custody" and "access" in favour of "residence and contact", these terms continued to be used in Ireland.

[3] The UN Convention on the Rights of the Child was ratified by Ireland in 1992.

relationship between the parents is legally terminated. As earlier studies on the impact of divorce on children found that the children of divorced parents are often exposed to parental conflict, and that contact with both parents is frequently disrupted, policy-makers became increasingly concerned with addressing these issues. The legal response was to support father-child contact, with courts in the UK and Ireland encouraging such contact (Smart et al. 2003; Mahon and Moore 2011).

Research on the quality of the parental relationship was also at the forefront of policy and the legal discourse on joint parenting. There appears to be general agreement in the literature that the relationship between the separated parents is a key determinant of whether joint parenting succeeds. Divorced parents frequently report having medium to high levels of conflict with each other, particularly with regard to contact issues (King and Head 1999). It has therefore been pointed out that parental relationship quality can seriously affect contact post-divorce (Braver and O'Connell 1998). Opponents of shared parenting argue that such an arrangement can disrupt the stability of a child's life, and can expose the child to ongoing parental conflict (Rhoades 2007). Although high levels of conflict are not always associated with low levels of contact (Wolchik et al. 1996), contact is generally found to be more likely if the relationship between the parents is positive (Bradshaw et al. 1999; Simpson et al. 1995; Smyth et al. 2001).

There are social and legal expectations that mothers and fathers will be responsible divorcees. For a mother, this means that she should encourage her child to have contact and a relationship with the father. Kaganas and Day Sclater (2004) observed that parents often have to position themselves within a range of competing legal, welfare, and human rights discourses; while coping with the personal pain that comes with the breakdown of a relationship. As the legal arena does not deal with the emotional side of divorce, parents are expected to behave as responsible divorcees; i.e., they are expected to behave as rational, altruistic actors, regardless of the emotion work required to manage multiple relationships. A decrease in hostility and the encouragement of joint parenting are crucial "building blocks" for creating an environment in which the welfare of the child is prioritised (Smart and Neale 1999). Joint custody and shared parenting is promoted because retaining contact with both parents protects the welfare of the child. Parents are expected to put aside their personal hostilities and continue communicating and cooperating as loving parents, and thus to manage the emotions involved in shared parenting. However, there is very little literature on how parents experience emotion work in relation to divorce, and specifically in relation to joint parenting. Collier and Sheldon (2008) pointed out that having an appreciation of the emotional context (of disputes) is critical to the development of effective interventions. Disputes over contact may be evidence of the inability of the parents to play the roles of rational, settlement-minded, and altruistic actors in the "new democratic family". Emotions cannot be ignored in the hopes that the parents will somehow become rational actors. Understanding the emotions divorcing parents experience, and recognising the emotion work required of the parents in a divorce, are crucial when seeking to resolve disputes and to provide support for divorcing parents.

Relative to this extensive literature on joint parenting and parental conflict, the body of literature on how parents manage this transition to becoming a responsible, post-divorce parent is much smaller. In contemporary society, "good mothering" is generally understood to be child-centred and-time intensive (Hays 1998). However, the model of good mothering in the context of divorce is less clear. Smart (1999) argued that good mothering is even more difficult to achieve in a divorced family than in a nuclear family, and that mothering or fathering in an "intact" family is poor preparation for parenting after a separation. For example, after a separation, the mother may be expected to trust the father to share in the care of their children, even though she remains ultimately responsible for a range of childcare tasks. A good divorced mother is also required to support the post-separated father in his attempt to carve a new dyadic relationship with his children. Thus, a divorced mother may have to "dislodge" herself from her core identity as the primary parent if there is a shared parenting arrangement. Within this context, the mother is made to believe that being a good divorced mother entails facilitating paternal involvement at all costs. Smart (1999) pointed out that after a separation, the previous primary caregiver is often still financially dependent on the other parent, but may derive fewer benefits from the workplace (including from social networks), and is usually compelled to seek part-time employment, often after a long absence from the workplace.

A father, on the other hand, may also have to work at post-divorce fathering in ways that force him to renew his relationship with the mother of his child, while simultaneously terminating his relationship with his ex-wife. As a father's relationship with his child is often centred around and negotiated by the mother, a poor mother-father relationship post separation will result in a poor father-child relationship. Mothering and fathering in a family – regardless of whether the family is "intact" or divorced – imposes a particular form of family life on men and women, whereby neither the mother nor the father can be considered an individual engaged in the self-interested pursuit of gain.

In this chapter, I examine the gendered experience of and the management of emotion in shared parenting arrangements. I have chosen to focus on the experience of fear for three reasons. First, there is little research on the emotional experience of divorce, and particularly on how it is shaped by the legal system. A second and related motivation is that there is a lack of knowledge about how fear is experienced and how it is gendered; i.e., whether men and women experience fear for different reasons. Third, I anticipate that these findings will be applicable across many jurisdictions, given the popularity of joint parenting principles and the existing evidence on the gendered experiences of caring for younger children. In particular, I focus on the following research questions: How do parents manage the transition to responsible divorced parenting? How do they manage their feelings when they are expected to focus on the best interests of the child?

Methods

The findings in this chapter are drawn from the author's book on divorce, families, and emotion work (Moore). The book is based on a longitudinal qualitative study of family practices post separation in Ireland. The main body of the research was based on qualitative interviews with a sample of 39 separated parents and ten family lawyers in 2008, and follow-up work with 19 parents in 2014. The sample of 39 separated and divorced parents, including 18 fathers and 21 mothers, were recruited through family law solicitors who work with private and legal aid clients. All of the parents in the sample were white, middle-class men and women with tertiary education. The only criteria for selection to participate in the main study was that the participant had to be a parent, and he or she had to have been separated for at least one year. The sample suffers from a number of limitations that readers should consider when interpreting the findings. Due to the highly selective social class and ethnic composition of the sample, I was unable to explore the relationship between social class, ethnicity, shared parenting, and emotional experience. Moreover, it may be assumed that compared to the median family income in Ireland, the participants in this sample had more joint and individual assets and higher total household income levels, and thus were better able to set up two households post separation.

A university ethics committee approved the study before interviewing commenced in 2008 and 2014. All participants consented to having the interviews recorded, and the duration of the interviews ranged from 90 to 120 min. The author adopted a largely open-ended, exploratory approach for large parts of the interviews. The aim was to cover aspects of the participant's marital relationship, divorce process, and financial and parenting arrangements post separation/divorce. The data were analysed using typologies that helped to describe and explain the different family practices that developed post separation. The parents were divided into four groups: egalitarians, dependents, deserted wives and excluded fathers, and conflicted couples. Several dimensions were used in the designation of categories, such as the ages of the children, the time since separation, the type of household income during the marriage, and the type of settlement reached (for more details, see Moore 2017: 8). This chapter is based on the experiences of the "dependents". It focuses on the findings of in-depth interviews with eleven parents about their experiences of judicial separation and divorce, and, in particular, about their experiences of being fearful of the consequences of their former spouse's actions. In each of these cases, the parents had a joint parenting arrangement that stipulated that their children were to stay overnight with both parents (at least one weekday overnight stay and one weekend overnight stay), but there was little direct communication between the divorced parents. The parents had to use solicitors/the courts to settle disputes and agree to a parenting arrangement. Table 7.1 describes the sample. In 2008, when the initial interviews were conducted, all of the parents were in their late thirties or early forties, and most had young children, including at least one child aged ten or younger. In the vast majority of cases, the father was the main breadwinner and the mother worked part-time while they were married (the household type of each

Table 7.1 Sample characteristics of dependents

Name	Age	Age of children	Length of marriage	Time Since separation	Household type	Settlement[b]
Josh	43	9, 5	11	5	One and a half	Solicitor
Cian[a]	42	15, 12, 6	10	6	One and a half	Solicitor
Rob	39	6	10	4	One and a half	Solicitor
Eoin	41	12, 8	12	5	One and a half	Solicitor
Ciaran[a]	37	7	6	6	Dual income	Solicitor
Larry[a]	45	20, 16	12	6	One and a half	Solicitor
Mike	45	17, 15, 12	12	8	One and a half	Court based
Peter[a]	52	20, 15	13	7	Dual income	Solicitor
Mairead	42	17, 15,12, 10	13	6	One and a half	Solicitor
Maria	39	14, 11	12	5	One and a half	Solicitor
Aine	52	18, 16, 10	18	12	One and a half	Court based

Notes:
[a]The following participants did not participate in the follow-up interviews in 2014
[b]The research differentiated three types of settlement reached: namely, (1) mediated, (2) solicitor-based (including "on the steps of the court"), and (3) court-based (adjudicated). Although additional applications were made by the participants (e.g., applications for discovery, relocation, interim maintenance, interim access) the settlement reached in this table refers to the separation or divorce settlement only

participant is shown in Table 7.1). Therefore, most of the mothers had been financially dependent on their former spouse while married, and continued to require financial assistance after the marriage ended. The parents had been separated approximately 4–12 years prior to the interviews.

Results

Post-separated Fathering, Mothering, and Fear

In the interviews, the dependents described their marital breakup as fraught with conflict from the beginning. In the following, I will concentrate on how the uncertainty surrounding housing, childcare, and financial arrangements generated fear during this extended period of uncertainty. The fathers reported being fearful of losing their father-child relationships and their place in the family. The mothers expressed fear about the anguish their children were experiencing, and about the financial costs of separation. Among the dependants, there were parents who remained (or attempted to remain) in the family home until a settlement had been reached, saying they were unwilling to move out for financial reasons and/or because they had been legally advised to remain in the family home. There were also mothers and fathers who did not remain in the family home following the decision to separate, as they had either been asked to leave the home by their former spouse or felt compelled to leave the home because of the misbehaviour of the other spouse. During this period of uncertainty, which lasted up to three or four years in most cases, financial and contact arrangements were not fixed.

The interim period was particularly complicated due to the multitude of changes that occurred in the spousal relationship. For couples who were unable to agree on interim parenting, financial, or housing arrangements, the period before such arrangements were formally regulated was characterised by uncertainty. The longer it took to formalise these arrangements, the longer the family members were held in a state of prolonged ambiguity. This uncertainty increased the level of emotional intensity that remained in the relationship with the former partner. The perception that these parents had of lacking control over their life, especially with regard to their parenting, was bound up with intimacy issues and power relations. Contact with their children during this period was unsatisfactory. For one of the fathers who continued to live with his child, the quality of the access was affected by the hostile environment in which it took place:

> But it was difficult as there were rows in front of Clara; well it became too much. I couldn't handle it. I couldn't take it. It wasn't good for anybody.

The parents who said they were asked to leave the family home or who felt compelled to leave the family home reported having restricted access to their children after moving out. This experience of having access restricted precipitated fears about losing contact with their children. None of the participants in this group had experienced the complete removal of access to their child, but many had lost some or a significant degree of access, and many more were haunted by the possibility of losing access in the future. None of the participants suffered from this fear more than a father in his thirties, whom I will call Rob. Rob told me that his ex-wife constantly threatened to remove his access to his children after he left the marital home:

> And you have to go and do it, and I left home, and that is when access to Mary stopped, you know. That was it, and that was part of my thinking, that if I walk out of here that I may not get to see Mary again.

Another father, Josh, described how threats and tensions played out in more subtle ways that stopped short of making him afraid, but still made it difficult for him to rely on and trust the co-parental relationship:

> Well, as I said, it got very serious, and my ex-wife threatened to take the kids away from me. But I just can't see her doing that; I know she couldn't do that. I think she just needed to let off.

One father explained how he was informed that his ex-wife was applying to relocate to another part of the country and to take the children with her. The courts are favourable to fathers, especially "in the circumstances where both parties are co-parenting and where the child is so happy and supported, the court would need serious proof that the welfare of the child would benefit from a move overseas", as one High Court Judge explained (Mahon and Moore 2011: 75). The father in this case, Cian, said that he couldn't believe that his ex-wife would be permitted to relocate, and sought immediate help from the courts. After a protracted battle, which took place before the couple were legally separated, the father won his case and the children and the former spouse did not relocate. Reflecting on this experience four years after the event, Cian said:

> My ex-wife's view of life was that I was taking her to court. How dare I take her to court? What had she done to deserve to be taken to court? 'You are taking my children away'. So, I said you know they are my children too.

The experiences reported by the participants highlight the lack of control fathers typically had over access to their children during this interim period. My interviews with solicitors also supported this finding. One solicitor explained how she managed this fear in her interactions with her male clients:

> Where they have this fear that they are going to lose their children, and when you explain to them, look, you will retain joint custody but being realistic, you're telling me that you work and travel abroad and you work till seven o'clock every day; I mean realistically can you pick up a five-year-old at seven o'clock and do you think it is wise that you take the child overnight during the week when they are at school and so on, and most of those parents come around very quickly. It sounds – I don't mean to use language that implies that I am persuading them – but it just kind of, when you shine that light on the situation for them, they then are more practical themselves, whereas they come in very worried and defensive, I suppose about themselves, like 'I am a good parent and I don't want to lose my children' but then you explain: 'Well this isn't a criticism of you and you are not losing joint custody but at a practical level, for your children and yourselves, it is impossible'. And I think they then see that very quickly and can live with that.

Some of the mothers in this group said they were afraid that access was detrimental during this period, as the young children in particular were upset about leaving their primary carer. One of the mothers explained her actions by saying that she was putting the safety and well-being of her child ahead of the needs of the father:

> I mean the little one was, my baby was three and my ex had worked away an awful lot – Monday, Friday, Wednesday, Saturday – so she had to be physically pulled out of my arms to hand to him. It was a fucking nightmare.

While the mothers said they were not against father-child contact, they indicated that they were unsure of how the younger children were managing the contact in the period immediately after the separation, especially if the children had never spent much time with their father. Maria talked at length about the emotional pain of witnessing her daughter's anguish when she spent nights with her father, which induced in Maria a sense of powerlessness over her mothering role:

> There was a period of about two to three years where I was, although I said okay in the beginning, and then I was constantly trying to pull back from that arrangement, but every time I said I would, he said he would go to court.

Maria undertook a considerable amount of emotion work in facilitating access even when she could see that her children were upset:

> They were upset and tired but there were lots of tears and hysterics, and I knew things weren't right because my daughter would often be upset with tummy aches in the mornings going to school; didn't want to go to school; didn't want to be separated from me.

The emphasis on constantly listening to and observing her children demonstrates Maria's approach to parenting, which is focused on working with her children in order to understand their feelings. Maria's "better judgement" was derogated, and her role as the primary parent was undermined. She had to manage her feelings and suppress her frustration with the father's insistence that it was not only in the children's best interests to spend nights with him, but that it was his right to see them; and with his threats of legal action. She felt compelled to facilitate her ex-husband's new involvement in parenting. Maria's need to manage the feelings that came up in her interactions with her ex-husband continued over a longer period of time. At the time of the second interview, which took place five years later, in 2014, Maria had just received a "nasty" email regarding the holiday arrangements. She reported feeling frustrated that her ex-husband was trying to control how she parented, and was preventing her from attending to the needs of the children:

> He was adamant that they would never be allowed near a therapist, I mean, even now, I would have had to go court to get them in to see a child psychologist, which is what I wanted to do. … [I was] so upset, and then it follows me around emotionally for days and I won't sleep for a few nights because I'm just so upset that somebody who would be co-parenting with me would not recognise that their child needs support.

For Maria, the question of why her ex-husband was not intuitive about the feelings of their children continued to frustrate her, especially given the time and energy she had devoted to developing maternal thought. According to Maria, her ex-husband lacked the awareness or the intellectual capacities that make up maternal thought. In her view, parenting involves not just having contact and caregiving, but monitoring the children's psychological needs and organising resources to meet those needs. Thus, Maria's notions about how the interests of her children would be best served clashed with those the children's father, and this conflict continued long after the separation. But Maria feared her ex-husband; he intimidated her because she felt threatened by an external authority (a court-appointed child psychologist) who could review the quality of her parenting, and who might undermine her maternal judgement and her entire identity as a competent mother.

Maria wanted her ex-husband to respect her caring work, and her opinion of what their children needed. She felt undermined and oppressed by his stance, and by the prospect that she could be held accountable by a court-appointed child psychologist. How did Maria resolve this problem? She said that she came to recognise the change in the fathering role her ex-husband took on following the separation, but added that she did not approve of the quality of his parenting.

> I mean in the sense, he is actually a much better father since we split up because he will always have a fear about losing the children if he messes up, or slips up, so he did almost always turn up to pick them up, you know, make arrangements. I think he is far more involved since the separation, that remained the case. … I mean I think…lots of people look at him and see a very devoted father. Lots of people who we know sort of…at an intermediate level rather than very close friends, they, they think he's just a great dad. Because he's really done stuff with his kids.

Maria acknowledged the work pressures and the responsibilities associated with providing for the family that her ex-husband faced, but said that this recognition and appreciation was destroyed when she found out that he was avoiding his financial responsibilities. Maria described how her ex-husband tried to control her and assert his authority over her by withholding child maintenance payments:

> Maintenance was always an issue. I think looking back at it now, it was his hold on the situation, and why he actually didn't want a legal agreement. He was constantly threatening to cut it (maintenance) off or cut it back and that was a common part of the arguments, so that was his way of keeping a hold on the situation…and he was the one with the money and power in that sense, and I think he used it.

In what I have called paternal banking (Moore 2012) practices, the father, as the primary breadwinner, often has the power over the family's financial resources, and can threaten to withhold support from the mother at any stage before the arrangements are formalised. A threat to cut off the mother's income is an indirect way of exercising control over her, especially if she is dependent on the father, and has little or no access to her own financial resources. Mairead talked about how her ex-husband paid the maintenance weekly as a means of exercising control over her role:

> I mean I never asked for maintenance for me, it was all just for the kids. He just kept paying that amount and he would pay weekly. He never paid it monthly because it's a control thing.

Disputes over child maintenance were often entangled with arguments about the father's commitment to his children. What the mothers in these cases were pointing to was that the father had little real commitment to his children, as he was not properly providing for them. Some viewed the father's care in terms of involvement and continued breadwinning, and thus saw child maintenance (alimony) as a currency representing commitment. In these cases, disputes over maintenance and costs continued to be an issue even twelve years after the separation. These parents had not learned to work together within their marriage, as they controlled separate spheres of marital and family life. Following their separation, the parents were expected to work together, albeit separately, to coordinate parenting across two households.

Legal Regulation as a Lifeline

In disputes over access to their children or maintenance, hope often arrived in the form of the legal system. Both the mothers and the fathers in this group reported clinging to the legal system almost like a lifeline, as they saw it as a means of asserting control over their role in the family. The parents in this group needed legal support to negotiate financial and parenting arrangements, and to avoid direct conflict with their former spouse. The majority of these parents did not end up in court. Instead, they agreed to a settlement either on the steps of the court, or through the help of solicitors. Most family law litigation ends in settlement (Coulter 2009). However, the settlement may not be achieved until late in the process; sometimes on the steps of the court and after a lengthy adversarial battle. One solicitor explained how s/he experiences and manages parents' expectations during the first encounter:

> It is the most difficult…the parents encounter when their relationship breaks down and it's the one where they really want the comfort at the beginning, you know, and does this get any better, and what is the norm and what should I agree, what's there? You will have people saying, what's normal? What would you say? Fathers will often say …for a father who isn't the primary carer to have, and I would say, well, there is not a norm; it's what is right for you and your family and what you can commit to, so why don't you tell me who can pick the kids up from school. If you are not able to do it, if you are abroad a lot, there is no point in saying that you are going to have them every weekend, you know.

In all cases in the sample, the father was eventually able to set up a second home. The men were generally able to obtain a mortgage based on their salary, and after having been awarded approximately 20–30% of the value of the marital home. Most of the fathers reported that were able to cut their ties to their former spouse by giving her the majority share in the house in lieu of providing spousal maintenance. In all of the cases, the fathers were paying child maintenance and covering their children's educational costs. The terms of some of these financial agreements created longer-lasting ties between the former spouses, as Cian described:

> Well the house is yours [wife] but if you ever sell it, you need my permission and I want 25 percent of the proceeds. So, the house is yours for the rest of your life as long as you want to live there but if you ever try and do anything funny, you're not going to walk away with all the embedded equity in the house.

In some cases, this kind of financial agreement allowed the father to reconcile the need to provide financially for the family and to ensure that the children's best interests were served by allowing them to remain in the family home, while also retaining his fair share of the matrimonial home. While this form of control was not exercised by all of the men in this group, it demonstrates that in some of the divorced couples, the parties remained financially connected after the end of the marriage. The participants reported other ways in which the father managed the financial arrangements so that he had more control over his children's lives. Rob said that he was satisfied with his financial settlement because it allowed him to control the educational expenses of his daughter:

> I look after her education, which I wanted to because, I just wanted to have control over her education; plus I pay ongoing maintenance.

Most of the fathers said they were more than willing to pay maintenance after an agreement was reached through the courts. However, many of the fathers reported that they faced difficulties in seeing their children regularly even after a separation agreement had been reached, as they perceived that their ex-wife continued to exert control by dictating when and how they could see their children. Although contact had been agreed between the parties, Rob explained that having flexible arrangements was unhelpful, as he and his ex-wife were unable to agree on the dates or times:

> It wasn't sufficient access, more correctly, it was down as 'every second weekend' and the phrase, you know 'in such way as the parties should agree between themselves' it will be 'shared' and in such way the parties agree themselves, the parties couldn't agree the day of Christmas, let alone share the child's time – so that was impossible, so the one thing that just needed to be tightened up…

One father, Ray, highlighted the problems with vague arrangements, such as an agreement that the father would have access from Friday to Sunday. He described the issues that had be clarified in making such arrangements:

> But no room for interpretation is the easiest thing up front…Friday to Monday, now what is Friday, is it 3 p.m.? I pick her up from school? Where do I pick her up? Is it regardless of sickness?

The fathers in this group reported facing ongoing challenges in maintaining access to their children. Ray, who described the emotion work involved in constantly negotiating arrangements, said he was trying to defend himself against the unspoken messages underlying these challenges, and the devaluation of his role as a father:

> I didn't know how to fight against that until it got to, and you are in a vulnerable situation until you get to a point where, well actually, if a child is sick you are more capable of looking after her so that is not a valid excuse.

Most of the fathers in this group said that their ex-wife continued to control when and how they saw their children. None of the mothers reported that they had been denied contact, but they all described experiencing ongoing difficulties with contact during this prolonged period. In most of these cases, the issues were settled, and the parents stuck to a fixed arrangement. These findings suggest that the system for ensuring steady contact is far more likely to fall short than the system for ensuring that maintenance is paid.

Concluding Discussion: Managing Fear and Joint Parenting

The parents whose experiences were described in this chapter were deeply fearful of losing their role in the family, and they were deeply insecure about the future of their personal relationships and financial well-being. They reported being unable to reach a parenting or a financial arrangement following the breakdown of their marriage, and relying on others to secure a satisfactory arrangement. The expectation that parents who are separating will be able to reach a satisfactory separation agreement that deals with all of the relevant legal, financial, and child-related matters lies at the heart of these experiences. When parents are unable to reach an agreement, they often report that they are feeling worried that their personal life is out of their hands, and that they are experiencing a great deal of fear.

The emotion of fear was expressed by all of the mothers and the fathers in this group, although the level of fear they said they experienced varied. When people are fearful, they are usually afraid of losing something they cherish because some other human or institution is blocking them from achieving their goals (Burkitt 2002). Contrary to previous reports that men are fleeing from commitment (Ehrenreich 1983), the fathers in this sample reported getting involved in caregiving in a context in which they were "outside", and trying to carve out a space for themselves in order to improve the quality of the father-child relationship. Scholars (Philip 2013; Simpson 1998) have argued that the fear of losing contact with a child often leads separated fathers to realise where their interests lie. As these fears reflect their vulnerability in the relationship, fathers frequently say that they are trying to change and to become more involved in parenting. It is for this reason that fear has special relevance when seeking to understand the changing practices of fathering.

The mothers in the sample reported that they continued to have the main responsibility for caregiving in a context in which their maternal judgement was being called into question both publicly and privately. Both the mothers and the fathers said they were afraid of losing their stronghold within the family. Resonating with existing research, some of the mothers said they felt "dislodged" (Smart 1999: 109): "when a father becomes more of a father, a mother becomes less of a mother". In light of these findings, it is important to ask why there appears to be a culture of fear following the breakdown of a marriage, and specifically among this group of parents for whom dependence is an issue. Both the mothers and the fathers in this group of parents expressed a firm commitment to parenting and to being involved with their children. Although the legal system has facilitated the involvement of the father as a provider, it cannot protect the quality of the father-child relationship, and it currently does not facilitate or protect the intimate ties between a father and his children. The legal system and the legal professionals within it add to this climate of fear by creating a mystique around the courts and uncertainty surrounding judgments and court processes. It is important to note that at the time the parents in this sample were separating and divorcing, there was a long-standing in camera rule that prohibited researcher access to family law courts. A reform of this law (Section 40 (3) of the Civil Liability and Courts Act 2004) has improved access for researchers, but the initial reports of what goes on in the courts did not start emerging until 2006.

Institutions such as the law and family therapy provide a framework of expectations of "futurity". When these institutions that govern relationships become unreliable or have a weaker hold over personal relationships, the emotions of the parents tend to guide their actions, and conflicts ensue. The dependents indicated that they enabled and constrained the actions and the movements of the other parent, but they also reported influencing the emotions experienced by the other parent. Burkitt (2002: 152) argued that emotions are an active response to a relational context. In this setting, the dependents' power rested in the threat of the withdrawal of financial support or of contact with the child. While all of the parents downplayed the power they had vis-à-vis their former spouse, they were often more powerful than their former spouse in conventional ways. By engaging in maternal gate-closing and paternal banking strategies, the dependents defined the parameters and the nature of their new relationship, and, in the process, the type of conduct they wanted to elicit from their former spouse. Ironically, the parents tried to manage their fears by turning to the courts to solidify their role in family life or to secure financial protection. They also attempted to quell their fears by turning to other experts, such as child and family psychologists, who were expected to ascertain what was in the child's best interests, and to support the co-parental relationship. Engagement with the legal system may have helped these parents offset the power relations that existed during the marriage, but they eventually came to realise that even the courts and the legal system could not ease their fears.

As Barbalet (2001: 160) has argued, a shift in power relations – for instance, when there is a relative decline in the power of the expert mother accompanied by a relative increase in the power of a newly involved actor, such as the court or a family therapist – is likely to lead the mother to fear that her position is in jeopardy, and may lead her to put in place new, constructive arrangements that were previously absent. In other words, a parent may be willing to compromise if s/he is faced with the fear of losing more than s/he is comfortable with losing. The fear that the mother experiences in this context leads to change. Not all experiences of fear lead to such changes, but this dynamic was observed among the sample of "dependent" parents discussed in this chapter.

These parents explained that in order to manage their own individual emotions of fear, they needed the support of others, such as lawyers, therapists, and family members. The sources of these fears lie in the structural inequalities of power that create vulnerabilities for both parents. My analysis has revealed that the structure of joint parenting laws and norms frame these emotions, and that parents engage in emotional power games as a way of protecting their sense of control during a period characterised by great uncertainty and potential loss. Although the social structure of the legal system can create feelings of security for parents, particularly for mothers seeking financial compensation, the uncertainty surrounding the legal system creates feelings of fear, which may push some fathers to accept the status quo, while encouraging others to fight against it. Mothers may also be fearful losing power if their actions are evaluated by outside legal or psychological "professionals", and these authorities enforce changes in their parenting. It appears that the parents profiled in this chapter managed their feelings of fear by developing new ways of parenting together with their ex-spouse. Thus, new parenting practices may reduce the threat posed by the other, and could shift power relations to remove the feelings of fear. This research on separated fathers' and mothers' responses to fear represents an important addition to sociological accounts of changes in family practices that have previously been overlooked. Further research in other contexts that have a longer history of divorce, and that are more ethnically diverse, could help to tease apart some of the idiosyncrasies of the Irish context.

Acknowledgments The research was funded by the DST-NRF Chair in Customary Law, Indigenous Values and Human Rights. The opinions, findings, and conclusions expressed in the chapter are those of the authors alone, and the NRF accepts no liability in this regard.

References

Barbalet, J. M. (2001). *Emotion, social theory, and social structure: A macrosociological approach*. Cambridge: Cambridge University Press.

Bauserman, R. (2002). Child adjustment in joint custody versus sole custody arrangements: A meta-analytic review. *Journal of Family Psychology, 16*(1), 91–102. https://doi.org/10.1037/0893-3200.16.1.91.

Bradshaw, J., Stimson, C., & Skinner, C. (1999). *Absent fathers?* London: Routledge.

Braver, S. L., & O'Connell, D. (1998). *Divorced dads: Shattering the myths*. New York: Putnam.

Burkitt, I. (2002). Complex emotions: Relations, feelings, and images in emotional experience. *The Sociological Review, 50*(S2), 151–167. https://doi.org/10.1111/j.1467-954X.2002.tb03596.x.

Collier, R., & Sheldon, S. (2008). *Fragmenting fatherhood*. Oxford: Hart Publishing.

Conneely, S. (2002). Research the Irish family mediation service: Women in mediation. *Irish Journal of Family Law, 2*(1), 1–9.

Coulter, C. (2009). *Family law in practice: A study of cases in the circuit court*. Dublin: Clarus Press Ltd.

Ehrenreich, B. (1983). *The hearts of men: American dreams and the flight from commitment*. New York: Anchor Books.

European Resolution. (2015). *Equality and shared responsibility: The role of fathers*. http://assembly.coe.int/nw/xml/XRef/Xref-XML2HTML-EN.asp?fileid=22220. Accessed 9 July 2019.

Hays, S. (1998). *The cultural contradictions of motherhood*. New Haven: Yale University Press.

Kaganas, F., & Day Sclater, S. (2004). Contact disputes: Narrative constructions of 'good' parents. *Feminist Legal Studies, 12*(1), 1–27. https://doi.org/10.1023/B:FEST.0000026077.03989.70.

King, V., & Head, H. (1999). Nonresident father visitation, parental conflict, and mother's satisfaction: What's best for child well-being? *Journal of Marriage and Family, 61*(2), 385–396. https://doi.org/10.2307/353756.

Mahon, E., & Moore, E. (2011). *Post separation parenting: A study of separation and divorce agreements made in the Family Law Circuit Courts of Ireland and their implications for parent child contact and family lives*. Dublin: Government Publications.

McGowan, D. (2018). Reframing the mediation debate in Irish all-issues divorce disputes: From mediation vs. litigation to mediation and litigation. *Journal of Social Welfare and Family Law, 40*(2), 181–194. https://doi.org/10.1080/09649069.2018.1444445.

Moore, E. (2012). Paternal banking and maternal gatekeeping: Gendered practices in postdivorce families. *Journal of Family Issues, 33*(6), 745–772. https://doi.org/10.1177/0192513X11428444.

Moore, E. (2016). Delaying divorce: Pitfalls of restrictive divorce requirements. *Journal of Family Issues, 37*(16), 2265–2293. https://doi.org/10.1177/0192513X14566620.

Moore, E. (2017). *Divorce, families, and emotion work: Only death will make us part*. Basingstoke: Palgrave Macmillan. http://www.palgrave.com/de/book/9781137438218.

Philip, G. (2013). Relationality and moral reasoning in accounts of fathering after separation or divorce: Care, gender, and working at 'fairness'. *Families, Relationships and Societies, 2*(3), 409–424. https://doi.org/10.1332/204674313X667407.

Rhoades, H. (2007). The changing face of contact in Australia. In M. Maclean (Ed.), *Parenting after partnering* (pp. 129–146). Oxford: Hart Publications.

Sclater, S. (1998). Divorce-Coping strategies, conflict and dispute resolution. *Family Law, 28*, 150–152.

Sclater, S. (2003). Families reunited. *FQ Magazine* (Issue 3, Winter).

Sclater, S., & Piper, S. (1999). *Undercurrents of divorce*. Aldershot: Ashgate.

Simpson, B. (1998). *Changing families: An ethnographic approach to divorce and separation*. Oxford: Berg.

Simpson, B., McCarthy, P., & Walker, J. (1995). *Being there: Fathers after divorce: An exploration of post-divorce fathering*. Newcastle: Relate Centre for Family Studies.

Smart, C. (1999). The new parenthood: Fathers and mothers after divorce. In E. B. Silva & C. Smart (Eds.), *The new family?* (pp. 102–114). London: Sage.

Smart, C., & Neale, B. (1999). *Family fragments?* Cambridge: Polity Press.

Smart, C., May, V., Wade, A., & Furniss, C. (2003). *Residence and contact disputes in court* (Vol. 1). London: Department for Constitutional Affairs.

Smyth, B., Sheehan, G., & Fehlberg, B. (2001). Patterns of parenting after divorce: A pre-reform act benchmark study. *Australian Journal of Family Law, 15*(2), 114–128.

Trinder, L., Beek, M., & Connolly, J. (2002). *Making contact: How parents and children negotiate and experience contact after divorce*. York: Joseph Rowntree Foundation.

Wolchik, S. A., Fenaughty, A. M., & Braver, S. L. (1996). Residential and nonresidential parents' perspectives on visitation problems. *Family Relations, 45*(2), 230–237. https://doi.org/10.2307/585295.

Chapter 8
The Consequences of Separation for Mothers' Perception of Their Parenting Capacity

Tina Haux and Lucinda Platt

Introduction

Separation and divorce have become a feature of many adult biographies in the western world. In England and Wales, 10.8 people per thousand of the married population divorced in 2012 (ONS 2014); and just under a third of all UK families with dependent children (32 percent) are post-separation families, with lone parent families making up 25 percent and stepfamilies accounting for seven percent of these families (ONS 2015). In the context of increasing normnalisation of parental separation and blended families, how do mothers evaluate themselves as parents following a separation? Does separation knock their confidence as parents? And, if so, does this confidence recover as mothers adjust to their new circumstances? Given that separated parents are being encouraged to, and increasingly express an interest in, entering into shared care arrangements, does it help the mother if the father stays involved? These are the questions that drive this chapter.

There is a substantial body of literature on the impact of separation on children. There is also a smaller body of work on the financial and mental health effects of separation on parents, including the extent to which poor maternal mental health affects parent-child relationships, and, in turn, the outcomes of children. We argue that the topic of perceived parenting competence has been neglected in this literature, despite being worthy of attention in its own right. Whether single mothers perceive themselves as good parents is indicative not only of their parenting capacity, but of the degree to which sole parenthood is endorsed or devalued in society. Since the vast majority of parents with primary custody of their children following

T. Haux (✉)
University of Kent, Kent, UK
e-mail: t.haux@kent.ac.uk

L. Platt
London School of Economics and Political Science, London, UK

M. Kreyenfeld, H. Trappe (eds.), *Parental Life Courses after Separation and Divorce in Europe*, Life Course Research and Social Policies 12,
https://doi.org/10.1007/978-3-030-44575-1_8

a separation are mothers, the context in which parents evaluate their parenting remains tied to gendered societal norms of the role of mothers, the problematisation of the absence of fathers, and the emphasis placed on the importance of male role models for children's development. Understanding how far mothers' evaluation of their competence as parents is impacted by separation can provide us with information about the wider context in which families are raising children, and about the ways in which persistent social norms are or are not internalised by parents. We use the terms "perceived parenting competence" and "parenting confidence" interchangeably throughout this chapter, as they reflect the fact that we are studying mothers' self-evaluation rather than their specific parenting practices.

We explore the relationship between separation and perceived parenting competence among a nationally representative UK longitudinal sample of families with children, some of whom are observed to experience parental separation. We focus on parents of young children, since that is the age when children are more likely to be considered the sole responsibility of their parents, and thus parenting confidence may be most susceptible to shocks, such as those associated with the breakdown in a relationship. We argue that mothers may draw on the unremarkable nature of parental separation to maintain confidence in their parenting, with no observed consequences. Alternatively, they may experience the fact of separation as an indictment of their competence, and lose confidence accordingly. Which of these outcomes is the case is an empirical question to which we currently do not know the answer.

The current evidence on the effects of separation on the mental health and life satisfaction of former partners indicates an initial shock, followed by a relatively rapid recovery. Thus, we also investigate whether any initial reduction in perceived parenting competence persists over time. On the one hand, parenting confidence might be expected to track mental health, with an initial drop followed by adaptation to pre-separation levels. On the other hand, to the extent that any loss of parenting confidence reflects the internalisation of societal judgements of sole parenthood, rather than the psychological impacts of relationship breakdown, it is possible that no such process of recovery occurs. Again, this is a question that is open to direct investigation.

The development of "new fathering" (Dermott 2014), and the increasing emphasis internationally on shared care arrangements and the involvement of fathers in their children's lives post-separation (Kitterød and Wiik 2017; Meyer et al. 2017; Nielsen 2018; Smyth 2017), might lead us to expect that where fathers remain involved and children therefore continue to experience parenting by both parents, mothers may evaluate their parenting more positively. We therefore explore the extent to which post-separation paternal involvement is associated with higher perceived parenting competence among separated mothers.

It is also important to consider the question of whether any observed impact on parenting confidence might be driven by selection. The literature on maternal mental health has indicated that those mothers who separate are more likely to be already suffering from mental distress, even if they experience further deteriorations following divorce (Wade and Pevalin 2004). Among mothers who separated, Tavares and

Aassve (2013) found post-separation mental distress to be negatively associated with pre-separation mental distress; that is, the impact of separation was less for already more distressed mothers. If parenting confidence differs between mothers who do and do not separate, this could potentially bias our results, even after controlling for prior perceived competence, given potential ceiling and floor effects. In addition, if parenting confidence is associated with other unmeasured characteristics of individuals who separate rather than the fact of separation, it would tell us less about the impact of internalised social norms relating to lone parenthood. It is therefore important to establish whether or not mothers who go on to separate already differ in their perceived competence from other mothers.

We address these questions using the Millennium Cohort Study, a nationally representative UK cohort study of around 19,000 children born at the beginning of the current millennium. We analyse a sample of nearly 12,000 mothers who were living in an intact family when their child was nine months old, of whom around 2000 had separated by the time their child was around seven years old. We first show that the perceived parenting competence of the mothers who subsequently separated did not differ from that of the mothers who remained in intact relationships. This finding suggests that separated mothers do not inherently struggle more than partnered mothers with their childrearing, or with how they feel their childrearing is perceived.

Estimating growth curve models, we then investigate whether those mothers who had separated by the time their child reached age seven experienced a reduction in parenting confidence after separating relative to the mothers who remained partnered. After re-estimating the growth curve models only for those mothers who experienced a separation, we then look at whether loss of confidence persisted or diminished with time since the separation, and whether it was reduced in cases in which the father remained more involved with his non-resident child. We frame our results in relation to theories regarding the stigmatisation of lone parents, personal efficacy, and the challenges a mother faces in maintaining post-separation contact with her child's father.

Background and Research Questions

Academics and policy-makers have long been interested in understanding whether – and, if so, to what extent and why – the children of separated parents have worse outcomes in adulthood than children who grow up in intact families (see among others Amato 2000, 2010; Mooney et al. 2009). Although the evidence that paternal involvement has positive consequences for children in post-separation families is somewhat equivocal (Amato 2010; Bernardi et al. 2013), the perception remains that growing up in an intact, couple parent family is the best situation for children. A smaller number of studies have examined the effects of separation on parents. Several studies have, for example, investigated the effects of separation on the mental health and well-being of mothers in the UK (see also Maslauskaite and Steinbach as well as Köppen, Kreyenfeld, and Trappe in this volume). This research has examined the impact of separation and divorce, the duration of this impact, and the speed at which the partners recover. Overall, the findings of these studies suggest that separation has a negative effect on former partners' mental health and life satisfaction, but that the separated partners tend to recover relatively swiftly; i.e. by the following year or so (Blekesaune 2008; Brewer and Nandi 2014; Gardner and Oswald 2006; Pevalin and Ermisch 2004; Tavares and Aassve 2013; Wade and Pevalin 2004). The theme of recovery is also evident in the literature for the US. Hetherington (2003) has argued that divorce affects the "psychological, social and physical well-being of adults" for a short period of time after the divorce. Most adults then adapt to their new life after separation, and only a minority experience long-term negative effects (ibid., p. 659, see also Amato 2010; Kalmijn and Monden 2006). Research on the impact of separation on the financial situation of the separated partners has suggested that the family incomes of women and of mothers in particular often decline immediately after a separation, but then later recover (Brewer and Nandi 2014; Jenkins 2009, 2011; but see also Harkness and Skipp 2013).

The question of what impact separation or divorce has on parenting is less well researched, particularly outside the US. The concept of "diminished capacity to parent" (see Wallerstein and Kelly 1980) refers to mothers being less able and less likely to engage with their children or to display positive parenting behaviour in the early stages of separation and divorce (Lovejoy et al. 2000). However, as in the case of mental health, it has been shown that parenting capacity tends to recover relatively soon after the transition (Hetherington 2003 in Amato 2010); although it can remain reduced in a minority of cases it can last for ten years and more (Strohschein 2007). The impact of separation on parenting capacity is likely to be attributable to the psychological effects of separation, which limit a mother's engagement in positive parenting (Kiernan and Huerta 2008; Lovejoy et al. 2000; Smith 2004).

While the relationship between parenting confidence, mental well-being, and parenting practices is clearly complex, we are concerned in this chapter specifically with the former issue, which has not been well researched. That is, we do not yet know whether the experience of separation and having sole responsibility for children affects the confidence of separated parents in their ability to parent; nor whether, if this is indeed the case, there is a subsequent reversion to earlier levels of perceived confidence or self-evaluated confidence over time. This gap in our knowledge is surprising given the prominence of the long-established, negative discourses around lone parent families (Klett-Davies 2016; Silva 1996) and the more recent focus on "good" parenting before and after separation (Fabricius et al. 2010; Fehlberg et al. 2011; Lamb 2012; Mahrer et al. 2016; Steinbach 2019). We argue that societal norms and discourses, and the specific stigmatisation (Link and Phelan 2001) of lone parenthood (Salter 2018), are likely to influence parents' self-conceptions or expressed confidence in their parenting. We cannot therefore assume that separated mothers' confidence tracks the patterns of impact and recovery found for psychological or behavioural consequences of separation. We draw on Rogers' (1959) definition of self-concept; i.e., the perception an individual has of him/herself, and of how others perceive him/her. An important contribution to our understanding of self-concept was made by Bandura (2006: 165), who, in his social cognition theory argued that self-concept is based on the "reciprocal interplay of intrapersonal, behavioural and environmental determinants"; i.e., that it is learned, organised, and dynamic. We apply this understanding of self-concept to account for how mothers respond to the circumstances that surround separation at the personal and the social level, and how that feeds into their own understanding of their status and their parenting.

Despite the striking rise in divorce and separation among families with children in the UK and internationally (Bernardi and Mortelmans 2018), sole parent and separated families continue to be frequently stigmatised as incomplete and less desirable family forms compared to married and cohabiting couples with children. Public opinion still endorses couple parent families as the optimum context for raising children (Park and Rhead 2013), Meanwhile, negative perceptions of lone parents remain common, with these parents often being accused of engaging in irresponsible behaviour, having poor parenting skills, or transmitting intergenerational patterns of "deviant" family forms (Klett-Davies 2016; Silva 1996). For example, a previous Secretary of State for Work and Pensions described lone parent families as "broken families" who are responsible for a "broken" society (CSJ 2006). More generally, the strong association between sole parenting and economic insecurity reinforces doubts about their efficacy as parents, given the assumed link between poor parents and "poor" parenting (Cooper 2017; McLanahan 2004; McLanahan and Jacobsen 2015; Stewart 2016). Many mothers find that their income drops and their risk of poverty increases following a separation, even if they had been comfortable before the breakup (Brewer and Nandi 2014; Jenkins 2009, 2011). Even if their income recovers subsequently, they may find themselves at least for a period in need of state support and directly encountering negative responses to their newfound status, real or perceived, as a result of their own internalisation of the dominant discourse.

The effect of such negative attitudes on lone parents' confidence is likely to be exacerbated by the current increased focus on parenting more generally. Parents' involvement, particularly in the early years of a child's life, is seen as increasingly instrumental in the social and cognitive outcomes of children (Lausten et al. 2013). Parenting "confidence" has emerged as a prominent concept, which can be defined as a set of skills and beliefs that parents do not necessarily have naturally, but need to acquire with the help of parenting experts (Daly 2015; Gauthier 2015). This may lead to anxiety as to how well mothers are performing as parents (Wall 2010). The combination of these social environmental influences may negatively affect a mother's confidence in her own parenting skills, especially after a separation. Given that separation will shift mothers from the validated couple category to the critiqued lone parent category, it is not clear that we would expect the impact of separation to lessen over time. Perceived self-competence therefore may act as a marker of the extent to which the home environment is more challenging all round, and can also be revealing about those factors that may ease (or perpetuate) such challenges over time.

Specifically, where fathers remain actively involved, mothers' parenting may be boosted both by the ongoing reinforcement they receive through co-parenting, through any financial support that may tend to accompany it (Ermisch and Pronzato 2008), and through retaining some element of their position as couple rather than sole parents. The contribution of fathers may therefore be highly relevant for how confidence is experienced after a split. Fathers today often aspire to spend more time and to be more involved with their children than fathers of previous generations (e.g., Bianchi et al. 2006; Brandth and Kvande 2018; Gauthier et al. 2004; Lamb 2010; Marsiglio et al. 2000). A number of qualitative studies (Lacroix 2006; Philip 2013, 2014) have compared fathers' experiences of parenting post-separation and parenting within a couple. These findings suggest that fathers felt more confident and took a more pro-active role in the parenting of their children and found the experience emotionally rewarding. Yet, despite the endorsement through policy emphasis on shared parenting, these fathers are likely to be highly selected, given the stubbornly high rates of contact breakdown in the UK (Lader 2008; Poole et al. 2016). Nevertheless, with current emphasis on "new fathering" (Dermott 2003, 2014; Ives 2015), and particularly on the positive consequences of fathering (Brandth and Kvande 2018; Craig 2006; Craig et al. 2014; Kalmijn 2015, 2016; Solomon 2014; Wilson and Prior 2010), where fathers have higher levels of contact, we might expect such involved fathers to improve mothers' confidence in their sole parenting.

At the same time, shared care arrangements are becoming increasingly common among both the most co-operative and the most conflicted couples (Smyth 2017). This could mean that any improvements in self-concept that arise from greater paternal involvement are undermined. On balance, we would expect to observe that greater paternal involvement has positive knock-on effects on the parenting confidence of separated mothers. However, this positive association cannot be assumed.

In sum, this chapter, which represents the first large-scale study of parenting confidence in the UK, addresses the following questions: Does parental separation in the early years of a child's life negatively affect the mother's perceived parenting competence? If so, does their parenting confidence recover over time? And, does the greater involvement of the father in the child's life increase the parenting confidence of separated mothers?

Data and Analytical Approach

Data and Analytical Sample

The data for this analysis come from the Millennium Cohort Study (MCS). The MCS is a UK-wide representative cohort study of around 19,000 children born to families resident in the UK between September 2000 and January 2002. The MCS employed a stratified clustered sampling design to ensure an adequate representation of all four UK countries, disadvantaged areas, and ethnic minority groups (Plewis 2007). The original cohort (MCS1) comprised 18,818 children whose parents were first interviewed at home when their child was around nine months old. Further surveys were completed when the cohort children were around three, five, seven, 11, and 14 years old. In this chapter, we draw on information from the first four surveys (University of London. Institute of Education. Centre for Longitudinal Studies 2012a, b, c, d), and on information provided in the interview and the self-completion questionnaire that was carried out with the main carer at each sweep.

Since we are interested in investigating the effects of separation on mothers, as these constitute the vast majority of parents with care (PWC) following a separation involving (young) children, we restrict our sample to those mothers who were both living with their child's father when the child was an infant (around nine months old) and who were the main respondent at the first and subsequent surveys (14,600 mothers). This approach ensures continuity in the information provided. The MCS includes a small number of twins and triplets whom we exclude from the analysis, as the factors linked to parenting and partnership dissolution are likely to differ for these cases (217 cases). We also exclude the small number of cases in which the father was known to have subsequently died (a further 91 cases). We use information on the remaining mothers collected up to the fourth survey when the child was aged around seven years old, as this enables us to capture the critical early years of parenting.[1] We restrict our sample to those respondents who completed the self-completion questionnaire (which contains the questions on parenting confidence) for at least one survey subsequent to the first survey (when the child was aged around three, five, or seven), and for whom we have non-missing information on the perceived parenting measure and all covariates employed in our analysis. For the perceived parenting measure, we treated as missing the small number of respondents who indicated that they could not evaluate their parenting (responding "can't say"). This results in a sample of 11,764 mothers nested in 29,646 person waves, of whom 2005 (3498 person waves) reported experiencing a separation by the time their child reached age seven. A comparison of key wave one characteristics of the full sample of 14,329 mothers and the 11,764 cases retained in our analytical sample did not suggest any systematic bias arising from our sample selection.

Variables

Our key dependent variable is the measurement of parental perceived self-confidence collected in the surveys conducted when the child was age three, age five, and age seven. The question wording is as follows: *"The next question is about how you feel*

[1] Note also that the question on perceived parenting competence was not asked after the child reached age seven.

about being a parent. For the next statement, choose your response from the choice 1 to 5: I feel that I am: 1 Not very good at being a parent; 2 A person who has some trouble being a parent; 3 An average parent; 4 A better than average parent; 5 A very good parent; 6 Can't say". We treat this as a continuous measure, excluding the final category ("can't say"), as noted above.

Our key independent variable is whether or not the mother has separated at the time that parenting confidence is measured. For separated mothers, we also include the time since separation in months, which was constructed using the retrospective information on partnership history collected at each survey. Furthermore, we included a measure of the frequency with which the child has contact with the non-resident parent (father) on a scale ranging from one (never) to seven (every day).

To capture other factors that might be correlated with both separation and parenting confidence, and which preceded the separation (see the discussion in Brewer and Nandi 2014), we include controls for mother's age at the birth of the child, her ethnic group (in six categories), her educational level (grouped into tertiary, higher secondary (advanced level exams taken at age 18), good lower secondary (end of compulsory schooling exams taken at age 16), lower or other qualifications, and no qualifications), housing tenure, and employment status at the time of the first (age nine months) survey. We include mothers who were both married and cohabiting at the first wave, since we have no reason to anticipate that their parenting confidence will be impacted differently by former marital status. Nevertheless, given the ongoing discussion in the literature (see e.g. Tavares and Aassve 2013), we include a dummy for married versus cohabiting. We additionally control for the sex of the child.

We also control for initial parenting confidence. At nine months, this was measured using a slightly different question, namely, '*When I am caring for [child], I feel…1 …very incompetent and lacking in confidence; 2 fairly incompetent and lacking in confidence; 3 fairly competent and confident; 4 very competent and confident; 5 Can't say*'. Again, we treat the measure as a continuous variable, omitting the small numbers who selected "can't say".

Analytical Approach

We first address the question of whether the mothers who separated are a select group. To do so, we examine whether mothers who did or did not separate before the child reached age seven differed in terms of their parenting competence in wave one (when the child was nine months old). We analyse the raw means, but also adjust for relevant covariates. We then estimate linear growth mixed models of maternal parenting confidence (Rabe-Hesketh and Skrondal 2012; Singer and Willett 2003). These models take advantage of the repeated measures of the mothers' confidence at three points in time, when their children were approximately three, five and seven years old. As noted above, we control for parenting confidence when the child was nine months old, as well as other potentially confounding characteristics. We estimate the effect of maternal separation as a time-varying covariate on mothers' confidence, and its development.

Level 1 represents the within-mother change in confidence from the child's third to seventh year of life. Level 2 represents the between-mother variation in confidence when the child was three years old (random intercept), and the linear change from the child's third to seventh year of life (random slope). We included a fixed quadratic on age to account for the curved shape of average parenting confidence trajectories. The composite model can be written as follows:

$$\text{Confidence}_{ij} = (\beta_{00} + \beta_{10}\text{AGE}_{ij} + \beta_{20}\text{AGE}_{ij}^{2} + \beta_{30}\text{time varying intact / separation status}_{ij} + \beta_{40-x}\text{time invariant controls}) + (u_{0i} + u_{1i}\text{AGE}_{ij} + e_{ij})$$

The components in the first set of parentheses represent the fixed effects, and the components in the second set represent the random intercept and slope for each mother, and thus reflect the between-mother variation in confidence, and its development over time. The coefficient that is of particular interest for our analysis is β_3.

We also estimate models only for the mothers who experienced separation. First, to determine whether there was evidence of recovery, we examine the impact of the time since separation on the mother's parenting confidence. Second, we look at the extent to which the child's contact with the non-resident parent affected the mother's parenting confidence, given our hypothesised expectation that the mother's confidence would be higher if the child had closer contact with the other parent; i.e., if the socially endorsed two-parent family structure was being partially maintained. Both of these measures are evaluated for the point in time at which the parenting confidence measure was assessed. These models again include a random intercept and a random slope for time since separation. Given the collinearity between the child's age and the time since separation, we centred the child's age and included it and its square as controls.

The models are estimated using the mixed procedure in Stata 13.1 (Rabe-Hesketh and Skrondal 2012). To adjust for the complex survey design of the MCS, we cluster the standard errors on the sample cluster variable, and include the strata variables as additional control variables. Table 8.1 shows the descriptive of all of the variables used in our pooled (person-wave) analytic sample by separation status.

Results

The means for parenting confidence (measured in wave 1) are found to be 3.68 (CI: 3.66–3.69) for the mothers who did not separate and 3.70 (CI: 3.67–3.73) for the mothers who subsequently separated. The distribution of responses is also very similar. After controlling for a full suite of relevant characteristics, we still observe

Table 8.1 Sample descriptive statistics, pooled sample, by separation status, means (standard error), and column percent

	Not separated	Ever Separated
Parenting competence	3.93 (0.01)	3.84 (0.02)
Child's age	5.09 (0.01)	5.73 (0.83)
Perceived competence when child was nine months old	3.67 (0.003)	3.70 (0.01)
Mother's age at birth (centred)	0.86 (0.03)	−2.51 (0.10)
Education		
Degree or above	0.23	0.09
A levels/diploma	0.23	0.17
O levels/GCSE	0.34	0.43
Less/other	0.11	0.14
None	0.09	0.17
Marital status		
Married	0.75	0.45
Cohabiting	0.25	0.55
Sex of child		
Boy	0.51	0.52
Girl	0.49	0.48
Older siblings	0.09 (0.01)	0.90 (0.02)
Mother has long-term limiting illness	0.21	0.25
Mother was in work and on leave when child was nine months old	0.59	0.46
Mother was not in work when child was nine months old	0.41	0.54
Housing tenure		
Owned/buying	0.77	0.49
Social rented	0.14	0.36
Private rented	0.06	0.11
Other	0.03	0.04
Time since separation (years)	–	2.72 (1.69)
Contact with non-resident parent (1 – None to 7 – Every day)	–	3.54 (0.03)
Person years	6074	3572

Source: MCS, sweeps 1–4: age nine months, three years, five years, and seven years (University of London 2012a, b, c, d)

Notes: The descriptives for the ever-separated are from all the observations they supply, including those before the separation

no statistically significant difference, and the coefficient on separation remains very small (see Appendix, Table 8.4). These findings indicate that prior to their separation, mothers who later separated did not differ in their understanding of their parenting from mothers who did not separate. Thus, this result is consistent with our expectation that parenting confidence is not a psychological trait or behaviour, but is instead a reflection of perceived self-efficacy in a specific context.

We next turn to the impact of separation on parenting confidence, reporting the key results from the growth curve model in Table 8.2 and Fig. 8.1. Table 8.2 shows

Table 8.2 Fixed and random effects estimates from a multi-level mixed effects linear regression of perceived parenting competence among mothers, beta coefficients from a growth curve model

Fixed effects parameters	
Child's age	−0.038*
	(0.017)
Age squared	0.005**
	(0.002)
Separated	−0.054**
	(0.019)
Confidence at first survey	0.277**
	(0.018)
Random effects parameters	
Level 2 (mother)	
Intercept variance	.584**
	(.037)
Slope (child's age) variance	.007**
	(.001)
Covariance	−.036 **
	(.006)
Level 1 (survey)	
Residual variance	0.345**
	(.008)
Person years	29, 646

Source: MCS, sweeps 1–4: age nine months, three years, five years, and seven years (University of London 2012a, b, c, d). 11,764 mothers nested in 29,646 observations

Notes: Analyses additionally control for maternal education, whether the mother was married or cohabiting at the first observation, family size, whether the mother was working, and the mother's health status at first observation, as well as MCS sample strata. Observations are clustered on the study clusters indicator. Standard errors in parentheses. * $p < 0.05$, ** $p < 0.01$

that, net of the control variables, there is a strong and statistically significant relationship between separation and mothers' negative evaluation of their parenting confidence. This result is net of (prior) perceived parenting confidence measured when the child was aged nine months, which is, as we might expect, also strongly associated with later confidence. The control variables (not shown) indicate that parenting confidence was also related to mother's employment status when the child was nine months old, as well as her socio-economic status (education and maternal employment at first sweep) and her marital status; but not with maternal age at birth or her overall health or the sex of the child (full table available on request).

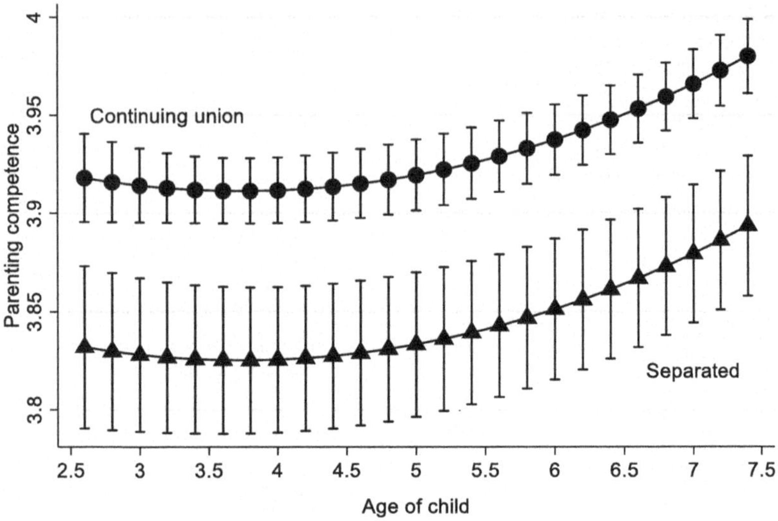

Fig. 8.1 Mothers' perceived parenting competence by separation status, predicted values from a growth curve model
Source: MCS, sweeps 1–4: age nine months, three years, five years, and seven years (University of London 2012a, b, c, d)
Notes: Results from a mixed model with a random intercept and a random slope for the age of the child, at mean values of the other covariates

Figure 8.1 illustrates graphically the results from this model. Looking at the figure, we can see that mothers who separated had lower self-evaluated parenting confidence across the range of the child's ages at which the mother's confidence was reported, even though perceived parenting confidence itself varied with age in a non-linear fashion.

We now consider to what extent the time since separation makes a difference for a mother who has separated; and to what extent contact with the non-resident parent influences the mother's parenting confidence. Given that the time since separation is correlated with the child's increasing age (a correlation coefficient of around 0.5), and that the child's age is also associated with different levels of perceived parenting confidence, we included the child's age centred at the mean age within the observation window in years (around 5.2 years) when estimating the impact of time since separation.

Looking at Table 8.3, which displays our findings on mental health and life satisfaction, we can see that there was no improvement in perceived parenting confidence among the separated mothers over time. This was the case whether or not we controlled for the child's age. That is, mothers who had been separated for longer periods of time did not tend to have higher parenting confidence than mothers who had separated more recently. This result may be partly a consequence of the relatively short time spans since separation in our sample: i.e., across the mothers, the average time since separation was only 2.7 years. However, research that examined

Table 8.3 Fixed and random effects estimates from a multi-level mixed effects linear regression of perceived parenting competence among separated mothers

	Model 1: Main effects plus time since separation	Model 2: plus child's contact with non-resident parent
Time since separation (months)	−0. 0002	−0.0000
	(0. 001)	(0.001)
Confidence at first survey	0.210**	0.209**
	(0.042)	(0.047)
Child's contact with non-resident parent		0.007
		(0.010)
Constant	2.990**	2.959**
	(0.160)	(0.164)
Level 2 (mother)		
Intercept variance	0.484**	0.482**
	(0.052)	(0.0521)
Slope variance	0.00007**	0.00007**
	(0.00003)	(0.00003)
Covariance	−0. 002**	−0.002**
	(0.001)	(0.001)
Level 1 (survey)		
Residual variance	0. 415**	0.415**
	(0.024)	(0.024)
Person years	3498	

Source: MCS, sweeps 1–4: age nine months, three years, five years, and seven years (University of London 2012a, b, c, d). 1893 individuals in 3498 observations

Notes: The numbers differ from those in Table 8.2 due to some missing values on paternal contact. The model includes a random slope on the time since separation. Analyses additionally control for the child's age (centred) and age squared, the child's sex, maternal education, whether the mother was married or cohabiting at the first observation, family size, whether the mother was working at the first observation, and the mother's health status at the first observation, as well as MCS sample strata. The model is also clustered on sample clusters. Standard errors in parentheses. * $p < 0.05$, ** $p < 0.01$

psychological impacts of separation has shown that recovery typically occurs within a short period of a few months to a year (Brewer and Nandi 2014; Tavares and Aassve 2013).[2] Other factors that remain associated with perceived parenting competence are perceived confidence and employment status at nine months and mothers' ethnicity.

Model 2 in Table 8.3 tests for whether the level of contact of the non-resident parent with the cohort child affected mothers' evaluation of their parenting

[2] To explore this point further we replicated the analysis with maternal depression as the dependent variable, and found that among separated mothers the level of depression did decrease over time since separation, other things being equal. Hence, the pattern for depression is consistent with other research, supporting the robustness of our null finding for duration effects for parenting confidence.

competence. Again, no relationship is found. Thus, there seems to be no indication that the mothers' parenting confidence recovered after declining in response to separation. This may be because of other factors that continued to render parenting itself more challenging without the presence of the child's father. At the same time, it appears that mothers' parenting confidence is not linked to how well contact between father and child is maintained. This may be because there were countervailing influences, as a higher level of contact may have eased the mother's parenting challenges in some cases, while complicating or exacerbating them in others. We return to these points in our discussion and conclusions.

Discussion and Conclusions

The aim of this chapter was to investigate changes in the perceived parenting competence of mothers who separated from their partner. In particular, our focus was on whether mothers who subsequently separate are likely to have lower confidence than mothers who remain in intact relationships. We set out to establish answers to three main questions: Does separation affect perceived parenting competence? If so, does it recover over time? Is greater paternal involvement associated with higher confidence among separated mothers?

We started by establishing that there was no selection on our dependent variable. Specifically, we found that in both the unadjusted and the adjusted analyses, mothers who subsequently separated and mothers who did not experience union dissolution had comparable levels of perceived parenting competence when they were living with the child's father and the child was around nine months old. This finding reassured us that any subsequent patterns were not driven by differential selection, rendering our claims about the impact of separation more robust. This result is also consistent with our argument that parenting confidence largely reflects an internalisation of social expectations that feed into self-efficacy, rather than a trait or a psychological state.

Following separation, the perceived parenting competence of mothers declined relative to that of their counterparts who did not separate, and we ascertained that this effect did not diminish with time since separation. That is, there was no evidence that parenting capacity recovered as mothers adjusted to their new status. This result suggests that the impact of separation on mothers' parenting confidence is not so much a psychological shock, but is instead linked to mothers having to reconceive of their parenting role as sole parents, deprived of the social endorsement of couples and subject to the widespread negative social perceptions of lone parents. This further suggests that the short term effects of separation found in other domains, such mental health, life satisfaction, and even income, could be further contextualised by considering how status changes may constitute a more permanent adjustment, with potentially long-term consequences for self-esteem and sense of self-worth and self-efficacy. While we were not able to investigate in this chapter how mothers' parenting confidence might play out in actual parent-child interactions, or wider economic and social outcomes, our findings suggest that this could be a relevant topic for future study.

We also found no support for our hypothesis that the ongoing involvement of the non-resident father would have a positive impact on the parenting confidence of mothers. We had anticipated that the greater involvement of fathers would boost mothers' self-confidence, both directly, through the father's engagement in co-parenting, and indirectly, as the mother would have the satisfaction of knowing that her child was continuing to receive attention from both parents. We thus expected to find that greater paternal involvement would compensate for some of the stigma and negative social responses associated with lone parenthood, as well as providing the mother with someone to share the burden of parenting. There was, however, no evidence in our study that this was the case. As we discussed above, shared care arrangements can occur in the most conflicted as well as in the most co-operative relationships. If a mother has to manage ongoing contact between her ex-partner and her child in a context of conflict, the involvement of the father could undermine rather than enhance her perceived competence. Our findings might therefore be capturing both positive and negative effects that cancel each other out. Alternatively, the positive effects of the non-resident parent's involvement might simply be drowned out by the negative effects of the stigma of lone parenthood.

In conclusion, we argue for an understanding of lone parenthood that is embedded in Bandura's (2006) concept of the self. In particular, we highlight some implications of society's largely negative views of lone parents. When a mother separates from the father of her children, her self-concept is disrupted, an impact which stems not only from the psychological shock but also through her interactions with significant others such as her children and ex-partner, and her experience of social perceptions of her status. It is then clear how this could translate into a drop in parenting confidence, and, as long as the lower status of lone parents is maintained, confidence is unlikely to recover, as lone parents continue to be regarded as less good environments for raising children in the UK.

Acknowledgments The researchers are grateful to the Nuffield Foundation for funding this research (CPF/40908). The research is based on analysis of the Millennium Cohort Study (www.cls.ioe.ac.uk/mcs), accessed from the UK Data Service (UKDS). We are grateful to the Centre of Longitudinal Studies (CLS) at the UCL Institute of Education for the use of these data, and to the UKDS and Economic and Social Data Service for making the MCS available. The Nuffield Foundation, the CLS, and the UKDS bear no responsibility for the analysis or the interpretation of these data. The researchers thank Rachel Rosenberg for her assistance in data preparation. The chapter benefited from comments from the University of Kent Social Policy Readings Group, the LSE Quantitative Social Policy Reading Group, and participants at presentations to the Ministry of Justice, the Social Policy Association conference, the Economic and Social Research Council Child Poverty seminar series, the Social Research Association seminar series, the Government Family Research Group, and the Parenting Cultures Centre conference.

Appendix

Table 8.4 OLS model of parenting confidence at the first MCS survey by subsequent separation status and control variables

	Beta-coefficient	Standard error
Mothers who subsequently separated (ref = remain intact)	0.009	(0.017)
Mother's age at birth (centred)	−0.006***	(0.001)
Qualifications (ref = degree)		
Higher degree	−0.000	(0.028)
Diploma	0.091***	(0.022)
A/AS level	0.063**	(0.021)
O levels/GCSE grades A-C	0.096***	(0.016)
O levels/GCSE grades D-G	0.071**	(0.025)
Other	−0.043	(0.051)
None	−0.003	(0.025)
Cohabiting (ref = married)	0.018	(0.014)
Child sex = girl	0.013	(0.011)
Number of siblings of cohort child	0.067***	(0.005)
Mother has longstanding illness	0.075***	(0.015)
Mother not in work (ref = in work)	−0.051***	(0.011)
Housing tenure (ref = owns/buying)		
Renting from LA HA	−0.071***	(0.019)
Private renter	0.006	(0.023)
Other	−0.054	(0.033)
Ethnic group (ref = white)		
Mixed ethnic groups	−0.035	(0.072)
Indian	−0.049	(0.048)
Pakistani and Bangladeshi	−0.205***	(0.033)
Black groups	0.173***	(0.030)
Other ethnic groups	−0.086	(0.057)
Constant	3.539***	(0.019)
R square	0.029	
Person-years	12,187	

Source: MCS, sweeps 1–4: age nine months, three years, five years, and seven years (University of London 2012a, b, c, d)

Notes: Analysis adjusted for the complex survey design of the MCS and non-response weights
Standard errors in parentheses. * $p < 0.05$, ** $p < 0.01$, *** $p < 0.001$

References

Amato, P. R. (2000). The consequences of divorce for adults and children. *Journal of Marriage and Family, 62*(4), 1269–1287. https://doi.org/10.1111/j.1741-3737.2000.01269.x.

Amato, P. R. (2010). Research on divorce: Continuing trends and recent developments. *Journal of Marriage and Family, 72*(3), 650–666. https://doi.org/10.1111/j.1741-3737.2010.00723.x.

Bandura, A. (2006). Toward a psychology of human agency . *Perspectives on Psychological Science, 1*(2), 164–180. https://doi.org/10.1111%2Fj.1745-6916.2006.00011.

Bernardi, L., & Mortelmans, D. (2018). Changing lone parents, changing life courses. In L. Bernardi & D. Mortelmans (Eds.), *Lone parenthood in the life course* (pp. 1–26). Cham: Springer.

Bernardi, F., Härkönen, J., Boertien, D., Andersson Rydell, L., Bastaits, K., & Mortelmans, D. (2013). State-of-the-art report. Effects of family forms and dynamics on children's well-being and life chances: Literature review. *Families and Societies, 4.*

Bianchi, S. M., Robinson, J. P., & Milke, M. A. (2006). *The changing rhythms of American family life*. New York: Russell Sage Foundation.

Blekesaune, M. (2008). Partnership transitions and mental distress: Investigating temporal order. *Journal of Marriage and Family, 70*(4), 879–890. https://doi.org/10.1111/j.1741-3737.2008.00533.x.

Brandth, B., & Kvande, E. (2018). Masculinity and fathering alone during parental leave. *Men and Masculinities, 21*(1), 72–90. https://doi.org/10.1177%2F1097184X16652659.

Brewer, M., & Nandi, A. (2014). *Partnership dissolution: How does it affect income, employment and well-being?* (ISER working paper series 2014–30). Colchester: University of Essex.

Cooper, K. (2017). *Poverty and parenting in the UK*. Doctoral dissertation. The London School of Economics and Political Science (LSE).

Craig, L. (2006). Does father care mean fathers share? A comparison of how mothers and fathers in intact families spend time with children. *Gender & Society, 20*(2), 259–281. https://doi.org/10.1177/0891243205285212.

Craig, L., Powell, A., & Smyth, C. (2014). Towards intensive parenting? Changes in the composition and determinants of mothers' and fathers' time with children 1992–2006. *The British Journal of Sociology, 65*(3), 555–579. https://doi.org/10.1111/1468-4446.12035.

CSJ. (2006). *Breakdown Britain: Interim report on the state of the nation*. London: Centre for Social Justice.

Daly, M. (2015). Parenting support as policy field: An analytic framework. *Social Policy and Society, 14*(4), 597–608. https://doi.org/10.1017/S1474746415000226.

Dermott, E. (2003). The 'intimate father': Defining paternal involvement . *Sociological Research Online, 8*(4). https://doi.org/10.5153%2Fsro.859.

Dermott, E. (2014). *Intimate fatherhood: A sociological analysis*. Basingstoke: Palgrave Macmillan.

Ermisch, J., & Pronzato, C. (2008). Intra-household allocation of resources: Inferences from non-resident fathers' child support payments. *The Economic Journal, 118*(527), 347–362. https://doi.org/10.1111/j.1468-0297.2007.02124.x.

Fabricius, W. V., Braver, S. L., Diaz, P., & Velez, C. E. (2010). Custody and parenting time: Links to family relationships and wellbeing after divorce. In M. E. Lamb (Ed.), *The role of the father in child development* (pp. 201–240). Hoboken: Wiley.

Fehlberg, B., Smyth, B., Maclean, M., & Roberts, C. (2011). Legislating for shared time parenting after separation: A research review. *International Journal of Law, Policy and the Family, 25*(3), 318–337. https://doi.org/10.1093/lawfam/ebr015.

Gardner, J., & Oswald, A. J. (2006). Do divorcing couples become happier by breaking up? *Journal of the Royal Statistical Society, 169*(2), 319–336. https://doi.org/10.1111/j.1467-985X.2006.00403.x.

Gauthier, A. H. (2015). Social class and parental investment in children. In R. Scott & S. Kosslyn (Eds.), *Emerging trends in the social and behavioral sciences* (pp. 1–14). Hoboken: Wiley Press.

Gauthier, A. H., Smeeding, T. M., & Furstenberg, F. F. (2004). Are parents investing less time in children? Trends in selected industrialized countries. *Population and Development Review, 30*(4), 647–672. https://doi.org/10.1111/j.1728-4457.2004.00036.x.

Harkness, S., & Skipp, A. (2013). *Lone mothers, work, and depression*. London: Nuffield Foundation.

Hetherington, E. M. (2003). Intimate pathways: Changing patterns in close personal relationships across time. *Family Relations, 52*(4), 318–331. https://doi.org/10.1111/j.1741-3729.2003.00318.x.

Ives, J. (2015). Theorising the 'deliberative father': Compromise, progress, and striving to do fatherhood well. *Families, Relationships and Societies, 4*(2), 281–294. https://doi.org/10.1332/204674314X14184029517584.

Jenkins, S. P. (2009). Marital splits and income changes over the longer term. In J. F. Ermisch & M. Brynin (Eds.), *Changing relationships* (pp. 214–237). London: Routledge.

Jenkins, S. P. (2011). *Changing fortunes*. Oxford: Oxford University Press.

Kalmijn, M. (2015). How childhood circumstances moderate the long-term impact of divorce on father-child relationships. *Journal of Marriage and Family, 77*(4), 921–938. https://doi.org/10.1111/jomf.12202.

Kalmijn, M. (2016). Father-child contact, interparental conflict, and depressive symptoms among children of divorced parents. *European Sociological Review, 32*(1), 68–80. https://doi.org/10.1093/esr/jcv095.

Kalmijn, M., & Monden, C. (2006). Are the negative effects of divorce on well-being dependent on marital quality? *Journal of Marriage and Family, 68*(5), 1197–1213. https://doi.org/10.1111/j.1741-3737.2006.00323.x.

Kiernan, K. E., & Huerta, M. C. (2008). Economic deprivation, maternal depression, parenting and children's cognitive and emotional development in early childhood. *British Journal of Sociology, 59*(4), 783–806. https://doi.org/10.1111/j.1468-4446.2008.00219.x.

Kitterød, R. H., & Wiik, K. A. (2017). Shared residence among parents living apart in Norway. *Family Court Review, 55*(4), 556–571. https://doi.org/10.1111/fcre.12304.

Klett-Davies, M. (2016). *Going it alone? Lone motherhood in late modernity*. London: Routledge.

Lacroix, C. (2006). Freedom, desire, and power: Gender processes and presumptions of shared care and responsibility after parental separation. *Women's Studies International Forum, 29*(2), 184–196. https://doi.org/10.1016/j.wsif.2006.03.004.

Lader, D. (2008). *Non-resident parental contact, 2007/8* (Omnibus survey report, 38). London: ONS.

Lamb, M. E. (Ed.). (2010). *The role of the father in child development*. (5th ed.). Hoboken: Wiley.

Lamb, M. E. (2012). Critical analysis of research on parenting plans and children's well-being. In L. Drozd, M. Saini, & N. Olese (Eds.), *Parenting plan evaluations: Applied research for the family court* (pp. 214–243). Oxford: Oxford University Press.

Lausten, M., Lee, R. H., & Waldfogel, J. (2013). Fathers' involvement and child development: Are they related? Evidence from four OECD countries. In *OECD social, employment and migration working papers, 140*. Paris: OECD.

Link, B. G., & Phelan, J. C. (2001). Conceptualizing stigma. *Annual Review of Sociology, 27*(1), 363–385. https://doi.org/10.1146/annurev.soc.27.1.363.

Lovejoy, C. M., Graczyk, P. A., O'Hare, E., & Neuman, G. (2000). Maternal depression and parenting behvaiour: A meta analytical review. *Clinical Psychology Review, 20*(5), 561–592. https://doi.org/10.1016/S0272-7358(98)00100-7.

Mahrer, N., Sandler, I., Wolchik, S., Winslow, E., Moran, J., & Weinstock, D. (2016). How do parenting time and interparental conflict affect the relations of quality of parenting and child well-being following divorce. In L. Drozd, M. Saini, & N. Olesen (Eds.), *Parenting plan evaluations: Applied research for the family court* (pp. 63–73). Oxford: Oxford University Press.

Marsiglio, W., Amato, P., Day, R., & Lamb, M. (2000). Scholarship on fatherhood in the 1990s and beyond. *Journal of Marriage and the Family, 62*(4), 1173–1191. https://doi.org/10.1111/j.1741-3737.2000.01173.x.

McLanahan, S. (2004). Diverging destinies: How children are faring under the second demographic transition. *Demography, 41*(4), 607–627. https://doi.org/10.1353/dem.2004.0033.
McLanahan, S., & Jacobsen, W. (2015). Diverging destinies revisited. In P. R. Amato, A. Booth, S. M. McHale, & J. Van Hook (Eds.), *Families in an era of increasing inequality* (pp. 3–23). Cham: Springer.
Meyer, D. R., Cancian, M., & Cook, S. T. (2017). The growth in shared custody in the United States: Patterns and implications. *Family Court Review, 55*(4), 500–512. https://doi.org/10.1111/fcre.12300.
Mooney, A., Oliver, C., & Smith, M. (2009). *Impact of family breakdown on children's well-being: Evidence review* (Research report DCSF-RR113). London: Department for Children, Schools and Families.
Nielsen, L. (2018). Preface to the special issue: Shared physical custody: Recent research, advances, and applications. *Journal of Divorce & Remarriage, 59*(4), 237–246. https://doi.org/10.1080/10502556.2018.1455303.
ONS (2014) *Divorces in England and Wales,* 2012. Statistical Bulletin. London: Office for National Statistics.
ONS (2015) *Families and Households,* 2014. Statistical Bulletin. London: Office for National Statistics.
Park, A., & Rhead, R. (2013). Personal relationships: Changing attitudes towards sex, marriage and parenthood. In A. Park, C. Bryson, E. Clery, J. Curtice, & M. Phillips (Eds.), *British social attitudes, the 30th report* (pp. 1–33). London: NatCen Social Research.
Pevalin, D. J., & Ermisch, J. (2004). Cohabiting unions, repartnering and mental health. *Psychological Medicine, 34*(8), 1553–1559. https://doi.org/10.1017/S0033291704002570.
Philip, G. (2013). Relationality and moral reasoning in accounts of fathering after separation or divorce: Care, gender and working at 'fairness'. *Families, Relationships and Societies, 2*(3), 409–424. https://doi.org/10.1332/204674313X667407.
Philip, G. (2014). Fathering after separation or divorce: Navigating domestic, public and moral spaces. *Families, Relationships and Societies, 3*(2), 219–233. https://doi.org/10.1332/204674314X14017856302453.
Plewis, I. (2007). *Millennium cohort study first survey: Technical report on sampling* (4th ed.). London: Centre for Longitudinal Studies, Institute of Education.
Poole, E., Speight, S., O'Brien, M., Connolly, S., & Aldrich, M. (2016). Who are non-resident fathers? A British socio-demographic profile. *Journal of Social Policy, 45*(2), 223–250. https://doi.org/10.1017/S0047279415000653.
Rabe-Hesketh, S., & Skrondal, A. (2012). *Multilevel and longitudinal modeling using Stata.* College Station: Stata Press.
Rogers, C. R. (1959). A theory of therapy, personality, and interpersonal relationships: As developed in the client-centered framework. In S. Koch (Ed.), *Psychology: A study of a science. Formulations of the person and the social context* (pp. 184–256). New York: McGraw-Hill.
Salter, E. (2018). A media discourse analysis of lone parents in the UK: Investigating the stereotype. In L. Bernardi & D. Mortelmans (Eds.), *Lone parenthood in the life course* (pp. 55–74). Cham: Springer.
Silva, E. B. (1996). *Good enough mothering? Feminist perspectives on lone motherhood.* London: Routledge.
Singer, J. D., & Willett, J. B. (2003). *Applied longitudinal data analysis: Modeling change and event occurrence.* New York: Oxford University Press.
Smith, M. (2004). Parental mental health: Disruptions to parenting and outcomes for children. *Child and Family Social Work, 9*(1), 3–11. https://doi.org/10.1111/j.1365-2206.2004.00312.x.
Smyth, B. M. (2017). Special issue on shared-time parenting after separation. *Family Court Review, 55*(4), 494–499. https://doi.org/10.1111/fcre.12299.
Solomon, C. R. (2014). 'I feel like a rock star': Fatherhood for stay-at-home fathers. *Fathering, 12*(1), 52–70.

Steinbach, A. (2019). Children's and parents' well-being in joint physical custody: A literature review. *Family Process, 58*(2), 353–369. https://doi.org/10.1111/famp.12372.
Stewart, K. (2016). The family and disadvantage. In H. Dean & L. Platt (Eds.), *Social advantage and disadvantage* (pp. 85–111). Oxford: Oxford University Press.
Strohschein, L. (2007). Challenging the presumption of diminished capacity to parent: Does divorce really change parenting practices? *Family Relations, 56*(4), 358–368. https://doi.org/10.1111/j.1741-3729.2007.00465.x.
Tavares, L. P., & Aassve, A. (2013). Psychological distress of marital and cohabitation breakups. *Social Science Research, 42*(6), 1599–1611. https://doi.org/10.1016/j.ssresearch.2013.07.008.
University of London Institute of Education Centre for Longitudinal Studies. (2012a). *Millennium Cohort study: First survey, 2001–2003 [computer file]* (10th ed.). Colchester: UK Data Archive [distributor], August 2012. SN: 4683.
University of London Institute of Education Centre for Longitudinal Studies. (2012b). *Millennium Cohort study: Fourth survey, 2008 [computer file]* (3rd ed.). Colchester: UK Data Archive [distributor], August 2012. SN: 6411.
University of London Institute of Education Centre for Longitudinal Studies. (2012c). *Millennium Cohort study: Second survey, 2003–2005 [computer file]* (7th ed.). Cochester: UK Data Archive [distributor], August 2012. SN: 5350.
University of London Institute of Education Centre for Longitudinal Studies. (2012d). *Millennium Cohort study: Third survey, 2006 [computer file]* (5th ed.). Colchester: UK Data Archive [distributor], August 2012. SN: 5795.
Wade, T. J., & Pevalin, D. J. (2004). Marital transitions and mental health. *Journal of Health and Social Behavior, 45*(2), 155–170. https://doi.org/10.1177/002214650404500203.
Wall, G. (2010). Mothers' experience with intensive parenting and brain development discourse. *Women's Studies International Forum, 33*(3), 253–263. https://doi.org/10.1016/j.wsif.2010.02.019.
Wallerstein, J. S., & Kelly, J. B. (1980). *Surviving the breakup: How children and parents cope with divorce*. New York: Basic books.
Wilson, K. R., & Prior, M. R. (2010). Father involvement: The importance of paternal solo care. *Early Child Development and Care, 180*(10), 1391–1405. https://doi.org/10.1080/03004430903172335.

Chapter 9
The Role of Gatekeeping in Non-Resident Fathers' Contact with Their Children: Mothers' and Fathers' Views

Sabine Walper, Stefanie Amberg, Carolin Thönnissen, and Sharon L. Christ

Introduction

In recent decades, normative expectations regarding fathers' involvement in parenting have changed substantially. Egalitarian gender role attitudes have become more widespread in many countries, endorsing not only women participating in the labor market, but also fathers actively contributing to child rearing (Knight and Brinton 2017; Scarborough et al. 2018). Even though family practices often lag behind these expectations, they have changed. Evidence from the U.S. and Europe suggests that fathers are investing more time in child care, not only in nuclear families, but also after parental separation (Amato et al. 2009; Westphal et al. 2014). Nevertheless, parental separation and divorce still put father-child relationships at substantial risk. In the majority of families with separated parents, the mother is the residential parent who takes primary responsibility for the children's everyday lives. Although joint physical custody or shared parenting has become a more common arrangement among separated parents, most separated fathers are relegated to the role of visiting parent, and thus often have only limited contact with their children.

This paper addresses the issue of non-resident fathers' contact with their children, and seeks to explore several hypotheses that may explain why some fathers manage to maintain frequent contact, while others rarely see their children. The factors affecting separated fathers' involvement have been widely debated, not only because access to fathers' economic, social, and emotional resources is considered

S. Walper (✉)
German Youth Institute and Ludwig-Maximilians-University (LMU), Munich, Germany
e-mail: walper@dji.de

S. Amberg · C. Thönnissen
Ludwig-Maximilians-University (LMU), Munich, Germany

S. L. Christ
Purdue University, West Lafayette, IN, USA

M. Kreyenfeld, H. Trappe (eds.), *Parental Life Courses after Separation and Divorce in Europe*, Life Course Research and Social Policies 12,
https://doi.org/10.1007/978-3-030-44575-1_9

important for children's well-being (Bastaits et al. 2012; Coley and Medeiros 2007; Jeynes 2015; King and Sobolewski 2006), but also because issues of visitation are often raised in legal conflicts between separated parents. This is the case in Germany, where our research is conducted. Even though there is considerable instability in couple relationships in Germany, with every third marriage ending in divorce (Statistisches Bundesamt 2018b), the available evidence on separated families is quite limited. Furthermore, as in many other countries, divorce rates in Germany no longer capture levels of family instability, as the rising share of nonmarital births has contributed to increased heterogeneity among separated parents. In 2017, every third childbirth (35 percent) in Germany was to unmarried parents (Statistisches Bundesamt 2018c). While around 80 percent of unmarried parents were cohabiting when their child was born (Langmeyer 2015), these couples were more likely to separate than married parents (Schnor 2012). In 2017, 19 percent of all German families with minor children were single-parent households, and the overwhelming majority of these families were headed by the mother (Statistisches Bundesamt 2018a). Almost half (43 percent) of these single mothers were never married (ibid.). In addition, estimates from surveys suggest that around 13 percent of all households with minor children are stepfamilies, with most being stepfather families (Bundesministerium für Familie, Senioren, Frauen und Jugend 2013).

The involvement of separated fathers in the lives of their children seems to be more limited in Germany than it is in other Western countries. In a cross-national study, Kalmijn (2015) compared 14-year-old students' post-divorce contact and relationship with their father in Germany, the Netherlands, England, and Sweden. The highest share of young people who had no contact with their father was found in Germany (21 percent). Conversely, the findings indicated that the rate of shared physical custody was lowest in Germany (ten percent), closely followed by England (eleven percent), and was highest in Sweden (36 percent). Since the pre-separation division of labor has been shown to affect fathers' post-separation involvement in child rearing (Poortman and van Gaalen 2017), these figures may reflect differences in gendered patterns of family roles. In Germany, the modernized provider model is most prevalent, as the high share of mothers in part-time employment and the substantial gender gap in the number of hours working mothers and fathers spend in employment demonstrate (OECD 2017).

Previous research on determinants of post-separation father-child contact in Germany has followed roughly two lines. From a sociological perspective, structural features that reflect parental resources and commitments have been investigated, including maternal employment, family SES, parents' educational resources, parents' former marital status, the father's legal custody rights, the father's current partnership status, and the children's ages and genders (e.g., Kalmijn 2015; Köppen et al. 2018). From a more psychological perspective, studies that were often inspired by issues raised in legal conflicts between separated parents have focused on the relationship dynamics between parents (e.g., Amendt 2004; Behrend 2010; Blesken 1998; Walper 2006, 2019). In this latter line of research, scholars have investigated not only the father's role identity and approach to coping with conflict, but also the role of the mother as the gatekeeper in the father-child relationship. Earlier debates that focused on extreme forms of maternal gatekeeping suggested that parental alienation is a common process through which the mother involves the child in a close alliance against the father, and thus causes the child to become distanced from the father (Kodjoe and Koeppel 1998). However, more recent research has shown that this description of post-separation family dynamics oversimplifies the processes involved, and neglects considerable variation between cases (Behrend 2010).

Our study seeks to provide a differentiated view of the factors linked to problems in the interparental relationship and their likely outcomes for the father-child relationship. Our focus is on the role of maternal gatekeeping, which has been proposed as a unifying concept that explains the disadvantages in social capital and resources of children whose parents have separated relative to children raised in nuclear families (Austin et al. 2013). In addition to looking at gatekeeping attitudes and behaviors, we will address the mother's and the father's attitudes toward each other and the issues surrounding coparenting, both of which may reflect each parent's resentment of his/her former partner, as well as more objective conditions linked to the father's failure in the role of provider.

Theoretical Background

Prior Research

In any dual parenting relationship, parents have to decide how to share their responsibilities to their children. Accordingly, engaging in negotiations about the extent and the type of involvement each parent has with the children, which may include making decisions about whether the children require protection from the other parent's behavior, is a natural part of coparenting (Austin et al. 2013). Such decisions are likely to be made more deliberately in separated families than they are in nuclear families, as the parents have to arrange the children's visits and overnight stays with each parent, at least as long as the children are too young to make these arrangements on their own. More importantly, since the often fraught process of separation and divorce does not necessarily facilitate the resolution of prior problems between parents, conflicts about parenting issues and attempts to limit or undermine the other parent's relationship with the child tend to be more common in separated than in nuclear families (Fagan and Barnett 2003; Walper et al. 2005).

As the findings discussed above indicate, the notion of parental gatekeeping is often cited as playing a major role in conflicts between separated parents over parenting time and the non-resident parent's access to the child (Austin et al. 2013). Parental gatekeeping has been defined as encompassing "attitudes and behaviors by either parent that affect the quality of the other parent-child relationship and/or level of involvement with the child" (Austin et al. 2013: 486). It comprises not only attitudes and behaviors that may restrict the other parent's interaction and relationship with the child, but also attitudes and behaviors that may facilitate this relationship (e.g., Altenburger et al. 2018). Restrictive gatekeeping would be evident in efforts to marginalize the other parent, refusals to communicate, and to deliver derogatory messages about the other parent in the presence of the child; while facilitative gatekeeping would be exemplified by efforts to include the other parent in communication and decision-making, and conveying a positive image of the other parent (Austin et al. 2013: 488). Most research that has focused on restrictive gatekeeping has provided evidence that it is linked to fathers being less involved with their children (e.g., Allen and Hawkins 1999; Fagan and Barnett 2003; Stevenson et al. 2014). Furthermore, some of these studies have found evidence that maternal encouragement of the father being involved with his children has positive effects, even after controlling for the quality of the interparental relationship (Fagan and Cherson 2017).

There is considerable overlap between the concepts of gatekeeping and coparenting. Coparenting refers to "the ways that parents and/or parental figures relate to each other in the role of parent" (Feinberg 2003: 96). The term is conceptualized as a multi-dimensional construct that includes features of cooperation, agreement, conflict, and triangulation/undermining (Feinberg 2003; Teubert and Pinquart 2010). The last of these features is at the core of restrictive gatekeeping; i.e., efforts to undermine the other parent in his/her parenting role. Using a typological approach to analyzing coparenting in separated families, Lamela et al. (2016) identified three groups of coparenting relationships: cooperative coparenting (48 percent), high-conflict coparenting (13 percent), and undermining coparenting (39 percent). While the undermining coparenting group were found to have levels of agreement and support that were as low as those of the high-conflict group, open conflict was reported less frequently in the undermining group. Interestingly, undermining behavior was similarly evident in the high-conflict group. These results are in line with findings from Germany indicating that undermining behavior is distinct from but related to interparental conflict (Walper et al. 2005).

Interparental conflict has often been cited as a risk factor that threatens a nonresidential father's levels of contact and relationship quality with his children (Coiro and Emery 1998; Walper and Beckh 2006; Walper and Krey 2009); although such effects have not always been found (e.g., Sobolewski and King 2005). There is also evidence that even in married or cohabitating couples, interparental conflict is linked to the father having reduced access to his young children (Hohmann-Marriott 2011). In line with the assumption that interparental conflict triggers restrictive gatekeeping by the mother, findings from a longitudinal study have shown that, over time, the parents having marital problems was linked to later maternal gatekeeping, which, in turn, reduced the level of father-child interaction (Stevenson et al. 2014). However, there is also evidence for reverse effects in intact families, which suggests that the father's involvement may have positive effects on later coparenting (Jia and Schoppe-Sullivan 2011).

While coparenting conflict is often accompanied by undermining or gate-closing behavior, cooperative coparenting can be understood as facilitative gatekeeping or gate-opening behavior. For a separated family, a cooperative coparental relationship may encourage the father to be more involved with his children. In a study that included separated as well as nuclear families, higher levels of coparental coordination were found to be associated with more paternal involvement across family types, whereas low coparental coordination was shown to be associated with less paternal involvement, especially among nonresidential divorced fathers (Finzi-Dottan and Cohen 2016). As might be expected, divorced fathers reported experiencing lower levels of coparental coordination than married fathers. Similar evidence from the Fragile Families Study showed that the father's level of involvement tended to be higher when the coparenting relationship was positive (McClain and DeMaris 2013). Some findings have suggested that in separated families, parental cooperation may play an even more important role than conflict (Sobolewski and King 2005). In this latter study, parental cooperation, but not conflict over child rearing, was found to predict the father's level of contact with his children, as well as his level of responsive fathering and the quality of his relationship with his children; with contact mediating the effects on the quality of his fathering and his relationship with his children.

In seeking to understand the emotional and attitudinal context of maternal gatekeeping, some studies have examined the mother's attitudes regarding the father and her perceptions of his role performance. As has been pointed out, the mother may restrict the father's access to their joint children because she is angry at the father, or because she feels he has opted out of his responsibilities to their children (Greif 1997). Similarly, the mother's continuing hostility toward her ex-spouse has been related to reduced or lost father-child contact (Buchanan et al. 1996), and to the father being driven away (Braver and O'Connell 1998). The mother is particularly likely to harbor feelings of disappointment and resentment if the father is not committed to his role as provider and withholds child support payments. Hence, it might be assumed that a father's access to his children would be restricted only if he was unable or unwilling to provide for them. Findings from the Fragile Families and Child Wellbeing Study supported this assumption in the case of separated families, but pointed to a different effect among fathers in intact families, with these fathers being less involved if their financial contributions to the family were high (Carlson et al. 2017). Other data also show a link between child support payments and father-child contact (Amato et al. 2009). While there is only very limited evidence regarding the impact of child support payments on father-child contact in Germany, findings from an online study of separated fathers also suggested that fathers with low economic resources have less access to their children (Amendt 2004). However, as these studies did not address issues of gatekeeping, the question of whether the mother restricts the father's access or the father withdraws because he is failing to provide remains unresolved. Indeed, there are qualitative data suggesting that gatekeeping work – regardless of whether it is gate-opening or gate-closing – can be a dynamic transactional process, rather than a linear and unidirectional process running from the mother to the father (Trinder 2008).

In addition to restrictive and facilitative gatekeeping, protective gatekeeping has been identified as a third type of approach a parent might use to manage the other parent's involvement (Austin 2018). Research has suggested that gate-closing behavior may reflect problems that go beyond the interparental relationship or a parent's feelings of resentment towards his/her former partner. The mother may also limit the father's access if she is worried about the children's well-being (Nixon and Hadfield 2018). Thus, under certain circumstances, the aim of gate-closing can be to protect the children when the other parent's behavior or a given parenting plan is seen as jeopardizing the children's well-being (e.g., Saini et al. 2017). Such concerns may motivate maternal gatekeeping, but they can also lead the father to withdraw in order to avoid exacerbating the children's stress levels and loyalty conflicts. Accordingly, a differentiated view on gatekeeping is needed that focuses not only on issues of parental resentment and conflict, but on parental worries about the children's well-being.

Aims of This Study

Although there is a large body of work on gatekeeping, the evidence on the role of maternal gatekeeping in shaping a father's post-separation access to his children is still limited. In particular, the factors mentioned above have not been jointly considered. Thus, the main aim of our study is to shed light on different features of maternal gatekeeping, as well as the likely predictors of maternal gatekeeping, and the effects of such efforts on the father's contact with his children. Furthermore, we seek to include multiple perspectives that address the mother's, the father's, and the children's views of family dynamics. Our analyses focus on four factors that may restrict a separated father's access to his children. Since our major aim is to explore the role of the interparental dynamic, we will not address cases in which there is no father-child contact (which would cause missing data on relationship problems), but will instead seek to explain situations in which the father-child contact is infrequent.

First, it is assumed that the father's failure to provide (i.e., missing support payments or failing to make payments on time) impedes his access (e.g., Amendt 2004), either because he withdraws in response to being unable to fulfil his financial obligations, or because the mother restricts the children's access to their father in response to his failure to comply with his obligations (*provider hypothesis*). Second, we expect to find that the mother having a negative view of the father undermines her willingness to facilitate the children's contact with their father, and is thus linked to the children having infrequent contact (*resentment hypothesis)*. We also test whether the father having a negative view of the mother is linked to infrequent contact with the child, based on the assumption that the father's resentment of the mother might lead him to avoid contact. Third, since interparental conflict and coparenting problems have often been identified as potential barriers to father-child contact, we assume that coparenting conflict contributes to infrequent contact, while successful cooperation facilitates contact (*coparenting hypothesis)*. Fourth, our focus is on maternal gatekeeping and parental worries about the children's well-being, which may inhibit the father's access to his children (*gatekeeping hypothesis*). Parental worries are of particular interest, since concerns about children's stress in the context of visitation and interparental problems can be expected to provide a

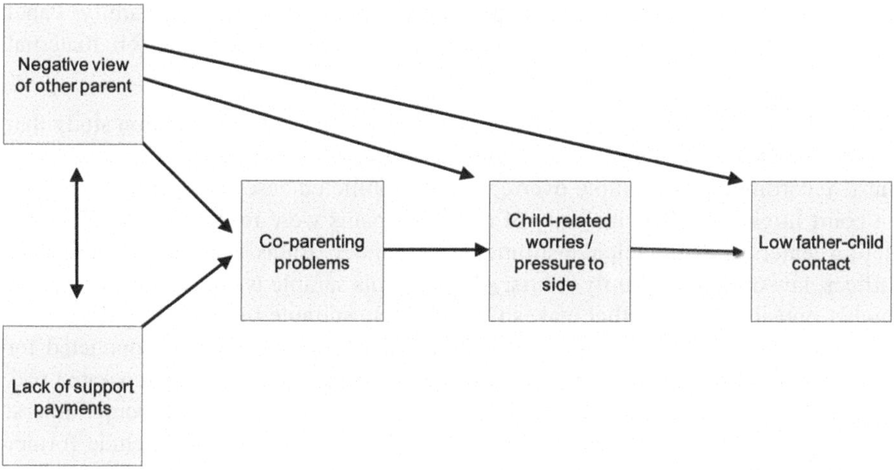

Fig. 9.1 Analytic model of interparental dynamics predicting low levels of father-child contact

powerful motivation for the mother to restrict father-child contact. At the same time, the father being worried about his children's well-being could lead him to have less contact with his children, as he may avoid contact in order to prevent the children from experiencing stress. Finally, the children's views on their mother's efforts to form an alliance with them against their father (i.e., maternal pressure to take sides) provides relevant information on gatekeeping behavior, since it may be more valid than maternal self-reports.

All of these factors are assumed to be interrelated, as Fig. 9.1 shows. We expect to find that coparenting problems mediate the effects of financial problems, based on the assumption that making insufficient support payments affects father-child contact only if this places stress on the interparental relationship. Similarly, we expect to observe that coparenting problems at least partly mediate the effects of negative attributions on infrequent contact. Furthermore, we assume that protective gatekeeping (which stems from a parent being worried) or restrictive gatekeeping (which places pressure on the children to choose sides) partly mediate the effects of both a negative view of the other parent and coparenting problems on the children's access to their father.

Method

Samples

We used two datasets to test our hypotheses: a small, intensive cross-sectional sample of separated mothers and fathers, most of whom sought counseling, mediation, or parenting training (*KiB*) and participated in an evaluation study (KiB sample);

and a two-wave longitudinal sample drawn from the German Family Panel (*pairfam*), which allows us to include the children's perspective on maternal gatekeeping.

KiB Sample The KiB sample was drawn from an ongoing intervention study that targets a broad range of separated parents, including those in highly conflicted families. Accordingly, this sample overrepresents conflicted cases (33 percent involved in court litigation[1]). The majority of the participants were recruited through counseling centers or at municipal institutions, like kindergartens, schools, youth welfare offices, law offices, or family courts. Although this sample is not representative, the higher prevalence of conflict makes it particularly suitable for exploring the role of interparental problems. The data used here come from the pre-test conducted for those parents involved in an intervention (KiB parenting course for separated parents; fathers: 80 percent, mothers: 71 percent) and the smaller control group (fathers: 20 percent; mothers: 29 percent). Since the KiB course does not include former couples in the same parenting group, the maternal and paternal subsamples are largely independent, and comprise a smaller subset of the former sample of couples (22 percent/19 percent of the fathers/mothers). As a prerequisite for the intervention, almost all of the non-resident parents still had contact with their children, but the contact frequency varied between shared parenting and weekly visits to less than one visit per year. Non-resident mothers (n = 18) and resident fathers (n = 22) were excluded due to their low numbers. Similarly, 14 mothers and twelve fathers who had no contact with their children's other parent were not included due to missing information on coparenting conflict. Furthermore, the sample was restricted to parents with a minor child between the ages of three and 17 years. The final sample comprised 160 fathers (non-resident or shared parenting) and 187 mothers (resident or shared parenting) who participated in the written questionnaire assessments.

Table 9.1 provides an overview of the sample, separately for fathers and mothers. The parents' reports on the children's ages and genders were based on a target child (randomly selected if the parents had more than one child in the age range three to 17 years). Substantial shares of the fathers and of the mothers reported engaging in shared parenting: 21 percent and 14 percent, respectively. These figures are considerably higher than those suggested by other data for Germany (Kalmijn 2015), and likely reflect high levels of paternal involvement. Furthermore, highly educated parents are overrepresented in this sample, as is typical for the outreach of such interventions. About half of the parents had successfully completed a higher level of general schooling; i.e. they had graduated from the advanced track of schooling required for entry into university or an advanced technical college ("Abitur" or "Fachabitur"). As expected based on other research, the per capita net household income (needs weighted according to the OECD) was substantially higher for the fathers (M = 2766 €, SD = 2094) than for the mothers (M = 1535 €, SD = 821.5).

[1]A question about ongoing legal conflict was not introduced until later in the course of the study, and is available for 81 parents only.

Table 9.1 Descriptives of the KiB and the pairfam sample

	KiB sample (Pretest)		Pairfam sample (Wave 7 and 8)
	Fathers' report (n = 160)	Mothers' report (n = 187)	Mothers' and children's report (N = 145)
Joint physical custody in % (n)[a]	21.3 (34)	14.4 (27)	2.8 (4)
High parental education in % (n)[b]	54.4 (87)	51.9 (97)	41.3 (59)
Boys in % (n)	48.8 (78)	43.3 (81)	50.0 (73)
Child age (years)			
Mean	7.2	7.1	11.0
Standard deviation	3.8	3.7	2.0
Parental age (years)			
Mean	42.9	39.7	38.5
Standard deviation	6.5	5.7	4.8
Equivalent household income in €			
Mean	2766.4	1535.0	1258.3
Standard deviation	2094.4	821.5	505.2

Notes: [a]The assessment of joint physical custody was based on the parents' estimates of whether the child was spending equal amounts of time at each parent's home in the KiB study, and was based on maternal reports of the number of overnights the child was spending with each parent in the pairfam study (50:50 up to 40:60)

[b] High education: General school qualification for university/university of applied sciences

The average ages of the children did not differ for the fathers (7.2 years, SD = 3.8) and the mothers (7.1 years, SD = 6.7).

Pairfam Sample The second sample was drawn from the German Family Panel pairfam (Huinink et al. 2011), a three-cohort longitudinal study on family development with annual assessments, which was started in 2008/2009 for three birth cohorts (see www.pairfam.de). The participants were recruited through register data provided by the local administration and personal visits of the interviewer, who conducted the interviews in the participants' homes. The data used here were drawn from waves seven and eight (Brüderl et al. 2017), and were restricted to separated mothers whose child(ren) participated in the child interview (for children aged eight to 15 years) in wave seven. If more than one child in a given family had participated in the child interview, we selected the youngest child for our analyses. In line with the approach used in the KiB, the cases in which there was no contact between the two parents and between the child and his/her non-resident father in wave seven were not included in the analyses, since the core predictors of contact (coparenting, maternal pressure to take sides) were filtered by contact. Omitting cases of parental reunion or recent parental separation (between waves seven and eight), the final sample included N = 145 separated mothers and their youngest child, who was eight to 15 years old.

Descriptive information for the pairfam sample is shown in Table 9.1 (right column). Unlike in the KiB results, but in line with other findings for Germany (Walper et al. 2020), only three percent of the mothers in the sample reported engaging in shared parenting, while 97 percent indicated that they had primary residential custody. Compared to the maternal subsample in the KiB study, a smaller share of the mothers in the pairfam sample reported having a high level of education (42 percent with high general school qualification; mean years of education: 12.6, SD = 2.7). Furthermore, the mothers in the pairfam sample had a lower average equivalent household income. Although the average age of the mothers (M = 38.6 years, SD = 4.7) was more than one year younger than it was in the KiB sample, the average age of the children was four years older (11.2 years, SD = 2.0), which suggests that the parents in the pairfam sample were substantially younger when their children were born than the parents in the KiB sample. Several factors may have contributed to this difference, including the smaller share of highly educated mothers in the pairfam sample (as higher education is linked to later childbearing) and the larger share of East German families in the pairfam sample (as the average maternal age at childbirth is lower in East than in West Germany). Of the mothers in the pairfam sample, 32 percent were living with a new partner (remarried or cohabitating), and ten percent were first- or second-generation migrants.

Indicators

KiB Data

Frequency of Father-Child Contact The frequency of contact between the child and the non-resident father was reported by the resident mother answering the question: “If your child lives with you, how often does the other parent see your child?”; and by the non-resident father answering the question: “If your child does not live with you, how often do you see him/her?” Parents selected a response from a four-point continuum ranging from “at least weekly” (coded one; mothers: 58 percent; fathers: 58 percent) across “every two weeks” (coded two; mothers: 25 percent, fathers: 31 percent), “once per month” (coded three; mothers: five percent; fathers: three percent), to “less often than once a month” (coded four; mothers: twelve percent, fathers: eight percent). Cases in which the parents reported engaging in shared parenting but their child’s moves between the two parental households were minimal (one father and three mothers), or in which there was a lack of data on contact frequency (nine fathers and nine mothers), were recoded as high contact.

The predictors used in our analyses were consistent with short scales (3–5 items) that had good to satisfactory internal consistency for both parents (Cronbach’s Alpha 0.75–0.90). All of the items were answered on a five-point scale (from 1 = never to 5 = very often). **Negative Attributions** of the other parent’s behavior were assessed by five items based on the “Relationship Attribution Measure”

(RAM) developed by Fincham and Bradbury (1992). The items indicated attributions of bad intent or dysfunctional behavior to the other parent (e.g., "She/he often hurts me on purpose." or "Most of our disputes are provoked by her/him."). Cronbach's Alpha for this index was 0.87 for fathers and 0.83 for mothers. **Coparenting Conflict** was indicated by three items based on Ahrons' Coparenting Conflict Scale (Ahrons 1981) (e.g., "Do you and your former spouse have basic differences of opinion about issues related to child rearing?" or "When you and your former spouse discuss parenting issues, how often does this result in an argument?"). Cronbach's Alpha was 0.87 for fathers and 0.88 for mothers. **Child-Related Worries** were assessed by a three-item indicator developed for this project (e.g., "Are you worried about the mental and/or physical well-being of your child because of the other parent?" or "Do you think that your child sometimes suffers from loyalty conflict?"). Cronbach's Alpha was 0.90 for fathers and 0.75 for mothers. Observations with missing information on any of these items (ranging from 1.3 percent to 13.1 percent) were retained in the models using the Full Information Maximum Likelihood (FIML) method (Arbuckle 1996).

Pairfam Data

Frequency of Father-Child Contact was reported by the mother (question: "How often does the other parent see child x?"). The frequency rating ranged from "daily" (coded one; seven percent) over "several times per week" (coded two; 17 percent), "once per week" (coded three; 15 percent), 1–3 times per month" (coded four; 37 percent), and "less often" (coded five; 19 percent), to "no contact" (coded six; six percent in wave eight; cases without contact in wave seven were excluded in this sample).

In order to test our hypotheses, the following predictors were included. **Father's Failure to Provide** was indicated by two dummy-coded variables based on information given by the mother on the child support payments made by the father. The first dummy indicator contrasts full payment with partial or no payment. The second dummy indicator contrasts no payment with partial or full payment. The no-payment category also includes cases in which the mother indicated that she was not entitled to child support payments. Although this may have been due to a shared parenting arrangement, the large share of mothers who reported that they were not entitled to receive child support payments (20 percent) suggests that some of the information on the father's inability to provide was false or based on a misinterpretation. Two indicators of coparenting quality were included that were selected from the "Parent Problem Checklist" (Dadds and Powell 1991). **Coparenting Conflict** was indicated by three items (e.g., "Discussions regarding parenting issues end in fights." Cronbach's Alpha = 0.86). **Coparenting Cooperation** was measured by a single item ("When there is a problem with your child or children: How often do you and the father of your child try to solve the problem together?"). **Maternal Pressure to Take Sides** was indicated by a single item ("My mother tries to get me to take sides against my father."). Although pairfam provides six items indicating the pressure to take sides exerted by both parents (see Thönnissen et al. 2019), the internal consistency for the maternal subscale was very weak (three items; Cronbach's Alpha = 0.48). Hence, we chose the item that most closely addressed the targeted maternal behavior. Except for indicators of family structure and contact frequency, missing information was imputed using the Full Information Maximum Likelihood (FIML) method.

Results

Findings from the KiB Data

The KiB data were used to estimate separate path models for maternal and paternal reports. Due to the lack of suitable indicators, these analyses could not address the provider hypothesis. Path models were estimated within a structural equation modelling framework using Maximum Likelihood Estimation (MLE). Indirect effects were calculated using a product-of-coefficients method (MacKinnon et al. 2002) and bootstrap standard errors with 1000 replicates. Mplus statistical software was used. The findings for the mothers and the fathers are shown in Figs. 9.2 and 9.3. In both models, control variables were included if their association with an outcome in the model was statistically significant at $p \leq 0.20$. For the mothers' report, the child's age was controlled for effects on coparenting conflict and father-child contact. For the fathers' report, the child's gender was controlled for effects on coparenting conflicts, and the child's age and the father's income were controlled for the effects on the father-child contact. To keep the figure parsimonious, these effects of the control variables are not displayed in Figs. 9.2 and 9.3.

As the figures show, both models have an excellent fit to the data, with many overall similarities, but also a few differences. At the same time, these models provide only partial support for our hypotheses. The model estimated for mothers provides evidence for only one significant predictor of low father-child contact. Supporting the resentment hypothesis, negative attributions were linked to low father-child contact. However, this effect was not found to be very strong ($\beta = 0.21$, $p < 0.05$), yielding a low explained variance for low contact ($R^2 = 0.06$). As expected, negative attributions were shown to be strongly linked to coparenting conflict ($\beta = 0.42$, $p < 0.001$), and to explain 18 percent of the variance in coparenting conflict, which was, in turn, linked to mothers' worries about the well-being of their children ($\beta = 0.32$, $p < 0.001$). In addition to coparenting conflict, negative attributions substantially predicted maternal worries ($\beta = 0.45$, $p < .001$). Hence, maternal worries could be well explained in this model ($R^2 = 0.42$). As expected, the model indicated that coparenting conflict partly mediated the effects of negative attributions on maternal worries (indirect effect: $b = 0.15$, $\beta = 0.13$, $p < 0.05$). However, contrary to our assumptions, neither coparenting conflict nor child-related worries were found to predict low contact. Accordingly, there was no significant indirect

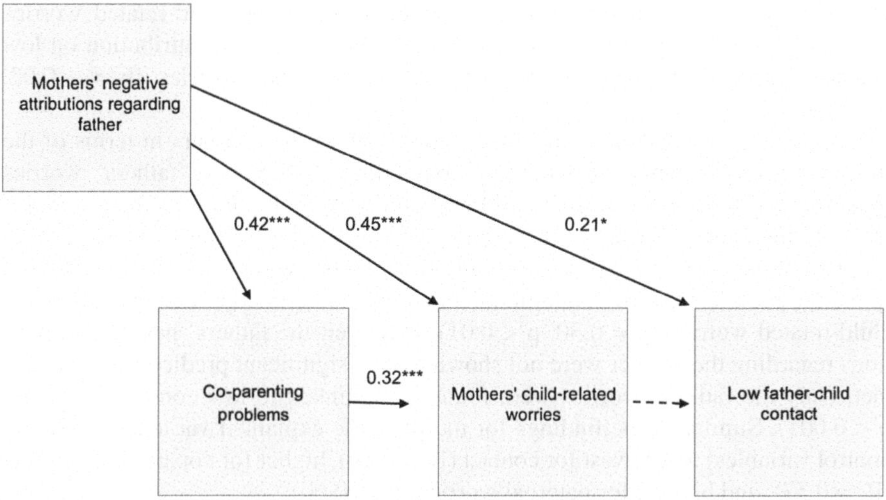

Fig. 9.2 Predictors of low levels of father-child contact. Mothers' perspective
Notes: Data from KiB Study; n = 187 separated mothers; standardized path coefficients. Solid lines indicate significant paths
Model fit: $\chi2 = 6.1$ (9), $p = 0.72$; CFI = 1.0, TLI = 1.0; RMSEA = 0.0

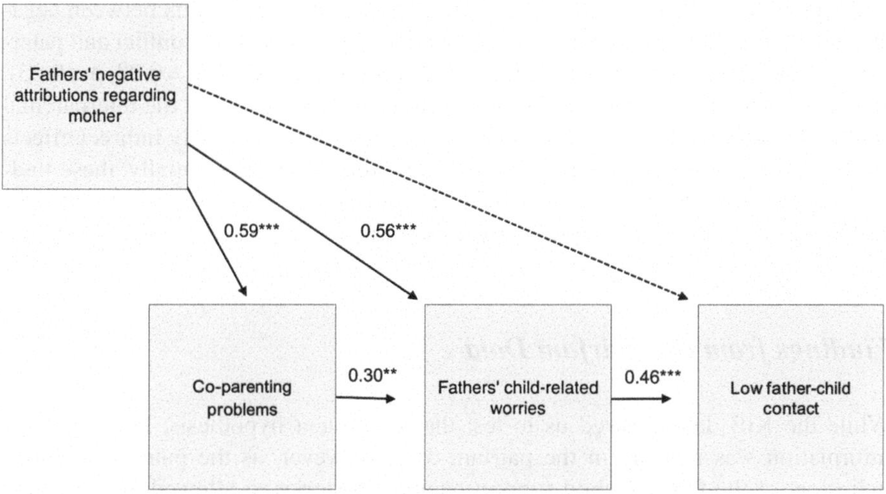

Fig. 9.3 Predictors of low levels of father-child contact. Fathers' perspective
Notes: Data from KiB study; n = 160 separated fathers; standardized path coefficients. Solid lines indicate significant paths
Model fit: $\chi2 = 2.0$ (11), $p = 1.0$; CFI = 1.0, TLI = 1.0; RMSEA = 0.0

effect of coparenting conflict on low contact mediated by child-related worries ($b = -0.04$, $\beta = -0.05$, n.s.), and no indirect effect of negative attribution on low contact mediated by coparenting conflict and maternal worries ($b = -0.02$, $\beta = -0.02$, n.s.).

The findings for fathers were very similar to those for mothers in terms of the links between negative attributions, coparenting conflict, and fathers' worries regarding the well-being of their children (see Fig. 9.3). In line with the results for mothers, the fathers' negative attributions were found to be strongly linked to coparenting conflict ($\beta = 0.59$, $p < 0.001$) and the fathers' worries about their children ($\beta = 0.56$, $p < 0.001$), with an additional direct link between coparenting conflict and child-related worries ($\beta = 0.30$, $p < 0.01$). However, the fathers' negative attributions regarding the mother were not shown to be a significant predictor of low contact. Only the fathers' worries were found to be linked to low contact ($\beta = 0.46$, $p < 0.001$). Similar to the findings for mothers, the explained variance (including control variables) was lowest for contact ($R^2 = 0.16$), higher for coparenting conflict ($R^2 = 0.37$), and highest for paternal worries ($R^2 = 0.60$).

For fathers, unlike for mothers, all of the indirect paths were significant. In line with our hypotheses regarding mediation, the effects of negative attributions on the fathers' worries about their children were significantly mediated by coparenting conflict (indirect effect $b = 0.20$, $\beta = 0.17$, $p < 0.01$). Furthermore, the effects of coparenting conflict on infrequent contact were mediated by child-related worries (indirect effect $b = 0.11$, $\beta = 0.14$, $p < 0.01$). Finally, the indirect link between negative attributions and infrequent contact, mediated by coparenting conflict and paternal worries, proved weak but significant (indirect effect $b = 0.06$, $\beta = 0.08$, $p < 0.05$). Hence, we found some support for the resentment hypothesis and the interparental conflict hypothesis, although both factors were shown to have only indirect effects on the fathers' levels of contact with their children. More substantially, these findings suggest that the fathers were likely to withdraw if they perceived that their children were stressed or caught in loyalty conflicts.

Findings from the Pairfam Data

While the KiB data allowed us to test the resentment hypothesis, the respective information was missing in the pairfam data. However, as the pairfam included indicators of the fathers' child support payment histories, it allowed us to address the provider hypothesis using the two dummy variables described in section "Pairfam data". Furthermore, we were able to draw on additional information regarding the coparenting relationship and to include coparenting cooperation as a likely resource for more frequent contact. Furthermore, the pairfam data provided us with a more conclusive test of maternal gatekeeping, as the data included reports from the children on maternal pressure to take sides; i.e., the mother's attempts to involve the child in an alliance with her against the father. Finally, the pairfam data allowed us to test our hypotheses longitudinally by predicting father-child contact

Table 9.2 Predictors of mediator variables: Standardized beta coefficients from linear regression analysis

	Main predictors or mediators (W7)				
	Child support payment		Coparenting		
	No versus some/full	Full versus. No/some	Conflict	Cooperation	Maternal press. To side (ordinal scale)
Child age	0.034	0.015	−0.205*	−0.069	−0.155+
Child gender (girl)	−0.173*	0.041	0.046	0.029	−0.107
Maternal education	0.010	−0.011	−0.111	0.006	−0.032
No child support payment[a]	–	–	0.082	0.004	0.018
Full child support payment[a]	–	–	−0.017	0.098	0.178+
Coparenting conflict	–	–	–	–	−0.008
Coparenting cooperation	–	–	–	–	−0.113
Maternal pressure to side	–	–	–	–	–
Low father-child contact W7	–	–	–	–	–
Adjusted R^2	0.011	−0.019	0.027	−0.020	0.020

Notes:[a]Child support payment dummy coded; reference category: irregular or only partial payment; the first column of effects on mediators shows coefficients for both dummy variables as dependent variable

Pairfam data (release 8.0.0) from waves 7 and 8, N = 145 separated mothers with child who participated in the child interview; significance: + $p < .10$, * $p < .05$, ** $p < .01$, ** $p < .001$

in wave eight by family dynamics at wave seven (one year earlier), controlling for previous father-child contact.

To shed more light on background factors, we used multiple regression analyses to test the extent to which infrequent father-child contact was linked to demographic factors such as maternal education, child age, and gender. Tables 9.2 and 9.3 present the findings from a series of multiple linear regression analyses based on the sample of separated mothers and their children (n = 146). The predictor variables are shown in rows, and the dependent variables are shown in columns. Based on the model assumptions (Fig. 9.1), we first analyzed the predictors of the explanatory factors assessed in wave seven: child support payments (dummy-coded as described in section "Indicators"), coparenting with two indicators of conflict and cooperation, and maternal pressure to take sides (based on the children's reports). Table 9.3 reports the findings for the predictors of the outcome; i.e., low frequency of contact with the father in wave eight, using four models. Model 1 (M1) included only demographic background factors and child support payments; Model 2 (M2) added both coparenting indicators; Model 3 (M3) added maternal pressure to take sides, and Model (M4) added infrequent contact with the father in wave seven.

Table 9.3 Predictors of infrequent father-child contact: Standardized beta coefficients from linear regression analysis

	M1	M2	M3	M4
Child age	0.014	−0.026	−0.004	0.031
Child gender (girl)	0.019	0.032	0.048	0.020
Maternal education	−0.183*	−0.192*	−0.189*	−0.145*
No child support payment[a]	−0.223*	−0.213*	−0.216*	−0.159+
Full child support payment[a]	−0.046	−0.018	−0.044	−0.101
Coparenting conflict	–	−0.093	−0.092	−0.028
Coparenting cooperation	–	−0.306***	−0.290***	−0.061
Maternal pressure to side	–	–	0.147+	0.143*
Low father-child contact W7	–	–	–	0.506***
Adjusted R^2	0.042	0.129	0.140	0.335

Notes: [a]Child support payment dummy coded; reference category: irregular or only partial payment; the first column of effects on mediators shows coefficients for both dummy variables as dependent variable

Pairfam data (release 8.0.0) from waves 7 and 8, N = 145 separated mothers with child who participated in the child interview; significance: + $p < .10$, * $p < .05$, ** $p < .01$, *** $p < .001$

As Table 9.2 shows, the demographic variables were largely unrelated to the main predictors of the frequency of contact with the father. Only two out of 15 regression coefficients proved significant with one additional marginal effect. Contrary to the assumption that fathers are often more willing to invest in male children, we found that girls were less likely than boys to be receiving no support payments; i.e., that girls were more likely than boys to be receiving at least some payments. However, the likelihood of receiving full versus no or only some child support payments was not found to differ by the child's age or gender. Negative family dynamics were reported more frequently by younger than older children. The findings indicated that coparenting conflicts declined significantly as the children's ages increased, and that older children reported marginally less maternal pressure to take sides than younger children. No other effects of age were found. Maternal education proved insignificant for any of the main predictors or mediators, but was shown to be negatively linked to the child having infrequent contact with the father; i.e., the children of better educated mothers had more frequent contact with their fathers than the children of less educated mothers (see Table 9.3). This effect was found to be robust for all models predicting child contact in wave eight.

Neither the child's age nor gender had any effect on whether the frequency of the child's contact with the father was reduced (see Table 9.3). The results showed that, in addition to maternal education, child support payments mattered, albeit in an unexpected way. We found that the fathers who were paying no child support were less likely to have infrequent contact than the fathers who were paying some or full child support. Indeed, the findings indicated that while 38 percent of the fathers who were paying no child support saw their children several times per week or daily, only 16 percent of those who provided at least some child support had such frequent access to their children (bivariate analysis, $X^2 = 13.95$, df = 5, $p < 0.05$). This effect remained largely unchanged when introducing the mediators, but was attenuated to marginal significance after controlling for the stability of contact. As was found for the maternal reports in the KiB data, coparenting conflict was not shown to be linked to a lower frequency of contact. However, the analysis found that the parents' cooperation in coparenting had a highly significant effect that was not reduced when the maternal pressure to take sides was also included. As expected, we found that higher levels of coparenting cooperation were linked to more frequent contact between the father and the child one year later. However, this effect disappeared in Model 4, which controls for previous contact. Finally, maternal pressure to take sides showed the expected effect. Although the bivariate link between maternal pressure to take sides and the child's later reduced frequency of contact with his/her father ($r = 0.188$, $p < 0.05$) was slightly reduced in the context of the other predictors, it remained significant even when controlling for previous contact ($\beta = 0.143$, $p < 0.05$).

In sum, the pairfam data supported neither the provider hypothesis nor the interparental conflict hypothesis. In fact, our findings on the effects of child support payments were contrary to our assumptions. While coparenting conflict appeared to have no impact on the likelihood of having infrequent contact, our data suggest that coparenting cooperation was significantly linked to later father-child contact, but did not predict changes in contact levels across time when previous contact levels were controlled for. However, some support was found for the maternal gatekeeping hypothesis, since maternal pressure to take sides predicted lower levels of father-child contact, even when controlling for previous contact levels.

Discussion

This study addressed different features of maternal gatekeeping in separated families. As we pointed out, there is considerable conceptual overlap between gatekeeping and the quality of coparenting (e.g., Austin et al. 2013; Cannon et al. 2008). While cooperative coparenting is likely to indicate gate-opening behavior, triangulation/undermining coparenting reflects gate-closing behavior. It has also been argued that protective gatekeeping is a special case of restrictive gatekeeping, whereby one parent is seeking to secure the well-being of the children when s/he perceives that the other parent or a particular visitation schedule puts the children at risk. Moreover, it has been suggested that conflict between parents, and coparenting conflict in particular, is a predictor of gate-closing behaviors and attitudes. Using two different datasets, we were able to investigate the extent to which coparenting quality was linked to protective or restrictive gatekeeping, and whether gatekeeping was, in turn, linked to less frequent father-child contact. The first dataset (KiB) allowed us to include information on the mother's and the father's attitudes toward the other parent as likely predictors of coparenting conflict, protective gatekeeping (i.e., each parent's worries about the children's well-being), and the father's access to his children. Our effort to address not only the mother's but the father's worries about the well-being of their children was intended to shed light on an alternative interpretation of infrequent father-child contact: i.e., that it might be driven by protective withdrawal by the father rather than by maternal gatekeeping. The second dataset (pairfam) provided information on the fathers' child support payments, and allowed us to test the extent to which a father's failure to provide was related to negative and positive features of coparenting, maternal gatekeeping, and father-child contact. Overall, the findings revealed a more differentiated picture of maternal gatekeeping than the one that is often presented in the literature.

First, our findings from the KiB sample highlighted the role of interparental attitudes, as several previous studies have pointed out (Braver and O'Connell 1998; Buchanan et al. 1996; Greif 1997). For mothers as well as for fathers, having a negative view of the other parent was found to be linked to higher levels of coparenting conflict, more child-related worries, and less frequent father-child contact. However, the effects of these views on father-child contact were shown to be much stronger for mothers than for fathers. The findings indicated that while the father's negative attributions regarding the mother were only indirectly related to infrequent contact, the mother's negative attributions had a direct effect, and proved to be the only significant predictor of infrequent father-child contact. Hence, these findings support the *resentment hypothesis*, particularly for mothers.

Second, we found only limited support for the maternal *gatekeeping hypothesis*. According to the KiB data, mothers' child-related worries were not related to infrequent father-child contact. Hence, these data did not confirm our assumption that *protective maternal gatekeeping* played a significant role in determining the father's access to his children. It should be emphasized that the KiB sample overrepresents highly conflicted cases, in which protective gatekeeping might be particularly likely to occur (e.g., Austin 2018; Trinder 2008). Interestingly, however, we found that the father's, and not the mother's worries about the well-being of the children were linked to reduced contact. This suggests that fathers may withdraw under such circumstances rather than being pushed out. Future research should aim to provide more conclusive evidence based on longitudinal data on the causal links between fathers' child-related worries and their tendency to withdraw. Nevertheless, our findings point to the salience of paternal attitudes, and should be of particular interest for custody evaluators.

Although we found no support for the claim that protective gatekeeping has significant effects, the pairfam data on restrictive maternal gatekeeping were in line with our assumptions. A mother's efforts to get her child involved in an alliance against the other parent (pressure to take sides), as reported by the child, were longitudinally linked to the father having less frequent contact with the child, even when controlling for father-child contact in the previous year. However, it should be noted that this effect was weak, which suggests that maternal gatekeeping is not a powerful tool in determining fathers' access to their children. Only two percent of the variance in father-child contact could be explained by maternal restrictive gatekeeping. At the same time, we have to caution that our indicator of restrictive gatekeeping was based on a single item only. More powerful indicators may yield different findings.

Third, the evidence on the *coparenting hypothesis* was similarly mixed. Although coparenting conflict was assumed to provide an important predictor of maternal gatekeeping and of the father having reduced access to his children, only the first part of this assumption found some support. In the KiB data, both parents' reports on coparenting problems were found to be linked to being more worried about their children's well-being, but they did not predict low levels of contact. In the pairfam data, coparenting conflict was not shown to be related to maternal restrictive gatekeeping, as reported by the children, or to contact. Hence, the coparenting hypothesis regarding conflict was not supported by our data. However, for coparenting cooperation, the pairfam data suggested that there was a substantial link to more frequent later contact. These findings are in line with other research that suggested that coparenting cooperation or gate-opening plays a more important role than coparenting conflict in contact frequency (Sobolewski and King 2005). At the same time, we have to point out that this link proved insignificant when controlling previous contact; i.e., positive parental cooperation did not appear to drive positive changes in father-child contact. Hence, any causal interpretation of these findings has to await further evidence on possible reciprocal or more long-term links between coparenting and father-child contact.

Fourth, the pairfam data did not support the provider hypothesis. Instead, they suggested that fathers with frequent access to their children were even less likely to pay child support. This finding is unexpected, and does not conform to current German family law, which requires non-resident parents to make financial payments to cover their children's needs, except in cases in which their earnings cover only their own basic needs. However, it is possible that a father who has particularly close contact with his children provides goods and services instead of financial payments to the mother.

Our data clearly have shortcomings. The KiB study does not yet allow for longitudinal analyses, and while the pairfam study enabled us to analyze longitudinal data in a one-year time frame, longer periods with multiple waves would be preferable. Furthermore, our indicators of coparenting cooperation and maternal pressure to take sides in the pairfam study were weak, since we had to rely on single-item indicators. Finally, neither of these datasets provided all indicators of interest. Nevertheless, both sets of analyses, when seen in a conjunction with each other, add to our knowledge of gatekeeping processes. Overall, since only little of the variance in levels of father-child contact could be explained by the predictors analyzed here, our findings suggest that other factors may be more powerful in encouraging or restricting father-child contact. Further research, preferably based on larger samples, should place features of the interparental dynamic in the larger context of the parents' current living conditions, their involvement with new partners, and the legal framework of parental responsibilities that have been found relevant for fathers' involvement with their children (see Köppen et al. 2018).

Acknowledgments This paper uses data from the German Family Panel pairfam, coordinated by Josef Brüderl, Sonja Drobnič, Karsten Hank, Bernhard Nauck, Franz Neyer, and Sabine Walper. pairfam is funded as long-term project by the German Research Foundation (DFG).

References

Ahrons, C. R. (1981). The continuing coparental relationship between divorced spouses. *American Journal of Orthopsychiatry, 51*(3), 415–428. https://doi.org/10.1111/j.1939-0025.1981.tb01390.x.

Allen, S. M., & Hawkins, A. J. (1999). Maternal gatekeeping: Mothers' beliefs and behaviors that inhibit greater father involvement in family work. *Journal of Marriage and the Family, 61*(1), 199–212. https://doi.org/10.2307/353894.

Altenburger, L. E., Schoppe-Sullivan, S. J., & Dush, C. M. K. (2018). Associations between maternal gatekeeping and fathers' parenting quality. *Journal of Child and Family Studies, 27*(8), 2678–2689. https://doi.org/10.1007/s10826-018-1107-3.

Amato, P. R., Meyers, C. E., & Emery, R. E. (2009). Changes in nonresident father-child contact from 1976 to 2002. *Family Relations, 58*(1), 41–53. https://doi.org/10.1111/j.1741-3729.2008.00533.x.

Amendt, G. (2004). *Scheidungsväter.* [Divorced fathers]. Bremen: Institut für Geschlechts- und Generationenforschung, Universität Bremen.

Arbuckle, J. L. (1996). Full information estimation in the presence of incomplete data. In G. A. Marcoulides & R. E. Schumacker (Eds.), *Advanced structural equation modeling: Issues and techniques* (pp. 243–277). Hillsdale: Erlbaum.

Austin, W. G. (2018). Parental gatekeeping and child custody evaluation: Part III: Protective gatekeeping and the overnights "conundrum". *Journal of Divorce & Remarriage, 59*(5), 429–451. https://doi.org/10.1080/10502556.2018.1454202.

Austin, W. G., Pruett, M. K., Kirkpatrick, H., Flens, J. R., & Gould, J. W. (2013). Parental gatekeeping and child custody/child access evaluation: Part I: Conceptual framework, research, and application. *Family Court Review, 51*(3), 485–501. https://doi.org/10.1111/fcre.12045.

Bastaits, K., Ponnet, K., & Mortelmans, D. (2012). Parenting of divorced fathers and the association with children's self-esteem. *Journal of Youth and Adolescence, 41*(12), 1643–1656. https://doi.org/10.1007/s10964-012-9783-6.

Behrend, K. (2010). *Kindliche Kontaktverweigerung (Umgangsverweigerung) aus psychologischer Sicht: Entwurf einer Typologie.* [Restricted contact from a psychological perspective: A typology]. Saarbrücken: Südwestdeutscher Verlag für Hochschulschriften.

Blesken, K. W. (1998). Der unerwünschte Vater: Zur Psychodynamik der Beziehungsgestaltung nach Trennung und Scheidung. [The unwanted father: The psychodynamic of relationships after separation and divorce]. *Praxis der Kinderpsychologie und Kinderpsychiatrie, 47*, 344–354.

Braver, S. L., & O'Connell, D. (1998). *Divorced dads: Shattering the myths.* New York: Tarcher Putnam.

Brüderl, J., Hank, K., Huinink, J., Nauck, B., Neyer, F. J., Walper, S., et al. (2017). *The German family panel (pairfam).* GESIS data archive, Cologne. ZA5678 data file version 8.0.0. https://doi.org/10.4232/pairfam.5678.8.0.0.

Buchanan, C. M., Maccoby, E. E., & Dornbusch, S. M. (1996). *Adolescents after divorce.* Cambridge: Harvard University Press.

Bundesministerium für Familie, Senioren, Frauen und Jugend. (2013). *Stief- und Patchworkfamilien in Deutschland. Monitor Familienforschung Nr. 31.* [Stepfamilies in Germany]. Berlin: BMFSFJ Referat für Öffentlichkeitsarbeit.

Cannon, E. A., Shoppe-Sullivan, S. J., Mangelsdorf, S. C., Brown, G., & Sokolowski, M. S. (2008). Parent characteristics as antecedents of maternal gatekeeping and fathering behavior. *Family Process, 47*(4), 501–519. https://doi.org/10.1111/j.1545-5300.2008.00268.x.

Carlson, M. J., Van Orman, A. G., & Turner, K. J. (2017). Fathers' investments of money and time across residential contexts. *Journal of Marriage and Family, 79*(1), 10–23. https://doi.org/10.1111/jomf.12324.

Coiro, M. J., & Emery, R. E. (1998). Do marriage problems affect fathering more than mothering? A quantitative and qualitative review. *Clinical Child and Family Psychology Review, 1*(1), 23–40. https://doi.org/10.1023/A:1021896231471.

Coley, R. L., & Medeiros, B. L. (2007). Reciprocal longitudinal relations between nonresident father involvement and adolescent delinquency. *Child Development, 78*, 132–147. https://doi.org/10.1111/j.1467-8624.2007.00989.x.

Dadds, M. R., & Powell, M. B. (1991). The relations of interparental conflict and global marital adjustment to aggression, anxiety, and immaturity in aggressive and nonclinic children. *Journal of Abnormal Child Psychology, 19*(5), 553–567. https://doi.org/10.1007/BF00925820.

Fagan, J., & Barnett, M. (2003). The relationship between maternal gatekeeping, paternal competence, mothers' attitudes about the father role, and father involvement. *Journal of Family Issues, 24*(8), 1020–1043. https://doi.org/10.1177/0192513X03256397.

Fagan, J., & Cherson, M. (2017). Maternal gatekeeping: The associations among facilitation, encouragement, and low-income fathers' engagement with young children. *Journal of Family Issues, 38*(5), 633–653. https://doi.org/10.1177/0192513X15578007.

Feinberg, M. E. (2003). The internal structure and ecological context of coparenting: A framework for research and intervention. *Parenting: Science and Practice, 3*(2), 95–131. https://doi.org/10.1207/S15327922PAR0302_01.

Fincham, F. D., & Bradbury, T. N. (1992). Assessing attributions in marriage: The relationship attribution measure. *Journal of Personality and Social Psychology, 62*(3), 457–468. https://doi.org/10.1037/0022-3514.62.3.457.

Finzi-Dottan, R., & Cohen, O. (2016). Predictors of involvement and warmth of custodial fathers in Israel: Comparison with married and noncustodial divorced fathers. *Family Process, 55*(1), 171–187. https://doi.org/10.1111/famp.12124.

Greif, G. L. (1997). When a divorced father does not visit. In J. Fagan & A. J. Hawkins (Eds.), *Clinical and educational interventions with fathers* (pp. 67–90). Binghamton: Haworth.

Hohmann-Marriott, B. (2011). Coparenting and father involvement in married and unmarried coresident couples. *Journal of Marriage and Family, 73*(1), 296–309. https://doi.org/10.1111/j.1741-3737.2010.00805.x.

Huinink, J., Brüderl, J., Nauck, B., Walper, S., Castiglioni, L., & Feldhaus, M. (2011). Panel analysis of intimate relationships and family dynamics (pairfam): Conceptual framework and design. *Journal of Familiy Research, 23*(1), 77–101.

Jeynes, W. H. (2015). A meta-analysis: The relationship between father involvement and student academic achievement. *Urban Education, 50*(4), 387–423. https://doi.org/10.1177/0042085914525789.

Jia, R., & Schoppe-Sullivan, S. J. (2011). Relations between coparenting and father involvement in families with preschool-age children. *Developmental Psychology, 47*(1), 106–118. https://doi.org/10.1037/a0020802.

Kalmijn, M. (2015). Father-child relations after divorce in four European countries: Patterns and determinants. *Comparative Population Studies, 40*(3), 251–276. https://doi.org/10.12765/CPoS-2015-10en.

King, V., & Sobolewski, J. M. (2006). Nonresident fathers' contributions to adolescent well-being. *Journal of Marriage and Family, 68*(3), 537–557. https://doi.org/10.1111/j.1741-3737.2006.00274.x.

Knight, C. R., & Brinton, M. C. (2017). One egalitarianism or several? Two decades of gender-role attitude change in Europe. *American Journal of Sociology, 122*(5), 1485–1532. https://doi.org/10.1086/689814.

Kodjoe, U. O., & Koeppel, P. (1998). The parental alienation syndrome (PAS). *Der Amtsvormund, 71*(1), 9–26.

Köppen, K., Kreyenfeld, M., & Trappe, H. (2018). Loose ties? Determinants of father–child contact after separation in Germany. *Journal of Marriage and Family, 80*(5), 1163–1175. https://doi.org/10.1111/jomf.12504.

Lamela, D., Figueiredo, B., Bastos, A., & Feinberg, M. (2016). Typologies of post-divorce coparenting and parental well-being, parenting quality and children's psychological adjustment. *Child Psychiatry & Human Development, 47*(5), 716–728. https://doi.org/10.1007/s10578-015-0604-5.

Langmeyer, A. (2015). *Sorgerecht, Coparenting und Kindeswohl: Eltern Sein in nichtehelichen Lebensgemeinschaften*. [Legal custody, co-parenting and child well-being: Being a parent in nonmarital unions]. Wiesbaden: Springer.

MacKinnon, D. P., Lockwood, C. M., Hoffman, J. M., West, S. G., & Sheets, V. (2002). A comparison of methods to test mediation and other intervening variable effects. *Psychological Methods, 7*(1), 83–104. https://doi.org/10.1037/1082-989X.7.1.83.

McClain, L. R., & DeMaris, A. (2013). A better deal for cohabiting fathers? Union status differences in father involvement. *Fathering, 11*(2), 199–220.

Nixon, E., & Hadfield, K. (2018). Construction of single mothers' roles as gatekeepers between children and nonresident fathers. *Journal of Family Issues, 39*(14), 3732–3752. https://doi.org/10.1177/0192513X18796051 .

OECD. (2017). *Dare to Share – Deutschlands Weg zur Partnerschaftlichkeit in Familie und Beruf*. [Dare to share – Germany's pathways into partnership in family and job]. Paris: OECD Publishing.

Poortman, A. R., & van Gaalen, R. (2017). Shared residence after separation: A review and new findings from the Netherlands. *Family Court Review, 55*(4), 531–544. https://doi.org/10.1111/fcre.12302.

Saini, M. A., Drozd, L. M., & Olesen, N. W. (2017). Adaptive and maladaptive gatekeeping behaviors and attitudes: Implications for child outcomes after separation and divorce. *Family Court Review, 55*(2), 260–272. https://doi.org/10.1111/fcre.12276.

Scarborough, W. J., Sin, R., & Risman, B. (2018). Attitudes and the stalled gender revolution: Egalitarianism, traditionalism, and ambivalence from 1977 through 2016. *Gender & Society, 33*(2), 173–200. https://doi.org/10.1177/0891243218809604.

Schnor, C. (2012). Trennungsrisiko von Paaren mit Kindern: Der Einfluss der Religion in West- und Ostdeutschland. [Separation risks of couples with children. The effect of religion in East and West Germany]. In J. Huinink, M. Kreyenfeld, & H. Trappe (Eds.), *Familie und Partnerschaft in Ost- und Westdeutschland: Ähnlich und doch immer noch anders* (Sonderheft 9 der Zeitschrift für Familienforschung) (pp. 229–255). Leverkusen: Verlag Barbara Budrich.

Sobolewski, J. M., & King, V. (2005). The importance of the coparental relationship for nonresident fathers' ties to children. *Journal of Marriage and Family, 67*(5), 1196–1212. https://doi.org/10.1111/j.1741-3737.2005.00210.x.

Statistisches Bundesamt. (2018a). Alleinerziehende in Deutschland 2017. [Single parents in Germany 2017]. Begleitmaterial zur Pressekonferenz am 2. August 2018. Wiesbaden: Statistisches Bundesamt. https://www.destatis.de/DE/Presse/Pressekonferenzen/2018/Alleinerziehende/pressebroschuere-alleinerziehende.pdf?__blob=publicationFile&v=3. Accessed 13 Aug 2019.

Statistisches Bundesamt. (2018b). Deutlich weniger Ehescheidungen im Jahr 2017. [Fewer divorces in 2017]. Pressemitteilung Nr. 251 vom 10.07.2018. Wiesbaden: Statistisches Bundesamt. https://www.destatis.de/DE/PresseService/Presse/Pressemitteilungen/2018/07/PD18_251_12631.html. Accessed 13 Aug 2019.

Statistisches Bundesamt. (2018c). Eheschließungen, Geborene und Gestorbene 2017 nach Kreisen. [Marriages, births and deaths 2017, by districts]. https://www.destatis.de/DE/Publikationen/Thematisch/Bevoelkerung/Bevoelkerungsbewegung/EheschliessungenGeboreneGestorbene5126001177004.pdf?__blob=publicationFile. Accessed 13 Aug 2019.

Stevenson, M. M., Fabricius, W. V., Cookston, J. T., Parke, R. D., Coltrane, S., Braver, S. L., et al. (2014). Marital problems, maternal gatekeeping attitudes, and father-child relationships in adolescence. *Developmental Psychology, 50*(4), 1208–1218. https://doi.org/10.1037/a0035327.

Teubert, D., & Pinquart, M. (2010). The association between coparenting and child adjustment: A meta-analysis. *Parenting: Science and Practice, 10*(4), 286–307. https://doi.org/10.1080/15295192.2010.492040.

Thönnissen, C., Wilhelm, B., Alt, P., Greischel, H., & Walper, S. (2019). Scales manual of the German Family Panel. Waves 1 to 10. Release 10.0). https://www.pairfam.de/fileadmin/

user_upload/uploads/Neu_10/Scales%20Manual%2C%20pairfam%20Release%2010.0.pdf. Accessed 27 Aug 2019.

Trinder, L. (2008). Maternal gate closing and gate opening in postdivorce families. *Journal of Family Issues, 29*(10), 1298–1324. https://doi.org/10.1177/0192513X08315362.

Walper, S. (2006). Das Umgangsrecht im Spiegel psychologischer Forschung. [Physcial custody in light of psychological research]. In Deutscher Familiengerichtstag e. V (Ed.), *Sechzehnter Deutscher Familiengerichtstag vom 14. bis 17. September 2005 in Brühl* (pp. 100–130). Gieseking Verlag: Bielefeld.

Walper, S. (2019). Die Beziehung zum getrennt lebenden Elternteil und das Wohlergehen von Kindern in verschiedenen Betreuungsmodellen. [The relationship with a separated parent and the well being of children in different care arrangements]. In K.-H. Brisch (Ed.), *Bindung, Scheidung, Neubeginn* (pp. 128–151). Stuttgart: Klett-Cotta.

Walper, S., & Beckh, K. (2006). Adolescents' development in high-conflict and separated families: Evidence from a German longitudinal study. In A. Clarke-Stewart & J. Dunn (Eds.), *Families count: Effects on child and adolescent development* (pp. 238–270). Cambridge: Cambridge University Press.

Walper, S., & Krey, M. (2009). Familienbeziehungen nach Trennungen. [Family relations after separation]. In K. Lenz & F. Nestmann (Eds.), *Persönliche Beziehungen* (pp. 715–744). Weinheim: Juventa.

Walper, S., Kruse, J., Noack, P., & Schwarz, B. (2005). Parental separation and adolescents' felt insecurity with mother: Effects of financial hardship, interparental conflict, and maternal parenting in East and West Germany. *Marriage & Family Review, 36*(3–4), 115–145. https://doi.org/10.1300/J002v36n03_07.

Walper, S., Entleitner-Phleps, C., & Langmeyer, A. N. (2020). Shared physical custody after parental separation: Evidence from Germany. In L. Bernardi & D. Mortelmans (Eds.), *Shared Physical Custody: Interdisciplinary theoretical and empirical insights in custody arrangements*. Cham: Springer.

Westphal, S. K., Poortman, A.-R., & Van Der Lippe, T. (2014). Non-resident father-child contact across divorce cohorts: The role of father involvement during marriage. *European Sociological Review, 30*(4), 444–456. https://doi.org/10.1093/esr/jcu050.

Part III
Parent and Child Well-Being

Chapter 10
Loneliness in Children Adapting to Dual Family Life

Inge Pasteels and Kim Bastaits

Introduction

In 2005, Belgium was among the frontrunners in terms of European divorce statistics, with a crude divorce rate of 2.9 per 1000 of the population (Eurostat 2015). The current rate of divorce in Belgium is lower, but this change is mainly due to a higher prevalence of unmarried cohabitation instead of marriage, and to selection effects for more recent marriage cohorts. Thus, the number of relationship break-ups has not decreased. Instead, there has been a shift away from high rates of divorce and toward high rates of separation, especially given that unmarried cohabitations are more likely to break up than marriages. Survey data for Flanders (the northern Dutch-speaking region of Belgium) from the Generations and Gender Programme (Neels et al. 2011) shows that by the age of 45, three out of ten men and four out of ten women had experienced a relationship break-up in the form of either a divorce or a separation (Pasteels et al. 2013). At the same time, unmarried cohabitation has become an acceptable context for bringing up children in Belgium. This evolution has accelerated in recent decades. The proportion of children born to unmarried parents in Belgium increased from 28% in 2000 to 51% in 2015 (ADSEI 2018). Although the statistics show a decrease in the number of divorces, these trends clearly suggest that a substantial percentage of children experience a parental relationship break-up. Lodewijckx (2005) calculated for 2004 that more than 20% of all Flemish children under age 18 had experienced a parental divorce. More recently, Pasteels (2012) calculated that the average number of children involved in each divorce is 1.1. This equates to 25,365 children experiencing a parental divorce in 2017 in Belgium (ADSEI 2018). However, this figure is an underestimation of the total number of children experiencing a parental relationship break-up, as the

I. Pasteels (✉) · K. Bastaits
PXL University of Applied Sciences and Arts, Hasselt, Belgium
e-mail: inge.pasteels@pxl.be

M. Kreyenfeld, H. Trappe (eds.), *Parental Life Courses after Separation and Divorce in Europe*, Life Course Research and Social Policies 12,
https://doi.org/10.1007/978-3-030-44575-1_10

proportion of children with separated parents has been increasing, and is expected to rise in the near future.

Parent-child relationships after divorce or separation develop in the context of single-parent families or new family structures formed through repartnering. Divorce or separation is not an endpoint in a parent's relationship trajectory. Due to repartnering dynamics, a single-parent family can turn into a different kind of family. For Flanders, Audenaert (2018) calculated that two out of ten families with at least one child younger than age 25 living in the household are single-parent families, and that one out of ten of these families is "newly composed," meaning that a parent co-resides with a new partner (and possibly his or her children). A previous Flemish study by Pasteels and Mortelmans (2013) showed that 20% of men and women who divorced between 2001 and 2005 had already begun a relationship with a new partner before leaving the marital home. Two years after living separately from the ex-spouse, 30% of fathers and mothers were living with a new partner, usually in an unmarried cohabitation. Second marriages are rare, and fewer than one in five parents had remarried within 5 years of a divorce. However, newly composed families are common. Four out of ten divorcees were cohabiting with a new partner and at least one child in the household, and one out of ten divorcees (14% of men and 12% of women) were living in a family with biological children and stepchildren. From a child's perspective, one out of four young adults whose parents divorced 20 years previously experienced a second relationship break-up on the mother's or the father's side (Pasteels and Mortelmans 2013).

A relationship break-up – whether in the form of a divorce or a separation – can be considered a complete transition for all of the individuals involved (Amato 2000). Research on the well-being of children after divorce clearly shows that their development can be damaged by the turbulence in their family life (Amato and Keith 1991), but that having satisfying parent-child relationships can mitigate the detrimental effects caused by the divorce itself (Amato and Gillbreth 1999). Overall, researchers agree that a lack of parental communication and the presence of parental conflict are the most damaging factors, and can have a huge impact on a child's well-being after divorce or separation (Amato 2000; Lansford 2009). Accordingly, Belgian divorce law, which is considered to be among the world's most progressive legal frameworks for marital dissolution, changed significantly in 1995 and in 2006. To discourage high-conflict divorces and to encourage positive parent-child relationships, Belgian lawmakers implemented two important legal changes aimed at ensuring continuous ties between parents and children. First, the Act of 13 April 1995 introduced the principle of the joint exercise of parental authority over the person and the property of children after divorce. Second, to facilitate proper parent-child bonds with both parents and to reduce the number of physical custody battles, the Act of 18 July 2006 introduced joint physical custody. Under this law, joint physical custody has to be considered prior to any other residence options if one of the parents requests this arrangement, or if the parents do not indicate any preference regarding the post-marital living arrangements for their children. The intention of the legislation is to improve the well-being of children after their parents divorce by increasing the frequency of their contact with both parents.

This chapter contributes to the literature on children's well-being after divorce by taking a child's perspective on family formation and family dissolution. To perform an in-depth investigation of the impact of divorce or separation on children, it is essential to consider the characteristics of the new family life a child experiences after a relationship break-up, which we refer to here as "dual family life." We strongly believe that after a divorce, the children have to be flexible and adaptive in order to adjust to a dual family life, as they become members of two families.

Children are supposed to be "**flexible**" after parental divorce or separation. Following the relationship break-up, they continue their childhood while living in two households. Decisions about their living arrangements, which are made by their parents or dictated by a judge, determine how much time the children will spend in the mother's and the father's household, and how many times per month the children will move between the two households. Children are expected to be flexible, which in this case means that they have to be prepared to live in two households and to be strong enough to handle the stress of frequently moving between them. In addition, each household may have its own rules and regulations based on the parents' own norms and beliefs about raising children. Children must adjust to the respective household in order to avoid conflicts with family members in daily life. This can be considered yet another way in which children are expected to be flexible after their parents' divorce. Moreover, the composition of each household can differ from day to day or week to week, as (step)siblings might also live all or part of the time in the same household. If the living arrangements differ for children and their (step)siblings, they are continuously confronted with a varying family constellations, because all of the children spend part of their time in the household of their parent and stepparent. This can result in children and their (step)siblings having common (step)parent-child activities, but also in each child spending time solely with his/her own parents and stepparents. The parental behavior of the children's own parents and of their stepparents might change if (step)siblings are present. Accordingly, children have to be flexible enough to adjust to a changing structure (constellation) and a changing culture (norms and beliefs) because of differences between the households of the mother and the father, and possibly because of continuous changes in each of these households.

Moreover, children are supposed to be "**adaptive**" after a parental divorce or separation. The concept of adaptive families refers to the family transitions that occur in the mother's or the father's household, and is also known as the multi-transitions perspective (Amato 2010). Due to repartnering dynamics, family constellations can change over time, and such changes can happen more than once, and on both the mother's and the father's side. Children accompany their parents on their relationship trajectories. Thus, if a child is co-residing with a parent, s/he experiences each start or end of a relationship as a new family transition that changes the family composition in the household. The start of a cohabiting relationship means that a stepparent and, in some cases, stepsiblings enter the household. When a marriage or an unmarried cohabitation dissolves, a stepfamily can disappear from the child's household, and even out of his/her life. The child only undergoes these transitions because adults have made decisions about their relationships. After each family transition, the parent-child relationships have to be re-balanced within the new family structures.

In the current study, we elaborate on the idea that after a parental divorce or separation, children live in adaptive and flexible families, and are forced by the circumstances of the divorce to adjust to a so-called dual family life. This adjustment can be more or less successful. On the one hand, having a dual family life can contribute positively to the social and emotional well-being of a child by adding to the richness of his/her ties and bonds, and by serving as a source of opportunities to improve his/her social, cultural, and economic capital. On the other hand, if a child finds adapting to a dual family life very difficult, s/he risks losing the attachment to his/her family in general, and to his/her parents in particular. Since the feeling of belonging permanently to one unique family or household is lacking, the child may experience loneliness. The child is likely to feel lonely especially if s/he does not subjectively experience his/her parent-child ties as warm and tender; or if the child observes that his/her parents are less supportive or less involved in his/her life than they were when they were still married.

Loneliness is an understudied indicator of children's well-being after divorce, and research into loneliness in children did not start to appear until the 1980s and 1990s. Prior to that time, loneliness in children was not seen as an independent area of research, as there was a belief that children did not experience strong feelings of loneliness (Bullock 1993). Studies in which loneliness was reliably measured in kindergarten and primary schools found that the concept of loneliness had meaning for young children, and could be considered similar to the feeling experienced by older children and adults (Cassidy and Asher 1992; Ladd et al. 1996). Recent studies have shown that one out of five children aged seven to twelve say they are lonely sometimes or often (Qualter et al. 2015), and that four out of five adolescents have experienced feelings of loneliness at some point in time, with one-third describing these feelings as persistent and painful (Houghton et al. 2016). Research on psychological well-being has provided empirical evidence for the association between loneliness during adolescence and the prevalence of depressive feelings (Koenig et al. 1994; Lau et al. 1999). Other studies have shown that loneliness is of major importance as a predictor of life satisfaction in later life (Chipuer et al. 2003; Neto 1993). More recently, Qualter et al. (2010) found that long-lasting peer-related loneliness during childhood acts as an interpersonal stressor that predisposes children to have depressive symptoms in adolescence. Although many studies about children's feelings of loneliness have been conducted in educational settings, teachers and other professionals who interact with children have mentioned several factors that occur outside of the school context as possibly contributing to children's feelings of loneliness, such as family conflict, moving to a new school or neighborhood, losing friends or pets, experiencing the divorce of parents, or experiencing the death of a significant person. We can certainly imagine that the impact of these factors will be increased if they occur simultaneously, as is likely to be the case in the context of a parental divorce.

Based on these observations, we explore how the characteristics of dual family life affects children's feelings of loneliness after a parental divorce. In particular, we examine how the structural characteristics of dual family life influence feelings of loneliness in children after a divorce. The main structural characteristics we consider are the child's living arrangements, the number of family transitions s/he experiences, and the presence of a stepparent in the household of either the mother or the father. These structural characteristics model a child's family life after a parental divorce as a framework within which parent-child relationships are continued and shaped. The number of family transitions a child experiences indicates the level of adaptation that is expected of the child after a divorce; the child's living arrangements reflect the level of flexibility that is required of the child after a divorce; and the presence of a stepparent indicates the levels of adaptation and flexibility that are demanded of the child in the context of a dual family life.

The contribution of the current study is threefold. First, the existing research on loneliness within the family context is sparse. This study adds to our scientific knowledge of children's feelings of loneliness after divorce by exploring the link between these feelings and the aforementioned structural components of dual family life using a gender-inclusive framework in which information about both the maternal and the paternal relationship trajectory of the child is included. Second, examining the complexity of the dual family life that children of divorced or separated parents are dealing with can help professionals who interact with children understand the impact these turbulent family trajectories might have on these children. Third, in the context of policy evaluation research, it is important to gain insights into the mechanisms that underlie children's well-being after divorce in order to provide accurate information to policy-makers and legislators considering future policy measures.

Literature Review

Theoretical Considerations

There are different theoretical approaches to the relationship between dual family life and children's well-being. First, the divorce-stress-adjustment perspective (Amato 2000) suggests that divorce and the subsequent transitions a family might undergo are stressful events that decrease the well-being of all the individuals involved. Second, there is the economic hardship perspective (Amato 1993). This theoretical framework posits that economic resources are greater in households with two cohabiting partners than in single-parent households because of a loss of scale advantages in the latter. Consequently, the reduction in economic resources due to a relationship dissolution might negatively influence a child's well-being, whereas starting a new relationship could lead to a recuperation of lost economic resources, and, in turn, to an increase in the well-being of the children (Amato 2000; Lansford 2009; Leon 2003). A third theoretical approach is the parental resource theory (Thomson and McLanahan 2012; Thomson et al. 1994). In addition to providing economic resources, parents should spend time with their children in order to be involved in their lives. Parental involvement is of major importance for a child's well-being, as the Flemish study by Bastaits et al. showed (2014). From the viewpoint of the parental resource theory, the presence of a stepparent as a second adult in the household in addition to the biological parent can have a different meaning than the two biological parents living together. The economic hardship perspective, by contrast, treats these two family structures as equivalent. In the parental resource framework, examining the quality of (step)parent-child relations and the quality of (ex-)partner relations in different family constellations can be helpful when seeking to understand the subjective experiences of parental resources in specific family structures. In line with the stress-related theory of Amato (2000), the **instability hypothesis** proposed by Fomby and Cherlin (2007) offers the relatively straightforward suggestion that children who experience multiple family transitions may fare worse developmentally. The economic hardship perspective and the parental resource theory are more ambiguous, as they argue that transitions can have different meanings when different types of resources are available, and that the effects of these transitions on children's well-being might vary. We label this overall perspective as the **change hypothesis**, which states that changing family structures can positively or negatively affect children's well-being depending on increasing or decreasing resources.

Prior Findings

There are only a few previous studies on the impact of a parental divorce or of the characteristics of post-divorce family life on loneliness in children. The effects of family characteristics were studied by Quay (1992), who found that living in a single-parent or a stepparent family increases a child's loneliness. Brage et al. (1993) reported that family effectiveness and communication between mothers and adolescents are negatively related to loneliness. Rotenberg (1999) emphasized the link between loneliness in children and perceived levels of parental warmth and parental involvement, but also pointed out that the effects differ between children and adolescents. Similarly, Civitci et al. (2009) found that adolescents with divorced parents are more susceptible to loneliness than adolescents with non-divorced parents.

There are, however, numerous studies on the effects of joint physical custody as a specific post-divorce living arrangement for children, and on the effects of (the number of) post-marital family transitions and the presence of a stepparent in the parent's household on other indicators of the well-being of children. Since the introduction of joint physical custody options, many researchers have focused on the effects of such arrangements on the well-being of children. Systematic literature overviews have been provided by Bauserman (2002, 2012), Nielsen (2011, 2013, 2014, 2015a, b, 2017), and Baude et al. (2016). In a study that focused on the father-child relationship, Bauserman (2012) found that children in joint physical custody arrangements have more qualitative father-child relationships, and that their fathers are more involved than those of children in sole custody arrangements. The meta-analysis by Baude et al. (2016) showed no significant differences between children in joint physical custody and sole (maternal) custody arrangements. Nielsen (2014) conducted a literature review of research on custodial arrangements and concluded that children living in joint physical custody arrangements have better relationships with their parents than those living in sole maternal custody arrangements. For Flanders, the findings of a recent study by Bastaits and Pasteels (2019) indicated that compared with sole custody (by either the mother or father), joint physical custody provides a better framework for shaping the child's relationships with both parents, as it facilitates open communication and mutual support.

With regard to family structure and family transitions, many empirical studies have shown that children living in a single-parent family or a stepfamily are at greater risk of experiencing a decreased level of well-being (for an overview, see Amato 2000; Lansford 2009). Studies that focus on family structure transitions have been carried out by Langton and Berger (2011), Lee and McLanahan (2015), Magnuson and Berger (2009), Robson (2010), and Ryan et al. (2015). Langton and Berger (2011) examined the associations between the family structure and the physical health, behavior, and emotional well-being of adolescents. Their results suggest that adolescents in two-biological-parent families tend to have better outcomes than those in most other family types. Lee and McLanahan (2015) concluded that the transition out of a two-parent family is more negative for a child's development than the transition into a two-parent family. Magnuson and Berger (2009) demonstrated that family structure transitions are associated with increases in behavioral problems, and are marginally associated with decreases in achievement. Robson (2010) showed that transitioning out of a two-parent biological family is associated with reduced happiness, self-esteem, and household income; and that transitioning into a stepfamily is also associated with decreased happiness, even when it is accompanied by an increase in household income. Ryan et al. (2015) found that changes in family structure that occurred early in life – particularly transitions from a two-biological-parent to a single-parent family – predicted increases in behavioral problems. Their findings also indicated that transitioning into a single or a stepparent family mattered more for children of higher-income than lower-income parents; and that for children of higher-income parents, moving into a stepfamily might improve, rather than undermine, behavior. For Flanders, Bastaits et al. (2018) recently found that the well-being of adolescents was lower if their mother was in a less stable partnership situation: i.e., if their mother had never repartnered, was in a LAT (living apart together) relationship, or had been in several relationships since her divorce. The opposite result was found for fathers, as the adolescents' well-being was shown to be lower if their father was in a seemingly stable partnership situation; i.e., if their father had remarried or started living with a new partner since his divorce.

Hypotheses

In this study, we contribute to our existing knowledge by testing the instability hypothesis and the change hypothesis while taking into account three post-divorce family characteristics: the number of family transitions, the presence of a stepparent in the household, and the living arrangements of the children. Since the dual family life experienced by children is the general context of this study, the tests are carried out simultaneously from the father's and the mother's perspective in each model. Based on the previous literature and theoretical frameworks, we propose a set of research hypotheses regarding the loneliness, the flexibility, and the adaptive behavior of children after a parental divorce:

- In line with the instability hypothesis, we expect to find that a greater number of maternal or paternal family transitions is linked to accumulated stress, and therefore leads to increased feelings of loneliness in children (hypothesis 1a).
- Based on the change hypothesis, we do not expect to find that the number of transitions influences a child's loneliness levels, since the current amount of economic and paternal resources may be more important than the number of family transitions experienced in the child's life course (hypothesis 1b).
- In line with the instability hypothesis, we expect to find that the child's level of loneliness increases if a stepparent lives in the household of a parent (either the biological mother or father), since repartnering is a new family transition that can be a stressful experience (hypothesis 2a).
- Based on the change hypothesis, we assume that the amount of economic and parental resources in a family determines the impact of a co-residing stepparent on the well-being of the children, and that this effect can be positive or negative. Since mothers tend to lose more economic scale advantages than fathers, we might expect to observe that the positive effect on children's well-being is stronger if the biological mother repartners. At the same time, we know from previous Flemish research that repartnered fathers are more likely than repartnered mothers to live in a household with stepchildren (Pasteels and Mortelmans 2013). This means that in a household with a repartnered mother, the parental resources will be more likely to benefit the mother's biological child or children. Thus, the negative impact of the presence of a stepparent on the parent-child relationship is likely to be smaller in such a household than in the household of a repartnered father, in which the parental resources are more likely to be shared between stepsiblings. This leads us to formulate the second competing hypothesis: i.e., that the effect of the presence of a stepparent in the household is more positive if the repartnered parent is the mother, and that it decreases feelings of loneliness in children (hypothesis 2b).
- Finally, we explore the effects of living in a joint physical custody on the well-being of children. Based on the instability hypothesis, we expect to find that children who commute between two parental households are at higher risk of experiencing feelings of loneliness (hypothesis 3a).

- However, in line with the change hypothesis, we anticipate that the risk of feeling lonely will be lower for these children because shared residence arrangements are more common in families with greater economic resources, and in which the two parents have equal amounts of time to spend with their children (hypothesis 3b).

Methods and Data

Data

We use data from the multi-actor study "Divorce in Flanders" (DiF) that were collected in 2009 and 2010 by interviewing 6470 (ex-)partners and 1257 children via Computer Assisted Personal Interviews (CAPI). The multi-actor design involved criteria used to select one child (if there were any) for each reference marriage (Mortelmans et al. 2011; Pasteels et al. 2011). For the current study, a subsample of 166 children from 166 broken marriages was selected. Our selection criteria were the age of the child, the living arrangements of the child, and the survey participation of both parents. The age range of the children included in the sample was between ten and 17, because only children in this age group answered specific questions about loneliness. Moreover, the children selected for the sample had been living with at least one of their parents at the time of the interview to allow for comparisons between children living in joint physical custody arrangements and children who were living with either their mother or their father most of the time. The participation in the survey of both parents was necessary to allow us to obtain information about their partnership status at the time of the interview and their relationship trajectory to that point. Based on these selection criteria, the analytical sample contains triadic data for 166 children and both of their parents. Since only the first marriages of heterosexual couples were selected in the DiF study, the parents can always be referred to as the mother and the father.

Variables

The dependent variable included in the analysis is the LLCA peers subscale, which measures children's feelings of loneliness by using 12 items (Goossens and Marcoen 1999).

- I think I have fewer friends than others
- I feel isolated from other people/I feel I don't belong
- I feel excluded by my classmates
- I want to be better integrated in the class group
- Making friends is hard for me

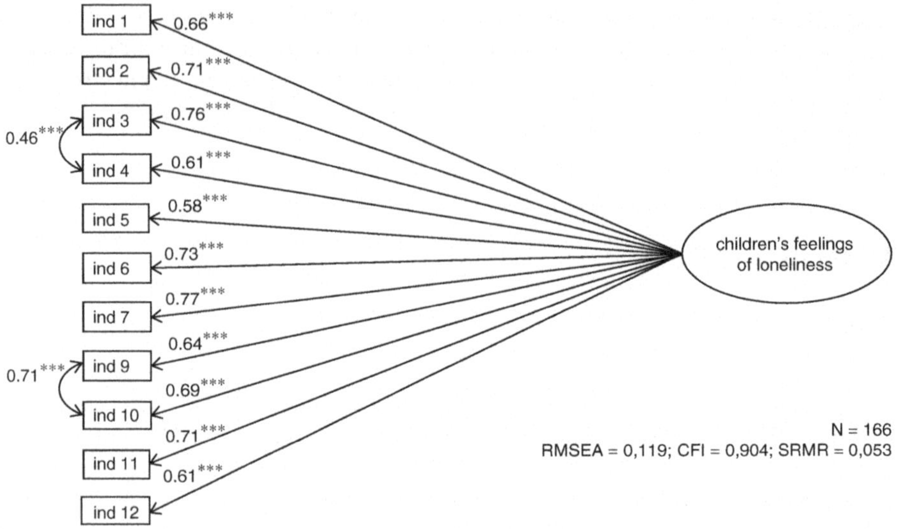

Fig. 10.1 Measurement model for the latent construct of children's feelings of loneliness

- I am afraid the others won't let me join in
- I feel alone at school
- I do not think there is any one friend I can tell everything to
- I feel abandoned by my friends
- I feel left out by my friends
- I feel sad because nobody wants to join in with me
- I feel sad because I have no friends

The children had to indicate on a four-point scale (often, sometimes, rarely, never) how often these statements applied to them. In line with the finding mentioned above that children's loneliness can be measured by using a single-factor structure, a confirmatory factor analysis on the LLCA peers subscale identified a single factor with factor loadings between 0.58 and 0.77 for our analytical sample. In order to improve the fit of this measurement, item eight was excluded from the measurement model and error variances were freed between two pairs of indicators. Items three and four on the one hand and items nine and ten on the other are worded very similarly in Dutch. The goodness of fit statistics show an adequate fit with CF = 0.904 and SRMR = 0.053, as these statistics are greater than 0.9 and less than 0.08, respectively (Brown 2006). The RMSEA of 0.119 is above the cut-off of 0.08, but this goodness of fit indicator may be of minor importance given the small sample size (N = 166), as Hu and Bentler (1999) have suggested. The single factor structure is in line with previous research. Recently, a Belgian study that employed the widely used measurement of children's feelings of loneliness developed by Asher et al. (1984), the Children's Loneliness Scale (CLS), showed that a single-factor structure is superior to alternative solutions proposed in the literature as a valid measurement of loneliness in children (Maes et al. 2017) (Fig. 10.1).

There are three main independent variables. First, there is a measurement of the living arrangements of the child that uses a monthly calendar (Sodermans et al. 2012). Based on the patterns indicated in this calendar by the mother (or father, if the information from the mother was lacking), we created a dummy variable containing information about the living arrangements of the child; i.e., whether the child was in a joint physical custody arrangement. If the proportions of time spent with the mother and with the father were each between 33% and 66%, we categorized the living arrangement as joint physical custody, and scored the dummy variable as one. If the time spent with the mother (father) was more than 66%, and, consequently, the time spent with the father (mother) was less than 33%, the dummy variable was given a score of zero. In addition to the living arrangements of the child, we also considered for both parents the current partnership status and the partnership trajectory up to the time of the interview.

The current partnership status was recoded as a dummy variable, with one indicating that the parent had a co-residential new partner after divorce, and zero indicating that the mother or father was living as a single parent without a new co-residing partner. Information about the partnership histories of both parents was included in the model by using the number of partnership transitions for both parents that the child had experienced. The number of transitions was deduced from the previously published partnership history clusters (Pasteels and Mortelmans 2015). Divorcees who remained single or were only in a LAT relationship after their divorce were classified as having been involved in one transition only. The children of divorcees who remarried or started cohabiting with a new partner after a short or a long period of being single were categorized as having experienced two transitions in the household of either their mother or father. If there was a relationship in the post-marital trajectory that subsequently broke up, resulting in three transitions and multiple relationships after divorce, the number of transitions was recoded as four or more transitions in the mother's or the father's household. The control variables included in the model were the age of the child, the gender of the child, and the educational level of the mother and the father (Table 10.1).

Analytical Strategy

We estimated structural equation models (SEM) for the indicator of loneliness in order to investigate the effects of living in a joint physical custody arrangements and the characteristics of the partnership trajectories of both parents on the child's feelings of loneliness, controlled for the age and the gender of the child and the educational level of the mother and the father. Statistical analyses were conducted with Mplus 6 software (Muthén and Muthén 2010), using ML estimation.

Table 10.1 Descriptive statistics

	Mean	Standard deviation
Number of maternal family transitions	1.86	0.92
Number of paternal family transitions	2.07	1.16
Age of child	13.74	2.14
	Column percent	
Living arrangements		
Joint physical custody	60.8	
Other arrangement	39.2	
New partner of father		
Not living with a new partner	43.5	
Living with a new partner	56.5	
New partner of mother		
Not living with a new partner	53.0	
Living with a new partner	47.0	
Gender of child		
Boy	53.6	
Girl	46.4	
Educational level of father		
Lower-secondary or below	25.0	
Upper-secondary	40.5	
Higher education	34.5	
Educational level of mother		
Lower-secondary or below	16.1	
Upper-secondary	38.1	
Higher education	45.8	

Results

The structural model for the child's feelings of loneliness related to the characteristics of dual family life is presented in Fig. 10.2. This model reveals a good fit (RMSEA = 0.055; CFI = 0.907; SRMR = 0.042). This structural equation model clearly shows that the child's feelings of loneliness are significantly and positively linked with two different characteristics of dual family life, at the $p < 0.01$ (**) and $p < 0.05$ (*) level. For the father, the number of paternal family transitions (0.11) influences the child's feelings of loneliness, with a greater number of family transitions in the father's household leading to increased feelings of loneliness for the child. The father's current partnership status, measured by a dummy variable that indicates whether a new partner is living in the household, has no impact on the child's loneliness. For the mother, the structural equation model reveals the opposite pattern. If the mother and her new partner are co-residing, the child has greater feelings of loneliness than if the mother is single or in a LAT relationship (0.22). The number of family transitions that occur in a maternal household has no impact on the dependent variable. The living arrangements of the child is found to have no

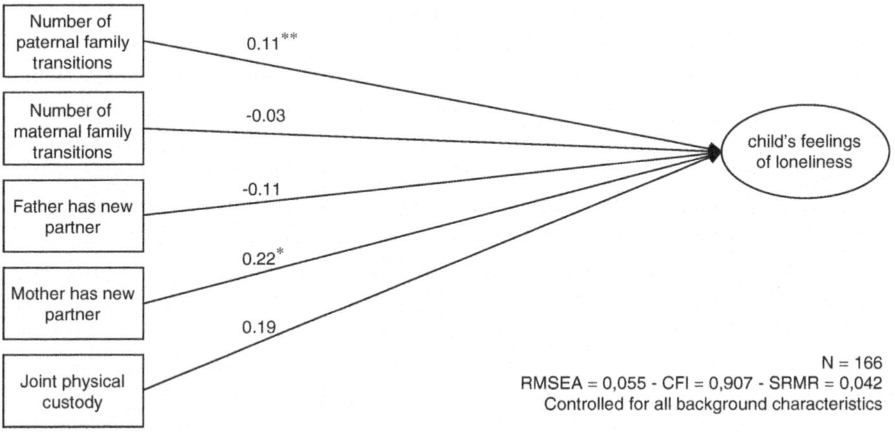

Fig. 10.2 Structural model for children's feelings of loneliness related to the characteristics of dual family life

effect: i.e., living in a joint physical custody arrangement, rather than living primarily with the mother or the father, does not appear to influence the child's feelings of loneliness. The effects of the main independent variables are controlled for the age and the gender of the child and the educational levels of both parents. None of these control variables has a significant effect on the child's feelings of loneliness.

Discussion

In this study, we explored children's feelings of loneliness when adapting to dual family life. The first perspective on the impact of dual family life suggests that children living in joint custody arrangements, as well as children with one or more subsequent stepparents in their family network on either their mother's or their father's side, experience less loneliness. This is assumed to be case because these children may have the subjective feeling of being strongly embedded in their parents' households, or they may forge family ties with multiple people and have increased opportunities to acquire social, cultural, and economic capital. The competing perspective suggests that children living in joint custody arrangements or in newly composed families, including stepfamilies, experience greater feelings of loneliness because a dual family life demands high levels of flexibility and adaptation, and may lead to the loss of their closest emotional bonds.

Using triadic data for 166 children and their mothers and fathers collected in the Divorce in Flanders study, we found that the number of post-divorce family transitions in the household of the father predicts the child's feelings of loneliness. If the father had multiple relationships after his divorce, or had another relationship break-up after the initial divorce, the child's feelings of loneliness were increased. This finding is in line with the instability hypothesis, which states that unstable family structures lead to decreased well-being (hypothesis 1a). By contrast, the number of family transitions in the mother's household was found to have no effect, which means that the change hypothesis (hypothesis 1b) concerning the effects of family transitions on feelings of loneliness in children was confirmed for the mother's side. It appears that the increase in resources associated with a maternal family transition was more important than the number of family transitions in the household.

As a post-marital relationship with a co-residing stepmother was not found to have any effect on a child's loneliness, the instability hypothesis is not supported in terms of the father's situation (hypothesis 2a). With regard to the mother's household, we found evidence to support the instability hypothesis (hypothesis 2a): i.e., the presence of a co-residing new partner in the mother's household increased the child's feelings of loneliness. The change hypothesis (hypothesis 2b), which suggests that the availability of increased economic resources as a result of repartnering is of major importance for the mother, and that parental resources are less frequently distributed among children and their siblings in the mother's household – has to be rejected. By contrast, we conclude that the presence of a co-residing stepfather led to increased feelings of loneliness in the child, which might mean that the new relationship between the biological mother and the stepfather adversely affected the mother-child bond. These findings concerning the impact of family structure on the well-being of children are contrary to those in previous research by Bastaits et al. (2018) based on the same DiF dataset. They found that the child's well-being – measured using self-esteem, life satisfaction, and depression as outcome indicators – was lower if the mother was single, in a LAT relationship, or had several relationships following her divorce; or if the father was sharing a household with a new partner. These opposite results clearly show that feelings of loneliness differ from other indicators of well-being, and are worth exploring.

With regard to living arrangements, we found that whether a child was in a joint physical custody arrangement had no effect on his/her feelings of loneliness. Thus, spending an equivalent amount of time in both the mother's and the father's household did not influence the child's loneliness in a positive or a negative way. Accordingly, our findings suggest that neither the instability hypothesis (hypothesis 3a) nor the change hypothesis can be confirmed (hypothesis 3b). The child's age and gender, as well as the educational levels of both parents, did not have any significant effect on the child's feelings of loneliness. This finding is contrary to the results of Rotenberg's (1999) study, which reported differences between children and adolescents in their feelings of loneliness based on their family context.

Returning to the theoretical frameworks mentioned above, we note that the economic hardship theory suggests that compared with children living in a two-parent household, children living in a single-parent household are always exposed to relative deprivation because they rely on the economic resources of a single household, regardless of whether the adults in the household are the two biological parents or a biological parent and a stepparent. By comparison, the parental resource theory introduces an aspect of parenting that we can label as emotional capital, which is fed by a strong parent-child bond. The idea of emotional capital was already mentioned in early research on loneliness in children. The hypothesis that the emotional capital provided by the family contributes to children's feelings of loneliness was confirmed by Honig and Wittmer (1996), who found that children who were supported, nurtured, and cherished by their family were less likely to be rejected and were more likely to interact positively with their peers. Interpreting changing family structures in terms of a change in emotional capital shows that the change hypothesis on the impact of the presence of a stepparent in the parent's household (hypothesis 2b) can be confirmed, especially if we consider a newly composed maternal family as involving a loss of parental resources that elicits feelings of loneliness in children, instead of as a gain of parental resources, as initially suggested in section "Hypotheses". Similarly, the increased feelings of loneliness evoked by an increasing number of paternal family transitions can be interpreted not only as an instable family structure (hypothesis 1a), but as a decrease in emotional capital, especially if we consider the fact that each time a father's relationship breaks up, the child's stepmother leaves the paternal household.

While this study contributes significantly to the existing literature on the well-being of children after divorce, it does have some limitations. First, we must recognize that only children of divorced people participated in the Divorce in Flanders (DiF) study. Although unmarried cohabitations are more likely to end in a break-up, and this family structure has become an increasingly accepted context for bringing up children, data on the children of separated couples are lacking in this study. Second, although more than 1000 children were interviewed in the DiF study, the analytical sample includes only 166 of them. This attrition was mainly due to non-response, as for most of these children only one parent participated in the study; whereas for the current research, triadic data were required. In addition to unit non-response, item non-response reduced the analytical sample size, as for some respondents, detailed and correct information on the partnership history as well as answers on the loneliness scale were missing. Third, and closely related to the second issue, is the limitation of the analytical model. Due to the small sample size, we did not have the opportunity to include mediating variables, such as parental involvement or the quality of the parent-child relationship. These variables could prove useful in explaining the mixed results for the different indicators of children's well-being. The last limitation concerns the measurement of the children's feelings of loneliness. All of the scales measuring loneliness in children focus primarily on social loneliness, as the items mainly refer to the respondent's wider social network of friends and classmates. Yet in the context of divorce, emotional loneliness, which refers to a bond with a specific person (such as a parent), could be more relevant. However, as we mentioned in the literature section, the existing studies on loneliness in children that primarily measured social loneliness emphasized that poor peer relationships during childhood is a contributory factor for social and emotional loneliness during adulthood, as lonely children may lack opportunities to interact with peers and to learn important skills that can improve their social interactions later in life.

Future research should investigate how feelings of loneliness experienced during childhood after a parental divorce affect people's relationship trajectories and/or subsequent feelings of loneliness during adulthood. Second, in addition to the effects of mediating variables such as parental involvement or parent-child relationship quality, the emotional and social loneliness of parents can be of major importance in understanding the impact of the characteristics of dual family life on loneliness in children. Research on the same DiF dataset has found evidence of an intergenerational effect of feelings of social loneliness; i.e., that parents who feel socially lonely are more likely to have lonely children (Heylen et al. 2013). Unfortunately, a gender-inclusive framework was lacking in this previous study. A study on feelings of loneliness in children adjusting to dual family life that also explores the loneliness of mothers and fathers as clarifying variables could shed light on the intergenerational transition of loneliness after divorce, separately for men and women and their children.

References

ADSEI. (2018). *Algemene Directie Statistiek en Economische Informatie – Thematische Directie Samenleving*. http://statbel.fgov.be/nl/statistieken/cijfers/bevolking. Accessed 25 May 2019.

Amato, P. R. (1993). Children's adjustment to divorce: Theories, hypotheses and empirical support. *Journal of Marriage and the Family, 55*(1), 23–38. https://doi.org/10.2307/352954.

Amato, P. R. (2000). The consequences of divorce for adults and children. *Journal of Marriage and Family, 62*(4), 1269–1287. https://doi.org/10.1111/j.1741-3737.2000.01269.x.

Amato, P. R. (2010). Research on divorce: Continuing trends and new developments. *Journal of Marriage and Family, 72*(3), 650–666. https://doi.org/10.1111/j.1741-3737.2010.00723.x.

Amato, P. R., & Gillbreth, J. (1999). Nonresident fathers and children's well-being: A meta-analysis. *Journal of Marriage and the Family, 61*(3), 557–573. https://doi.org/10.2307/353560.

Amato, P. R., & Keith, B. (1991). Parental divorce and the well-being of children: A meta-analysis. *Psychological Bulletin, 110*(1), 26–46. https://doi.org/10.1037/0033-2909.110.1.26.

Asher, S. R., Hymel, S., & Renshaw, P. D. (1984). Loneliness in children. *Child Development, 55*(4), 1456–1464.

Audenaert, V. (2018). *De samenstelling van het gezin – Fact Sheet Gezinsenquête* [Constellation of the family – Fact Sheet Family Survey]. Brussels: Departement Welzijn, Volksgezondheid en Gezin, Vlaamse Overheid.

Bastaits, K., & Pasteels, I. (2019). Is joint physical custody in the best interests of the child? Parent-child relationships and custodial arrangements. *Journal of Social and Personal Relationships*, Online First. https://doi.org/10.1177/2F0265407519838071.

Bastaits, K., Ponnet, K., & Mortelmans, D. (2014). Do divorced fathers matter? The impact of parenting styles of divorced fathers on the well-being of the child. *Journal of Divorce and Remarriage, 55*(5), 1–27. https://doi.org/10.1080/10502556.2014.920682.

Bastaits, K., Pasteels, I., & Mortelmans, D. (2018). How do post-divorce paternal and maternal family trajectories relate to adolescents' subjective well-being? *Journal of Adolescence, 64*, 98–108. https://doi.org/10.1016/j.adolescence.2018.02.005.

Baude, A., Pearson, J., & Drapeau, S. (2016). Child adjustment in joint physical custody versus sole custody: A meta-analytic review. *Journal of Divorce and Remarriage, 57*(5), 338–360. https://doi.org/10.1080/10502556.2016.1185203.

Bauserman, R. (2002). Child adjustment in joint-custody versus sole-custody arrangements: A meta-analytic review. *Journal of Family Psychology, 16*(1), 91–102. https://doi.org/10.1037//0893-3200.16.1.91.

Bauserman, R. (2012). A meta-analysis of parental satisfaction, adjustment and conflict in joint custody and sole custody following divorce. *Journal of Divorce and Remarriage, 53*(6), 464–488. https://doi.org/10.1080/10502556.2012.682901.

Brage, D., Meredith, W., & Woodward, J. (1993). Correlates of loneliness among Midwestern adolescents. *Adolescence, 28*(111), 685–693.

Brown, T. A. (2006). *Confirmatory factor analysis for applied research*. New York: The Guilford Press. https://doi.org/10.1177/1094428108323758.

Bullock, J. (1993). Children's loneliness and their peer relationships with family and peers. *Family Relations, 42*(1), 46–49. https://doi.org/10.2307/584920.

Cassidy, J., & Asher, S. R. (1992). Loneliness and peer relations in young children. *Child Development, 63*(2), 350–365. https://doi.org/10.1111/j.1467-8624.1992.tb01632.x.

Chipuer, H. M., Bramston, P., & Pretty, G. (2003). Determinants of subjective quality of life among rural adolescents: A developmental perspective. *Social Indicators Research, 61*(1), 79–95. https://doi.org/10.1023/A:1021271831731.

Civitci, N., Civitci, A., & Fiyakali, N. C. (2009). Loneliness and life satisfaction in adolescents with divorced and non-divorced parents. *Educational Sciences: Theory and Practice, 9*(2), 513–525.

Eurostat. (2015). *Crude divorce rate, selected years, 1960–2015 (per 1000 persons)*. http://ec.europa.eu/eurostat/statistics-explained/index.php/File:Crude_divorce_rate,_selected_years,_1960–2015_(per_1_000_persons).png. Accessed 25 May 2019.

Fomby, P., & Cherlin, A. J. (2007). Family instability and child well-being. *American Sociological Review, 72*(2), 181–204. https://doi.org/10.1177/000312240707200203.

Goossens, L., & Marcoen, A. (1999). Relationships during adolescence: Constructive versus negative themes and relational dissatisfaction. *Journal of Adolescence, 22*(1), 65–79. https://doi.org/10.1006/jado.1998.0201.

Heylen, L., Pasteels, I., & Mortelmans, D. (2013). Eenzaamheid over generaties heen? Eenzaamheid bij kinderen na de scheiding van hun ouders. [Loneliness across generations? Loneliness in children after the divorce of their parents]. In I. Pasteels, D. Mortelmans, P. Bracke, K. Matthijs, J. Van Bavel, & C. Van Peer (Eds.), *Scheiden in Meervoud* (pp. 153–158). Leuven: Acco.

Honig, A. S., & Wittmer, D. S. (1996). Helping children become more prosocial: Ideas for classrooms, families, schools, and communities. *Young Children, 51*(2), 62–70.

Houghton, S., Hattie, J., Carroll, A., Wood, L., & Baffour, B. (2016). It hurts to be lonely! Loneliness and positive mental wellbeing in Australian rural and urban adolescents. *Journal of Psychologists and Counsellors in Schools, 26*(1), 52–67. https://doi.org/10.1017/jgc.2016.1.

Hu, L., & Bentler, P. (1999). Cutoff criteria for fit indices in covariance structure analysis: Conventional criteria versus new alternatives. *Structural Equation Modeling, 6*(1), 1–55. https://doi.org/10.1080/10705519909540118.

Koenig, L. J., Isaacs, A. M., & Schwartz, J. A. (1994). Sex differences in adolescent depression and loneliness: Why are boys lonelier if girls are more depressed? *Journal of Research in Personality, 28*(1), 27–43. https://doi.org/10.1006/jrpe.1994.1004.

Ladd, G. W., Kochenderfer, B. J., & Coleman, C. C. (1996). Friendship quality as a predictor of young children's early school adjustment. *Child Development, 67*(3), 1103–1118. https://doi.org/10.1111/j.1467-8624.1996.tb01785.x.

Langton, C. E., & Berger, L. M. (2011). Family structure and adolescent physical health, behavior, and emotional well-being. *Social Service Review, 85*(3), 323–357. https://doi.org/10.1086/661922.

Lansford, J. E. (2009). Parental divorce and children's adjustment. *Perspectives on Psychological Science, 4*(2), 140–152. https://doi.org/10.1111/j.1745-6924.2009.01114.x.

Lau, S., Chan, D. W., & Lau, P. S. (1999). Facets of loneliness and depression among Chinese children and adolescents. *Journal of Social Psychology, 139*(6), 713–729. https://doi.org/10.1080/00224549909598251.

Lee, D., & McLanahan, S. (2015). Family structure transitions and child development: Instability, selection and population heterogeneity. *American Sociological Review, 80*(4), 738–763. https://doi.org/10.1177/0003122415592129.

Leon, K. (2003). Risk and protective factors in young children's adjustment to parental divorce: A review of the research. *Family Relations, 52*(3), 258–270. https://doi.org/10.1111/j.1741-3729.2003.00258.x.

Lodewijckx, E. (2005). *Kinderen en scheiding bij hun ouders in het Vlaams Gewest. Een analyse op basis van Rijksregistergegevens* [Children and the divorce of their parents in Flanders. An analysis of National Register data]. Brussels: Centrum voor Bevolkings- en Gezinsstudies, CBGS-Werkdocument, 7.

Maes, M., Van den Noortgate, W., Vanhalst, J., Beyers, W., & Goossens, L. (2017). The children's loneliness scale: Factor structure and construct validity in Belgian children. *Assessment, 24*(2), 244–251. https://doi.org/10.1177/1073191115605177.

Magnuson, K., & Berger, L. M. (2009). Family structure states and transitions: Associations with children's well-being during middle childhood. *Journal of Marriage and Family, 71*(3), 575–591. https://doi.org/10.1111/j.1741-3737.2009.00620.x.

Mortelmans, D., Pasteels, I., Bracke, P., Matthijs, K., Van Bavel, J., & Van Peer, C. (2011). *Divorce in Flanders. Codebook and questionnaires*. Antwerp: University of Antwerp.

Muthén, L. K., & Muthén, B. O. (2010). *Mplus user's guide* (6th ed.). Los Angeles: Muthén & Muthén. https://doi.org/10.4236/sm.2012.24052.

Neels, K., Van Rossem, R., De Winter, T., & Lauwereys, G. (2011). *GGS Wave 1 Belgium. Sample design* (GGP Belgium Paper Series, 1).

Neto, F. (1993). The satisfaction with life scale: Psychometrics properties in an adolescent sample. *Journal of Youth and Adolescence, 22*(2), 125–134. https://doi.org/10.1007/BF01536648.

Nielsen, L. (2011). Shared parenting after divorce: A review of shared residential parenting research. *Journal of Divorce and Remarriage, 52*(8), 586–609. https://doi.org/10.1080/10502556.2011.619913.

Nielsen, L. (2013). Shared residential custody: Review of the research. *American Journal of Family Law, 27*(1), 123–137.

Nielsen, L. (2014). Shared physical custody: Summary of 40 studies on outcomes for children. *Journal of Divorce and Remarriage, 55*(8), 614–636. https://doi.org/10.1080/10502556.2014.965578.

Nielsen, L. (2015a). Shared physical custody: Does it benefit most children? *Journal of the American Academy of Matrimonial Lawyers, 28*, 79–138.

Nielsen, L. (2015b). Pop goes the woozle: Being misled by research on child custody and parenting plans. *Journal of Divorce and Remarriage, 56*(8), 595–633. https://doi.org/10.1080/10502556.2015.1092349.

Nielsen, L. (2017). Re-examining the research on parental conflict, coparenting, and custody arrangements. *Psychology, Public Policy, and Law, 23*(2), 211–231. https://doi.org/10.1037/law0000109.

Pasteels, I. (2012, May 8). *Nota ter voorbereiding van de Hoorzitting ontwerpdecreet houdende wijziging van het tarief op het recht op verdelingen en gelijkstaande overdrachten* [Report in preparation of the public hearing regarding the draft decree on changing the tariff for divisions and equivalent transfers]. Vlaams Parlement.

Pasteels, I., & Mortelmans, D. (2013). Gescheiden en dan? Herpartneren in Vlaanderen anno 2010 [Divorced, and then? Repartnering in Flanders in 2010]. *Relaties en Nieuwe Gezinnen, 3*(3), 1–66.

Pasteels, I., & Mortelmans, D. (2015). Dyadic analysis of repartnering after divorce: Do children matter? *Journal of Family Research, 10*, 143–164. https://doi.org/10.2307/j.ctvddzmht.11.

Pasteels, I., Mortelmans, D., Bracke, P., Matthijs, K., Van Bavel, J., & Van Peer, C. (2011). *Divorce in Flanders: Methodology*. Antwerp: University of Antwerp.

Pasteels, I., Lodewijckx, E., & Mortelmans, D. (2013). Gezinstransities in de levensloop van mannen en vrouwen. [Family transitions in the life course of men and women]. In M. Corijn & C. Van Peer (Eds.), *Gezinstransities in Vlaanderen [Family transitions in Flanders]* (pp. 37–72). Brussels: Studiedienst van de Vlaamse Regering.

Qualter, P., Brown, S. L., Munn, P., & Rotenberg, K. J. (2010). Childhood loneliness as a predictor of adolescent depressive symptoms: An 8-year longitudinal study. *European Child & Adolescent Psychiatry, 19*(6), 493–501. https://doi.org/10.1007/s00787-009-0059-y.

Qualter, P., Vanhalst, J., Harris, R., Van Roekel, E., Lodder, G., Bangee, M., et al. (2015). Loneliness across the life span. *Perspectives on Psychological Science, 10*(2), 250–264. https://doi.org/10.1177/1745691615568999.

Quay, L. (1992). Personal and family effects on loneliness. *Journal of Applied Developmental Psychology, 13*(1), 97–110. https://doi.org/10.1016/0193-3973(92)90008-6.

Robson, K. (2010). Changes in family structure and the well-being of British children: Evidence from a fifteen-year panel study. *Child Indicators Research, 3*(1), 65–83. https://doi.org/10.1007/s12187-009-9057-3.

Rotenberg, K. J. (1999). Parental antecedents of children's loneliness. In K. J. Rotenberg & S. Hymel (Eds.), *Loneliness in childhood and adolescence* (pp. 176–200). Cambridge: Cambridge University Press. https://doi.org/10.1017/CBO9780511551888.

Ryan, R. M., Markowitz, A. J., & Claessens, A. (2015). Associations between family structure change and child behavior problems: The moderating effect of family income. *Child Development, 86*(1), 112–127. https://doi.org/10.1111/cdev.12283.

Sodermans, A. K., Vanassche, S., Matthijs, K., & Swicegood, G. (2012). Measuring residential arrangements with the residential calendar. *Journal of Family Issues, 35*(1), 125–145. https://doi.org/10.1177/0192513X12464947.

Thomson, E., & McLanahan, S. S. (2012). Reflections on "Family structure and child well-being: Economic resources vs. parental socialization". *Social Forces, 91*(1), 45–53. https://doi.org/10.1093/sf/sos119.

Thomson, E., Hanson, T. L., & McLanahan, S. S. (1994). Family structure and child well-being: Economic resources vs. parental behaviors. *Social Forces, 73*(1), 221–242. https://doi.org/10.1093/sf/73.1.221.

Chapter 11
Paternal Psychological Well-being After Union Dissolution: Does Involved Fatherhood Have a Protective Effect?

Aušra Maslauskaitė and Anja Steinbach

Introduction

While the literature on the extent to which the involvement of a non-resident father can affect a child's developmental outcomes has been expanding (e.g., Elam et al. 2016; Kalmijn 2016; Poortman 2018; Sarkadi et al. 2008), the extent to which a father's engagement level affects his own well-being is an issue that has barely been examined (for an exception, see Waldvogel and Ehlert 2016). The question of whether involved fatherhood has a protective effect on a man's psychological well-being after a union dissolution becomes even more relevant if we consider the recent increase in fathers' involvement in childrearing after divorce or separation (Westphal et al. 2014), and the high or growing rates of family dissolution in many countries (Andersson et al. 2017). In addition, numerous studies conducted in Europe and the US have reported that union dissolution has negative effects on the mental health and well-being of men as well as women (e.g., Brockmann and Klein 2004; Williams and Dunne-Bryant 2006). Some studies have suggested that the magnitude of these effects varies significantly across countries: i.e., the negative effects tend to be weaker in "familialistic" than in "individualistic" countries, and in countries where divorce is more common (Kalmijn 2009). Various individual-level factors that contribute to the reduction in men's well-being after separation or divorce have been analyzed (i.e., income, employment, re-partnering) (Wang and Amato 2000). However, the moderating role of fatherhood in the well-being of men after union dissolution is a topic that has, surprisingly, been under-researched (Amato and Dorius 2010).

A. Maslauskaitė (✉)
Vytautas Magnus University, Kaunas, Lithuania
e-mail: ausra.maslauskaite@vdu.lt

A. Steinbach
University of Duisburg-Essen, Duisburg, Germany

M. Kreyenfeld, H. Trappe (eds.), *Parental Life Courses after Separation and Divorce in Europe*, Life Course Research and Social Policies 12,
https://doi.org/10.1007/978-3-030-44575-1_11

In brief, this chapter examines the effects of non-resident fathers' involvement with their children on two psychological well-being outcomes for men: depressive feelings and overall life satisfaction. We analyze the extent to which fathers' involvement levels – measured by frequency of contact, emotional closeness, payment of child support, and co-parenting relationship quality – are associated with their self-reported psychological well-being. By adopting Amato's (2000) divorce-stress-adjustment perspective and fatherhood identity theory (Marsiglio et al. 2005), we consider the role of paternal resources and the father's family context, as well as the socio-demographic characteristics of the father and the child.

Our analyses are based on the cross-sectional survey "Fathering after Union Dissolution," which was conducted in Lithuania in 2016 (N = 1500) with divorced and separated men who had non-resident children under age 18. Using this database has several advantages. First, the survey has a relatively large sample size and provides detailed measurements on partnership dynamics, the divorce process, the father-child relationship, and father and child characteristics. Moreover, to our knowledge, the dataset is the only one of its kind in the Baltic and the Central and Eastern European countries, where research on the implications of divorce and separation is still in its early stages.

Our study focuses on Lithuania, an EU country characterized by both a high divorce rate and a long tradition of divorce (Maslauskaitė et al. 2015). Divorce expanded rapidly in Lithuania after 1965, following the liberalization of the country's divorce laws. Over the past four decades, the crude divorce rate in Lithuania has fluctuated at around 3.0–3.3 (ibid). Currently, around 35% of children under age of 15 in Lithuania have experienced parental separation – a share that is among the highest in Europe, and that is comparable to values observed in France (35%) and Estonia (36%) (Andersson et al. 2017). The legal framework for divorce in Lithuania does not encourage joint physical custody. After a divorce, the children usually reside with one of the parents, while the non-resident parent receives visitation rights. In 95% of such cases, the children live with their mother (Kudinavičiutė-Michailovienė 2013). The visitation order tends to be based on an oral or a written agreement, and the visitation schedule is not legally binding. Generally, a court intervenes in visitation matters only if a mutual agreement is not reached. Joint physical custody is an exceptionally rare arrangement in Lithuania. In a survey of non-resident fathers, 29% reported meeting with their children at least once a week, and another 37% said they see their children at least once a month. In the majority of cases, these visits did not include overnight stays (Maslauskaitė and Tereškinas 2017). When considering the country context, it should be noted that in Lithuania, discursive and social policy shifts in fatherhood-related issues are occurring that place more weight on paternal involvement in childrearing. Lithuania could also be characterized as a familialistic society, as family ties play a substantial role in the provision of social support in the country (Stankuniene and Maslauskaite 2008).

This chapter contributes to the literature in several ways. First, it adds empirical evidence on the role of paternal involvement in fathers' adjustment to divorce or separation, an issue that currently remains under-researched. Second, it makes a theoretical contribution by building on the divorce-stress-adjustment perspective

(DSA) (Amato 2000) and the fatherhood identity framework (Marsiglio et al. 2005). Previous studies that examined divorce stress using the coping perspective did not explicitly consider the specifics of non-resident fathers' adjustment to union dissolution. In addition, by integrating paternal involvement and the father-child bond, the interpersonal resources that moderate men's adjustment to divorce can be expanded beyond the kin, friendship, or re-partnering relationships. Third, evidence is presented from an Eastern European region that is covered far less in the literature on divorce outcomes than Western European countries or the United States.

The remainder of this chapter is structured as follows. First, we lay out our theoretical considerations regarding the effects of fathers' involvement with their children on their mental health and well-being. In the next section, we provide an overview of the previous empirical research and develop our hypotheses. After describing our data and methods, we present our bivariate descriptive findings as well as multiple results of linear regression models. We conclude with a discussion of our findings, the limitations of the data, and perspectives for future research.

Theoretical Framework

Our theoretical framework draws on Amato's (2000) divorce-stress-adjustment perspective (DSA), fatherhood identity theory (Marsiglio and Roy 2013; Marsiglio et al. 2005), and the paternal involvement framework (Pleck 2010b). The DSA perspective is based on stress and coping theories (Hill 1949; McCubbin et al. 1982), and combines various elements of the stress framework. Overall, the DSA perspective suggests that divorce or union dissolution sets in motion numerous stressors, such as the loss of emotional support, conflict with the ex-partner, the transition to sole parenting or the loss of child custody, downward economic mobility, and pressure to move out of the family home. Stressors that the DSA perspective labels as mediators have detrimental effects on the well-being of ex-spouses. However, even though many people who divorce do not fully recover or experience chronic stress for long periods of time, others adjust to being divorced and might even return to the level of well-being they experienced before the dissolution of the union (Amato 2000).

Accordingly, successful forms of adjustment, such as the development of new roles and identities, are indicated by the absence of psychological, behavioral, and health problems. The length of the ex-spouses' processing intervals and their adjustment levels depend on moderating or protective factors "which act as shock absorbers and weaken the links between divorce related events and people's experience of stress" (Amato 2000: 1272). Furthermore, the DSA perspective distinguishes between individual resources, such as coping and social skills; structural resources, like employment and education; and interpersonal resources that come from kin and friendship networks, but also from new partnership relationships. Although the DSA perspective does not explicitly include the non-resident father-child relationship among the moderating factors, it is likely that these relationships help to buffer the disruptive life changes linked to divorce or separation, and thus contribute positively to psychological well-being.

Complementing the DSA perspective, the fatherhood identity theory addresses the gender-specific challenges experienced by fathers when adjusting to divorce or separation. As fatherhood identity theory articulates the processes through which a man constructs his role as a father, it helps to explain how the changes in childrearing arrangements that occur in a divorce or separation affect paternal well-being. According to the identity theory, a father's identity is bound up with perpetually processing the meaning of paternal status and role assignment (Marsiglio and Roy 2013). A man creates and recreates his identity as a father through the constant flux of fathering practices that shape his everyday life. The self-crafted dynamic narrative of a father's identity guides his behavior and feelings, and is situated in a proximal context (family, neighborhood environment), but is also maintained through the broader culture and institutions (Marsiglio et al. 2005).

As divorce or separation triggers changes in fathering practices, it can challenge a father's identity. Thus, a partnership break-up reshapes the proximal context of fathering: living in separate households requires a father and his child to establish new routines in their relationship. Since in many cases this happens in a context that is characterized by conflict and disagreement, the stress related to changes in the father's identity might intensify. Potential conflict with the child's mother increases the likelihood of maternal "gatekeeping" (Allen and Hawkins 1999), and might result in additional constraints on a man's participation in childrearing – or, in extreme cases, in the father's withdrawal from having a relationship with his child.

The successful restoration of a man's identity as a father after a divorce or separation is also relevant for his well-being, as there is a culturally synchronous link between masculinity and fatherhood. In the cultural script of normative masculinity, fatherhood is an essential narrative element (Pleck 2010a). In contemporary societies, fatherhood is associated with diverse discursive notions and practices, such as involved fatherhood or a more traditionally oriented role of the father as provider. Nonetheless, fatherhood remains a relevant constituent of masculine identity. Engaging in everyday fathering practices affords men a general sense of meaning and purpose in life, and signals the fulfilment of cultural expectations for masculine behavior. Thus, renegotiating paternal identity after a divorce or separation can be stressful, which should in turn have an impact on a father's psychological well-being.

Identity-related challenges also indirectly affect other life domains, which can, in turn, influence a father's psychological well-being. A desire to comply with the social norms of fatherhood can motivate a man to engage in socially acceptable behavior like working, and to avoid "risky behavior" like binge drinking or using illicit drugs (Edin et al. 2004). As we mentioned above, fatherhood identity theory posits that a father's identity is (re-)created through a wide range of related practices, which could be conceptualized as paternal involvement. The literature has defined paternal involvement as attitudes and behavior that "promote interaction and healthy relationships with the child" (Ihinger-Tallman et al. 1995: 58). Although many attempts to operationalize paternal involvement have been made, one of the most widely used concepts distinguishes between three components (Lamb and

Tamis-Lemonda 2004; Lamb et al. 1987): accessibility, engagement, and responsibility. *Accessibility* indicates the time a father spends with his children; *engagement* refers to the quality of the father-child relationship and activities that contribute to child development (Pleck 2010b); and *responsibility* refers to the father's role not only in meeting the material needs of and securing resources for his children, but in "taking initiative and monitoring what is needed" (Pleck 2010b: 66).

In discussing the association between the well-being of non-resident fathers and their involvement with their children, it is also important to consider social selection. Having certain personality traits and social characteristics that elevate the risk of separation or divorce can also be associated with a father being less involved with his children and having lower levels of adjustment and well-being. For example, it has been shown that in the U.S. context, men who are less educated have a higher divorce risk (Teachman 2002) and are generally less involved fathers than highly educated men, as they tend to provide less financial support and spend less time with their children (Stykes et al. 2013). There is also evidence that less educated men have lower levels of psychological well-being (Courtenay 2003). Therefore, our findings on the association between paternal involvement and psychological well-being should be interpreted with caution.

Previous Empirical Findings and Hypotheses

Divorce and Well-being Although several studies have found that divorce has a negative effect on fathers' well-being (e.g., Amato 2010; Williams and Dunne-Bryant 2006), there is also evidence that leaving an unhappy marriage is better than staying in it (Hawkins and Booth 2005; Waite et al. 2009). Additionally, several factors have been found to moderate the association between divorce and well-being. A break-up that involves younger children is often associated with very high stress levels, and can lead to secondary stressors like parenting strain, economic strain, and co-parenting issues (Williams and Dunne-Bryant 2006). Meanwhile, higher levels of adjustment to divorce and well-being have been shown to be positively associated with education and employment (for an overview, see Amato 2000, 2010; Härkönen 2014). Adjustment levels may also be influenced by the nature of the previous marriage. For example, ending a high-conflict marriage appears to have less detrimental effects on psychological well-being than ending a low-conflict marriage (Wang and Amato 2000). Re-partnering has been identified as another moderating factor in the divorce adjustment process (Amato 2000, 2010). Embracing new family roles (e.g., as a partner or as a partner/father to new biological or stepchildren) can serve as a source of emotional support and improve a father's psychological well-being (Wang and Amato 2000).

Fatherhood and Well-being Previous empirical findings suggest that the association between fatherhood and well-being is not straightforward. While some studies have found that being a father is positively associated with psychological and physical health (Helbig et al. 2006; Knoester and Eggebeen 2006), others have reported that the mental health of fathers suffers, especially during the early parenting period (Evenson and Simon 2005; Giallo et al. 2012). One potential explanation for these inconsistent results is that selection effects on parenthood are at work (Kalucza et al. 2015). Another possible factor is that the effects of fatherhood on a man's well-being depend on his marital and residential context (Eggebeen and Knoester 2001), with a stepfather or non-resident biological father being more likely to have poor outcomes than a co-resident biological father. However, all of those studies compared fathers with childless men, without differentiating between the various contexts of fatherhood.

As we mentioned above, there is plenty of empirical evidence suggesting that children with involved fathers have more positive outcomes (e.g., Choi et al. 2014; Sarkadi et al. 2008). Researchers have also recognized that the quality of the relationship between the non-resident father and his children is more important than the simple frequency of contact (Amato and Gilbreth 1999; Whiteside and Becker 2000). These findings might apply to the well-being of fathers, too. The paper that comes closest to answering this question is by Knoester et al. (2007), who used data from the first two waves of the Fragile Families Study to examine how changes in commitments to fathering in different family contexts are related to changes in fathers' well-being over a 1-year period. They found that changes in fathers' attitudes towards and engagement with their children between birth and 1 year were generally associated with small but significant improvements in their well-being with respect to health, depression, substance abuse, religious conviction, and paid labor; but also that increased paternal engagement was linked to lower work hours, presumably due to time demands (Knoester et al. 2007).

Non-resident Father's Involvement and Well-being The only existing study that relates to our research question examined the association between different contemporary forms of fatherhood (biological fathers, stepfathers, adoptive fathers, and foster fathers) and paternal psychological well-being (chronic stress, life satisfaction, and psychological distress) (Waldvogel and Ehlert 2016). The main finding of this study was that biological fathers who were living with the mother of their children had higher levels of well-being than other types of fathers (such as single, non-resident fathers or stepfathers). Even after controlling for several sociodemographic characteristics, the results indicated that fathers who were separated or divorced had the worst outcomes on multiple dimensions of psychological well-being. The findings further suggested that maintaining regular contact with their non-resident children seemed to protect divorced and separated fathers from negative outcomes. However, after controlling for contact frequency, the psychological well-being of separated fathers was still found to be worse than that of other kinds of fathers. The authors argued that one potential explanation for this result is that although most of the separated or divorced fathers had regular contact with their non-resident children, they were significantly less involved in day-to-day childcare activities than fathers in stable families: "Thus, regular contact within the limits of visitation arrangements may not be sufficiently rewarding to compensate for the emotional costs of family separation, meaning that these fathers might still feel burdened by their lack of involvement in everyday childcare" (Waldvogel and Ehlert 2016: 12).

A number of studies have shown that there is a growing cultural expectation that non-resident fathers become more involved in their children's lives economically and socially. There is also evidence that over the past few decades, this shift in attitudes has led to a substantial increase in father-child contact after a parental break-up (Amato et al. 2009). Moreover, in addition to having more frequent contact with their non-resident children, it appears that fathers have become more conscientious about paying child support (Amato et al. 2009). Thus, the standards of active fatherhood seem to have risen not only for men who are in a partnership with the mother of their children, but for men who are divorced.

Given the evidence that men with higher educational levels provide more regular support for their children after a parental dissolution than men with less education (Schnor et al. 2017), education is an important overall factor to be considered in the analyses. Likewise, there is evidence that poor fathers are more likely than higher-income fathers to lose contact with their children (Skevik 2006). This could be because poor fathers who live farther away after the parental break-up do not have the resources to stay in contact (Dommermuth 2016), or because poor fathers have fewer resources to spend on their children when they see them. So-called "recreational fatherhood" – i.e., taking children to participate in leisure or "Disneyland" activities, such as going out to restaurants, movies, or sporting events – requires resources that men who are struggling financially do not possess (Amato and Dorius 2010; Stewart 1999).

Similarly, re-partnering and founding a new family with additional children could have an impact on a father's involvement with his children from a previous partnership. However, the results of studies that have examined whether this is the case are not consistent. Some authors have found that re-partnered fathers "swap" their older children for their new children (Manning and Smock 2000), or are less involved with their older children because of the time constraints and financial and emotional demands that come with having two families (Manning et al. 2003; Swiss and Le Bourdais 2009). Others have argued that re-partnering facilitates paternal involvement, either because having a new partner releases a man from household duties, and thus allows him to intensify his commitment to his children (Hetherington 2006); or because it signals a man's attachment to traditional family customs and duties (Cooksey and Craig 1998).

Against this background, the association between custody arrangements and paternal well-being should be taken into account. Compared to other divorced parents, parents with joint physical custody (JPC) often report being more satisfied with their situation (Bergström et al. 2014; Cashmore et al. 2010), feeling less time pressure (Van der Heijden et al. 2016), and having more time for both leisure time activities and labor force participation (Botterman et al. 2015). One study from the U.S. has shown that JPC parents are also in better physical and emotional health than parents with sole physical custody (Melli and Brown 2008). However, another study from Belgium found no direct association between custody status and parental subjective well-being (Sodermans et al. 2015).

The divorce-stress-adjustment perspective (Amato 2010) states that adjustment to divorce, as indicated by, for example, the level of psychological well-being, is moderated by interpersonal resources. Following father identity theory, we argue that non-resident father-child relationships constitute an important element of interpersonal resources, and, thus, that the father-child bond plays an essential role in moderating divorce-related stress. Based on the theoretical considerations and previous findings mentioned above, we hypothesize that higher levels of paternal involvement in all three components (accessibility, engagement, and responsibility) contribute positively to the psychological well-being of non-resident fathers (*Hypothesis 1*). Furthermore, based on the results reported by Waldvogel and Ehlert (2016), we expect to find that out of all the components of paternal involvement, engagement has the clearest positive effect on paternal well-being, because it reflects the qualitative side of the relationship (*Hypothesis 2*). In addition, we argue that psychological well-being is associated with the interpersonal resources linked to a man's family trajectory after divorce or separation. Accordingly, our next hypothesis states that having a higher level of psychological well-being could be explained by a man's family context after divorce or separation. Therefore, we expect to find that re-partnered fathers are better adjusted than single fathers, and thus have elevated levels of psychological well-being (*Hypothesis 3*).

Data and Methods

Data and Analytical Sample

We used data derived from the cross-sectional survey "Fathering after Union Dissolution," which was conducted in Lithuania in 2016. The primary unit in the sample was a male respondent with non-resident children under the age of 18 from a previous marriage or cohabiting union. The sample was obtained using multi-stage stratified sampling methods. In the first stage, the sample was stratified by all ten administrative districts in Lithuania, while distinguishing between the largest towns in the district and other urban and rural areas. The size of each stratum was set proportionally to the distribution of the male population aged 25–54. In the second stage, we applied a random sampling procedure. The final sample consisted of 1505 respondents. Face-to-face interviews with the respondents were conducted in their homes using a standardized questionnaire. Since we excluded from these analyses men who had never shared a household with their children, our effective sample included 1225 non-resident fathers who were not the primary custodians of their children.

The survey recorded information on a wide range of themes related to the men's life course events (partnership and fertility histories were recorded on a calendar-based information), including information on the divorce process and the post-divorce relationship with the child's mother, the respondents' subjective and psychological well-being, payment of child support, levels and types of father-child contact, father-child relationship characteristics, current partnerships, and socio-demographic and structural well-being indicators. Baltic Survey Ltd. conducted the sampling and fieldwork. Up to the present time, this dataset remains unique, as it contains very detailed information on post-divorce fathers in Lithuania; and is, to our knowledge, the only dataset of its kind in the Baltic and Eastern European countries.

Variables

We employed two indicators of psychological well-being. First, we measured *depressive feelings* using the Center for Epidemiological Studies Depression Scale (CES-D 8 scale) (Radloff 1977). The CES-D 8 is a self-reported inventory of seven emotional states indicating depression that the respondent may have experienced during the week before the interview. Each item was measured on a four-point frequency scale with values ranging from one (never or almost never) to four (very often or almost all the time). From these items, we composed an index summary variable. The values ranged from one to 22, with lower values indicating the absence of depressive feelings. The second dependent variable was *general life satisfaction*, measured by the Cantril ladder (Cantril 1965) with values between one (complete dissatisfaction with life) and ten (complete satisfaction with life).

Based on our theoretical model, the existing findings, and our hypotheses, we considered three sets of independent variables. The first set included four measures of *paternal involvement*. (1) We used an indicator of non-resident father and child face-to-face *contact frequency* in the year preceding the interview. The variable indicated the accessibility component of paternal involvement, and ranged from one (no contact) to six (contact at least once a week). (2) In addition, we considered the father's assessment of the *quality of his relationship with the child*. This variable approximated the engagement component of paternal involvement. The variable ranged from one to five, with low values indicating poor relationship quality. (3) We also included an indicator on the *co-parenting relationship*; i.e., the father's subjective perception of the quality of his relationship with the child's mother. The quality of co-parenting was measured on a five-point scale, with higher values indicating higher quality. (4) The last variable on paternal involvement was *child support payments*. We used a dichotomous variable indicating the payment (=1) or the non-payment (=0) of child support in the year preceding the interview. The last two variables expressed the responsibility component of paternal involvement.

Following our theoretical model, we also took into account *a father's individual resources* that might facilitate psychological well-being after separation. First, we used an *education* variable with three categories: below upper secondary (low, ISCED 0-2), upper secondary (middle, ISECD 3-4), and tertiary (high, ISCED

6-8).[1] Next, we included a variable on *material living conditions* with values ranging from one to five, with low values indicating material deprivation ("I lack money even for food."), and high values indicating material sufficiency ("I can afford all I want."). In addition, we incorporated a variable on the father's family context. Three *living situations* were distinguished: living with a new partner but without (new) children, living with a new partner and with (new) children (stepchildren or new biological children), and living without a partner (=single).

For our controls, we included several variables. Time is a relevant factor in the adjustment process. Thus, we used a variable that measures *time since union dissolution* (in years). We also included a variable on *divorce conflict*, because experiencing a higher level of conflict in the process of divorce might affect a man's levels of adjustment to divorce and post-separation well-being. Divorce conflict was measured on a 10-point scale, with lower values indicating an absence of conflict (=1), and the highest value indicating extensive conflict (=10). Based on the existing evidence, we incorporated additional controls, such as the *father's age*, the *child's age,* and the *child's sex*. If a father had multiple children, we only considered the first child from the dissolved union. However, the majority of the sample (80%) reported having only one child. Descriptive information on all of the variables is provided in Table 11.1.

We performed multiple stepwise OLS-regression analyses for each of the two paternal psychological well-being outcomes (general life satisfaction and depressive feelings) separately. For each outcome, we included in the first model only the set of independent variables that measure paternal involvement. In the second model, we added the father's resources. In the third model, we added the variable on the father's living situation. The fourth and last model presents the results with all of the control variables included. The results of tests of multicollinearity were satisfactory (statistics for tolerance are above 0.4 and VIF below 2.5). Given the different measurement scales of some explanatory variables, we decided to test the regression models with standardized variables; however, the statistically significant predictors remained the same as those identified in the models with the unstandardized variables.

Results

Table 11.2 shows the results of the regression analysis with father's *general life satisfaction* as the outcome variable. Controlling only for paternal involvement (Model 1), we observe that general life satisfaction is significantly associated only with the quality of the father-child relationship and child support payments. Thus, the fathers who reported having positive feelings about the quality of their relationship with a non-resident child also scored higher on general life satisfaction. In

[1] ISCED 2011 category five does not exist in the Lithuanian education system.

Table 11.1 Descriptive sample statistics. Column percent and means (standard errors)[a]

	Column percent	Means (standard error)
Paternal psychological well-being		
Depressive feelings (1–22)		3.8 (0.09)
General life satisfaction (1–10)		2.1 (0.05)
Paternal involvement		
Frequency of contact with the child (1–6)		4.2 (0.03)
Quality of the relationship with the child (1–5)		3.5 (1.06)
Quality of the co-parenting relationship (1–5)		3.0 (0.03)
Child support payment: yes	80.0	
Paternal resources		
Education (ISCED)		
Education: low	46.6	
Education: middle	31.0	
Education: high	22.4	
Material living conditions (1–5)		2.9 (0.02)
Paternal living situation		
Re-partnered without children	18.8	
Re-partnered with children	29.0	
Single	52.2	
Controls		
Time since union dissolution (years)		5.3 (0.10)
Divorce conflict (1–10)		6.5 (0.06)
Father's age (years)		37.6 (0.19)
Child's age (years)		10.6 (0.14)
Child's sex: female	47.3	
Number of subjects	1225	

Source: Fathering after Union Dissolution in Lithuania, 2016
Notes: [a]The sample statistics are not weighted

addition, the fathers who indicated they were paying child support had better psychological outcomes, as measured by general life satisfaction, than the fathers who indicated they were not paying for their child's maintenance. Furthermore, the quality of the co-parenting relationship is shown to be positively linked to the father's general life satisfaction. Contrary to our expectations, we find that the frequency of a father's contact with his child did not contribute to his overall life satisfaction.

In addition to paternal involvement, Model 2 in Table 11.2 includes explanatory variables on paternal resources. The significant effects of paying child support and the quality of co-parenting disappeared after adding variables on education and material living conditions. Thus, it appears that resources mediated the effects of these two dimensions of paternal involvement on a father's general life satisfaction. Having a higher educational level and better material living conditions enabled fathers to pay child maintenance and to develop a positive co-parental relationship

Table 11.2 OLS regression results for father's general life satisfaction, unstandardized beta-coefficients, std. errors

	Model 1		Model 2		Model 3		Model 4	
	b	Std. errors	b	Std. errors	b	Std. errors	b	Std. errors
Paternal involvement								
Frequency of contact with the child (1–6)	−0.04	(0.05)	−0.04	(0.04)	−0.01	(0.04)	0.01	(0.07)
Quality of the relationship with the child (1–5)	0.41***	(0.08)	0.25***	(0.07)	0.22***	(0.07)	0.24***	(0.07)
Quality of the co-parenting relationship (1–5)	0.12*	(0.06)	0.07	(0.06)	0.06	(0.05)	0.05	(0.05)
Child support payment (ref. yes)	0.59***	(0.18)	0.14	(0.17)	0.01	(0.16)	0.01	(0.16)
Paternal resources								
Education (ref. high):								
Middle			−0.22	(0.15)	−0.09	(0.14)	−0.12	(0.14)
Low			−0.58***	(0.15)	−0.37***	(0.14)	−0.42***	(0.14)
Material living conditions (1–5)			0.76***	(0.07)	0.66***	(0.06)	0.67***	(0.06)
Paternal living situation (ref. single)								
Re-partnered without children					1.45***	(0.12)	1.45***	(0.12)
Re-partnered with children					1.57***	(0.14)	1.52***	(0.15)
Controls								
Time after union dissolution							0.05**	(0.01)
Divorce conflict (1–10)							0.01	(0.02)
Father's age							−0.02**	(0.03)
Child's age							−0.01	(0.01)
Child's sex (ref. female)							−0.21**	(0.11)
R^2	0.08		0.20		0.33		0.34	
Subjects	1225		1225		1225		1225	

Source: Fathering after Union Dissolution in Lithuania, 2016
Notes: ***$p < 0.01$, **$p < 0.05$, *$p < 0.1$

with the mother, which, in turn, added to their general life satisfaction. However, we observe a persistent positive association between the quality of the relationship with the child and a father's general life satisfaction, even if the effect size decreased after the introduction of resources. The results for education show that fathers with less education reported lower general life satisfaction than more educated fathers, and that there was no difference in the level of general life satisfaction between medium and highly educated men. However, material living conditions are found to be relevant in predicting fathers' general life satisfaction, as fathers who were better off were more likely report being happy with their life.

In Model 3 (Table 11.2), we additionally include the father's living situation. A positive association is shown to remain between the reported quality of a father's relationship with his child and his general life satisfaction. Effects of education and material living conditions are also still detectable, although the effect sizes are only slightly smaller. The results further indicate that re-partnered men with or without (new) children had higher levels of general life satisfaction than men who remained single. Thus, it appears that being single was most detrimental to men's general life satisfaction, while the formation of a partnership with or without new (biological or step-children) was most beneficial to men's general life satisfaction.

The last model (Model 4 in Table 11.2) controls not only for all of the independent variables discussed above, but for factors such as time since the union dissolution, the level of conflict in the divorce process, the father's age, the child's age, and the child's sex. All of the previously identified associations remain, with marginal variation in the effect sizes. Although they are not of primary interest in this chapter, we will briefly discuss the effects of the included control variables. A man's age is shown to be negatively related to his general life satisfaction. A father with a non-resident daughter was more likely to report lower life satisfaction than a father with a son. In contrast to our expectations, the findings indicate that the intensity of conflict in the divorce process did not affect a man's general life satisfaction after a union dissolution.

Table 11.3 presents results for the second dimension of paternal psychological well-being: *depressive feelings*. As we explained above, this dependent variable measures the frequency of depressive feelings, with higher values indicating more frequent depressive symptoms (in the week before the interview). In the initial model (Model 1), we again include only the four variables on paternal involvement. Two aspects of involvement are shown to be related to a father's well-being. A man who reported having a higher quality relationship with his non-resident child was more likely to score low on depressive feelings. A similar pattern is observed for paying child support. Again, we see no statistically significant effects of contact frequency and the quality of the co-parenting relationship on paternal well-being.

In the next step (Model 2 in Table 11.3), we also consider the father's educational background and material living conditions. The results show that the effects of relationship quality and paying child support persist, but that resources also have an impact on depressive feelings. Separated men with less education were more likely than their highly educated counterparts to report having frequent depressive feelings. Again, we observe no statistically significant difference between men with medium and high levels of education. Material living conditions are shown to be

Table 11.3 OLS regression results for father's depressive feelings, unstandardized b, std. errors

	Model 1		Model 2		Model 3		Model 4	
	b	Std. errors	b	Std. errors	b	Std. errors	b	Std. errors
Paternal involvement								
Frequency of contact with the child (1–6)	0.05	(0.08)	0.04	(0.08)	−0.01	(0.07)	0.00	(0.07)
Quality of the relationship with the child (1–5)	−0.55***	(0.13)	−0.36**	(0.13)	−0,29**	(0.12)	−0.32***	(0.12)
Quality of the co-parenting relationship (1–5)	0.007	(0.10)	0.05	(0.10)	0.08	(0.09)	0.16*	(0.09)
Child support payment (ref. yes)	−1.87***	(0.29)	−1.35***	(0.29)	−1.16***	(0.09)	−1.12***	(0.27)
Paternal resources								
Education (ref. high):								
Middle			0.30	(0.26)	0.13	(0.24)	0.13	(0.24)
Low			1.21***	(0.25)	0.85***	(0.10)	0.9***	(0.23)
Material living conditions (1–5)			−0.72***	(0.12)	−0.60***	(0.11)	−0.61***	(0.11)
Paternal living situation (ref. single)								
Re-partnered without children					−1.90***	(0.2)	−2.10***	(0.26)
Re-partnered with children					−2.70***	(0.23)	−3.00***	(0.25)
Controls								
Time after union dissolution							0.00	(0.00)
Divorce conflict (1–10)							0.11***	(0.04)
Father's age							0.04**	(0.03)
Child's age							0.03	(0.03)
Child's sex (ref. female)							−0.03	(0.17)
R^2	*0.09*		*0.16*		*0.28*		*0.30*	
Subjects	1225		1225		1225		1225	

Source: Fathering after Union Dissolution in Lithuania, 2016
Notes: ***p < 0.01, **p < 0.05, *p < 0.1

inversely associated with depressive feelings; meaning that fathers who described their material conditions as disadvantaged scored higher on this dimension of psychological well-being.

Model 3 in Table 11.3 also considers the father's living situation. Adding this predictor did not significantly change the effects of any related variable on paternal involvement and resources. Men who reported having better quality relationships, a history of paying child support, and materially advantageous living conditions are also shown to have higher well-being; i.e., fewer depressive symptoms. Having less education is found to be positively related to frequently having depressive feelings. Again, as in the case of general life satisfaction, we observe that having a new partnership with or without (biological or step-) children was beneficial to a man's well-being. A man who remained single was more likely to report having frequent depressive feelings than a man who was re-partnered. All of the significant associations discussed above remained after we added the control variables in Model 4 (Table 11.3). It is worth mentioning that the age of the father is shown to be positively related to depressive feelings. Of equal interest is the finding that the intensity of the divorce conflict contributes to the model; i.e., that having a high level of conflict during the divorce or separation process was positively associated with having depressive feelings. However, we see no effects on paternal depressive feelings of child-related characteristics or the length of time since the union dissolution.

Conclusion

The involvement of fathers with their non-resident children after union dissolution is a topic that is receiving increasing attention in the literature on divorced and separated families. For example, studies that examined why some fathers are more involved than others (e.g., Köppen et al. 2018) have shown that this is a policy-relevant issue. Moreover, scholars have been increasingly investigating the impact of paternal involvement on the well-being of children (e.g., Poortman 2018). Nevertheless, the question of the extent to which a father's involvement with his non-resident children affects his own psychological well-being is considered only very rarely, even though the issue of the well-being of parents should be of no less importance. Accordingly, our research question was as follows: Does a father's involvement with his non-resident children protect him psychologically from the adverse effects of union dissolution? In explaining the theoretical association between paternal involvement and psychological well-being, we drew upon the divorce-stress-adjustment perspective (Amato 2000), the fatherhood identity theory (Marsiglio and Roy 2013; Marsiglio et al. 2005), and the paternal involvement framework (Pleck 2010b). In brief, we argued that the successful recreation of the fatherhood identity after a divorce or separation is relevant for a man's well-being because there are very close cultural links between masculinity and fatherhood. Involvement with his children can help to recreate fatherhood, and can buffer a father from break-up-related stress.

Our regression results are based on the cross-sectional survey "Fathering after Union Dissolution," which was conducted in 2016 in Lithuania with divorced or separated men who had non-resident children under age 18. As information on two dependent variables for psychological well-being was available, we ran two separate analyses for "depressive feelings" and for "general life satisfaction." Our findings indicated that the quality of a father's relationship with his child was the most important factor in paternal psychological well-being. Even after controlling for the father's resources, living situation, and other socio-demographic characteristics, we found clear evidence that the quality of this relationship had a negative impact on a father's depressive feelings and a positive impact on his general life satisfaction. Thus, our second hypothesis has been confirmed. We also found that paying child support was associated with a reduction in depressive feelings. Yet contrary to our expectations, the results indicated that neither frequent contact with the non-resident child nor the quality of the co-parenting relationship with the mother played a role in either the frequency of depressive feelings or general life satisfaction for the father. Thus, our initial hypothesis was only partially supported. However, our third hypothesis was confirmed, as we found evidence that re-partnering had a positive impact on paternal psychological well-being.

As every study suffers from some limitations, we should mention that, first, the cross-sectional design of our data did not allow us to control for the father's social characteristics prior to the union dissolution. However, in order to partially control for selection, we included in the analysis some social indicators that were likely the same before and after the union dissolution. Second, we examined only two dimensions of psychological well-being (depressive feelings and general life satisfaction), even though other dimensions (e.g., loneliness) might have been studied as well. Further research should be able to clarify these issues.

Although researchers are increasingly interested in exploring the effects of paternal involvement on the well-being of children, they appear to be less interested in investigating the effects of this involvement on the well-being of fathers themselves. This represents a large research gap, given that parental health and well-being are as important as the well-being of children. It should also be emphasized that the well-being of parents is linked to the well-being of their children. Thus, it is clear that a society needs healthy and functioning adults, as well as children. Our results reveal that a father's involvement with his children can greatly affect his psychological well-being. Again, however, it must be stressed that for both children and their fathers, the quality of the father-child relationship has a greater effect on well-being than the quantity of contact.

Acknowledgments This research has received funding from European Social Fund (project No. 09.3.3-LMT-K-712-01-0020) under grant agreement with the Research Council of Lithuania (LMTLT).

References

Allen, S. M., & Hawkins, A. J. (1999). Maternal gatekeeping: Mothers' beliefs and behaviors that inhibit greater father involvement in family work. *Journal of Marriage and Family, 61*(1), 199–212. https://doi.org/10.2307/353894.

Amato, P. R. (2000). The consequences of divorce for adults and children. *Journal of Marriage and Family, 62*(4), 1269–1287. https://doi.org/10.1111/j.1741-3737.2000.01269.x.

Amato, P. R. (2010). Research on divorce: Continuing trends and new developments. *Journal of Marriage and Family, 72*(3), 650–666. https://doi.org/10.1111/j.1741-3737.2010.00723.x.

Amato, P. R., & Dorius, C. (2010). Fathers, children, and divorce. In M. E. Lamb (Ed.), *The role of the father in child development* (pp. 177–200). Hoboken: Wiley.

Amato, P. R., & Gilbreth, J. G. (1999). Nonresident fathers and children's well-being: A meta-analysis. *Journal of Marriage and the Family, 61*(3), 557–573. https://doi.org/10.2307/353560.

Amato, P. R., Meyers, C. E., & Emery, R. E. (2009). Changes in nonresident father-child contact from 1976 to 2002. *Family Relations, 58*(1), 41–53. https://doi.org/10.1111/j.1741-3729.2008.00533.x.

Andersson, G., Thomson, E., & Duntava, A. (2017). Life-table representations of family dynamics in the 21st century. *Demographic Research, 37*(35), 1081–1230. https://doi.org/10.4054/DemRes.2017.37.35.

Bergström, M., Fransson, E., Hjern, A., Köhler, L., & Wallby, T. (2014). Mental health in Swedish children living in joint physical custody and their parents' life satisfaction: A cross-sectional study. *Scandinavian Journal of Psychology, 55*(5), 433–439. https://doi.org/10.1111/sjop.12148.

Botterman, S., Sodermans, A. K., & Matthijs, K. (2015). The social life of divorced parents. Do custody arrangements make a difference in divorced parents' social participation and contacts? *Leisure Studies, 34*(4), 487–500. https://doi.org/10.1080/02614367.2014.938768.

Brockmann, H., & Klein, T. (2004). Love and death in Germany: The marital biography and its effect on mortality. *Journal of Marriage and Family, 66*(3), 567–581. https://doi.org/10.1111/j.0022-2445.2004.00038.x.

Cantril, H. (1965). *The pattern of human concerns*. New Brunswick: Rutgers University Press.

Cashmore, J., Parkinson, P., Weston, R., Patulny, R., Redmond, G., Qu, L., et al. (2010). *Shared care parenting arrangements since the 2006 family law reforms: Report to the Australian government attorney-general's department Sydney*. Social Policy Research Centre, University of New South Wales. https://www.ag.gov.au/FamiliesAndMarriage/Families/FamilyLawSystem/Documents/SharedCareParentingArrangementssincethe2006FamilyLawreformsreport.pdf. Accessed 30 June 2019.

Choi, J. K., Palmer, R. J., & Pyun, H. S. (2014). Three measures of non-resident fathers' involvement, maternal parenting, and child development in low-income single-mother families. *Child & Family Social Work, 19*(3), 282–291. https://doi.org/10.1111/cfs.12000.

Cooksey, E. C., & Craig, P. H. (1998). Parenting from a distance: The effects of paternal characteristics on contact between nonresidential fathers and their children. *Demography, 35*(2), 187–200. https://doi.org/10.2307/3004051.

Courtenay, W. H. (2003). Key determinants of the health and well-being of men and boys. *International Journal of Men's Health, 2*(1), 1–30. http://menshealth.org/code/KEY-DTR.pdf. Accessed 30 June 2019.

Dommermuth, L. (2016). Children as family commuters. The geographical distance between non-resident parents and children in Norway. *Discussion Papers Statistics Norway, 841*(5). https://www.ssb.no/en/forskning/discussion-papers/_attachment/267802. Accessed 30 June 2019.

Edin, K., Nelson, T. J., & Paranal, R. (2004). Fatherhood and incarceration as potential turning points in the criminal careers of unskilled men. In M. Pattillo, D. Weiman, & B. Western (Eds.), *Imprisoning America* (pp. 46–75). New York: Russell Sage Foundation.

Eggebeen, D. J., & Knoester, C. (2001). Does fatherhood matter for men? *Journal of Marriage and Family, 63*(2), 381–393. https://doi.org/10.1111/j.1741-3737.2001.00381.x.

Elam, K. K., Sandler, I., Wolchik, S., & Tein, J.-Y. (2016). Non-residential father-child involvement, interparental conflict, and mental health of children following divorce: A person-focused approach. *Journal of Youth and Adolescence, 45*(3), 581–593. https://doi.org/10.1007/s10964-015-0399-5.

Evenson, R. J., & Simon, R. W. (2005). Clarifying the relationship between parenthood and depression. *Journal of Health and Social Behavior, 46*(4), 341–358. https://doi.org/10.1177/002214650504600403.

Giallo, R., D'Esposito, F., Christensen, D., Mensah, F., Cooklin, A., Wade, C., et al. (2012). Father mental health during the early parenting period: Results of an Australian population based longitudinal study. *Social Psychiatry and Psychiatric Epidemiology, 47*(12), 1907–1916. https://doi.org/10.1007/s00127-012-0510-0.

Härkönen, J. (2014). Divorce: Trends, patterns, causes, and consequences. In J. Treas, J. Scott, & M. Richards (Eds.), *The Wiley Blackwell Companion to the sociology of families* (pp. 303–322). Chichester: Wiley.

Hawkins, D. N., & Booth, A. (2005). Unhappily ever after: Effects of long-term, low-quality marriages on well-being. *Social Forces, 84*(1), 451–471. https://doi.org/10.1353/sof.2005.0103.

Helbig, S., Lampert, T., Klose, M., & Jacobi, F. (2006). Is parenthood associated with mental health? *Social Psychiatry and Psychiatric Epidemiology, 41*(11), 889–896. https://doi.org/10.1007/s00127-006-0113-8.

Hetherington, E. M. (2006). The influence of conflict, marital problem solving, and parenting on children's adjustment in nondivorced, divorced and remarried families. In A. Clarke-Stewart & J. Dunn (Eds.), *Families count: Effects on child and adolescent development* (pp. 203–237). New York: Cambridge University Press.

Hill, R. (1949). *Families under stress: Adjustment to the crises of war separation and reunion.* New York: Harper & Brothers.

Ihinger-Tallman, M., Pasley, K., & Buehler, C. L. (1995). Developing a middle-range theory of father involvement post-divorce. In W. Marsiglio (Ed.), *Fatherhood: Contemporary theory, research, and social policy* (pp. 57–77). Thousand Oaks: Sage.

Kalmijn, M. (2009). Country differences in the effects of divorce on well-being: The role of norms, support, and selectivity. *European Sociological Review, 26*(4), 475–490. https://doi.org/10.1093/esr/jcp035.

Kalmijn, M. (2016). Father-child contact, interparental conflict, and depressive symptoms among children of divorced parents. *European Sociological Review, 32*(1), 68–80. https://doi.org/10.1093/esr/jcv095.

Kalucza, S., Hammarström, A., & Nilsson, K. (2015). Mental health and parenthood – A longitudinal study of the relationship between self-reported mental health and parenthood. *Health Sociology Review, 24*(3), 283–296. https://doi.org/10.1080/14461242.2015.1051079.

Knoester, C., & Eggebeen, D. J. (2006). The effects of the transition to parenthood and subsequent children on men's well-being and social participation. *Journal of Family Issues, 27*(11), 1532–1560. https://doi.org/10.1177/0192513X06290802.

Knoester, C., Petts, R. J., & Eggebeen, D. J. (2007). Commitments to fathering and the well-being and social participation of new, disadvantaged fathers. *Journal of Marriage and Family, 69*(4), 991–1004. https://doi.org/10.1111/j.1741-3737.2007.00426.x.

Köppen, K., Kreyenfeld, M., & Trappe, H. (2018). Loose ties? Determinants of father-child contact after separation in Germany. *Journal of Marriage and Family, 80*(5), 1163–1175. https://doi.org/10.1111/jomf.12504.

Kudinavičiūtė-Michailovienė, I. (2013). Santuokos nutraukimo teisinės pasekmės ir jų išsprendimo problematika ištuokos bylose. In E. Tamošiūnienė & I. Kudinavičiūtė-Michailovienė (Eds.), *Šeimos bylų nagrinėjimo ir teismo sprendimų vykdymo ypatumai* (pp. 59–103). Vilnius: MRU.

Lamb, M. E., & Tamis-Lemonda, C. S. (2004). The role of the father: An introduction. In M. E. Lamb (Ed.), *The role of the father in child development* (pp. 1–31). Hoboken: Wiley.

Lamb, M. E., Pleck, J. H., Charnov, E. L., & Levin, J. A. (1987). A biosocial perspective on paternal behavior and involvement. In J. B. Lancaster, J. Altmann, A. S. Rossi, & L. R. Sherrod (Eds.), *Parenting across the lifespan: Biosocal dimensions* (pp. 111–142). New York: De Gruyter.

Manning, W. D., & Smock, P. J. (2000). "Swapping" families: Serial parenting and economic support for children. *Journal of Marriage and the Family, 62*(1), 111–122. https://doi.org/10.1111/j.1741-3737.2000.00111.x.

Manning, W. D., Stewart, S. D., & Smock, P. J. (2003). The complexity of father's parenting responsibilities and involvement with nonresident children. *Journal of Family Issues, 24*(5), 645–667. https://doi.org/10.1177/0192513X03252573.

Marsiglio, W., & Roy, K. (2013). Fathers' nurturance of children over the life course. In G. Peterson & K. Bush (Eds.), *Handbook of marriage and the family* (pp. 353–376). Boston: Springer.

Marsiglio, W., Roy, K., & Fox, G. L. (2005). Situated fathering: A spatially sensitive and social approach. In W. Marsiglio, K. Roy, & G. L. Fox (Eds.), *Situated fathering: A focus on physical and social spaces* (pp. 3–26). Lanham: Rowan Littlefield Publishers.

Maslauskaitė, A., & Tereškinas, A. (2017). Involving nonresident Lithuanian fathers in child-rearing: The negative impact of income inequalities and sociolegal policies. *Men and Masculinities, 20*(5), 609–629. https://doi.org/10.1177/1097184X17727798.

Maslauskaitė, A., Jasilioniene, A., Jasilionis, D., Stankuniene, V., & Shkolnikov, V. M. (2015). Socio-economic determinants of divorce in Lithuania: Evidence from register-based census-linked data. *Demographic Research, 33*(30), 871–908. https://doi.org/10.4054/DemRes.2015.33.30.

McCubbin, H. I., Cauble, A. E., & Patterson, J. M. (1982). *Family stress, coping, and social support*. Springfield: Thomas.

Melli, M. S., & Brown, P. R. (2008). Exploring a new family form. The shared time family. *International Journal of Law, Policy and the Family, 22*(2), 231–269. https://doi.org/10.1093/lawfam/ebn002.

Pleck, J. H. (2010a). Fatherhood and masculinity. In M. E. Lamb (Ed.), *The role of the father in child development* (pp. 27–57). Hoboken: Wiley.

Pleck, J. H. (2010b). Paternal involvement: Revised conceptualization and theoretical linkages with child outcomes. In M. E. Lamb (Ed.), *The role of the father in child development* (pp. 58–93). Hoboken: Wiley.

Poortman, A.-R. (2018). Postdivorce parent-child contact and child well-being: The importance of predivorce parental involvement. *Journal of Marriage and Family, 80*(3), 671–683. https://doi.org/10.1111/jomf.12474.

Radloff, L. S. (1977). The CES-D scale: A self-report depression scale for research in the general population. *Applied Psychological Measurement, 1*(3), 385–401. https://doi.org/10.1177/014662167700100306.

Sarkadi, A., Kristiansson, R., Oberklaid, F., & Bremberg, S. (2008). Fathers' involvement and children's developmental outcomes: A systematic review of longitudinal studies. *Acta Paediatrica, 97*(2), 153–158. https://doi.org/10.1111/j.1651-2227.2007.00572.x.

Schnor, C., Vanassche, S., & Van Bavel, J. (2017). Stepfather or biological father? Education-specific pathways of postdivorce fatherhood. *Demographic Research, 37*(51), 1659–1694. https://doi.org/10.4054/DemRes.2017.37.51.

Skevik, A. (2006). 'Absent fathers' or 'reorganized families'? Variations in father-child contact after parental break-up in Norway. *The Sociological Review, 54*(1), 114–132. https://doi.org/10.1111/j.1467-954X.2006.00604.x.

Sodermans, A. K., Botterman, S., Havermans, N., & Matthijs, K. (2015). Involved fathers, liberated mothers? Joint physical custody, and the subjective well-being of divorced parents. *Social Indicators Research, 122*(1), 257–277. https://doi.org/10.1007/s11205-014-0676-9.

Stankuniene, V., & Maslauskaitė, A. (2008). Family transformations in the post-communist countries: Attitudes toward changes. In C. Höhn, D. Avramov, & I. E. Kotowska (Eds.), *People, population change and policies* (pp. 113–138). Wiesbaden: Springer.

Stewart, S. D. (1999). Disneyland dads, Disneyland moms? How nonresident parents spend time with absent children. *Journal of Family Issues, 20*(4), 539–556. https://doi.org/10.1177/019251399020004006.
Stykes, J. B., Manning, W. D., & Brown, S. L. (2013). Nonresident fathers and formal child support: Evidence from the CPS, the NSFG, and the SIPP. *Demographic Research, 29*(46), 1299–1330. https://doi.org/10.4054/DemRes.2013.29.46.
Swiss, L., & Le Bourdais, C. (2009). Father-child contact after separation: The influence of living arrangements. *Journal of Family Issues, 50*(5), 623–652. https://doi.org/10.1177/0192513X08331023.
Teachman, J. D. (2002). Stability across cohorts in divorce risk factors. *Demography, 39*(2), 331–351. https://doi.org/10.1353/dem.2002.0019.
Van der Heijden, F., Poortman, A.-R., & Van der Lippe, T. (2016). Children's postdivorce residence arrangements and parental experienced time pressure. *Journal of Marriage and Family, 78*(2), 468–481. https://doi.org/10.1111/jomf.12283.
Waite, L. J., Luo, Y., & Lewin, A. C. (2009). Marital happiness and marital stability: Consequences for psychological well-being. *Social Science Research, 38*(1), 201–212. https://doi.org/10.1016/j.ssresearch.2008.07.001.
Waldvogel, P., & Ehlert, U. (2016). Contemporary fatherhood and its consequences for paternal psychological well-being – A cross-sectional study of fathers in central Europe. *Frontiers in Public Health, 4*, 199. https://doi.org/10.3389/fpubh.2016.00199.
Wang, H., & Amato, P. R. (2000). Predictors of divorce adjustment: Stressors, resources, and definitions. *Journal of Marriage and Family, 62*(3), 655–668. https://doi.org/10.1111/j.1741-3737.2000.00655.x.
Westphal, S. K., Poortman, A.-R., & Van der Lippe, T. (2014). Non-resident father-child contact across divorce cohorts: The role of father involvement during marriage. *European Sociological Review, 30*(4), 444–456. https://doi.org/10.1093/esr/jcu050.
Whiteside, M. F., & Becker, B. J. (2000). Parental factors and the young child's postdivorce adjustment: A meta-analysis with implications for parenting arrangements. *Journal of Family Psychology, 14*(1), 5–26. https://doi.org/10.1037//0893-3200.14.1.5.
Williams, K., & Dunne-Bryant, A. (2006). Divorce and adult psychological well-being: Clarifying the role of gender and child age. *Journal of Marriage and Family, 68*(5), 1178–1196. https://doi.org/10.1111/j.1741-3737.2006.00322.x.

Chapter 12
Gender Differences in Parental Well-being After Separation: Does Shared Parenting Matter?

Katja Köppen, Michaela Kreyenfeld, and Heike Trappe

Introduction

Mothers and fathers face "gendered realities" after union dissolution. Mothers usually continue to live with their children, and thus have to juggle work and parental responsibilities. Moreover, mothers typically experience a significant drop in (equivalent) household income in the aftermath of separation and divorce (Andreß and Bröckel 2007; Bayaz-Ozturk et al. 2018), which is reflected in a decline in their satisfaction with their financial situation (Leopold and Kalmijn 2016). In contrast, the well-being of fathers is more strongly affected by their reduced opportunities to see their children and to interact with them on a regular basis (Huß and Pollmann-Schult 2018). While the economic well-being of fathers does not, on average, decline as much as that of mothers, fathers commonly report substantial drops in satisfaction with family life when they separate (Leopold 2018). Thus, these gendered realities after separation and divorce are mirrored in gendered patterns of well-being. However, recent changes in gender role attitudes and fathers' behaviour suggest that a change

K. Köppen (✉)
University of Rostock, Rostock, Germany
e-mail: katja.koeppen@uni-rostock.de

M. Kreyenfeld
Hertie School, Berlin, Germany
e-mail: kreyenfeld@hertie-school.org

H. Trappe
Institut für Soziologie und Demographie, Universität Rostock,
Rostock, Mecklenburg-Vorpommern, Germany
e-mail: heike.trappe@uni-rostock.de

M. Kreyenfeld, H. Trappe (eds.), *Parental Life Courses after Separation and Divorce in Europe*, Life Course Research and Social Policies 12,
https://doi.org/10.1007/978-3-030-44575-1_12

is occurring. Fathers have become more active in the upbringing of their children. In addition, a growing percentage of separated parents are practising "shared parenting".[1]

Shared parenting is on the rise in many European countries (Smyth 2017; Steinbach 2019). Germany has been a laggard in this trend, as only about 5% of separated parents with minor children in Germany practise shared parenting arrangements (Kindler and Walper 2016; Walper 2016). Nevertheless, there has been a lively scholarly and public discussion on the "*Wechselmodell*" in Germany (Sünderhauf 2013; Walper 2016). In particular, the question of whether (equally) shared parenting should be integrated into the legal framework as the standard physical custody arrangement is being debated. Those who favour making (equally) shared parenting the default option typically argue that this change in the law would be a logical response to the increased involvement of fathers in childrearing, while those who oppose such a change generally counter that German family patterns are still traditional, and that it would be premature to define shared parenting as the default model.

Child well-being is an important dimension in the debate on shared parenting. There is a large body of existing literature on the effects of parental separation on the emotional and the economic well-being of children and adolescents (Härkönen et al. 2017; Lee and McLanahan 2015; McLanahan et al. 2013; Walper and Beckh 2006; Walper et al. 2015). For example, a number of studies have looked at how child well-being is affected by the frequency of contact and the quality of the relationship with the non-resident parent (Amato and Rezac 1994; Kalmijn 2016; Poortman 2018). Recent research has examined more specifically the well-being of children involved in shared parenting arrangements (Bauserman 2002; Beckmeyer et al. 2014; Bergström et al. 2015; Braver and Votruba 2018; Nielsen 2018; Steinbach 2019). These studies have suggested that shared parenting can have positive effects on the well-being of children, provided the relationship between the ex-partners is characterised by low levels of conflict (ibid.).

While child well-being has been in the focus of a number of studies, less is known about how shared parenting relates to parental well-being. This study seeks to close part of this research gap by examining how practising shared parenting affects the well-being of fathers and mothers after separation and divorce. We analyse two spheres of life: namely, satisfaction with family life and satisfaction with the financial situation of the household. Our analysis is based on 10 years of longitudinal data from the German Family Panel (pairfam). Fathers and mothers are included, regardless of whether they were married or cohabiting or whether they had ever lived with the other parent. We investigate how separation affected mothers and fathers' well-being. For the group of separated parents, we examine whether practising shared parenting affected their well-being after separation. We add to the literature in the following ways. First, our analysis provides nuanced evidence on

[1] We use the term "shared parenting" in this chapter. Apart from "shared parenting", "joint parenting", "joint physical custody", "shared residence", and "shared residential custody" have been used to describe these arrangements in the literature. In the German context, "*Wechselmodell*" or "*geteilte Betreuung*" are often used interchangeably for the same arrangements (Schumann 2018). "*Umgang*" is a legally defined term in German that refers to the non-resident parent seeing the child on a regular basis. Some scholars have argued that "shared parenting" may be captured by the German legal concept of "*erweiterter Umgang*" (Henneman 2017).

parental well-being by examining different spheres of life satisfaction. Second, we exploit a recent set of rich longitudinal data. While there is a large body of longitudinal research on life satisfaction, less is known about parents' well-being after separation. Third, our study can be added to the small number of studies that have examined the relationship between shared residence and parental well-being in the German context.

Institutional Context, Prior Research, and Hypotheses

Institutional Context

In Germany, as in many other European countries, the divorce rate has risen in recent decades. Although the divorce rate has decreased slightly since 2004, the current level suggests that every third marriage in Germany is likely to end in divorce (Statistisches Bundesamt 2018a). In about half of all divorces, children of minor age are involved (ibid.). There are no official statistics on the separation rates of non-marital unions with children, but evidence from social science surveys suggests that the risk of separation is higher among unmarried than among married couples (Schnor 2014). In the large majority of cases, children continue to reside with their mother after a separation. This is evident from the small share of single fathers reported in the official statistics. About 90% of lone parents are women (Statistisches Bundesamt 2018b). The prevalence of shared parenting arrangements is not covered in the official statistics. Estimates based on social science surveys by Kindler and Walper (2016: 821) and Walper (2016: 124) indicate that in Germany, only about 5% of all parents with minor children practice shared parenting after a separation. A government-initiated survey conducted among separated parents in 2016 and 2017 reported substantially higher values of around 15% (Institut für Demoskopie Allensbach 2017), and found that another 17% of these parents would consider such an arrangement in the future (ibid.). However, the survey also found that around one-third of the separated parents had never heard of shared parenting (*Wechselmodell*) (ibid.: 24). As shared parenting is still an ill-defined concept in Germany, estimates of how common such arrangements are seem to be very sensitive to the phrasing of the question. However, regardless of which operational definition is used, the estimates clearly show that the prevalence of shared parenting in Germany is well below the levels that are generally reported in countries such as the Netherlands, Sweden, Norway, and Belgium, where the percentage of separated parents who practice shared parenting ranges from 20% to 40% (Smyth 2017; Steinbach 2019).

Shared parenting is not yet legally defined in the German system. German family law regulates visitation rights (*Umgangsrecht*), based on the assumption that the child lives with one resident parent, while the non-resident parent has the right to see the child on a regular basis. The registration law (*Melderecht*) stipulates that the child can be registered with the local authorities at only one main place of residence. The parent with whom the child is registered receives the child benefits (Ruetten 2016). As child benefits can only be collected by the resident parent, this area of family law ignores the possibility of shared parenting. Other parts of the legal regime are less restrictive, and acknowledge shared parenting. This is, for example, the case for social welfare regulations, which stipulate that child supplements are allocated according to the number of overnight stays the child has at each parent's residence. Furthermore, the non-resident parent is not legally required to pay child alimony if the child lives at the mother's and the father's residences for equal amounts of times (Dethloff and Kaesling 2018). A particularity of the German system is that it provides for a sharp distinction between legal and physical custody. Legal custody (*Sorgerecht*) confers on a parent the rights and duties associated with making important decisions in the child's life, such as decisions about the child's education or medical care. Joint legal custody has become the default arrangement for divorced parents since 1998 (Dethloff 2015). Unmarried fathers have the legal right to apply for joint legal custody (ibid.). While joint legal custody is the standard legal custody arrangement when parents separate and divorce, there is considerable controversy surrounding the question of whether shared parenting should be made the default physical custody arrangement in the German system.

Prior Research and Theoretical Considerations

A large body of research has documented that separation and divorce reduces well-being (Clark et al. 2008; Diener 2009; Lucas 2007). As separation and divorce are often anticipated and preceded by partnership conflict, the life satisfaction levels of the partners tend to decline before the divorce or separation, and usually do not recover until several years later. Clark et al. (2008), using data from the German Socio-Economic Panel, found that the life satisfaction levels of men recover from divorce more quickly than those of women. Leopold (2018) confirmed this finding, while adding that men tend to experience a greater decrease in life satisfaction around the time of divorce than women. Leopold (2018) also examined other life course domains. His results indicated that between the ex-partners, there are large gender differences in the decline in household income, but only modest differences in levels of satisfaction with the financial situation and the standard of living of the household, and no gender differences in levels of satisfaction with health. Although there is a substantial body of research on life satisfaction levels based on German panel data, most of these studies only included divorcees, while leaving out the large and growing share of the separated population who were in unmarried unions. Furthermore, many of these studies were rather general, and did not address the particular situations of parents, or the "gendered realities" mothers and fathers are subject to after union dissolution.

The gendered realities after separation are closely linked to the division of paid and unpaid work that existed before these unions were dissolved (Leopold and Kalmijn 2016). In societies in which gendered family models are prevalent – i.e., the man is the main breadwinner while the woman works part-time and is in charge of the bulk of the housework and the childcare – mothers face a particularly high risk of experiencing a decline in household income in the wake of a separation. The economic costs of union dissolution usually fall more heavily on women than on men because mothers often have lower earnings than fathers, and are more restricted in their labour market opportunities due to their fragmented work careers after entering parenthood (Bröckel and Andreß 2015). The incompatibility of work and family life can also limit the ability of mothers to expand their employment activities after a separation (van Damme et al. 2009). Thus, compared to men, women face greater poverty risks after separation or divorce, and are more likely to be dependent on public transfers (Andreß and Bröckel 2007; Bröckel and Andreß 2015; Geisler and Kreyenfeld 2019; Popova and Navicke 2019). In contrast, men, and especially fathers, tend to experience larger declines in immaterial domains of life satisfaction than women; e.g., in the domains of health satisfaction and mental health (Biotteau et al. 2019; Leopold 2018; Yuan 2016), emotional well-being (Kessler 2018), and satisfaction with family life (Huß and Pollmann-Schult 2018; Leopold 2018; Leopold and Kalmijn 2016). Fathers' diminished levels of emotional and family-related well-being appear to be largely attributable to their reduced opportunities to see their children and to interact with them on a regular basis (Grätz 2017), particularly if the children continue to live with their mother (Steinbach 2019).

Kessler (2018) has made the intriguing argument that as the gender revolution progresses (Goldscheider et al. 2015), and, correspondingly, women's and men's roles in the public and the private sphere converge, the gendered consequences of separation and divorce on parental well-being will decrease. Although the existing empirical evidence does not support this claim (Kessler 2018; Radenacker in this volume), the underlying theoretical idea is appealing because it assumes that the gendered division of paid and unpaid work before and after parental separation, and the parental care arrangements that support a certain division of labour, will moderate the relationship between parental separation and the gendered realities that follow. Empirical research from the Netherlands has shown that separated parents who were practising shared parenting reported having higher life satisfaction than other parents (van der Heijden et al. 2015), while a study from Belgium found no direct effects of joint physical custody on parents' subjective well-being (Sodermans et al. 2015). Mothers who were practising shared parenting reported having less time pressure than resident mothers, whereas fathers who were practising shared parenting reported having slightly greater time pressure than other fathers (van der Heijden et al. 2016). A recent study based on data from the German micro-census found that the welfare benefits mothers were receiving declined significantly if their children were also living with the other parent (Geisler and Kreyenfeld 2019).

While shared parenting has the potential to improve the well-being of parents after separation, this arrangement has so far been adopted by only a small minority of separated parents in Germany. It should also be stressed that there are factors beyond custody arrangements that affect the lives of separated parents. Re-partnering, (re)-marriage, and the birth of a new child are critical events that can redefine the relationship of separated parents with their children from a previous union, and that can affect the separated parents' well-being (Ivanova and Balbo 2019; Soons et al. 2009). In addition, there are several factors that influence parental well-being that are also correlated with shared parenting. Fathers and mothers are not selected randomly into shared parenting. Instead, the choice to practise shared parenting depends on parental resources, as joint residence is more expensive than sole residence (Lettmaier and Dürbeck 2019). In order to practise shared parenting, both parents need to have sufficient housing space and equipment for the children. In addition, separated parents who live apart need to budget for the costs of transporting the children between the parents' residences. It is, therefore, not surprising that shared parenting is more common among highly educated than among less educated parents (Steinbach 2019). This selectivity is particularly pronounced under societal conditions in which joint physical custody is uncommon, as is the case in Germany (Walper 2016).

Following the abovementioned line of thought, we may assume that the gendered realities after separation would be mirrored in gendered differences in well-being. Mothers may experience a greater decline in economic well-being than fathers after separation (*Hypothesis 1a*). Conversely, levels of satisfaction with family life should decrease more among fathers than among mothers after separation (*Hypothesis 1b*). Practising shared parenting after separation is assumed to increase mothers' financial well-being, because it tends to improve their employment opportunities, reduce their time pressures, and provide them with a better work-life-balance (*Hypothesis 2*). Fathers who practise shared parenting are, by contrast, assumed to have a more intense and satisfying relationship with their children, because they are spending relatively long and regular periods of time with their children. Thus, we expect that practising shared parenting has a positive effect on fathers' well-being (*Hypothesis 3*). However, as choosing to practise shared parenting is not a random event, it is important to account for socio-economic factors that may select parents into shared parenting.

Data, Variables, and Research Strategy

Data and Analytical Sample

This chapter uses data from the German Family Panel (pairfam), a multidisciplinary, longitudinal study of partnership and family dynamics in Germany (Brüderl et al. 2019; Huinink et al. 2011). The German Family Panel is an annual survey that includes respondents of the birth cohorts 1971–73, 1981–83, and 1991–93. The first wave was conducted in 2008/09, and the most recent wave available is from 2017/18. In 2009/10, an oversample of eastern German respondents was added to the data (Kreyenfeld et al. 2012). The total number of observations for the ten survey waves, including the oversample, is 75,186 observations for 13,891 subjects. One of the exceptional features of this survey is that it collects detailed monthly partnership histories. Respondents are queried about the start and end dates of all partnerships that had a duration of more than 3 months, including living-apart-together relationships. If children resulted from a relationship, respondents were asked to report the start and end points of the partnership, regardless of its duration.

We have restricted this investigation to respondents whose first child was aged 17 or younger at the time of the survey. We focus on first-born children in order to simplify the analysis. We have dropped respondents with incomplete birth or partnership histories, as well as respondents whose first child was already aged 18 or older. An individual respondent could contribute several person-years to the data. In our analytical sample, we observe 5,776 subjects over 27,190 person-years. Parts of the analysis are restricted to separated parents. In order to identify whether a respondent was separated from the parent of his/her first-born child, we have combined the respondents' partnership and fertility histories. If the respondent was in a partnership when his/her first child was born, but separated from that partner later on, we assume that the person was a *separated parent*. Our procedure relies on the assumption that the respondent's partner at the time the child was born was the biological parent.[2] We observe 550 separated fathers and 1,062 separated mothers in the data. The large difference in the sample sizes of separated fathers and separated mothers can be attributed to the differences in the ages at which women and men experience separation. However, under-coverage of fathers (Joyner et al. 2012) – and especially of separated fathers, given their high levels of attrition following separation – may have also contributed to this gap (Müller and Castiglioni 2015).

Variables

The two outcome variables are **satisfaction with family life** and **satisfaction with the financial situation of the household**. Both variables are measured on a scale that ranges from zero (very dissatisfied) to ten (very satisfied). While satisfaction with family life is surveyed every year, satisfaction with the financial situation of the household was not yet surveyed in the first wave; thus, the sample size for the analysis of this variable is slightly smaller than the sample size for the analysis of satisfaction with family life. Table 12.6 in the appendix provides the sample descriptives. The table shows that satisfaction with family life (mean 8.51 in the total sample) was substantially higher than satisfaction with the financial situation of the household (mean 6.31 in the total sample).

A key independent variable of interest is the **duration since the separation** from the parent of the first-born child. A few respondents were not in a relationship when their first child was born. In such cases, we assume that separation occurred at the time of childbirth. We include the **family status at first birth**, distinguishing between married and unmarried respondents. The latter group is further distinguished by whether they were cohabiting or were not living with a partner (denoted

[2] The German Family Panel includes information on the filiation of the respondents' biological children to their past partners. We did not, however, refer to this information to verify whether the partner at childbirth was indeed the biological parent of the child, as this information is often missing in the data. We also did not consider whether the respondents re-partnered with the biological parent of their first child, because only a fraction of the respondents separated from and then re-partnered with the biological father later in the life course (Bastin 2016).

as "single"). A key variable that depicts changes in the post-separation partnership trajectory is a variable for the **current family status**. This covariate is time-varying, and distinguishes between respondents who were (a) single, (b) who had a partner (living-apart-together relationship, LAT), (c) who had a partner and were living with their (new) partner (cohabiting), and (d) who were married and living with their partner. Married individuals who were not living with their partner are not considered married here, as some of the respondents may have been separated but not yet officially divorced. We also account for whether the respondent had a (new) **child with the current partner**. This variable is again time-varying, and indicates whether the respondent has a child with the current partner. The standard control variables are **age** and **gender**. We also include a binary variable for region to account for possible differences between East and West Germany. **East Germany** is defined here as the eastern German states, including Berlin. We also consider the highest level of **education**. This variable is time-varying, and distinguishes between low (ISCED1997 0-3), medium (ISCED1997 4-6), and high (ISCED1997 7-8) levels. **Employment status** is also time-varying, and distinguishes between individuals who were employed, unemployed, and not in the labour force (e.g., students, home-makers, or parents taking leave).

The main variable of interest is the **parenting arrangement** after separation and divorce. There is currently no legal definition of shared parenting. Some researchers have defined shared parenting as an arrangement in which children spend between 25% and 50% of their time with each parent (Steinbach 2019). This definition leaves open the question of whether the children in such an arrangement have to stay over-night with both parents. It is also unclear whether shared parenting must involve face-to-face contact with the children. Moreover, this definition does not specify how shared parenting is aligned with the children's activities that take place outside of the time they spend with their parents. Teenage children in particular may spend only a limited share of their time with either of their parents. If we assume that shared parenting is defined by the amount of time children spend with each of their parents, we would ideally draw on time use data to measure the prevalence of shared parenting. The German family panel does not include such information. However, there are two major sources in the data that allow us to reconstruct the place of residence of a given child, and to infer the amount of time the child was spending with each parent. In a first step, we seek to determine whether the child was living with the respondent, the other parent, or in another arrangement.[3] If the child was not

[3] The following categories are distinguished: 1 = only with the respondent; 2 = with the respondent, but also alone/in a dwelling shared with others; 3 = with the respondent and with the other parent, but mostly with the respondent; 4 = with the respondent, but also with the other parent, more or less equally often with the respondent and the other parent; 5 = with the respondent but also with the other parent, but mostly with the other parent; 6 = with the respondent, but also with other relatives; 7 = with the respondent, but also in the child's home; 8 = with the respondent, but also somewhere else not listed; 9 = only alone/in a dwelling shared with others; 10 = only with the other parent; 11 = only with other relatives; 12 = only in a children's home; 13 = only somewhere else not listed.

living with the respondent, we use the survey data to assess how often the parent was seeing the child. If the child was living with the respondent, we attempt to determine how often the other parent was seeing the child.[4] Based on these two sources of information, we have generated a variable that distinguishes four categories:

- **Resident parenting:** This category includes respondents who were living with the child and were not practising shared parenting.
- **Non-resident parenting:** This category includes respondents who were not living with the child and were not practising shared parenting.
- **Shared parenting**: This category includes respondents who reported that the child was living with the respondent and with the other parent "more or less equally often". It also includes respondents who said that the child was mainly living with them, but was also living with the other parent. Conversely, it also includes respondents who reported that the child was mainly living with the other parent, but was also living with them. Moreover, we include respondents who reported that the non-resident parent was seeing the child every day, and respondents who characterised themselves as a non-resident parent who was seeing the child every day.
- **Other**: This category includes respondents who reported that the child was in another arrangement, such as living in a relative's home, in his/her own flat, or in a children's home.

Figure 12.1 shows that 12% of the respondents in the sample were practising shared parenting.[5] The figure also indicates that shared parenting was socially selective. As expected, we find that respondents who were highly educated and employed, and who thus likely had high earnings, were more likely than other respondents to be practising shared parenting. The findings further indicate that shared parenting was slightly more prevalent in West than in East Germany, and was much more

[4] The survey collects information on how often the non-resident parent sees the child. In addition, the resident parent is asked how often the other parent sees the child. The following response categories are distinguished: (1) daily; (2) several times per week; (3) once per week; (4) 1–3 times per month, (5) several times per year; (6) less often; (7) contact broken off; and (8) contact never established (9).

[5] The values are very sensitive to the operational definition of shared parenting. If shared parenting is defined only as those situations in which the child is living "more or less equally often" with both parents, we find that just 3% of the respondents were practising shared parenting. If we include those respondents who reported that they were "mostly" living with the child, the value increases to 5%. If we include those respondents who see the child daily, the value increases to 12% (which is the definition adopted in this study, see above). If we also include those respondents who see the child several times per week, the value rises to 20%. If we adopt the latter definition, we find highly significant results for the impact of shared parenting on fathers' satisfaction with family life. However, the effect is not stable to the inclusion of socio-economic covariates. We have also conducted sensitivity analysis for the other operational definitions of shared parenting. The results of this analysis were strongly affected by the very low number of "positive events" in the data, and hardly any of the covariates were found to be significant.

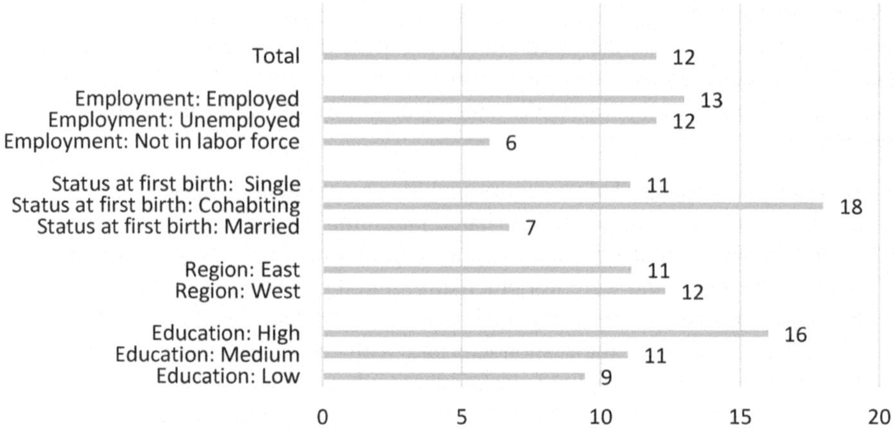

Fig. 12.1 % shared parenting by socio-economic characteristics of separated parents

prevalent among parents who were cohabiting at the first birth than among parents who were previously married.

Table 12.1 reports the distribution of the other control variables for the sample of separated parents (for the full sample, see Table 12.6 in the appendix). The table shows that the sample includes more women than men. As we noted earlier, this gap is largely attributable to the differences between men and women in the ages at birth and separation, but it may also be linked to the under-coverage of separated fathers in the survey. About 40% of the individuals in the sample are eastern Germans. This high share of eastern Germans is due to the oversampling of eastern Germans in pairfam. The regression analysis accounts for this bias by controlling for region. The data include respondents of the birth cohorts 1971–73, 1981–83, and 1991–93. Thus, the age structure of our respondents was fairly young. The respondents were, on average, 35 years old. It is important that we control for age, given that the respondents we are observing experienced a separation at an early stage of their life course. The sample statistics also reveal gender differences in educational attainment, with the women in the sample being less likely than the men to hold a university degree. Although women in Germany reached parity in higher education in the early 2000s, this pattern does not show up in our data, most likely because we have limited the analysis to parents, and there appears to be a negative educational gradient in women's childlessness. Thus, highly educated women are more likely to remain childless (Bujard 2015). Likewise, we observe stark gender differences in employment patterns. Although women tend to expand their employment activities in anticipation of and after a divorce or separation (Bröckel and Andreß 2015; de Regt et al. 2013; Thielemans and Mortelmans 2019), the share of employed women in our sample is much lower than that of employed men. Among the separated parents in the sample, only a quarter were living in a marital union at first birth, while the majority were either single or living in a non-marital union. We can also see that about 60% of our sample members (or rather 60% of the person-years) were already

Table 12.1 Sample composition, separated parents, person-years by column percent

	Satisfaction with family life			Satisfaction with financial situation		
	Men	Women	Total	Men	Women	Total
Gender						
Male	–	–	0.33	–	–	0.33
Female	–	–	0.67	–	–	0.67
Region						
Western Germany	0.53	0.61	0.58	0.53	0.60	0.58
Eastern Germany	0.47	0.39	0.42	0.47	0.40	0.42
Duration since separation						
0–1 years after separation	0.17	0.15	0.16	0.17	0.15	0.16
2–3 years after separation	0.14	0.14	0.14	0.14	0.14	0.14
4–5 years after separation	0.13	0.13	0.14	0.13	0.13	0.13
6–7 years after separation	0.13	0.13	0.13	0.12	0.13	0.13
8–9 years after separation	0.13	0.13	0.13	0.12	0.13	0.12
10 or more years after separation	0.30	0.32	0.31	0.32	0.32	0.32
Education						
Low	0.11	0.20	0.17	0.10	0.19	0.16
Medium	0.63	0.61	0.62	0.63	0.61	0.62
High	0.26	0.19	0.21	0.27	0.20	0.22
Employment status						
Employed	0.79	0.62	0.68	0.80	0.64	0.69
Unemployed	0.12	0.12	0.12	0.11	0.11	0.11
Not in labour force	0.08	0.25	0.19	0.08	0.24	0.19
Missing	0.01	0.01	0.01	0.01	0.01	0.01
Family status at first birth						
Married	0.25	0.29	0.28	0.26	0.29	0.28
Cohabiting	0.39	0.31	0.34	0.40	0.32	0.34
Single	0.36	0.40	0.38	0.34	0.39	0.38
Current family status						
Single	0.35	0.37	0.36	0.36	0.37	0.36
LAT	0.12	0.20	0.17	0.12	0.19	0.17
Cohabiting	0.23	0.19	0.21	0.23	0.20	0.21
Married	0.30	0.24	0.26	0.29	0.24	0.26
Child with current partner						
Child with current partner	0.30	0.25	0.26	0.29	0.25	0.26
No child with current partner	0.70	0.75	0.74	0.71	0.75	0.74
Parenting arrangement						
Residence with child	0.23	0.87	0.66	0.21	0.85	0.65
Shared parenting	0.14	0.08	0.10	0.17	0.10	0.12
Non-resident parent	0.56	0.02	0.20	0.55	0.02	0.19
Other	0.07	0.03	0.04	0.07	0.03	0.04

(continued)

Table 12.1 (continued)

	Satisfaction with family life			Satisfaction with financial situation		
	Men	Women	Total	Men	Women	Total
Continuous covariates (Mean, std. error)						
Age (Mean)	36.69	34.81	35.43	37.19	35.20	35.85
Age (std. error)	(0.12)	(0.09)	(0.07)	(0.13)	(0.09)	(0.08)
Age of child (Mean)	10.26	10.28	10.28	10.45	10.40	10.42
Age of child (std. error)	(0.09)	(0.07)	(0.06)	(0.11)	(0.07)	(0.06)
Satisfaction (Mean)	7.65	8.05	7.91	5.42	5.30	5.34
Satisfaction (std. error)	(0.05)	(0.03)	(0.03)	(0.06)	(0.04)	(0.04)
Sample size						
Subjects	550	1062	1612	437	844	1281
Person years	2128	4371	6499	1739	3579	5318

Notes: Unweighted values

living with a new partner, and that the likelihood of re-partnering did not differ by gender. This latter finding seems to contradict the widely held view that mothers have lower chances of re-partnering than fathers (Ivanova et al. 2013). It appears, however, that women were more likely than men to choose less institutionalised forms of partnerships, such as living-apart-together relationships. About a quarter of the respondents reported that they have a child with their current partner. Again we find that the likelihood of having another child did not vary by gender.

Research Strategy

The analysis consists of two major parts. In the first part of our analysis, we estimate the **effect of separation on satisfaction with family life and satisfaction with the household's financial situation**. We do so by using pooled linear regression models to analyse the total sample of mothers and fathers (including separated and non-separated parents). The results are reported as unstandardized coefficients. We treat the dependent variables as cardinal, and thus assume that the 11 satisfaction categories carry a meaning. It has been shown that assuming cardinality as opposed to ordinality is largely irrelevant for the results (Ferrer-i-Carbonell and Frijters 2004). As subjects may have entered the analysis several times, we have generated robust standard errors that account for the multiple occurrence of the respondents in the sample. Model 1 only includes an indicator for separation (as well as region to account for the oversampling of East Germans). Model 2 controls for the major socio-economic control variables, such as education, employment, age, age of child, and family status at first birth. Since unobserved characteristics may still bias our investigations, we estimate another model (Model 3) that employs fixed-effects modelling that accounts for time-constant individual heterogeneity (Allison 2009).

In the fixed-effects model, we only control for traits that vary substantially across time: namely, age, age of child, and employment status. We also insert dummy variables for calendar year, which is generally recommended for fixed-effects models in order to account for overall trends. We conduct all investigations separately by gender. To better compare the estimates for women and men, we also pool the male and the female sample, and introduce an interaction effect of separation and gender. We insert the categorical variable for "duration since separation" into this specification in order to examine how life satisfaction develops in the aftermath of separation. To make the gender differences easier to gauge, we display the results in a graph as predicted values, along with their 95% confidence intervals.

The second part of the investigation focuses on separated parents. Specifically, we examine how **shared parenting affects satisfaction with family life, and satisfaction with the household's financial situation.** The investigation is restricted to the period after separation. We again estimate OLS-regressions. We first estimate a model without socio-economic covariates (Model 1). We then estimate a model that includes the socio-economic controls in order to assess how the association of shared parenting and life satisfaction was affected by the particular characteristics of the parents who opted for shared parenting (Model 2). The final model (Model 3) adopts a fixed-effects modelling approach. Again, all of the analyses are conducted separately by gender, and for the two different spheres of life satisfaction.

Results

Separation and Parental Life Satisfaction

Table 12.2 reports the regression results for satisfaction with family life. Model 1 includes the OLS-regression that only controls for whether the respondent is a separated parent. The model shows that fathers' life satisfaction levels decline by 1.05 units after separation. The effect is rather stable to the inclusion of further covariates (Model 2). The fixed-effects model corroborates this finding, showing a negative effect of separation on satisfaction with family life. However, the effect size is slightly smaller in magnitude than in the OLS-regression. The model results for the female sample also show that separation affects satisfaction with family life, but the strength of the parameter is weaker than it is for the male model. The parameter is now only 0.41.

Table 12.3 reports the regression results for satisfaction with the household's financial situation. The OLS model without the socio-economic controls again shows a strong negative parameter. The level of satisfaction with the household's financial situation drops by about one unit after separation for males. However, the parameter is not stable across specifications. The inclusion of the socio-economic characteristics reduce the parameter to 0.60. The fixed-effects model reduces the parameter even further, to 0.38. In the latter model, the parameter is no longer significant. The model results suggest that socio-economic characteristics as well as

Table 12.2 Regression results

	Men						Women					
	Model 1		Model 2		Model 3		Model 1		Model 2		Model 3	
	OLS		OLS		FE		OLS		OLS		FE	
Separation												
No separation	Ref.		Ref.		Ref.		Ref.		Ref.		Ref.	
Separation	−1.05	***	−1.10	***	−0.84	***	−0.65	***	−0.65	***	−0.41	***
Region												
Western Germany	−0.12	*	−0.15	*			−0.05		−0.09			
Eastern Germany	Ref.		Ref.				Ref.		Ref.			
Marital status at first birth												
Married			Ref.						Ref.			
Cohabiting			−0.10						−0.15	**		
Single			0.07						.0.04			
Education												
Low			Ref.						Ref.			
Medium			−0.04						0.07			
High			−0.05						0.03			
Employment												
Employed			Ref.		Ref.				Ref.		Ref.	
Unemployed			−0.21		−0.20				−0.33	***	−0.11	
Not in labour force			−0.10		−0.02				0.11	**	0.08	
Constant	8.76	***	9.68	***	9.00	***			9.57	***	8.89	***

Outcome variable: Satisfaction with family life (scale 0–10)

Notes: ***$p < 0.01$; **$p < 0.05$; *$p < 0.1$. Robust standard errors. Flag variable for missing values (employment status and education) was included. Further control variables are age and age of first child in the OLS-model. The FE-model includes dummy variables for calendar year

Table 12.3 Regression results

	Men						Women					
	Model 1		Model 2		Model 3		Model 1		Model 2		Model 3	
	OLS		OLS		FE		OLS		OLS		FE	
Separation												
No separation	Ref.		Ref.		Ref.		Ref.		Ref.		Ref.	
Separation	−0.99	***	−0.60	***	−0.38		−1.36	***	−0.99	***	−0.67	***
Region												
Western Germany	0.58	***	0.28	***			−0.39		0.25	**		
Eastern Germany	Ref.		Ref.				Ref.		Ref.			
Marital status at first birth												
Married			Ref.						Ref.			
Cohabiting			−0.37	***					−0.08			
Single			0.04						0.06			
Education												
Low			Ref.						Ref.			
Medium			0.03						−0.23	*		
High			0.97	***					−1.63	***		
Employment												
Employed			Ref.		Ref.				Ref.		Ref.	
Unemployed			−2.37	***	−1.20	***			−0.15		−0.92	***
Not in labour force			−0.47	**	−0.45	**			−0.20	*	−0.19	***
Constant	6.10	***	5.46	***	6.24	***	6.43	***	5.13	***	6.98	

Outcome variable: Satisfaction with financial situation (scale 0–10)

Notes: ***$p < 0.01$; ** $p < 0.05$; * $p < 0.1$. Robust standard errors. Flag variable for missing values (employment status and education) was included. Further control variables are age and age of first child in the OLS-model. The FE-model includes dummy variables for calendar year

time-constant traits of the separated fathers, explain much of the decline in satisfaction with the financial situation after separation. The overall pattern for women is similar. In this case as well, western German respondents who were highly educated and employed reported being more satisfied with their financial situation. However, the parameter for separation is stable and highly significant across all models. The fixed-effects model shows that a separation is associated with a decline in satisfaction with the financial situation of 0.67 units. Thus, the drop in satisfaction among women cannot be explained by changes in employment patterns around the time of the divorce, or by unobserved characteristics that select people into separation. There must be other unobserved factors (such as a drop in household income or low alimony payments) that explain the decline in mothers' economic well-being.

The models above analysed men and women separately, which makes it difficult to compare the parameters for men and women across models. In order to better compare the effect sizes for both genders, we pool the male and the female sample in a final step. We estimate an OLS-model, and include an interaction variable for gender and separation in the model. Instead of a simple dummy variable for separation, we include time since separation. This approach allows us to examine gender differences in the recovery of well-being following separation. The model results are displayed as average predicted values. Figure 12.2 shows the results for satisfaction with family life. We find that fathers experienced a steeper decline in their satisfaction with family life after separation than mothers, which is in line with previous research (Huß and Pollmann-Schult 2018; Leopold 2018; Leopold and Kalmijn 2016). A comparison of non-separated fathers and fathers in the first 2 years after

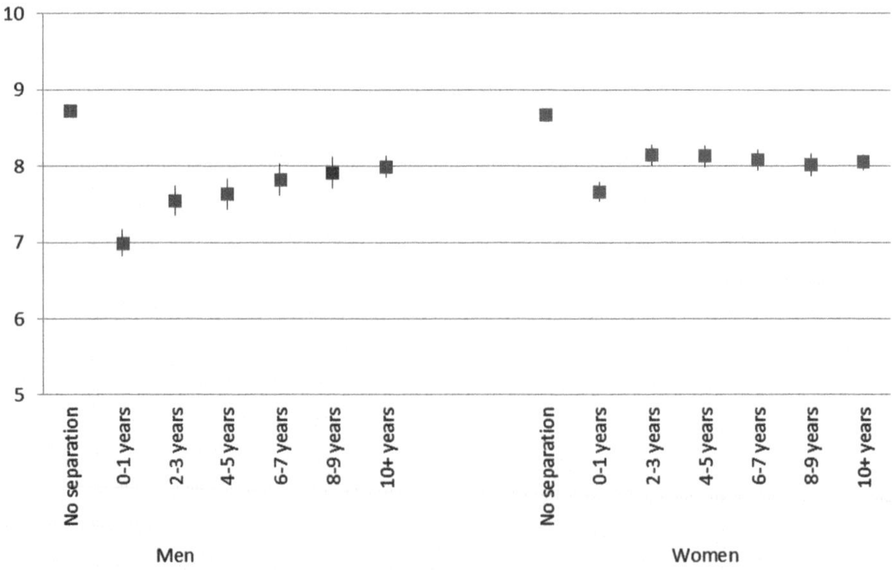

Fig. 12.2 Linear predictions from OLS-regression and 95%-confidence interval. Outcome variable: satisfaction with family life (scale 0–10)
Notes: Further covariates in the model are: region (East/West), education, employment, age, age of first child, marital status at first birth

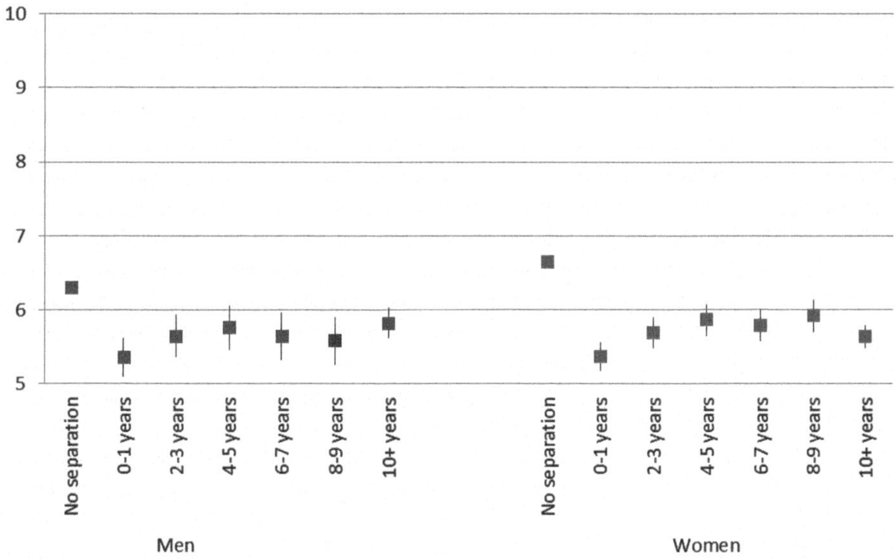

Fig. 12.3 Linear predictions from OLS-regression and 95%-confidence interval. Outcome variable: satisfaction with financial situation (scale 0–10)
Notes: Further covariates in the model are: region (East/West), education, employment, age, age of first child, marital status at first birth

separation indicates that separated fathers' satisfaction with family life declined by almost two units. The corresponding value for mothers was one unit. The results also show that although the decline was more severe for fathers, the family satisfaction levels of fathers recovered more quickly than those of mothers. The findings for the financial situation (Fig. 12.3) show the opposite pattern. Here, we see that the financial satisfaction levels of women decreased more than those of men following separation. This observation is generally in line with previous research that has shown that mothers experience a more drastic reduction in their household income after separation than fathers (Bröckel and Andreß 2015). However, compared to these previous findings, the gender differences in satisfaction with the household's financial situation seem to be more modest than the gender differences in the (equivalent) household income.

Satisfaction with Family Life and the Financial Situation After Separation

Table 12.4 reports the results for the models that examine separated parents' satisfaction with family life. We expected to find that practising shared parenting increased the family-related well-being of separated fathers. Our investigation does not support this hypothesis. Model 1 suggests that the level of satisfaction with family life of resident fathers was 0.50 units higher than that of non-resident fathers, but that there was hardly any difference in family satisfaction levels between non-resident fathers and fathers who practise shared parenting. Model 2, which controls for socio-economic confounders, further suggests that there was no relationship between where the children lived and fathers' satisfaction with family life, as resident and non-resident fathers did not differ after controlling for major confounders. The model results indicate, however, that cohabitation with or marriage to a new partner increased the fathers' satisfaction with family life. The fixed-effects model (Model 3) supports this finding, and additionally suggests that having a new child played a decisive role in fathers' satisfaction with family life. As fathers commonly do not live with their children from prior partnerships, a new child may have another meaning for fathers than for mothers.

The results for mothers reveal a similar pattern. However, Model 1 indicates that practising shared parenting had some positive and weakly significant impact on satisfaction with family life. The parameter was, however, not robust to the inclusion of further variables. Model 2, which controls for major socio-economic characteristics, shows no significant relationship between the parental arrangement and the level satisfaction with family life. In this case as well, having a cohabiting or married partner is shown to substantially increase satisfaction with family life. Unlike the model results for men, the model results for women indicate that the birth of a new child did not significantly affect their satisfaction levels. It might be more important for fathers than for mothers to support their idea of a "real" family. The outcomes of the fixed-effects model (Model 3) support the notion that there was no relationship between women's parenting arrangements and their levels of satisfaction with family life.

Table 12.5 reports the results for the parents' levels of satisfaction with their financial situation. The findings of Model 1 suggest that practising shared parenting positively influenced men's satisfaction with their financial situation. However, this association does not appear to be stable across the models. After the socio-economic confounders are included, the relationship between the residential arrangement and well-being disappears (Model 2). This pattern is also found in the model that includes the partnered parents as well (see Table 12.3): i.e., the results show that fathers who were married or cohabiting, were from western Germany, or were highly educated and employed were more satisfied with their financial situation than other fathers. The results of the fixed-effects model (Model 3) suggest that the birth of a new child was associated with lower levels of satisfaction with the financial situation.

We had speculated that shared parenting would have affected the well-being of mothers in particular. Again, we have to reject our hypothesis, as we do not find any association between the parenting arrangement and mothers' satisfaction with their financial situation, even before controlling for the socio-economic characteristics (Model 1). The results of Model 2 indicate that being unemployed or non-employed had a very large negative effect on women's satisfaction with their financial situation. We also find that mothers who were cohabiting or had married a new partner reported higher levels of satisfaction with their financial situation than single

Table 12.4 Regression results

	Men						Women					
	Model 1		Model 2		Model 3		Model 1		Model 2		Model 3	
	OLS		OLS		FE		OLS		OLS		FE	
Parenting arrangement												
Residence with child	0.50	***	0.09		0.03		0.54		0.54		−0.03	
Shared parenting	0.02		0.08		−0.11		0.78	*	0.58		−0.07	
Non-resident parent	Ref.		Ref.		Ref.		Ref.		Ref.		Ref.	
Region												
Western Germany	−0.18		−0.27	*			−0.20	*	−0.25	**		
Eastern Germany	Ref.		Ref.				Ref.		Ref.			
Marital status at first birth												
Married			Ref.						Ref.			
Cohabiting			0.10						−0.18			
Single			−0.05						0.01			
Education												
Low			Ref.						Ref.			
Medium			0.04						0.09			
High			−0.20						−0.20			
Employment												
Employed			Ref.		Ref.				Ref.		Ref.	
Unemployed			−0.16		−0.19				−0.05		−0.05	*
Not in labour force			0.12		−0.07				0.21	**	0.05	

(continued)

Table 12.4 (continued)

	Men						Women					
	Model 1		Model 2		Model 3		Model 1		Model 2		Model 3	
	OLS		OLS		FE		OLS		OLS		FE	
Current family status												
Single			Ref.		Ref.				Ref.		Ref.	
LAT			0.41	*	0.35	***			0.35	***	0.09	***
Cohabiting			0.97	***	1.17	***			0.74	***	0.50	***
Married			1.53	***	0.98	***			1.03	***	0.47	***
Child with current partner												
Child with current partner			0.30		0.92	***			0.16		0.05	
No child with current partner			Ref.		Ref.				Ref.		Ref.	
Constant	7.65	***	7.26	***	6.85	***	7.64	***	7.13	***	8.01	***

Outcome variable: Satisfaction with family life (scale 0–10), separated parents

Notes: $***p < 0.01$; $**p < 0.05$; $*p < 0.1$. Robust standard errors. Flag variable for missing values (employment status, education, parenting arrangement) was included. Further control variables are age and age of first child in the OLS-model. The FE-model includes dummy variables for calendar year

Table 12.5 Regression results

	Men						Women				
	Model 1		Model 2		Model 3		Model 1	Model 2		Model 3	
	OLS		OLS		FE		OLS	OLS		FE	
Parenting arrangement											
Residence with child	0.22		−0.21		0.31		0.52	0.43		−0.32	
Shared parenting	0.55	*	0.25		0.02		0.84	0.50		−0.37	
Non-resident parent	Ref.		Ref.		Ref.		Ref.	Ref.		Ref.	
Region											
Western Germany	0.48	***	0.17				0.07	0.00			
Eastern Germany	Ref.		Ref.				Ref.	Ref.			
Marital status at first birth											
Married			Ref.					Ref.			
Cohabiting			−0.27					−0.06			
Single			0.23					0.13			
Education											
Low			Ref.					Ref.			
Medium			0.04					0.15			
High			0.88	***				0.59	*		
Employment											
Employed			Ref.		Ref.			Ref.			
Unemployed			−2.12	***	−1.12	***		−1.61	***	−0.90	***
Not in labour force			−0.38		−0.41	***		−0.59	***	−0.30	*

(continued)

Table 12.5 (continued)

	Men						Women				
	Model 1		Model 2		Model 3		Model 1	Model 2		Model 3	
	OLS		OLS		FE		OLS	OLS		FE	
Current family status											
Single			Ref.		Ref.			Ref.		Ref.	
LAT			0.03		−0.14			0.32	*	0.07	
Cohabiting			0.75	***	0.79	***		1.19	***	0.96	***
Married			1.00	***	0.71	***		1.14	***	0.73	***
Child with current partner											
Child with current partner			0.04		−0.69	**		0.44	*	0.52	*
No child with current partner			Ref.		Ref.			Ref.		Ref.	
Constant	5.05	***	4.22	***	5.75	***	4.74	3.65	***	5.76	***

Outcome variable: Satisfaction with financial situation (scale 0–10), separated parents

Notes: ***$p < 0.01$; **$p < 0.05$; *$p < 0.1$. Robust standard errors. Flag variable for missing values (employment status, education, parenting arrangement) was included. Further control variables are age and age of first child in the OLS-model. The FE-model includes dummy variables for calendar year

mothers. Unlike among men, the birth of a new child is not shown to affect levels of satisfaction with the household's financial situation among women. The results of the fixed-effects model support this finding (Model 3).

Discussion

In this chapter, we have examined parental well-being after separation. The analysis was based on data from the German Family panel (pairfam) spanning a total of 10 years. We argued that mothers and fathers face "gendered realities" after union dissolution. As children commonly live with their mother after their parents split up, separated fathers tend to be negatively affected by having reduced contact with their offspring. Conversely, separated women often face a rapid drop in their (equivalent) household income, especially if they had not been previously employed or had been working part-time only. Against this background, we assumed that men would report a strong decline in their levels of satisfaction with family life, while mothers would report reduced levels of satisfaction with their financial situation. The results of our investigation support these assumptions. We found that men's satisfaction with family life decreased by about one unit after separation; and that women also experienced a deterioration in family well-being, but that the effect was less pronounced among women than among men. The pattern we observed for satisfaction with the household's financial situation was reversed, with women experiencing a more rapid decline in satisfaction than men. These results were largely robust to different model specifications, with the exception of our findings for men's financial well-being. After several major socio-economic characteristics were included in the model, the effect size declined. Furthermore, the fixed-effects model showed no significant effects of separation. Thus, it appears that much of the correlation was due to particular kinds of fathers (i.e., fathers with low wages or other characteristics that would cause them to be concerned about their finances) who selected themselves into separation.

In addition to investigating the effects of separation on parents' levels of satisfaction with their family life and financial situation, we looked at how practising shared parenting affected their well-being. Our findings indicated that practising shared parenting was only weakly correlated with parental well-being. After socio-economic variables were included in the model, no significant association could be detected. Instead, we found that cohabiting with or having married a new partner was the decisive determinant of the well-being of separated parents. The results also showed that for men, having had another child increased their family well-being, but reduced their financial well-being. Financial well-being was also found to be strongly associated with employment status, as being unemployed or non-employed reduced the well-being of both men and women to a similar extent.

Like in other European countries, shared parenting is becoming increasingly common in Germany. While shared legal custody has been the default legal custody arrangement for divorced parents in Germany since 1998, the question of whether (equally) shared parenting should be made the default physical custody arrangement after separation is now being debated. The current discussion has primarily focused on the question of how shared parenting affects the well-being of children, while paying little attention to the impact of shared parenting on the well-being of parents. Our study adds to this debate by showing that practising shared parenting neither positively nor negatively affects parental well-being. One potential explanation for this rather unexpected "non-finding" is the heterogeneity of the parents who practise shared parenting. On the one hand, parents who practise shared parenting must maintain a cooperative relationship, which may be positively associated with well-being. On the other hand, these parents are forced to interact with their ex-partner. Depending on the level of conflict between the ex-partners and their ability to co-parent, this pressure to engage with each other may be a source of stress that reduces their well-being.

This study has several limitations. Most importantly, there is no common legal definition of shared parenting in the social sciences. The lack of a clear concept has resulted in radically different operational definitions and values for shared parenting being reported in different studies. In the German case, for example, estimates of the percentage of separated parents who practice shared parenting range from 5% to 15% (Institut für Demoskopie Allensbach 2017). In this study, we have defined shared parenting as an arrangement in which the child lives with both of his/her parents, or in which the non-resident parent sees the child every day. Using this definition, we found that 12% of separated parents were practising shared parenting in Germany, which is in line with the abovementioned prior estimates. Even though our findings are stable across different operational definitions of shared parenting, the discussion of shared parenting and its effect on children and parents is greatly hampered by the lack of a shared understanding of the concept.

Our analyses were very much focused on determining the causal influence of shared parenting on well-being. While the fixed-effect analysis was able to account for unobserved time-invariant characteristics, including variables that depict the gendered realities before separation would have been desirable. In particular, it would have been intriguing to explore how the parents' division of work before they separated affected their arrangements after they separated, and how this association, in turn, affected the well-being of fathers and mothers. It is possible that having experienced a more egalitarian division of paid and unpaid labour before they separated was beneficial for the well-being of the parents (Kessler 2018). If, for example, the mother was more engaged in paid employment while the father was more engaged in childcare and housework before the separation, the reduction in the mother's household income might have been less dramatic, and a more equal parenting arrangement might have emerged. Both of these factors might have increased either the financial or family well-being. Moreover, prior research has shown that the quality of the relationship between the ex-partners is decisive for the success of their parenting arrangements and for their well-being after separation (Cornelißen and Monz 2016; Markham et al. 2017). Although information of this kind is surveyed in the German Family Panel, there are currently too few cases in the dataset to allow us to investigate this issue. Finally, a drawback that we share with other studies that examine the behaviour and well-being of separated parents is selective panel attrition, which is a particular problem for the sample of separated fathers (Müller and Castiglioni 2015).

Acknowledgments The research leading to these results received funding from the German Research Foundation (project number: 266395921). This chapter uses data from the German Family Panel pairfam, coordinated by Josef Brüderl, Sonja Drobnič, Karsten Hank, Bernhard Nauck, Franz Neyer, and Sabine Walper. pairfam is funded as long-term project by the German Research Foundation (DFG).

Appendix

Table 12.6 Sample composition, all parents, person-years by column percent

	Satisfaction with family life			Satisfaction with financial situation		
	Men	Women	Total	Men	Women	Total
Gender						
Male	–	–	0.40	–	–	0.40
Female	–	–	0.60	–	–	0.60
Region						
Western Germany	0.64	0.67	0.66	0.64	0.67	0.66
Eastern Germany	0.36	0.33	0.34	0.36	0.33	0.34
Duration since separation						
No separation	0.80	0.73	0.76	0.81	0.74	0.76
0–1 years after separation	0.03	0.04	0.04	0.03	0.04	0.04
2–3 years after separation	0.03	0.04	0.03	0.03	0.04	0.03
4–5 years after separation	0.03	0.04	0.03	0.03	0.03	0.03
6–7 years after separation	0.02	0.04	0.03	0.02	0.03	0.03
8–9 years after separation	0.03	0.03	0.03	0.02	0.03	0.03
10 or more years after separation	0.06	0.08	0.08	0.06	0.08	0.08
Education						
Low	0.09	0.11	0.10	0.08	0.11	0.10
Medium	0.54	0.58	0.56	0.54	0.57	0.56
High	0.37	0.31	0.34	0.38	0.32	0.34
Employment status						
Employed	0.90	0.65	0.75	0.90	0.68	0.77
Unemployed	0.05	0.05	0.05	0.05	0.05	0.05
Not in labour force	0.05	0.29	0.19	0.05	0.26	0.18
Missing	0.00	0.01	0.01	0.00	0.01	0.01
Family status at first birth						
Married	0.54	0.55	0.54	0.54	0.55	0.54
Cohabiting	0.35	0.32	0.33	0.36	0.32	0.34
Single	0.11	0.13	0.13	0.10	0.13	0.12

(continued)

Table 12.6 (continued)

	Satisfaction with family life			Satisfaction with financial situation		
	Men	Women	Total	Men	Women	Total
Current family status						
Single	0.07	0.10	0.09	0.07	0.10	0.09
LAT	0.03	0.06	0.05	0.03	0.06	0.05
Cohabiting	0.17	0.16	0.16	0.17	0.15	0.16
Married	0.73	0.68	0.70	0.73	0.68	0.70
Child with current partner						
Child with current partner	0.54	0.53	0.54	0.55	0.54	0.54
No child with current partner	0.46	0.47	0.46	0.45	0.46	0.46
Parenting arrangement						
Residence with child	0.82	0.95	0.90	0.82	0.94	0.90
Shared parenting	0.04	0.03	0.04	0.05	0.04	0.04
Non-resident parent	0.12	0.01	0.05	0.11	0.01	0.05
Other	0.02	0.01	0.01	0.02	0.01	0.01
Continuous covariates (Mean, std. error)						
Age (Mean)	36.72	35.39	35.92	37.19	35.87	36.39
Age (std. error)	(0.05)	(0.04)	(0.03)	(0.06)	(0.05)	(0.04)
Age of child (Mean)	7.65	8.37	8.09	7.82	8.59	8.29
Age of child (std. error)	(0.05)	(0.04)	(0.03)	(0.05)	(0.04)	(0.03)
Satisfaction (Mean)	8.48	8.52	8.51	6.28	6.33	6.31
Satisfaction (std. error)	(0.02)	(0.01)	(0.01)	(0.02)	(0.02)	(0.02)
Sample size						
Subjects	2351	3425	5776	1886	2716	4602
Person years	10,768	16,422	27,190	10,768	16,422	22,535

Notes: Unweighted values

References

Allison, P. D. (2009). *Fixed effects regression models*. Los Angeles: Sage.

Amato, P. R., & Rezac, S. J. (1994). Contact with nonresident parents, interparental conflict, and children's behavior. *Journal of Family Issues, 15*(2), 191–207. https://doi.org/10.1177/0192513X94015002003.

Andreß, H.-J., & Bröckel, M. (2007). Income and life satisfaction after marital disruption in Germany. *Journal of Marriage and Family, 69*(2), 500–512. https://doi.org/10.1111/j.1741-3737.2007.00379.x.

Bastin, S. (2016). *Partnerschaftsverläufe alleinerziehender Mütter: Eine quantitative Untersuchung auf Basis des Beziehungs- und Familienpanels*. [Repartnering of single mothers: A quantitative study based on the German Family Panel]. Wiesbaden: Springer VS.

Bauserman, R. (2002). Child adjustment in joint-custody versus sole-custody arrangements: A meta-analytic review. *Journal of Family Psychology, 16*(1), 91–102. https://doi.org/10.1037/0893-3200.16.1.91.

Bayaz-Ozturk, G., Burkhauser, R. V., Couch, K. A., & Hauser, R. (2018). The effects of union dissolution on the economic resources of man and women: A comparative analysis of Germany and the United States, 1985–2013. *The Annals of the American Academy of Political and Social Science, 680*(1), 235–258. https://doi.org/10.1177/0002716218793608.

Beckmeyer, J. J., Coleman, M., & Ganong, L. H. (2014). Postdivorce coparenting typologies and children's adjustment. *Family Relations, 63*(4), 526–537. https://doi.org/10.1111/fare.12086.

Bergström, M., Fransson, E., Modin, B., Berlin, M., Gustafsson, P. A., & Hjern, A. (2015). Fifty moves a year: Is there an association between joint physical custody and psychosomatic problems in children? *Journal of Epidemiology and Community Health, 69*(8), 769–774. https://doi.org/10.1136/jech-2014-205058.

Biotteau, A.-L., Bonnet, C., & Cambois, E. (2019). Risk of major depressive episodes after separation: The gender-specific contribution of the income and support lost through union dissolution. *European Journal of Population, 35*(3), 519–542. https://doi.org/10.1007/s10680-018-9488-y.

Braver, S. L., & Votruba, A. M. (2018). Does joint physical custody "cause" children's better outcomes? *Journal of Divorce and Remarriage, 59*(5), 452–468. https://doi.org/10.1080/10502556.2018.1454203.

Bröckel, M., & Andreß, H.-J. (2015). The economic consequences of divorce in Germany: What has changed since the turn of the millennium? *Comparative Population Studies, 40*(3), 277–312. https://doi.org/10.12765/CPoS-2015-04en.

Brüderl, J., Drobnič, S., Hank, K., Nauck, B., Neyer, F. J., Walper, S., et al. (2019). *The German Family Panel (pairfam).* GESIS Data Archive, Cologne. ZA5678 Data file Version 10.0.0. https://doi.org/10.4232/pairfam.5678.10.0.0.

Bujard, M. (2015). Kinderlosigkeit in Deutschland: Wie interagieren Bildung, Wohnort, Migrationshintergrund, Erwerbstätigkeit und Kohorte? [Childlessness in Germany: How do education, place or residence, migration background, occupation, and cohort interact?]. *Zeitschrift für Familienforschung/Journal of Family Research, 27*(3), 270–296. https://doi.org/10.3224/zff.v27i3.21275.

Clark, A. E., Diener, E., Georgellis, Y., & Lucas, R. E. (2008). Lags and leads in life satisfaction: A test of the baseline hypothesis. *The Economic Journal, 118*(529), F222–F243. https://doi.org/10.1111/j.1468-0297.2008.02150.x.

Cornelißen, W., & Monz, A. (2016). Coparenting: Wie kooperieren Eltern in Bezug auf die Versorgung, Betreuung und Erziehung ihrer Kinder nach einer Trennung? Vier Fallbeispiele. [Co-parenting: How do parents cooperate after separation regarding their children's provisioning, care and education? Four case studies]. *Zeitschrift für Soziologie der Erziehung und Sozialisation, 36*(1), 23–38. https://doi.org/10.3262/ZSE1601023.

de Regt, S., Mortelmans, D., & Marynissen, T. (2013). Financial consequences of relationship dissolution: A longitudinal comparison of formerly married and unmarried cohabiting men and women. *Sociology, 47*(1), 90–108. https://doi.org/10.1177/0038038512453793.

Dethloff, N. (2015). From separation to stepfamily. A legal perspective. In U. Zartler, V. Heintz-Martin, & O. Arránz Becker (Eds.), *Family dynamics after separation: A life course perspective on post-divorce families* (Vol. Special Issue/Sonderheft 10 der Zeitschrift für Familienforschung/Journal of Family Research, pp. 205–218). Opladen/Berlin/Toronto: Barbara Budrich.

Dethloff, N., & Kaesling, K. (2018). Kindesunterhalt und Wechselmodell – Eine vergleichende Perspektive. [Child support and shared parenting – A comparative perspective]. *FamRZ, 2*, 73–78.

Diener, E. (2009). Subjective well-being. In E. Diener (Ed.), *The science of well-being: Social indicators research series* (pp. 11–58). Dordrecht: Springer. https://doi.org/10.1007/978-90-481-2350-6_2.

Ferrer-i-Carbonell, A., & Frijters, P. (2004). How important is methodology for the estimates of the determinants of happiness? *The Economic Journal, 114*(497), 641–659. https://doi.org/10.1111/j.1468-0297.2004.00235.x.

Geisler, E., & Kreyenfeld, M. (2019). Why do lone mothers fare worse than lone fathers? Lone parenthood and welfare benefit receipt in Germany. *Comparative Population Studies, 44*(2019), 61–84. https://doi.org/10.12765/CPoS-2019-09en.

Goldscheider, F., Bernhardt, E., & Lappegård, T. (2015). The gender revolution: A framework for understanding changing family and demographic behavior. *Population and Development Review, 41*(2), 207–239. https://doi.org/10.1111/j.1728-4457.2015.00045.x.

Grätz, M. (2017). Does separation really lead fathers and mothers to be less involved in their children's lives? *European Sociological Review, 33*(4), 551–562. https://doi.org/10.1093/esr/jcx058.

Härkönen, J., Bernardi, F., & Boertien, D. (2017). Family dynamics and child outcomes: An overview of research and open questions. *European Journal of Population, 33*(2), 163–184. https://doi.org/10.1007/s10680-017-9424-6.

Henneman, H. (2017). Das Wechselmodell als Umgangsregelung – eine überzeugende Lösung? [Shared parenting as a physical custody arrangement – A convincing solution?]. *NJW, 70*(25), 1787–1790.

Huinink, J., Brüderl, J., Nauck, B., Walper, S., Castiglioni, L., & Feldhaus, M. (2011). Panel analysis of intimate relationships and family dynamics (pairfam): Conceptual framework and design. *Zeitschrift für Familienforschung, 23*(1), 77–101.

Huß, B., & Pollmann-Schult, M. (2018). *Lebenszufriedenheit von getrennt lebenden Müttern und Vätern* [Life satisfaction of separated mothers and fathers]. Berlin/Rostock/Magdeburg. https://doi.org/10.25673/5206.

Institut für Demoskopie Allensbach. (2017). *Getrennt gemeinsam erziehen: Kernergebnisse einer Befragung von Trennungseltern* [Joint parenting despite separation: Main results of a survey among separated parents]. Allensbach. https://www.ifd-allensbach.de/uploads/tx_studies/Abach_Trennungseltern_Bericht.pdf. Accessed 26 Aug 2019.

Ivanova, K., & Balbo, N. (2019). Cementing the stepfamily? Biological and stepparents' relationship satisfaction after the birth of a common child in stepfamilies. *Journal of Family Issues, 40*(10), 1346–1363. https://doi.org/10.1177/0192513X19836456.

Ivanova, K., Kalmijn, M., & Uunk, W. (2013). The effect of children on men's and women's chances of re-partnering in a European context. *European Journal of Population, 49*(4), 417–444. https://doi.org/10.1007/s10680-013-9294-5.

Joyner, K., Peters, H. E., Hynes, K., Sikora, A., Taber, J., & Rendall, M. (2012). The quality of male fertility data in major U.S. surveys. *Demography, 49*(1), 101–124. https://doi.org/10.1007/s13524-011-0073-9.

Kalmijn, M. (2016). Father-child contact, interparental conflict, and depressive symptoms among children of divorced parents. *European Sociological Review, 32*(1), 68–80. https://doi.org/10.1093/esr/jcv095.

Kessler, D. (2018). *The consequences of divorce for mothers and fathers: Unequal but converging?* (LIVES Working Paper 71). Lausanne: https://doi.org/10.12682/lives.2296-1658.2018.71.

Kindler, H., & Walper, S. (2016). Das Wechselmodell im Kontext elterlicher Konflikte. [Shared parenting in the context of parental conflicts]. *Neue Zeitschrift für Familienrecht, 3*(18), 820–824.

Kreyenfeld, M., Huinink, J., Trappe, H., & Walke, R. (2012). DemoDiff: A dataset for the study of family change in eastern (and western) Germany. *Schmollers Jahrbuch, 132*(4), 653–660. https://doi.org/10.3790/schm.132.4.653.

Lee, D., & McLanahan, S. (2015). Family structure transitions and child development: Instability, selection, and population heterogeneity. *American Sociological Review, 80*(4), 738–763. https://doi.org/10.1177/0003122415592129.

Leopold, T. (2018). Gender differences in the consequences of divorce: A study of multiple outcomes. *Demography, 55*(3), 769–797. https://doi.org/10.1007/s13524-018-0667-6.

Leopold, T., & Kalmijn, M. (2016). Is divorce more painful when couples have children? Evidence from long-term panel data on multiple domains of well-being. *Demography, 53*(6), 1717–1742. https://doi.org/10.1007/s13524-016-0518-2.

Lettmaier, S., & Dürbeck, W. (2019). Die Behandlung elterlicher Umgangskosten im Unterhalts-, Sozial- und Steuerrecht. [Treatment of costs of parent-child contact in the legal regulations concerning maintenance, social rights and taxes]. *FamRZ, 2*, 81–88.

Lucas, R. E. (2007). Adaptation and the set-point model of subjective well-being: Does happiness change after major life events? *Current Directions in Psychological Science, 16*(2), 75–79. https://doi.org/10.1111/j.1467-8721.2007.00479.x.

Markham, M. S., Hartenstein, J. L., Mitchell, Y. T., & Aljayyousi-Khalil, G. (2017). Communication among parents who share physical custody after divorce or separation. *Journal of Family Issues, 38*(10), 1414–1442. https://doi.org/10.1177/0192513X15616848.

McLanahan, S., Tach, L., & Schneider, D. (2013). The causal effects of father absence. *Annual Review of Sociology, 39*(1), 399–427. https://doi.org/10.1146/annurev-soc-071312-145704.

Müller, B., & Castiglioni, L. (2015). Stable relationships, stable participation? The effects of partnership dissolution and changes in relationship stability on attrition in a relationship and family panel. *Survey Research Methods, 9*(3), 205–219. https://doi.org/10.18148/srm/2016.v10i1.6207.

Nielsen, L. (2018). Joint versus sole physical custody: Children's outcomes independent of parent-child relationships, income, and conflict in 60 studies. *Journal of Divorce and Remarriage, 59*(4), 247–281. https://doi.org/10.1080/10502556.2018.1454204.

Poortman, A.-R. (2018). Postdivorce parent–child contact and child well-being: The importance of predivorce parental involvement. *Journal of Marriage and Family, 80*(3), 671–683. https://doi.org/10.1111/jomf.12474.

Popova, D., & Navicke, J. (2019). The probability of poverty for mothers after childbirth and divorce in Europe: The role of social stratification and tax-benefit policies. *Social Science Research, 78*(1), 57–70. https://doi.org/10.1016/j.ssresearch.2018.10.007.

Ruetten, B. (2016). Das paritätische Wechselmodell und Streitfragen des Kindergeldes sowie anderer kindbezogener Leistungen. [Equally shared parenting and the controversial issue of child allowance and other child related benefits]. *Neue Zeitschrift für Familienrecht, 8*, 337–341.

Schnor, C. (2014). *The contexts of partnership and childbearing as determinants of union stability: A quantitative analysis on western and eastern German partnerships with data from the German Family Panel.* Rostock: Max Planck Institute for Demographic Research. https://www.demogr.mpg.de/en/projects_publications/publications_1904/dissertations/the_contexts_of_partnership_and_childbearing_as_determinants_of_union_stability_a_quantitative_5344.htm. Accessed 26 Aug 2019.

Schumann, E. (2018). *Gemeinsam getragene Elternverantwortung nach Trennung und Scheidung –Reformbedarf im Sorge-, Umgangs- und Unterhaltsrecht?* [Joint parental responsibility after separation and divorce – Reform need of legal regulations concerning custody, contact, and maintenance?]. München: C.H. Beck.

Smyth, B. M. (2017). Special issue on shared-time parenting after separation. *Family Court Review, 55*(4), 494–499. https://doi.org/10.1111/fcre.12299.

Sodermans, A., Botterman, S., Havermans, N., & Matthijs, K. (2015). Involved fathers, liberated mothers? Joint physical custody and the subjective well-being of divorced parents. *Social Indicators Research, 122*(1), 257–277. https://doi.org/10.1007/s11205-014-0676-9.

Soons, J. P. M., Liefbroer, A. C., & Kalmijn, M. (2009). The long-term consequences of relationship formation for subjective well-being. *Journal of Marriage and Family, 71*(5), 1254–1270. https://doi.org/10.1111/j.1741-3737.2009.00667.x.

Statistisches Bundesamt. (2018a). *Bevölkerung und Erwerbstätigkeit. Statistik der rechtskräftigen Beschlüsse in Eheauflösungssachen (Scheidungsstatistik) und Statistik der Aufhebung von Lebenspartnerschaften (Berichtsjahr: 2016)* [Population and employment. Statistic on divorce and statistic on the dissolution of civil unions]. Wiesbaden: Statistisches Bundesamt.

Statistisches Bundesamt. (2018b). *Alleinerziehende in Deutschland 2017. Begleitmaterial zur Pressekonferenz am 2. August 2018* [Lone parents in Germany 2017. Accompanying information with a press conference on August 2nd, 2018]. Wiesbaden: Statistisches Bundesamt.

Steinbach, A. (2019). Children's and parents' well-being in joint physical custody: A literature review. *Family Process, 58*(2), 353–369. https://doi.org/10.1111/famp.12372.

Sünderhauf, H. (2013). *Wechselmodell: Psychologie-Recht-Praxis: Abwechselnde Kinderbetreuung durch Eltern nach Trennung und Scheidung* [Joint physical custody: Psychology-law-practice: Alternate parental child care after separation and divorce]. Wiesbaden: Springer.

Thielemans, G., & Mortelmans, D. (2019). Female labour force participation after divorce: How employment histories matter. *Journal of Family and Economic Issues, 40*(2), 180–193. https://doi.org/10.1007/s10834-018-9600-9.

van Damme, M., Kalmijn, M., & Uunk, W. (2009). The employment of separated women in Europe: Individual and institutional determinants. *European Sociological Review, 25*(2), 183–197. https://doi.org/10.1093/esr/jcn042.

van der Heijden, F., Gähler, M., & Härkönen, J. (2015). Are parents with shared residence happier? Children's postdivorce residence arrangements and parents' life satisfaction. *Stockholm Research Reports in Demography, 17*(2015).

van der Heijden, F., Poortman, A.-R., & van der Lippe, T. (2016). Children's postdivorce residence arrangements and parental experienced time pressure. *Journal of Marriage and Family, 78*(2), 468–481. https://doi.org/10.1111/jomf.12283.

Walper, S. (2016). Arrangements elterlicher Fürsorge nach Trennung und Scheidung: Das Wechselmodell im Licht neuer Daten aus Deutschland. [Arrangements of parental custody after separation and divorce: Joint physical custody in light of new data from Germany]. In Deutscher Familiengerichtstag (Ed.), *21. Deutscher Familiengerichtstag vom 21. bis 24. Oktober 2015 in Brühl* (Vol. Brühler Schriften zum Familienrecht, Band 19, pp. 99–143). Bielefeld: Gieseking Verlag.

Walper, S., & Beckh, K. (2006). Adolescents' development in high-conflict and separated families: Evidence from a German longitudinal study. In A. Clarke-Stewart & J. Dunn (Eds.), *Families count: Effects on child and adolescent development* (pp. 238–270). Cambridge: Cambridge University Press.

Walper, S., Thönnissen, C., & Alt, P. (2015). Effects of family structure and the experience of parental separation: A focus on adolescents' well-being. *Comparative Population Studies – Zeitschrift für Bevölkerungsforschung, 40*(3), 335–364. https://doi.org/10.12765/CPoS-2015-12en.

Yuan, A. S. V. (2016). Father-child relationships and nonresident fathers' psychological distress: What helps and what hurts? *Journal of Family Issues, 37*(5), 603–621. https://doi.org/10.1177/0192513X14526394.

Part IV
Health-Related Consequences of Divorce and Separation

Chapter 13
Heterogeneous Effects of Family Complexity in Childhood on Mental Health: Testing the "Good Divorce" and the "Good Stepparent" Hypotheses

Katya Ivanova and Matthijs Kalmijn

Introduction

As the instability of adult intimate unions has grown in recent decades, there has been ongoing scientific and popular interest in the impact of parental partnership dissolution (referring both to marital and non-marital cohabiting unions) on children (Amato 2010; Amato and James 2010; Wang and Amato 2000). Much has been written about the effects of divorce on a range of short- and long-term child outcomes, such as psychosocial adjustment (Sands et al. 2017), educational attainment (Bernardi and Radl 2014; Brand et al. 2019), and (adult) children's own experiences with intimate partnerships (Amato and DeBoer 2001; Ivanova et al. 2011; Wolfinger 2011). Considerable efforts have been made by researchers in this field to assess the magnitude of and the heterogeneity in the possible disadvantages children of divorce might be facing, and to identify the mechanisms that drive the potential association between parental separation and maladjustment (Härkönen 2014; Kim 2011). Importantly, the initial general consensus that family dissolution has negative effects has evolved into a recognition of the difficulties associated with distinguishing the specific effects of parental separation (i.e., the moment when one of the parents leaves the parental household) from the complex interplay of events and processes that lead up to and are precipitated by that family transition (Härkönen 2014). In other words, viewing divorce as an event might be an unjustified oversimplification, given that it is often preceded by the longer process of the disintegration of the relationship, and is followed by the need to negotiate relations between multiple single or stepparent households.

K. Ivanova (✉)
Department of Sociology, Tilburg University, Tilburg, The Netherlands
e-mail: k.o.ivanova@uvt.nl

M. Kalmijn
Netherlands Interdisciplinary Demographic Institute, Den Haag, The Netherlands

M. Kreyenfeld, H. Trappe (eds.), *Parental Life Courses after Separation and Divorce in Europe*, Life Course Research and Social Policies 12,
https://doi.org/10.1007/978-3-030-44575-1_13

The importance of post-divorce relations for the adjustment levels of the children involved has been highlighted by the notion of the "good divorce" (Ahrons 1994, 2007; Ahrons and Tanner 2003). The argument made by proponents of this concept is that as long as "parents – as they did when they were married – continue to be responsible for the emotional, economic, and physical needs of their children" (Ahrons 1994: 3) and maintain a cooperative relationship, any negative consequences of their separation can be minimized. In her work, Ahrons developed a typology of ex-couples based on the nature of their interactions after separation, and reported that about half of the ex-partners could be classified as having high-quality communication. However, the claim that the children of these couples could be successfully sheltered from the negative repercussions of the parental separation has certainly been challenged (e.g., Amato et al. 2011). Furthermore, studies that have paid closer attention to the timing of separation have shown that the vast majority of couples with children report having antagonistic contact, especially in the years immediately following the divorce (Fischer et al. 2005). In other words, although there certainly are some "good divorces," a substantial number of children are still exposed to a hostile interparental relationship in the years following the separation.

Given that the majority of parents repartner after the dissolution of their union (Thomson 2014), children often grow up not only with two ex-partners as parents, but also with one or two stepparents. Therefore, much attention has been paid to the effects of living in a stepfamily on child well-being. The findings of these studies have been rather mixed, with some authors reporting that living in a stepfamily has positive effects on children's adjustment levels, while others have found either negative or no effects (Sweeney 2007; for a review, see Sweeney 2010). One reason why these findings differ (in addition to the wide range of outcomes studied) is that the comparison groups used were not consistent. For example, whereas some researchers compared children in stepfamilies with children in their original, two-parent families, others compared single-parent and stepparent households. It is, however, important to note that there is considerable heterogeneity among stepfamilies, as some stepfamilies are stable and cooperative, while others are characterized by conflict. This variability should matter for child outcomes as well.

In this chapter, we contribute to the ongoing debate about the concept of the "good divorce," and examine the levels of depressive feelings reported by young adults who experienced parental separation in childhood. We begin by addressing the question of whether growing up with separated biological parents can be linked to higher levels of maladjustment in young adulthood. We then examine whether any association found in the first part of our study might be driven by the quality of the post-divorce tie between the ex-partners. In other words, we explicitly look at whether separations that are not followed by elevated levels of conflict are detrimental to the long-term adjustment of children. We go a step further than earlier investigations of the "good divorce" hypothesis by also considering the quality of a young adult's stepparent-child relationships in childhood, and proposing a "good stepparent" hypothesis. It should be pointed out that when we refer to "effects" in the analyses and in the title, the term is meant in a statistical sense, as it is clear that these effects are only approximations of the causal effects that a divorce may have.

In our work, we utilize data from the recently collected OKiN survey (Ouders en Kinderen in Nederland; Parents and Children in the Netherlands; Kalmijn et al. 2018), which was specifically designed to address questions about the long-term repercussions of family complexity. We focus on young adults (aged 25–35) born in the 1980s who were not living with their two biological parents by age 15. Like many other Western countries, the Netherlands has experienced a marked increase in divorce since the 1960s. Therefore, the cohorts of young adults included in our analyses are among the first group of children who were affected by the Dutch "divorce revolution" while growing up – although they are certainly not the first cohorts to experience the impact of that substantial shift in matrimonial patterns.

Background

Parental Separation and Post-divorce Interparental Conflict

Considerable efforts have been made to identify the mechanisms that might explain the association between divorce and the adjustment levels of individuals. In particular, many authors have closely examined the question of whether there is negative selection into divorce (for example, based on socioeconomic status; Gennetian 2005; Ginther and Pollak 2004; Grätz 2017). In other words, scholars have been attempting to determine the extent to which the link between divorce and (child) maladjustment is causal or spurious. A number of researchers have indeed found that the magnitude of the effect of parental divorce on (adult) children's well-being decreases after a range of characteristics that might function as confounders are taken into account. Moreover, some authors have used person fixed-effect models to show that there is no association between changes in family structure and changes in behavioral problems for children (Aughinbaugh et al. 2005). However, the majority of studies that have looked at this question have found that at least some of the negative effects of marital separation on individual adjustment persist after accounting for selection (Amato 2010; Amato and Sobolewski 2001; Kim 2011). Therefore, in line with previous work, we expect to find that when we compare adults whose parents separated while they were children to adults with continuously married parents, the well-being of the adults in the former group will be lower.

In addition to differing on methodology, scholars have debated the theoretical mechanisms that underlie this association, which might include the loss of resources (e.g., financial resources, but also parental time and ability to provide support) following parental separation, and the stress precipitated by the family transition. Whereas the resource model has often been used in investigations of how child educational attainment is affected by parental divorce (Bernardi and Boertien 2016; Bernardi and Radl 2014; Jonsson and Gähler 1997; Thomson et al. 1994), the stress model has frequently been applied in studies of child and parental psychological well-being following separation (Lansford 2009; Pearlin et al. 2005). Importantly, evidence of the detrimental effects of the stress precipitated by family transitions has led some researchers to argue that a child's level of adjustment may be highly dependent on the level of interparental conflict (and the resulting stress and anxiety for children) that surrounded the marital separation.

Exposure to interparental discord has been shown to have clear, long-term negative repercussions for individual well-being (Amato and Sobolewski 2001; Musick and Meier 2010). A number of studies have shown that conflict within a marriage can be detrimental for children. For example, children may perceive that they play a role in creating the tensions between their parents (Pryor and Rodgers 2001), or they may suffer because the ability of their parents to engage in warm and effective parenting is compromised (Amato 2000). This line of reasoning in turn implies that ending an acrimonious relationship might be beneficial for everyone involved, as it limits the risk of conflictual interactions occurring. Indeed, researchers have shown that when a partnership is of poor quality, the negative effects of divorce on adjustment are diminished for both the adults (e.g., Monden and Kalmijn 2006) and the children involved (Strohschein 2005). It is, however, important to note that dissolving a discordant relationship does not necessarily mean that the ties between the ex-partners are severed, especially when there are children involved. Whereas couples without children can have a "clean break" from a problematic relationship, parents have to maintain some form of communication while parenting their shared offspring (Fischer et al. 2005).

The magnitude of post-divorce conflict has been highlighted as an important moderator in the association between the dissolution of the partnership of the parents and the maladjustment of their children. It has been a key reason why researchers have pointed out that shared post-divorce residence for children might be harmful, as it can expose them continuously to heightened interparental discord (Harris-Short 2010; Poortman and van Gaalen 2017). Post-divorce conflict can affect children in a myriad of ways. It can, for example, intensify feelings of conflicting loyalties for children, as it could force them to choose between the contending parents. This pressure may, in turn, undermine the children's relationship with one or both of their biological parents (usually the father; Hornstra et al. 2020). It has, however, been argued that if parents are able to maintain a low-conflict, collaborative relationship following the dissolution of their partnership, the stress associated with the divorce could be temporary. Thus, any negative effects of the dissolution on the child's well-being would be short-lived (Ahrons 1994; Kelly and Emery 2003). This line of reasoning implies that the child should experience no long-term negative effects if the parents have a "good divorce." The "good divorce" became the ideal of the cultural elite during the 1970s and 1980s, when social science research was warning of the potentially negative effects of divorce on children (Dronkers 1997).

The existing evidence on this potential buffering effect has been mixed (for an overview, see Kelly and Emery 2003). Some authors have reported that children with collaborative divorced parents display fewer behavioral problems in adolescence (Amato et al. 2011; Beckmeyer et al. 2014), but others have found little evidence to support the good divorce hypothesis (Amato et al. 2011). In their analysis of ten child outcomes, Amato et al. (2011) identified only one significant difference that seems to indicate that cooperative parenting after a divorce confers an advantage. However, since their analysis was based on a small sample of approximately 300 young adults, the chances of finding insignificant results was high. In our contribution, we use a much larger sample; and, importantly, we also account for the parents' own behavioral problems while the child was young. Although we do expect to find a negative association between parental separation and adjustment in adulthood (*divorce hypothesis*), we also expect that once the level of conflict is considered, we will observe no differences in the long-term well-being of adult children raised in households with separated parents and those raised in households with continuously married or cohabiting parents (*good divorce hypothesis*).

Most of the previous studies that tested this hypothesis did so primarily for children who were still living at home. In our work, we generalize this idea to long-term effects (i.e., to the consequences for the children of divorced parents when they are adults and living independently). Whether any effects that were operating in an individual's childhood and youth last into his/her adulthood remains an open question. When children become young adults, their well-being is usually less dependent on the behavior of their parents, and they tend to be less exposed to their parents' conflicts. We therefore would not expect large effects but there are also reasons to believe that effects will still be present. Children need practical and emotional support from parents when making the transition to adulthood. Moreover, early mental health problems may lead to an accumulation of adverse experiences, and could therefore persist into adulthood.

Stepparents: The "Good Stepparent" Hypothesis

The majority of separated parents go on to re-partner (Thomson 2014). Thus, studying the long-term effects of parental union dissolution on child well-being in isolation from the possible addition of a stepparent to the household in which the child lives might lead to erroneous conclusions. It is, for example, possible to misrepresent the consequences of divorce by conflating the impact of two distinct transitions: namely, the separation of the parents and the re-partnering of the resident parent. Therefore, in this chapter, we not only address the "good divorce" hypothesis as presented above, but also consider how the addition of a stepparent to a single-parent household might affect the well-being of the child in young adulthood.

The assumption that stress is a key mechanism underlying the association between household transitions and adjustment levels has also been made in studies that examined the extent to which living with a stepparent affects a child's well-being (Fomby and Cherlin 2007). Similar to the argument made about parental union dissolution, this hypothesis suggests that adding a new parental figure to a single-parent household involves a number of potentially stressful adjustments for both the parent and the child. In line with this argument (and, albeit to a less extent, with the resource hypothesis), a number of studies have shown that the transition from a single- to a stepparent household is not associated with more positive outcomes for the children involved (Coleman et al. 2000; Hanson et al. 1996; Thomson et al. 1994). Therefore, we expect to find that young adults who experienced the addition of a stepparent to the household were worse off than their counterparts who experienced only the transition from two-parent to a single-parent household (*stepfamily hypothesis*).

We believe, however, that the effects on a child of the simple transition from one type of household to another are less important than the quality of the tie between the child and the new co-resident parental figure. In other words, as in the case of divorce, we need to recognize the likely heterogeneity in the ties that are created as a result of the transition. While a large number of studies have highlighted the challenges stepparents face in establishing a positive relationship with their stepchildren (Stewart 2007), there is also evidence of considerable diversity in the quality of these dyadic ties (King 2007; White and Gilbreth 2001). It has, moreover, been shown that high-quality stepparent-child relationships are associated with higher adjustment levels well beyond childhood (Jensen and Harris 2017). Therefore, in this contribution we propose a "good stepparent" hypothesis: i.e., we expect to find that adult children who grew up with a stepparent with whom they had a high-quality relationship fare better than children who were raised by a single, separated parent. Again, these expectations apply to the long-term effects of stepfamily experiences.

Method and Data

Data

We use data from the recently collected Dutch survey *Parents and Children in the Netherlands* (*Ouders en Kinderen in Nederland*, OKiN; Kalmijn et al. 2018). The sampling frame was based on the Dutch population register (Bakker et al. 2014; Prins 2017). A systematic oversample was created based on with whom the targeted respondents (adults born between 1971 and 1991) were living when they were 15 years old. Three sampling strata were defined: (a) households with non-separated parents (both parents, as listed on the birth certificate, were present in the household; 25%); (b) households with one separated parent and no new partner (i.e., only one biological parent was present in the household; 33%); and (c) households with a separated parent and a new partner (i.e., one biological parent and the partner of the parent were registered as living in the household; 42%). Although the officially registered household constellation did not always match the actual situation of the household, using the strata was a highly effective way to oversample children whose parents were not continuously together throughout their childhood. The actual household situation of the respondent during youth was assessed in the questionnaire.

The fieldwork was carried out by Statistics Netherlands in 2017. The targeted respondents (also referred to as anchors) received an introduction letter inviting them to participate using an internet link. The invitation included an unconditional incentive (€5 gift certificate), and non-respondents received several reminders. If they did not respond after a month following the last letter, they were asked to participate in a face-to-face computer-assisted interview. The final response rate was 62% (N = 6485 adult children), which is above average for the Netherlands (De Leeuw and De Heer 2001). Given that our focus is on young adults, we decided to limit the sample to 25–35-year-old respondents. This led to a subsample of 4056 individuals. Of those, we dropped the anchors who reported that they either did not know or could not provide any information about their father or mother, as they were not asked questions about the level of interparental conflict after separation (n = 166 observations lost). We kept the respondents who experienced the death of a parent while young and those who were born to a single parent in order to give the reader the opportunity to compare the association between separation and maladjustment with the effects of living in other household constellations. The final analytical sample consisted of 3890 individuals (57.4% of whom experienced parental separation in childhood). On average, the participants with separated parents experienced the dissolution of their parents' partnership at 7.61 years of age (with a standard deviation of 4.08 years), which is, on average, 22 years prior to the interview (range 9–34; median: 22 years). Descriptive information about all of the variables described below is provided in Tables 13.1a and 13.1b (Table 13.1a shows the unweighted descriptives and Table 13.1b shows the weighted descriptives).

Variables

Depression In this contribution, we operationalized maladjustment as the self-reported level of depressive feelings using the eight-item version of the Centre of Epidemiological Studies-Depression Scale (Van de Velde et al. 2009). The respondents were asked to rate how well eight statements described how they felt during the past week on a scale from 1 = *rarely or never* to 4 = *most of the time or always* (e.g., "I felt depressed"; "My sleep was restless"; "I was unable to get going"). The scale was calculated by taking the mean of the eight items, with higher values denoting more depressive feelings. The reliability of the scale was $\alpha = .86$ and the mean in our analytical sample was $M = 1.62$ ($SD = 0.56$).

Family and Household Composition in Childhood Information about the family and household transitions in childhood were obtained through retrospective questions. The respondents were asked whether their parents were together at the time of the respondent's birth (single parent, n = 264 of analytical sample), whether either of their parents had died (deceased parent, n = 286 of analytical sample), and whether their parents had separated (separated parents, n = 2233 of analytical sample). The last two questions referred to the period before the anchor turned 18 (or

Table 13.1a Unweighted descriptive statistics of variables used in the multivariate analysis, column percent, mean (M) and standard deviation (SD)

	Parents together in youth		Separated in youth		One parent deceased		Parents not together at birth	
	M (SD)	*range*	*M (SD)*	*range*	*M (SD)*	*range*	*M (SD)*	*range*
Self-reported depressive feelings (1–4)	1.52 (0.49)	1–3.63	1.66 (0.58)	1–4	1.57 (0.51)	1–3.75	1.73 (0.63)	1–4
In top 15% of depression distribution (0/1)	0.10		0.17		0.13		0.24	
Parents separated in youth, low-conflict (0/1)			0.68					
Parents separated in youth, high-conflict (0/1)			0.32					
Lived with a stepparent for part of youth (0/1)			0.75		0.53		0.68	
Lived with a stepfather for part of youth (0/1)			0.65		0.27		0.65	
Low conflict with stepfather (0/1)			0.69		0.65		0.63	
High conflict with stepfather (0/1)			0.31		0.35		0.37	
Lived with a stepmother for part of youth (0/1)			0.27		0.26		0.08	
Low conflict with stepmother (0/1)			0.67		0.58		0.45	
High conflict with stepmother (0/1)			0.33		0.42		0.55	
Age respondent (25–35)	30.07 (3.03)	25–35	29.64 (3.10)	25–35	30.03 (3.03)	25–35	29.78 (3.08)	25–35
Respondent is a woman (0/1)	0.50		0.55		0.56		0.60	
Father is a non-Western migrant (0/1)	0.10		0.09		0.08		0.16	
Father problem behaviors (0–3)	0.21 (0.50)	0–3	0.48 (0.75)	0–3	0.25 (0.54)	0–3	0.38 (0.67)	0–3
Mother problem behaviors (0–3)	0.16 (0.41)	0–3	0.41 (0.64)	0–3	0.23 (0.50)	0–3	0.42 (0.67)	0–3
Subjects	1107		2233		286		264	

Table 13.1b Weighted descriptive statistics of variables used in the multivariate analysis

	Parents together in youth		Separated in youth		One parent deceased		Parents not together at birth	
	M	*SD*	*M*	*SD*	*M*	*SD*	*M*	*SD*
Self-reported depressive feelings (centered)	−0.09	0.93	0.20	1.07	0.14	0.94	0.41	1.33
In top 15% of depression distribution	0.11		0.19		0.20		0.27	
Parents separated in youth, low-conflict			0.63					
Parents separated in youth, high-conflict			0.30					
Lived with a stepparent for part of youth			0.56		0.28		0.47	
Lived with a stepfather for part of youth			0.44		0.14		0.45	
Low conflict with stepfather			0.29		0.09		0.27	
High conflict with stepfather			0.15		0.05		0.18	
Lived with a stepmother for part of youth			0.22		0.14		0.06	
Low conflict with stepmother			0.14		0.08		0.04	
High conflict with stepmother			0.08		0.06		0.02	
Age respondent	29.83	2.99	29.57	3.18	30.01	3.01	30.13	3.15
Respondent is a woman	0.49		0.49	0.50	0.57		0.51	
Father is a non-Western migrant	0.10		0.14	0.34	0.14		0.19	
Father problem behaviors	0.20	0.49	0.46	0.74	0.27	0.51	0.54	0.70
Mother problem behaviors	0.16	0.41	0.42	0.65	0.21	0.48	0.64	0.84

moved out of the household, if preceding 18). If their parents were not together throughout their childhood, the respondents were asked whether their father or mother had any new partners at that time. Identical questions were then asked about the partners with whom the father and the mother had the longest relationships. The respondents were asked whether they lived with any of these new partners, and what the relationship between the anchor and the stepparent was like. Of the respondents aged 25–35 in our sample, 1690 had lived with a stepfather and 687 had lived with a stepmother for at least part of their childhood. Note that the data were collected retrospectively. This means that the new unions of the anchor's parents may have been terminated. In retrospective surveys, there is some danger of the underreporting of dissolved partnerships. In addition, a respondent's evaluation of an anchor-stepparent relationship may depend on whether the union was still ongoing (see below).

Post-separation Interparental Conflict If the participants reported that their parents separated during their childhood, they were asked to assess the level of conflict between their parents using the following question, "Were there serious fights between your parents in the first years following the separation?" on a four-point scale (1 = *never* to 4 = *often*). Those respondents who reported that their parents never or sometimes fought were rated as "low conflict," while those who reported that their parents fought regularly or frequently were coded as "high conflict." A total of 327 respondents in our analytical sample said that they did not know how much conflict there was between the parents. We decided to code these participants as having experienced a low level of conflict, based on the assumption that regular or frequent fighting would have been noted by the respondent. Of the anchors whose parents had separated, 1519 (68.0%) reported observing low levels of conflict, while 714 (32.0%) reported observing high levels of conflict.

Conflict with Stepparent The respondents who reported that either of their parents had a new partner were asked to assess the level of conflict they had with that person by answering the following question about the period before they started living independently: "Were there tensions and/or conflicts between you and that new partner of your [mother/father] during that time?" (1 = *never* to 4 = *often*). As in the case of the interparental conflict items, we coded the "never" and "sometimes" categories as "low conflict" and the other two as "high conflict." Of the anchors who had lived with a stepparent, 68.0% (n = 1149) of those who lived with a stepfather and 65.2% (n = 448) for those who lived with a stepmother reported experiencing a low level of conflict.

Control Variables In our analyses, we accounted for a number of potential confounders in the key association of interest. First, we controlled for the father's and the mother's problem behaviors during the anchor's childhood. Three indicators were considered: namely, frequent alcohol use (1 = *yes*, 0 = *no*), mental health problems (1 = *yes*, 0 = *no*), and addiction (1 = *yes* 0 = *no*). The three health behaviors were combined into a single scale that represented the count of problem behaviors of the parent during the adult child's youth. We also accounted for the socioeconomic status of both parents, which was based on a scale composed of each parent's standardized highest educational attainment and occupational status during the anchor's childhood (as reported by the participant, and indicated by the International Socio-Economic Index of Occupational Status, ISEI). In cases in which the information needed to estimate the SES status of the parent was missing, we used the Dutch register data to impute these values based on each parent's origin (native Dutch, Western foreigner, non-Western foreigner), current income, age, and estimated home value. We had to implement this procedure for 177 fathers and 116 mothers (out of a full analytical sample of 3890). We also controlled for whether the respondent reported having lived in an institution (and not with family members) at any point during his or her youth (of our full analytical sample, only 53 anchors fit in this category). We also included controls for having a father of non-Dutch origin, the current age of the respondent, and gender.

Analytical Approach

We estimate a number of linear regression models, with the self-reported level of depressive feelings as the dependent variable. The first model only examines the association between experiencing parental separation and maladjustment. The second model addresses the "good divorce" hypothesis by focusing on the level of post-separation conflict between the parents. The reference category consists of children whose parents remained together during their childhood. The third model adds an effect for having lived in a stepfamily. The coding is cumulative; hence, this effect compares children from stepfamilies with children from single-parent divorced families. The fourth model adds variables for high- and low-conflict stepfamilies, separately for stepfathers and stepmothers. Again, the coding is cumulative. We present predictive margins to facilitate the interpretation of these more complex models.

Additionally, given that the level of depressive feelings was rather low in our analytical sample ($M = 1.62$, $SD = 0.56$ for a variable which ranged from one to four), we also estimated logistic regression models, with the probability of reporting depressive symptoms in the top 15% of the distribution. In our analyses, all of the continuous variables (including the dependent variable in the linear regression models) were standardized to $M = 0$, $SD = 1$, which means that the findings can be interpreted as standardized effect sizes. As we had a number of missing values for the parents' problem behaviors ($n = 273$ for mothers and $n = 558$ for fathers), we implemented sequential imputation using chained equations that included all of the variables from the main analyses and a number of anchor characteristics (educational level, unemployment status, current partnership status, parenthood status, and whether the respondent had experienced a partnership dissolution).

Results

We first focus on some descriptive results (presented in Table 13.1a unweighted and Table 13.1b weighted), separately for the young adults who grew up living continuously with their two biological parents and those who did not. First, we can see that, as expected, the anchors who experienced the separation of their parents reported higher levels of depression than their counterparts with parents who were continuously together though the difference is certainly not large. The highest average levels of depression were reported by the anchors who were born into a single-parent household. If we look at the weighted percentage of anchors who reported very high levels of depression (in the top 15% of the distribution), we can see that 19% of the young adults with separated parents, but just 11% of the young adults with parents who were continuously together, reported having high levels of depression. In other words, the results of these basic bivariate analyses suggest that there are some persistent differences in the mental well-being of young adults based on whether their parents had separated.

Another interesting finding displayed in Tables 13.1a and 13.1b is that although the majority of young adults with separated parents reported observing low levels of conflict after parental separation, one in three respondents indicated experiencing a conflictual interparental relationship. An additional check showed that those who observed low levels of post-divorce conflict did not differ substantially in terms of the age at which they experienced a separation from the high-conflict group ($M = 7.56$, $SD = 4.12$ for the low-conflict group and $M = 7.72$, $SD = 3.98$ for the high-conflict group). As we implied in the introduction, the vast majority of the OKiN participants were living with a stepparent following the breakup of their parents' union and unsurprisingly, more participants were living with a stepfather than with a stepmother. The results shown in Tables 13.1a and 13.1b indicate is that there was indeed considerable heterogeneity in the quality of the child-stepparent tie: about one-third of the participants reported having regular and frequent confrontations with a stepparent, regardless of whether the new partner was male or female.

We now turn to Table 13.2, which displays the results from the linear regression analysis with self-reported depressive feelings as the dependent variable. It is important to point out that although we refer here to "effects," we cannot, of course, ascertain a causal relationship per se given the nature of our data. In the first model, we see a positive and significant effect of experiencing parental separation on depressive symptoms in young adulthood, although the magnitude of the effect is not large (.11 of a standard deviation; compared to, for example, the effect of being born to a single parent, which is .22). It is, however, important to keep in mind that this association was found for a sample of young adults who experienced that transition an average of 22 years ago. We would be surprised if we found a very large effect of a single important life event in childhood so many years later. Therefore, this result supports previous findings about the long-lasting repercussions of parental separation on the children involved. Another interesting result is the finding that the participants who had experienced the death of a parent did not report higher levels of depression in adulthood than those whose parents were continuously together.

Yet the findings of the subsequent models are also essential to our work. Model 2 shows that the association between divorce and maladjustment is only present if it is followed by high levels of interparental conflict. The magnitude of the effect is larger than it is in the first model (.260 vs .109), and it is comparable to the detrimental effect of being born to a single parent. No statistically significant association is found between having experienced a low-conflict parental separation and maladjustment, which suggests that children who experienced low-conflict separations are doing as well as children in families with stable parental unions. Thus, the "good divorce" hypothesis posited by Ahrons (1994) is supported.

Model 3 and Model 4 focus on the "good stepparent" hypothesis. Looking at Model 3, we observe an association between adding a stepparent to the single-parent post-divorce household and maladjustment. In other words, the results of this model suggest that having experienced an additional transition to a stepparent

Table 13.2 Linear regression models of depressive symptoms in young adults (aged 25–35)

	Model 1	Model 2	Model 3	Model 4
Parental union in youth (ref. = parents together continuously)				
Parents separated in youth	.109**			
	(2.91)			
Parents separated, low-conflict		.051	.054	.063
		(1.29)	(1.07)	(1.28)
Parents separated, high-conflict		.260**	.263**	.256**
		(5.20)	(4.42)	(4.42)
Parent deceased	.050	.053	.055	.044
	(.76)	(.81)	(.80)	(.66)
Parent alone (at birth)	.222**	.231**	.234**	.226**
	(3.22)	(3.36)	(3.13)	(3.07)
Anchor lived in a stepfamily in youth			−.004	
			(−.10)	
Lived with a stepfather, low conflict				−.110*
				(−2.54)
Lived with a stepfather, high conflict				.207**
				(3.93)
Lived with a stepmother, low conflict				−.046
				(−.89)
Lived with a stepmother, high conflict				.157*
				(2.32)
Age respondent	−.082**	−.082**	−.082**	−.078**
	(−5.17)	(−5.17)	(−5.17)	(−4.94)
Woman	.035	.025	.025	.020
	(1.10)	(.80)	(.80)	(.64)
Father is a non-Western migrant	.208**	.215**	.214**	.217**
	(3.89)	(4.03)	(3.99)	(4.06)
Father SES	.016	.017	.017	.014
	(.83)	(.88)	(.88)	(.72)
Mother SES	−.020	−.018	−.018	−.016
	(−1.02)	(−.91)	(−.91)	(−.81)
Mother problem behaviors	.175**	.165**	.165**	.155**
	(10.25)	(9.64)	(9.63)	(9.05)
Anchor lived in an institution in youth	.641**	.594**	.594**	.571**
	(4.65)	(4.31)	(4.31)	(4.16)
Constant	−.083*	−.083*	−.083*	−.084*
	(−2.39)	(−2.41)	(−2.40)	(−2.44)
R squared	.07	.08	.08	.09
Subjects	3890	3890	3890	3890

Notes: t-values in parentheses. Continuous variables standardized
*$p < 0.05$, **$p < 0.01$

household (and potential stress associated with it) is not necessarily detrimental in the long run. However, as Model 4 shows, the failure to find a significant association is due to the clearly diverging effects of having a low-conflict or a high-conflict relationship with the co-resident stepparent. For example, having lived with a stepfather with whom the anchor had a low-conflict relationship is shown to be associated with having *lower* levels of depressive feelings than if the anchor had not lived with a stepparent in childhood. However, having lived with a stepfather with whom the tie was strained is found to be associated with a significant and sizeable increase in depressive symptomatology (about a fifth of a standard deviation). For the young adults who reported living with a stepmother, the story was slightly different. The negative impact of having had a conflictual relationship with a stepmother is still clearly visible, but the protective effect of having had a low-conflict tie is not. In other words, the results of this model indicate that whereas having a positive tie with a stepfather can buffer against depressive symptoms in young adulthood, having a negative tie with a stepfather is associated with maladjustment. In the case of a coresident stepmother, at best, the experience does not result in harm in the long run.

In addition to performing these analyses, we examined the question of whether having experienced family complexity in childhood is strongly predictive of high levels of maladjustment in adulthood (i.e., reporting depressive feelings in the top 15% of the distribution). The logistic regression models, displayed in Table 13.3, show the association between the experience of having lived in different household constellations during childhood and the probability of reporting very high levels of depressive feelings in adulthood. The results of the first model indicate the young adults whose parents split had 39% higher odds ($b = 0.335$) of reporting extreme levels of depression compared to their counterparts with continuously married parents. In other words, whereas the baseline probability of reporting such high levels of depression for the participants with non-separated parents was about 10%, those with separated parents had a probability of about 14%. Again, the reader should keep in mind that we are referring the impact of family events that happened, on average, two decades ago. In Model 2, we again see that the negative repercussions of divorce are only visible if the parents had frequent conflicts following the divorce. Having experienced that situation increased the odds of extreme depression by 80% ($b = 0.59$) compared to having had continuously married parents.

Model 3 and Model 4 examined the association between having lived with a stepparent and extreme levels of depression. It is clear that even though the direction of the coefficients is consistent with the analyses displayed in Table 13.2, the associations are not statistically significant. In other words, neither living with a stepparent nor the quality of the respondent-stepparent tie is found to have a significant effect on the risk of experiencing extreme depression in early adulthood. Still, in order to give the reader an impression of the associations, we estimated the predicted probabilities of reporting high levels of depression depending whether the respondents experienced their parents' divorce as good or bad, and whether they had a good or a bad relationship with the co-resident stepfather (the more likely co-resident stepparent figure). These associations are plotted in Fig. 13.1. We can see that for an individual who experienced a low-conflict parental separation and had a low-conflict tie

Table 13.3 Logistic regression analysis for the probability of reporting very high levels of depressive symptoms (Top 15% of the distribution), young adults (aged 25–35)

	Model 1	Model 2	Model 3	Model 4
Parental union in youth (ref. = parents together continuously)				
Parents separated in youth	.335**			
	(2.77)			
Parents separated, low-conflict		.209	.227	.256
		(1.63)	(1.47)	(1.69)
Parents separated, high-conflict		.590**	.609**	.614**
		(4.08)	(3.58)	(3.70)
Parent deceased	.243	.249	.261	.250
	(1.18)	(1.21)	(1.22)	(1.19)
Parent alone (at birth)	.708**	.726**	.742**	.737**
	(3.83)	(3.93)	(3.69)	(3.70)
Anchor lived in a stepfamily in youth			−.025	
			(−.21)	
Lived with a stepfather, low conflict				−.212
				(−1.70)
Lived with a stepfather, high conflict				.260
				(1.89)
Lived with a stepmother, low conflict				−.178
				(−1.15)
Lived with a stepmother, high conflict				.267
				(1.50)
Age respondent	−.214**	−.215**	−.216**	−.209**
	(−4.53)	(−4.55)	(−4.56)	(−4.39)
Woman	.125	.106	.106	.091
	(1.33)	(1.12)	(1.12)	(.96)
Father is a non-Western migrant	.451**	.467**	.464**	.470**
	(3.19)	(3.30)	(3.25)	(3.29)
Father SES	−.008	−.006	−.007	−.009
	(−.15)	(−.11)	(−.11)	(−.16)
Mother SES	−.092	−.087	−.088	−.086
	(−1.61)	(−1.52)	(−1.53)	(−1.51)
Father problem behaviors	.134**	.121*	.121*	.120*
	(2.71)	(2.42)	(2.42)	(2.36)
Mother problem behaviors	.348**	.334**	.333**	.319**
	(8.30)	(7.89)	(7.89)	(7.45)
Anchor lived in an institution in youth	1.104**	1.023**	1.021**	.994**
	(3.72)	(3.43)	(3.42)	(3.31)
Constant	−2.235**	−2.230**	−2.230**	−2.225**
	(−19.31)	(−19.29)	(−19.28)	(−19.25)
Subjects	3890	3890	3890	3890

Notes: t-values in parentheses. Continuous variables standardized
*$p < 0.05$, ** $p < 0.01$

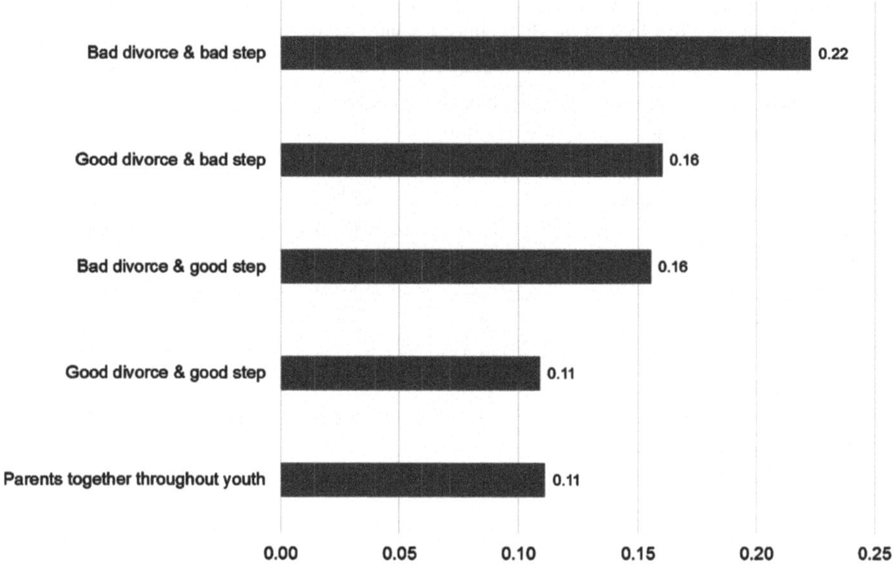

Fig. 13.1 Predicted probability of reporting a very high level of depression (top 15% of distribution) by the type of household transition and the level of post-separation interparental conflict experienced in childhood. (Notes: Average predicted probabilities of reporting a high level of depression (see Table 13.3 for full model))

with the stepfather, the predicted probability of having severe depression was 0.11, which is very comparable to the probability for an individual whose parents were together throughout his or her childhood. However, for a young adult who experienced a high-conflict parental separation and then had a high-conflict tie with his or her stepfather, the predicted probability of having severe depression was twice as high, at 0.22. In summary, although the logistic regression does not provide statistically significant findings in support of the "good stepparent" hypothesis, we consistently find that conflict between the biological parents and conflict within the stepparent-child tie are much more detrimental to an individual's long-term well-being than simply having experienced specific household transitions.

Discussion

In this chapter, we used a unique survey among young Dutch adults to study the long-term association between parental union instability and maladjustment. We first examined the question of whether parental separation had a negative effect on individual well-being into adulthood, and then paid specific attention to the role conflict played in this association. Our work thus explored a hypothesis presented by Ahrons (1994), which states that as long as parents are able to maintain a cooperative relationship after separation, children will be shielded from the long-term effects of divorce (the "good divorce" hypothesis). We built on this proposition by also considering whether the effects of the subsequent – and potentially stressful – addition of a stepparent to the household were also contingent on the level of conflict between the child and the stepparent. Our findings support both the "good divorce" hypothesis and what we have called the "good stepparent" hypothesis.

First, in line with previous work, we found evidence that parental union dissolution has long-term effects on the children involved (Amato 2010; Amato and Cheadle 2005; Härkönen 2014). The young Dutch adults in our sample who saw their parents separate (which took place, on average, two decades earlier) reported having somewhat higher levels of depression than their counterparts whose parents were continuously together. However, our findings also indicated that it was not the separation itself that left that a lasting mark, but rather the level of conflict following the transition. The results of our analysis can be interpreted as providing clear support for the "good divorce" (Ahrons 1994) hypothesis: when the parents were able to minimize their overt disagreements after separating, their adult children's levels of adjustment did not differ from those of adults whose parents did not separate; whereas when the parents had heightened post-separation conflict, the mental well-being of their adult children clearly suffered. To the best of our abilities, we controlled for possible confounding factors, such as the parents' own problematic behaviors and socioeconomic positions while the young adults were children, and still found a negative association between having experienced a high-conflict separation and an adult child's well-being.

Another interesting outcome of our work is that we did not necessarily find an additional negative effect of parental repartnering after separation, which could have been expected based on the assumption that multiple household transitions lead to additional stress, and, thus, to maladjustment for the children involved (Amato 2010). We also did not find an automatic benefit of adding another adult to the household in which the child was living after the parental divorce. Previous studies that examined the adjustment levels of children reported there is no parental repartnering benefit (Hanson et al. 1996). In other words, in contradiction to the "resource hypothesis," we found that the addition of another parent figure and their resources to the household did not necessarily offset the disadvantage of having separated parents relative to having a stable two-parent family. Similarly, we did not find that simply having lived in a stepfamily after the parental separation was associated with high levels of depression. However, we uncovered important differences in the well-being of adult children after taking the quality of the stepparent-child tie in childhood into account.

In line with earlier work that pointed to the benefits of a high-quality stepparent-child tie (Jensen and Harris 2017), our findings supported what we coined "the good stepparent" hypothesis. We found that having a low-conflict relationship with a resident stepfather could act as a buffer against depressive symptomatology in adulthood. In contrast, when the relationship between the child and the stepparent was characterized by conflict, we observed cumulative negative effects. Of the young adults who experienced both a high-conflict divorce and a conflict-ridden tie with a resident stepparent in childhood, 22% reported very high levels of depression, compared to 11% of the young adults whose parents stayed together throughout their childhood. We consider this to be a noteworthy finding, especially given the extreme levels of depression reported in this specific case and the amount of time that had passed since the family transitions.

However, we also observed an interesting gender difference: whereas a high-quality stepfather-child tie was a protective factor and a low-quality stepfather-child tie was linked to higher levels of depression, at best, the stepmother-child tie was not associated with maladjustment. In other words, having a high-quality relationship with a stepmother does not appear to confer the same benefits as a having high-quality relationship with a stepfather. The precise reason for this gender difference is unclear. It is worth noting that although shared custody arrangements are on the rise in the Netherlands (Poortman and van Gaalen 2017), the majority of the adults we studied lived primarily with their mother (and thus with a stepfather, and not with a stepmother) after separation. Yet having had more exposure to one stepparent figure than another cannot explain why we found comparable disadvantages of having a high-conflict stepfather- or stepmother-child tie, but that only stepfathers could act as a buffer. This remains an open question in our work.

We conclude by noting certain limitations of our study, and opportunities for further research. One limitation is that we were unable to control for child effects. It is, for example, possible that the deterioration in a child's psychological well-being resulted in the child having a poor relationship with the stepparent. Hence, some of the evidence we found in support of the "good stepparent" hypothesis may be due to reverse causation (Kalmijn et al. 2019). A second limitation is that we did not have measures of potential conflicts between the parent and the stepparent. While there is likely some correlation between the conflicts the child had with the stepparent and the conflicts the parent had with the stepparent, this correlation is far from perfect. To check this bias, we estimated an extra model in which we controlled for stepfamily instability (whether the parent and stepparent separated later). Our results were robust even after considering this additional control variable. Related to this second limitation, we have to acknowledge that all of our measures of conflict were based on retrospective information from a single source – the adult child. We cannot eliminate the possibility that a participant's current state of mind was affecting his or her perception of the past. However, our findings are very much in line with those of other studies that were based on prospective data, and that also examined the impact of conflict on individual well-being (e.g., Musick and Meier 2010). Despite these limitations, our study has several advantages, including our use of a systematic oversample of children from stepfamilies and elaborate measures of confounding parent and stepparent traits, and our focus on the generation who grew up during the divorce revolution. Our finding that family turmoil affected the depressive symptoms of adults so many years after their parents divorced and re-partnered is striking, and can be seen as bad news, given that the young adults we studied were in a life course phase that can be particularly challenging, as it tends to be characterized by the clustering of multiple transitions (becoming a parent, entering employment, etc.). But the good news is that we found no divorce effects at all when the level of conflict between the separated parents of the anchor was low, and when the stepparent-child ties were harmonious, as was often the case for these young adults.

Acknowledgements This work was supported by the European Research Council under the European Union's Seventh Framework Programme [FP7/2007-2013/ERC grant agreement no. 669334].

References

Ahrons, C. R. (1994). *The good divorce: Keeping your family together when your marriage comes apart*. New York: Harper Collins.

Ahrons, C. R. (2007). Family ties after divorce: Long-term implications for children. *Family Process, 46*(1), 53–65. https://doi.org/10.1111/j.1545-5300.2006.00191.x.

Ahrons, C. R., & Tanner, J. L. (2003). Adult children and their fathers: Relationship changes 20 years after parental divorce. *Family Relations, 52*(4), 340–351. https://doi.org/10.1111/j.1741-3729.2003.00340.x.

Amato, P. R. (2000). The consequences of divorce for adults and children. *Journal of Marriage and Family, 62*(4), 1269–1287. https://doi.org/10.5559/di.23.1.01.

Amato, P. R. (2010). Research on divorce: Continuing trends and new developments. *Journal of Marriage and Family, 72*(3), 650–666. https://doi.org/10.1111/j.1741-3737.2010.00723.x.

Amato, P. R., & Cheadle, J. (2005). The long reach of divorce: Divorce and child well-being across three generations. *Journal of Marriage and Family, 67*(1), 191–206. https://doi.org/10.1111/j.0022-2445.2005.00014.x.

Amato, P. R., & DeBoer, D. D. (2001). The transmission of marital instability across generations: Relationship skills or commitment to marriage? *Journal of Marriage and Family, 63*(4), 1038–1051. https://doi.org/10.1111/j.1741-3737.2001.01038.x.

Amato, P. R., & James, S. (2010). Divorce in Europe and the United States: Commonalities and differences across nations. *Family Science, 1*(1), 2–13.

Amato, P. R., & Sobolewski, J. M. (2001). The effects of divorce and marital discord on adult children's psychological well-being. *American Sociological Review, 66*(6), 900–921. https://doi.org/10.2307/3088878.

Amato, P. R., Kane, J. B., & James, S. (2011). Reconsidering the "good divorce". *Family Relations, 60*(5), 511–524. https://doi.org/10.1111/j.1741-3729.2011.00666.x.

Aughinbaugh, A., Pierret, C. R., & Rothstein, D. S. (2005). The impact of family structure transitions on youth achievement: Evidence from the children of the NLSY79. *Demography, 42*(3), 447–468. https://doi.org/10.1353/dem.2005.0023.

Bakker, B. F. M., van Rooijen, J., & van Toor, L. (2014). The system of social statistical datasets of statistics Netherlands: An integral approach to the production of register-based social statistics. *Statistical Journal of the United Nations ECE, 30*(4), 411–424.

Beckmeyer, J. J., Coleman, M., & Ganong, L. H. (2014). Postdivorce coparenting typologies and children's adjustment. *Family Relations, 63*(4), 526–537. https://doi.org/10.1111/fare.12086.

Bernardi, F., & Boertien, D. (2016). Understanding heterogeneity in the effects of parental separation on educational attainment in Britain: Do children from lower educational backgrounds have less to lose? *European Sociological Review, 32*(6), 807–819. https://doi.org/10.1093/esr/jcw036.

Bernardi, F., & Radl, J. (2014). The long-term consequences of parental divorce for children's educational attainment. *Demographic Research, 30*(61), 1653–1680. https://doi.org/10.4054/DemRes.2014.30.61.

Brand, J. E., Moore, R., Song, X., & Xie, Y. (2019). Parental divorce is not uniformly disruptive to children's educational attainment. *Proceedings of the National Academy of Sciences, 116*(15), 7266–7271. https://doi.org/10.1073/pnas.1813049116.

Coleman, M., Ganong, L., & Fine, M. (2000). Reinvestigating remarriage: Another decade of progress. *Journal of Marriage and Family, 62*(4), 1288–1307. https://doi.org/10.1111/j.1741-3737.2000.01288.x.

De Leeuw, E., & De Heer, W. (2001). Trends in household survey nonresponse: A longitudinal and international comparison. In R. M. Groves, D. A. Dillman, J. L. Eltinge, & R. J. A. Little (Eds.), *Survey nonresponse* (pp. 41–54). New York: Wiley.

Dronkers, J. (1997). Zoals de ouden zongen, piepen de jongen: Intergenerationele overdracht van de kans op scheiding in Nederland. *Mens en Maatschappij, 72*(2), 149–165.

Fischer, T. F. C., Graaf, P. M. D. E., & Kalmijn, M. (2005). Friendly and antagonistic contact between former patterns and determinants. *Journal of Family Issues, 26*(8), 1131–1163. https://doi.org/10.1177/0192513X05275435.

Fomby, P., & Cherlin, A. J. (2007). Family instability and child well-being. *American Sociological Review, 72*(2), 181–204. https://doi.org/10.1177/000312240707200203.

Gennetian, L. A. (2005). One or two parents? Half or step siblings? The effect of family structure on young children's achievement. *Journal of Population Economics, 18*(3), 415–436. https://doi.org/10.1007/s00148-004-0215-0.

Ginther, D. K., & Pollak, R. A. (2004). Family structure and children's educational outcomes: Blended families, stylized facts, and descriptive regressions. *Demography, 41*(4), 671–696. https://doi.org/10.1353/dem.2004.0031.

Gratz, M. (2017). Does separation really lead fathers and mothers to be less involved in their children's lives? *European Sociological Review, 33*(4), 551–562. https://doi.org/10.1093/esr/jcx058.

Hanson, T. L., McLanahan, S. S., & Thomson, E. (1996). Double jeopardy: Parental conflict and stepfamily outcomes for children. *Journal of Marriage and Family, 58*(1), 141–154. https://doi.org/10.2307/353383.

Härkönen, J. (2014). Divorce: Trends, patterns, causes, consequences. In J. Treas, J. Scott, & M. Richards (Eds.), *The Wiley-Blackwell companion to the sociology of families* (pp. 303–322). Chichester: Wiley-Blackwell.

Harris-Short, S. (2010). Resisting the march towards 50/50 shared residence: Rights, welfare and equality in post-separation families. *Journal of Social Welfare & Family Law, 32*(3), 257–274. https://doi.org/10.1080/09649069.2010.520519.

Hornstra, M., Kalmijn, M., & Ivanova, K. (2020). Fatherhood in complex families: Studying the tie between children, biological fathers and stepfathers. *Journal of Marriage and Family.*

Ivanova, K., Mills, M., & Veenstra, R. (2011). The initiation of dating in adolescence: The effect of parental divorce. The TRAILS study. *Journal of Research on Adolescence, 21*(4), 769–775. https://doi.org/10.1111/j.1532-7795.2010.00734.x.

Jensen, T. M., & Harris, K. M. (2017). Stepfamily relationship quality and stepchildren's depression in adolescence and adulthood. *Emerging Adulthood, 5*(3), 191–203. https://doi.org/10.1177/2167696816669901.

Jonsson, J. O., & Gähler, M. (1997). Family dissolution, family reconstitution, and children's educational careers: Recent evidence from Sweden. *Demography, 34*(2), 277–293. https://doi.org/10.2307/2061705.

Kalmijn, M., Ivanova, K., van Gaalen, R., de Leeuw, S. G., van Houdt, K., van Spijker, F., & Hornstra, M. (2018). A multi-actor study of adult children and their parents in complex families: Design and content of the OKiN survey. *European Sociological Review, 34*(4), 452–470. https://doi.org/10.1093/esr/jcy016.

Kalmijn, M., de Leeuw, S., Hornstra, M., Ivanova, K., van Gaalen, R., & van Houdt, K. (2019). *Family complexity into adulthood: A double multi-actor analysis of intergenerational ties*. Under Review.

Kelly, J. B., & Emery, R. E. (2003). Children's adjustment following divorce: Risk and resilience perspectives. *Family Relations, 52*(4), 352–362. https://doi.org/10.1111/j.1741-3729.2003.00352.x.

Kim, H. S. (2011). Consequences of parental divorce for child development. *American Sociological Review, 76*(3), 487–511. https://doi.org/10.1177/0003122411407748.

King, V. (2007). When children have two mothers: Relationships with nonresident mothers, stepmothers, and fathers. *Journal of Marriage and Family, 69*(5), 1178–1193. https://doi.org/10.1111/j.1741-3737.2007.00440.x.

Lansford, J. E. (2009). Parental divorce and children's adjustment. *Perspectives on Psychological Science, 4*(2), 140–152. https://doi.org/10.1111/j.1745-6924.2009.01114.x.

Monden, C. W. S., & Kalmijn, M. (2006). Are the negative effects of divorce on well-being dependent on marital quality? *Journal of Marriage and Family, 68*(5), 1197–1213. https://doi.org/10.1111/j.1741-3737.2006.00323.x.

Musick, K., & Meier, A. (2010). Are both parents always better than one? Parental conflict and young adult well-being. *Social Science Research, 39*(5), 814–830. https://doi.org/10.1016/j.ssresearch.2010.03.002.

Pearlin, L. I., Schieman, S., Fazio, E. M., & Meersman, S. C. (2005). Stress, health, and the life course: Some conceptual perspectives. *Journal of Health and Social Behavior, 46*(2), 205–219. https://doi.org/10.1177/002214650504600206.

Poortman, A.-R., & van Gaalen, R. (2017). Shared residence after separation: A review and new findings from the Netherlands. *Family Court Review, 55*(4), 531–544. https://doi.org/10.1111/fcre.12302.

Prins, K. (2017). *Population register data, basis for the Netherlands' population statistics: Bevolkingstrends*. Statistics Netherlands. https://www.cbs.nl/-/media/_pdf/2017/38/population-register-data.pdf. Accessed 15 June 2019.

Pryor, J., & Rodgers, B. (2001). *Children in changing families: Life after parental separation*. Oxford: Blackwell Publishers.

Sands, A., Thompson, E. J., & Gaysina, D. (2017). Long-term influences of parental divorce on offspring affective disorders: A systematic review and meta-analysis. *Journal of Affective Disorders, 218*, 105–114. https://doi.org/10.1016/J.JAD.2017.04.015.

Stewart, S. D. (2007). *Brave new stepfamilies*. London: Sage.

Strohschein, L. (2005). Parental divorce and child mental health trajectories. *Journal of Marriage and Family, 67*(5), 1286–1300. https://doi.org/10.1111/j.1741-3737.2005.00217.x.

Sweeney, M. M. (2007). Stepfather families and the emotional well-being of adolescents. *Journal of Health and Social Behavior, 48*(1), 33–49. https://doi.org/10.1177/002214650704800103.

Sweeney, M. M. (2010). Remarriage and stepfamilies: Strategic sites for family scholarship in the 21st century. *Journal of Marriage and Family, 72*(3), 667–684. https://doi.org/10.1111/j.1741-3737.2010.00724.x.

Thomson, E. (2014). Family complexity in Europe. *The Annals of the American Academy of Political and Social Science, 654*(1), 245–258. https://doi.org/10.1177/0002716214531384.

Thomson, E., Hanson, T. L., & McLanahan, S. S. (1994). Family structure and child well-being: Economic resources versus parental behaviors. *Social Forces, 73*(1), 221–242. https://doi.org/10.1093/sf/73.1.221.

Van de Velde, S., Levecque, K., & Bracke, P. (2009). Measurement equivalence of the CES-D 8 in the general population in Belgium: A gender perspective. *Archives of Public Health, 67*, 15–29. https://doi.org/10.1186/0778-7367-67-1-15.

Wang, H., & Amato, P. R. (2000). Predictors of divorce adjustment: Stressors, resources, and definitions. *Journal of Marriage and Family, 62*(3), 655–668. https://doi.org/10.1111/j.1741-3737.2000.00655.x.

White, L., & Gilbreth, J. G. (2001). When children have two fathers: Effects of relationships with stepfathers and noncustodial fathers on adolescent outcomes. *Journal of Marriage and Family, 63*(1), 155–167. https://doi.org/10.1111/j.1741-3737.2001.00155.x.

Wolfinger, N. H. (2011). More evidence for trends in the intergenerational transmission of divorce: A completed cohort approach using data from the general social survey. *Demography, 48*(2), 581–592. https://doi.org/10.1007/s13524-011-0025-4.

Chapter 14
Work Disability and Divorce

Daniel Brüggmann

Introduction

Research has suggested that married people enjoy better mental and physical health than their divorced peers (Williams et al. 2008). The explanations for this pattern refer to two different (but not necessarily mutually exclusive) modes of action between the state of health and the event of divorce. The social causation argument posits that changes associated with divorce or separation have a negative impact on health (Wade and Pevalin 2004). According to this logic, experiences typically associated with divorce – such as having to adapt to the loss of the spouse, a deterioration in living standards, the disruption of social networks, the loss of social support, and having to bear the double burden of single parenting and employment – are detrimental to health and/or are promote unhealthy behaviours. The literature has also posed the question of whether these effects are of a short-term nature (i.e., individuals become accustomed to their new conditions) or are longer lasting (Couch et al. 2015; Tamborini et al. 2016). The social selection argument states that with declining health, the quality of a couple's marriage decreases and their risk of divorce increases (Goldman 1993; Wade and Pevalin 2004). According to this logic, the effects of a divorce should be minor, and the relatively poor health observed among people who are divorced is a consequence of selection.

In this chapter, we use register data from the statutory German pension fund to examine the health consequences of divorce in West Germany. The outcome of interest is the uptake of work disability, which is defined as sick leave starting after 6 weeks of illness. Work disability is an important measure because at an individual level, taking work disability limits the scope of an individual's labour market participation, and reduces his/her income. Taking extended periods of sick leave might

D. Brüggmann (✉)
Hertie School, Berlin, Germany
e-mail: d.brueggmann@phd.hertie-school.org

M. Kreyenfeld, H. Trappe (eds.), *Parental Life Courses after Separation and Divorce in Europe*, Life Course Research and Social Policies 12,
https://doi.org/10.1007/978-3-030-44575-1_14

also significantly reduce a worker's retirement income, and lead to social isolation, depression, and low self-esteem. At the macro level, work disability claims create public costs in the form of sick pay, medical expenses, rehabilitation costs, lost working days, and reduced productivity. The aim of this study is twofold. First, we provide easily accessible statistics that illustrate how the likelihood of taking work disability leave changes around divorce. Second, we examine the question of whether individuals' health status after divorce is partially related to selection into divorce. As a method, we employ the nearest neighbor matching approach, which allows us to generate a comparable control group for the divorced population. We have restricted the analysis to West German men and women who separated between 2000 and 2010. We analyse men and women separately. For women, we differentiate between mothers and childless women, as we assume that divorce weighs more heavily on the health status of mothers than of childless women.

Theoretical Considerations

Benefits of Marriage

Apart from the reasonable assumption that healthier and wealthier individuals are privileged in the partner market – i.e., that those individuals might be more likely to select into marriage – marriage is found to improve health (Lillard and Panis 1996) and material well-being (Wilmoth and Koso 2002). Material well-being increases because married couples benefit from economies of scale by sharing housing, food, and utilities. Sharing resources minimises the partners' cost of living and provides them with insurance against unexpected events, like unemployment or illness (Wilmoth and Koso 2002). Moreover, in some countries, including in Germany, marriage can provide institutional support that is not available to non-married individuals, like free health insurance for spouses or tax benefits. Thus, on average, married couples have lower poverty rates and more assets than their unmarried counterparts. These effects of marriage are usually assumed to reduce stress and to increase security, which may, in turn, have positive effects on health. Additionally, marriage provides a healthy social environment that inhibits individuals from engaging in self-destructive acts; i.e., a married person is more likely than a single person to have someone in his/her life who regulates his/her behaviour, either by imposing sanctions or by causing the person to internalise norms that encourage conventional behaviour (Umberson 1987). For these reasons, marriage has been found to be one of the most important categories of social ties that help to buffer people from the effects of negative life events (Umberson 1987).

Although marriage offers a range of socio-emotional and economic resources that can enhance the partners' health and well-being, the benefits of marriage for a given individual depend on the person's gender, socio-demographic characteristics, and relationship characteristics. Compared to men, women seem to gain more from marriage in material terms, and but are less likely to rely exclusively on their partner for emotional support (Williams et al. 2008). In contrast, compared to women, men are less likely to benefit from marriage economically, but are more likely to rely on their partner for emotional support and social integration (Gerstel et al. 1985). The benefits of marriage also depend on the duration and the timing of the marriage. There is evidence that marriage duration is correlated with longevity. However, it has also been shown that the benefits of marriage are diminished if the partners form the union while very young, because early marriage tends to be associated with reduced financial resources and greater marital distress (Dupre et al. 2009). In particular, marital distress has been found to counteract the protective effects of marriage, as conflict-ridden marriages are associated with emotional loneliness, drinking, and depression (Waite 1995; Dykstra and Fokkema 2007; Umberson et al. 2006).

To sum up, marriage seems to provide the partners with financial resources and social support that promotes health by either reducing their economic uncertainty or prompting them to adopt a healthier lifestyle. Conversely, men and women who are experiencing marital disruption tend to have substantially higher stress levels, worse subjective well-being, a higher risk of drinking, and lower body weight (Waite 1995; Umberson 1992). Research has also shown that divorcees have an elevated risk of psychiatric illness, suicide, motor vehicle accidents, homicide, physical illness, and misuse of various substances; and tend to report higher levels of depression, anxiety, and unhappiness (Booth and Amato 1991). In general, it seems that compared to married people, divorcees are more likely to engage in negative health behaviours, and are less likely to have an orderly lifestyle. These unpleasant outcomes are addressed in the "divorce-health" literature, and are condensed in the social causation framework.

Health Consequences of Divorce

The "divorce-health" literature has shown that separation and divorce are stressful events with adverse effects on health. There are many reasons why divorce has a negative impact on health, but among those that are mentioned most frequently are that divorcees often experience a deterioration in living standards, a change in residence, the disruption of their social networks, the loss of social support, and the pressure to take on the double burden of single parenting and employment. The stress associated with these changes and with the loss of a partner seem to promote unhealthy behaviours, which, in turn, increases the risk of poor health and mortality (Zhang and Hayward 2006). Divorcees are especially likely to report symptoms of poor mental health, in part because a divorce can lead to the loss of supportive social networks, and force them to reorganise their network outside of their marriage. Moreover, the networks people build after a divorce are often not of the same quality as the networks they had while married. It has, for example, been shown that divorcees' new networks are often burdensome, and may undermine their health, rather than supporting it (Gerstel et al. 1985). There is, however, evidence that women are better than men at developing new networks and maintaining their ties (Gerstel et al. 1985). The differences in the network structures of men and women might also be responsible for their different health outcomes after divorce. To the extent that network size and quality correlates with loneliness, the greater decline in social support found among men than among women could mean that for men, divorce has especially negative effects on their levels of social control and lifestyle choices. Shor et al. (2012) suggested that the risk of death is higher for divorced men than for divorced women because men are more likely to experience a substantial decline in social support. Similarly, Umberson (1987) found that men suffer more than women from the loss of social control, which may cause them to develop drinking problems. By contrast, compared to their male counterparts, divorced women are more prone to experiencing financial strain, and having a lower household income coupled with increased parental responsibilities increases the likelihood of having poor mental health. Although men also frequently have a lower household income after a divorce, men's income losses tend to be smaller than those of women (Andreß and Bröckel 2007; see also Mortelmans, Chap. 2 in this volume). Research on the impact of the time that has elapsed since the union dissolution on the well-being of divorcees has shown that the negative consequences of divorce are most pronounced around the time of the event itself, and then usually attenuate and lose their effect. It has, for example, been found that getting divorced more than doubles mortality for men (133%) and women (132%) in the first 2 years after the divorce, but that this effect peters out in later years (Brockman and Klein 2004). Having been recently divorced has also been shown to be associated with lower life satisfaction for men and women. It appears, however, that this effect is stronger for men than for women, as women tend to have smaller reductions in life satisfaction, and generally return to their baseline values more quickly (Leopold and Kalmijn 2016). However, while some of the negative consequences of divorce seem to be short-lived or to diminish over time, there is also evidence that divorce can have long-term consequences. Divorce has been linked to an increased cumulative probability of taking work disability leave and of receiving disability benefits for many years after the divorce (Couch et al. 2015; Tamborini et al. 2016). These results strengthen the view that life-changing events can lead to cumulative health strains that emerge slowly.

Selection into Divorce

While the "divorce-health" literature has highlighted the stressful nature of divorce, the "health-divorce" literature has pointed out that poor health, psychological problems, and financial hardship increase the risk of divorce (Fu and Goldman 2000; Wade and Pevalin 2004). Hence, the often-observed poor health condition of divorcees is not necessarily attributable to the event itself, but may instead be a result of selection. If the decline in a spouse's health leads to constraints in his/her everyday functioning, the healthy spouse might have to take over more of the cleaning, cooking, maintenance, and childcare (Booth and Johnson 1994). The change in the division of household tasks may be a source of marital unhappiness. The persisting poor health of one of the partners might also lead to a reduction in the couple's shared activities, changes the set of assumptions the marriage was based on, and a reduction in family income that increases financial stress (Teachman 2010). These shifts might, in turn, lead to a renegotiation of marital tasks, a reduction in the benefits of marriage for the healthy spouse, and an increased risk of divorce (ibid.).

The assumption that one of the spouses being in poor health worsens the quality of the marriage may be overly pessimistic. The poor health of one of the spouses might also be perceived as a common experience with the power to strengthen the couple's existing bonds. Syse and Kravdal (2007), for example, have found that a spouse having an illness like cancer does not necessarily increase the risk of divorce, and may even reduce it. However, this result might be driven by the normative pressure not to leave a seriously ill partner, or by the rationale that leaving a seriously ill spouse might not make sense if death is anticipated (Syse and Kravdal 2007).

To the extent that social selection precedes separation, any measured health consequence after divorce cannot be linked directly to divorce, because divorcees are then a selected group in especially poor or especially good health. The "health-divorce" literature has provided support for the selection argument, with one study showing that some of the excess mortality and health problems observed among divorcees result from a health-related selection process out of marriage (Fu and Goldman 2000). Another study found that work-related health limitations are associated with marital instability rather than the reverse, but this result referred only to the health of the husband, and not to the health of the wife (Teachman 2010). These results are in line with the findings of Yorgason et al. (2008): i.e., that when a wife's health declines, the husband is more likely to report a decline in marital happiness; but that when the husband's health declines, the wife is more likely to report not only a decline in happiness, but increases in disagreement levels, marital problems, and divorce proneness (Yorgason et al. 2008).

To sum up, the "divorce-health" literature provides evidence that divorce has an impact on health, and the "health-divorce" literature provides evidence of a selection into divorce due to poor health. Both frameworks are important, and need to be addressed in the empirical investigation.

Data and Analytical Approach

Data and Analytical Sample

In the present study, we used linked data from the statutory German pension system. We linked the records of the Sample of Active Pension Accounts (VSKT) with the records of the Pension Rights Adjustments Statistic (EHRCSY). The VSKT is a random sample of individuals with a pension account. It provides detailed pension-relevant information, such as information on the individuals' employment and earnings history, spells of parental leave, and childbirths (Stegmann and Himmelreicher 2008). The EHRCSY contains the dates of separation and divorce (Keck and Mika 2016). The pension fund collects these data, because Germany has a system of "income splitting", whereby pension entitlements are split after divorce (for more details, see Keck et al. 2017). The great advantage of using these data is that they provide us with a reasonably large sample size. Unlike prospective survey data, register data do not suffer from attrition, which is especially likely to occur after a separation or a divorce. However, there are other caveats that we need to mention. One limitation of the data is that the register data do not include the full resident population, but cover only those who have a pension account. About 90% of the resident population are included in the data, but people in certain professions, such as civil servants and farmers, are not included (Kruse 2007). Furthermore, not all divorces are included in the data because the register data only contain information on divorces that result in pension splitting. Pension splitting is, in theory, mandatory, but certain couples – and particularly those with short marriages – can avoid pension splitting (Keck et al. forthcoming). Thus, the observed divorcees might not be a representative subpopulation of all divorcees in Germany.

The analytical sample consists of individuals who separated between 2000–2010. Separation (t_0) is defined as the year that the divorce file was opened; i.e., the year when the defendant received the divorce petition.[1] In the following, we use the term "divorce" to refer to the date the file was opened to make the text easier to read. Note, however, that a divorce may not be legally finalised until months or even years after the file was opened. We restricted the analysis to individuals living in West Germany, who are persons who have never worked in the Eastern states of Germany. East Germany was excluded, in part because the case numbers were low, especially for childless women; and in part because there are considerable differences between the two parts of Germany in terms of female labour market participation and marriage and divorce patterns. We have furthermore limited the investigation to the time window of 7 years before the separation up to 4 years after the separation. Thus, we followed individuals from t_{-7} to t_{+4}. We chose t_{-7} to address separation and the anticipation of separation, and to properly isolate prior health selection (see, for example, Johnson and Skinner (1986) for changes in labour market participation). The choice of t_{+4} was driven by constraints in the data availability for the most recent years. We organised the data as a person-year dataset. Thus, each individual contributes several years of data to the investigation. We furthermore restricted the sample to individuals who were divorced for the first time and who were married at the beginning of the observation period in t_{-7}. Thus, shorter marriages are not included in this investigation. Time is defined as the exact time since separation. The final sample includes 4467 men and 6192 women (see Table 14.1). The subsamples of

[1] Instead of calendar year, we defined years by the exact time since divorce. If the divorce file was opened in, for example, April 2003, then t_0 spans the period 16 April 2002 to 15 April 2003; and t_{-1} is from 16 April 2001 to 15 April 2002; and so on.

Table 14.1 Covariate mean values before and after four nearest neighbour matching at t_{-7}

Variable		Men		Women		Women with children		Women without children	
		Divorced	Control	Divorced	Control	Divorced	Control	Divorced	Control
Foreign citizenship	Raw	0.30	0.58	0.32	0.52	0.29	0.39	0.40	0.62
	Matched	0.30	0.30	0.32	0.32	0.29	0.30	0.40	0.40
Age	Raw	35.3	30.4	32.6	30.3	33.7	37.9	31.2	27.8
	Matched	35.3	35.5	32.6	33.0	33.7	33.8	31.2	31.4
Number children <3	Raw			0.310	0.089	0.398	0.279		
	Matched			0.310	0.298	0.398	0.392		
Number children 3–6	Raw			0.280	0.083	0.359	0.261		
	Matched			0.280	0.278	0.359	0.357		
Number children >6	Raw			0.883	0.454	1.133	1.425		
	Matched			0.883	0.921	1.133	1.144		
Parental leave	Raw			199.9	43.2	256.4	135.1		
	Matched			199.9	195.2	256.4	258.2		
Unemployment rate	Raw	9.06	9.04	9.04	9.04	9.03	9.05	9.08	9.04
	Matched	9.06	9.07	9.04	9.04	9.03	9.02	9.08	9.06
Employment	Raw	4094	1627	1940	1416	2032	2731	2063	839
	Matched	4094	4104	1940	2042	2032	2057	2063	2093
Earnings employment	Raw	12.21	4.67	3.66	2.80	3.76	5.07	4.32	1.84
	Matched	12.21	12.15	3.66	3.88	3.76	3.83	4.32	4.39
Military service	Raw	132	63						
	Matched	132	135						
Vocational training	Raw	480	184	363	180	365	260	315	102
	Matched	480	469	363	359	365	364	315	307
N	Raw	4467	165,621	6192	154,269	4826	49,187	729	80,246
	Matched	4467	15,104	6192	19,333	4826	14,030	729	2757

Notes: Further matching variables were: year and month the file was opened, age squared, employment, and earnings squared

mothers and childless women consist of 4826 and 729 women, respectively. The numbers do not sum up to 6192 because the mothers were women who already had children in $t_{-7,}$ and the childless women were childless until t_{+4}. The women who gave birth between t_{-7} and t_{+4} account for the remaining difference.

Analytical Approach

The aim of this study is to describe the work disability uptake pattern around separation by comparing the health status of divorcees to the health status of an appropriate control group. In order to design a control group, we relied on matching techniques. The use of matching techniques was necessary because the characteristics of the people who did not undergo a divorce differed sharply from the characteristics of the divorcees. This becomes clear when looking at Table 14.1, which compares the socio-demographic characteristics of the "raw sample" and the "matched sampled" (see the row "matched" and "raw"). The most important aim of matching is to exclude all of the individuals from the control group who are not similar to the individuals from the divorced group.

For our purposes, we relied on four nearest neighbour matching, with the common support restriction and a caliper of 0.02 (i.e., we chose only individuals from the comparison group whose propensity scores did not differ by more than +/– 0.02). All of the individuals from the control group who were not a valid "neighbour" were deleted, and have not been included in our analysis. The lines marked "matched" in Table 14.1 show the mean values for the selected covariates after matching, and demonstrate that dropping the non-comparable resulted in a much more balanced control sample. Additionally, in Table 14.3 in the Appendix, we provide further details of our matching procedure. These findings suggest that after matching, the two groups (divorced and control sample) were highly comparable. Obviously, we could only match on observable characteristics; which means that unobserved factors could still bias our investigation. Finally, as the people in the control group obviously did not have a date of divorce, we had to randomly assign them a date of divorce.

In the first step of the investigation, we display sample statistics at the start of the observation period (t_{-7}) and at the end of the observation period (t_{+4}). We also provide the mean values of our key dependent variables (the cumulated days of work disability and the yearly work disability rate) for these two time points. The second step of the investigation contains a pooled OLS-regression analysis. Here, we use the person-year data that was pooled over the entire observation period. We interact a dummy for the control group with our time variable (t_{-7} to t_{+4}) to illustrate how disability changes around divorce. All of these analyses are done separately for men and women. For women, we also conduct a separate analysis for mother and childless women.

Variables

Health is defined based on an individual's history of work disability. It is important to note that this term refers only to long-term disability, because the pension data only includes information on work disability if the individual or the employer was paying social security contributions to the pension system. During the first 42 days of illness, employees in Germany are entitled to sick pay benefits that cover their full income. After 42 days of illness, employees are entitled to receive a reduced sickness benefit that usually amounts to 70% of their former income, and that is recorded in the pension data. There are two other important shortcomings in our data that pertain to the outcome variable. The outcome variable may be biased upwards because sick pay for children is also included in the pension data, and is recorded from the first day of sickness. The uptake of sick pay for children is, however, very low in Germany. Analyses of health data have shown that the sick pay days for children account for less than 2% of all recorded sick pay days, and those days that are recorded are mainly granted for mothers (> 85%) and very rarely for fathers (< 15%) (Sondergutachten 2015). While children's sick days bias the absolute values upwards, the outcome variable does not include the health impairments of unemployed and non-working individuals, which biases the absolute days of sick leave downwards. This aspect has to be taken into account when we discuss the absolute values of sick leave. However, our interest is less in the absolute number of disability days taken. Instead, the analysis compares the work disability days taken by divorcees and a control group. Thus, the difference is of greater interest than the absolute values (see below).

We use two outcome variables for this investigation:

- The main variable of interest is the **cumulated days of work disability.** This variable was constructed by cumulating the number of work disability days taken since age 15.
- The yearly **work disability rate**. It was calculated by the number of work disability days taken in the respective year divided by 365.

We used several socio-demographic variables in matching the control group. These variables are also employed later in the OLS regression. We controlled for German **citizenship**, distinguishing between German citizens and persons with foreign citizenship. We included **age** (and squared) in years to account for different health risks across the life course. We controlled for the **unemployment rate** in West Germany, because the uptake of work disability correlates with times of recessions and prosperity (Benítez-Silva et al. 2010). We also used **cumulated days in employment with social security contributions** (and squared), because employment is a protective factor against the economic risk of marriage dissolution, as well as a source of self-esteem and social support.[2] For a woman, being employed may increase her economic independence, thereby lowering her exit costs. Thus, a

[2] Cumulated covariates accumulate the outcome from age 15 up to the respective year.

woman's employment could make it easier for her to dissolve an unsatisfactory, conflict-ridden marriage. Moreover, a woman's employment might increase her psychological independence and strengthen her belief that she is competent and capable of establishing an independent household (Kalmijn and Poortman 2006). We also accounted for **cumulated earnings** (and squared). Earnings are measured in individual pension points. An individual earns one pension point if the yearly gross income equals the average gross income in West Germany of the respective year. We also added **cumulated days of vocational training** to the models as a proxy for education. The **month and the year the divorce file was opened** was included to control for seasonality. We controlled for the **number of children**, because the presence of children increases a family's economic needs and stress. We controlled for **cumulated days in parental leave** to account for how soon after childbirth the women returned to the labour market. This variable might reflect financial necessity or a desire to participate in the labour force. The latter two variables were only available for the women, and are thus used only for the analysis of the women. For the men, time spent in military service was also included.

Descriptive Findings

Table 14.1 gives an overview of the selected baseline covariates at the beginning of our observation period at t_{-7}. We display their mean values before (raw) and after matching (matched). We can see that the average age of the men in the matched sample was approximately 35.5 years at t_{-7}. The men had accumulated up to that date roughly 4100 days in employment with social security contributions. The days spent in military service are less relevant, and mainly refer to days spent in basic military service. The women were, on average, younger than the men, and had accumulated only half of the men's lifetime employment. The income (measured in earning points) of the average woman was roughly one-third of the income accumulated by the average man. This finding suggests that the women earned less and were less likely to be in full-time employment than the men. On average, the mothers were 1 year older and the childless women were 1 year younger than all of the women in the sample. The mothers and the childless women both accumulated roughly 2000 days in employment; thus, the labour market participation and income levels of childless women were higher. At t_{-7}, the mothers had, on average, at least one child over age six.

Table 14.2 provides summary statistics for the outcome variables for t_{-7} and t_{+4}. The upper panel of the table shows the cumulated days of work disability. Looking at the table, we first note that the number of cumulated work disability days was much lower for the women than for the men. It is, however, important to consider that the lifetime employment participation of the men was twice that of the women. On average, a divorced man had accumulated 32 work disability days at t_{-7}. Four years after the divorce, the value has increased to 79 days. In relative terms, this represented an increase of 146%. For the control group, we observe an increase of

Table 14.2 Average cumulated days of work disability (in days) and yearly work disability rate (in 100)

	Men		Women		Women with children		Women without children	
	Divorced	Control	Divorced	Control	Divorced	Control	Divorced	Control
Cumulated work disability at t_{-7}	32.2	30.3	17.0	13.8	18.0	14.1	18.0	13.3
Cumulated work disability at t_{+4}	79.1	58.6	36.7	26.7	37.8	28.0	40.8	23.3
Ratio (t_{+4}) / (t_{-7})	2.46	1.93	2.16	1.93	2.11	1.98	2.26	1.76
Ratio divorced / control	1.27		1.12		1.06		1.29	
Yearly work disability rate at t_{-7}	0.0096	0.0069	0.0043	0.0039	0.0043	0.0036	0.0052	0.0023
Yearly work disability rate at t_{+4}	0.0114	0.0078	0.0066	0.0041	0.0065	0.0052	0.0094	0.0029
Ratio (t_{+4}) / (t_{-7})	1.19	1.13	1.53	1.06	1.51	1.44	1.81	1.28
Ratio divorced / control	1.05		1.45		1.04		1.42	

Notes: Presented are the sample mean values for the cumulated work disability days and the yearly work disability rate. For each individual, the cumulated work disability days are measured since age 15 up to the respective year. T_0 represents the opening of the divorce file. Each individual's yearly work disability rate is measured by the number of work disability days in the respective year divided by 365

only 93%. Thus, the increase in the number of work disability days was 27% higher for the divorced men than for the control group. While similar increases are found for childless women, all of the women and the mothers had substantially smaller increases.

The lower panel displays the yearly work disability rate at t_{-7} and t_{+4}. Note that, in contrast to the cumulated outcome, the yearly focus might be more volatile and prone to outliers. Changing the base year, for example, from t_{-7} to t_{-6} might substantially alter the result. However, comparing t_{+4} with t_{-7} shows that the divorced men had a rate that was 5% higher than that of the control group. The sample of all women had a rate that was 45% higher than that of the control group, and the mothers had the smallest increase.

Regression Results

Cumulated Work Disability

The results from the pooled OLS regression on the matched sample are displayed in Table 14.4 in the Appendix. We do not discuss the effect of the control variables, but instead focus on the effect of the time since separation, which is displayed in a graph. The aim of using the pooled OLS regression is simply to standardise for the covariates applied and to retrieve the net effect; i.e., the net, for example, of ageing, childbirth (women only), and labour market participation. We start with the pattern for the cumulated receipt of work disability benefits. Figure 14.1 displays the

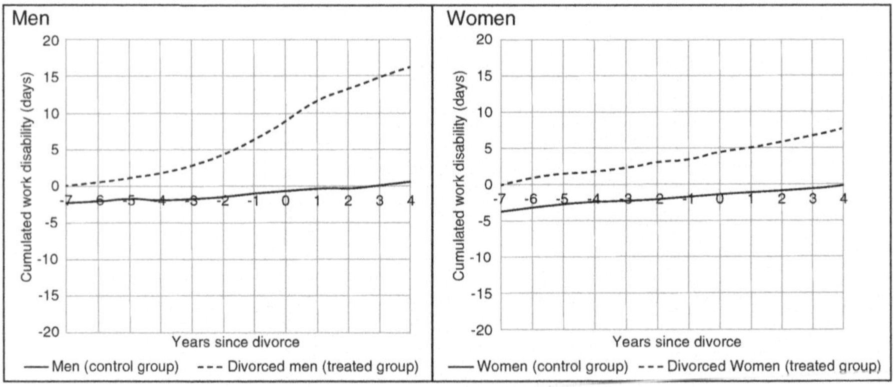

Fig. 14.1 Beta coefficient from the OLS model. Outcome variable: Cumulated days of disability since age 15 (Reference category: Divorced at t_0)

Notes: Pooled OLS models of cumulated work disability days around the time the divorce file was opened. Displayed are the coefficients of group and time interaction from Table 14.4 (Appendix). The control group is chosen by four nearest neighbour matching, with common support and caliper 0.02 at baseline covariates in t_{-7}. Coefficients are shown separately for men and women

pattern for the male and female sample. The slope of the figure for the control group reflects the general trend. As we can see, already at t_{-7} the health of the men and women from the divorced population was worse than that of the control group. At t_{-7}, the difference in all of the accumulated work disability days since age of 15 was 2.3 days for men and 3.7 days for women. These findings strongly support the selection argument, and highlight the importance of controlling for health selection *before* separation. However, we also note that the difference at t_{-7} was statistically significant ($p < 0.01$) for women, but not for men (see Table 14.5, Appendix). Wald tests for the equality of two coefficients show that the control/divorce and time interaction coefficients displayed in Fig. 14.1 were statistically equal for men until t_{-3}, but differed thereafter (t_{-2} $p < 0.05$; t_{-1} to t_{+4} $p < 0.01$). For women, the coefficients were statistically different for all time points ($p < 0.01$) (Table 14.5, Appendix). Given the change between t_{-7} and t_{+4} in the control group and the divorced sample, we calculate a difference-in-difference (DiD) effect of 13.4 days for men ($p < 0.01$) and 4.1 days for women ($p < 0.05$).

Figure 14.2 displays the results for the mothers and the childless women. The figures again show that the divorcees tended to be in poor health before their divorce. Against our expectations, we find that divorce had a greater impact on the health of the childless women than on the health of the mothers, as the curve was much steeper for the childless women than for the divorced mothers. We again calculated a DiD for the period t_{-7} and t_{+4}. We obtained a value of 3.7 days for the mothers and a value of 7.5 days for the divorced women without children. Thus, the increase seems to have been more pronounced for the childless women. However, as the p-values were 0.09 and 0.17, respectively; we have to conclude that neither of the changes was of statistical significance.

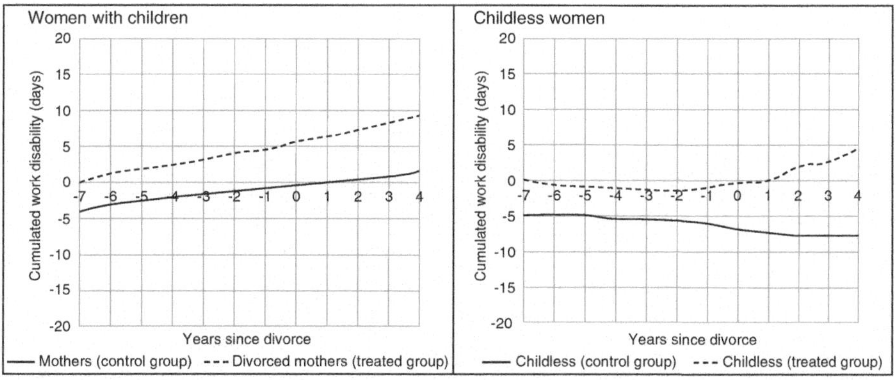

Fig. 14.2 Beta coefficient from the OLS model. Outcome variable: Cumulated days of disability since age 15 (Reference category: Divorced at t_0)

Notes: Pooled OLS models of cumulated work disability days around the time the divorce file was opened. Displayed are the coefficients of group and time interaction from Table 14.4 (Appendix). The control group is chosen by four nearest neighbour matching, with common support and caliper 0.02 at baseline covariates in t_{-7}. Coefficients are shown separately for mothers and childless women.

Work Disability Rate

The analysis of cumulated work disability days revealed that the divorced women were already a select group before their separation. We now display the standardised yearly rate in order to highlight the fluctuation around t_0. In Fig. 14.3, we display the results for the men and the women. For the mothers and the childless women, the sample sizes are, unfortunately, too small to allow us to conduct an equivalent analysis. The figure shows that the disability rate of the control group was always lower than that of the divorcees. Indeed, it appears that the health status of the control group improved slightly over time. The increase in the disability rate over time can very likely be attributed to a shift in job profiles to the service sector, improvements in workplace security, and better medication and rehabilitation over time. The initial difference between the divorced and the control sample was small, amounting to 0.0027 for the men and to 0.00048 for the women. However, beginning with t_{-4} for the men and t_{-3} for the women, the rates started to dynamically diverge from those of the control group ($p < 0.01$). We interpret this pattern as signalling the beginning of the separation process or the anticipation of the separation. For the men, this process peaked at t_{+1} which coincides with the median date when the divorce was legally finalised. The pattern for the women was more irregular. The disability rate had already peaked at t_0 and had declined considerably at t_{-1} (p-value of 0.35, Table 14.5, Appendix). The results of the analysis suggest that the health of the men (as shown in the pension data) was more affected by divorce than that of the women. We should, however, point out that our approach does not allow for a direct comparison of effect sizes, because we analysed the men and the women separately.

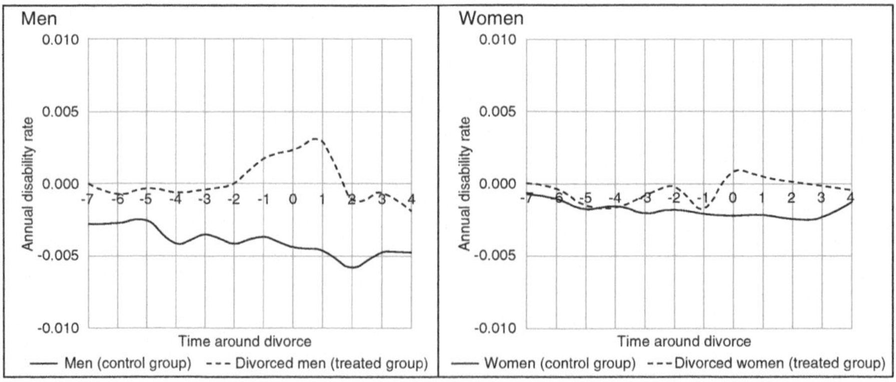

Fig. 14.3 Beta coefficient from the OLS model. Outcome variable: Yearly work disability rate (Reference category: Divorced at t_0)

Notes: Pooled OLS models of the yearly work disability rate around the time the divorce file was opened. Displayed are the coefficients of group and time interaction from Table 14.4 (Appendix). The control group is chosen by four nearest neighbour matching, with common support and caliper 0.02 at baseline covariates in t_{-7}. Coefficients are shown separately for men and women.

The effect sizes for the men were greater because most of the men worked full-time. As the women were often working part-time or only marginally, they may have adopted different strategies for coping with health impairments. In addition, many of the women entered employment after their divorce, and may have shied away from taking large numbers of days off for health reasons.

Discussion

Using administrative pension data, this study examined work disability patterns among divorcees in West Germany. We provided an estimate of the effect of divorce on health impairments. We did so by calculating the difference between divorcees and a control group in the uptake of work disability. This value summed up to 13.4 days for the men, 4.1 days for the women, 3.7 days for the mothers, and 7.5 days for the childless women compared to the control group, and holding control variables constant. This increase was, however, statistically significant only for the men and the sample of all of the women. Although our findings suggest that men's health was more affected by divorce than that of women, we want to emphasise that direct comparisons of effect sizes were not possible in our framework. In particular, it is important to keep in mind that most of the men were working full-time, while most of the women were in part-time or marginal work. It is therefore possible that the women were less likely than the men to register as sick with an employer, even if they were grappling with similar health impairments. In addition, many women started working around the time of their divorce. As they had to establish themselves in the labour market, they may have shied away from taking long periods of sick leave. While we could not compare the size of the effect across our subsample, we were able to compare the temporal ordering of divorce and health impairments. The findings indicate that, on average, the women adapted to their new life earlier (peak at t_0), while the men's health did not start to improve until after t_{+1}.

The study also examined health selection. The results of our analysis show that the women, and particularly the mothers, were, at t_{-7}, already showing signs of poor health, as they had four more cumulated work disability days (counted since the age of 15) than a control group with similar baseline characteristics. These values are significant, and seem to support the argument that social selection contributes to the likelihood of a divorce. Thus, our results stress the point made by Fu and Goldman (2000), who observed that if selection is important, then researchers might have been overstating the negative effects of dissolution on health and exaggerating the benefits of marriage. In other words: "*... sample selection temper conclusions about divorce being causal in driving health. The primary argument is that worse health outcomes among the divorced reflect elevated divorce risks among individuals with worse health*" (Couch et al. 2015: 1491).

However, although we found some evidence of selection, we also observed that divorce had a large impact on health status. The findings from this investigation allow us to draw some policy-relevant conclusions. First, we note that the uptake of work disability is an important outcome, because work disability limits the scope of labour market participation and of access to secure income. Spending longer periods in work disability might even reduce an individual's employability, retirement income, and material well-being. As well as having personal costs, long-term disability creates public costs, including the loss of working days and the costs associated with providing sick pay, health services, and rehabilitation services. Our results show that separation and the anticipation of separation had immediate effects on health for all of the subsamples. Thus, we conclude that to ensure that spouses and their children emerge from the divorce process less compromised and healthier, psychological help or mediation services should be made available (Hannighofer et al. 2017).

Finally, there are several caveats to this study. First, the register data do not constitute a full sample of the population. For example, civil servants and farmers are not included. It is possible that these groups behave very differently. Most importantly, our approach was based on a nearest neighbour matching method that relied on the observable covariates in the data. Variables such as psychological disposition, lifestyle factors, and work characteristics were not included in our data, but may be important for understanding health impairments after divorce. Furthermore, to allow for a causal interpretation of our results, more rigorous testing and further sensitivity analysis would be needed.

Acknowledgments I am grateful to Anke Radenacker for her valuable comments. I would also like to acknowledge the Research Data Centre at the statutory German pension fund as my data distributer, and, in particular, Tatjana Mika. I am thankful for the valuable comments at the conference "18. Graduierten-Kolloquium des Forschungsnetzwerk Alterssicherung" held at the statutory German pension fund in Berlin. Finally, I want to thank the Forschungsnetzwerk Alterssicherung for providing me with financial support.

Appendix

Table 14.3 Four nearest neighbour matching summary parameter

Mean bias	1.2	2.5	0.8	1.9
Median bias	0.8	2.7	0.9	2.0
Max. difference in propensity score	.002372	.0114435	.0060626	.0004681

Notes: The mean and median bias are summary indicators of the standardised percentage bias. The bias refers to the percent difference of the sample means in the divorced and control sub-samples (for details see Rosenbaum and Rubin 1985)

Table 14.4 Weighted pooled OLS estimation with cumulated work disability and disability rate as the dependent variable over 12 years (t_{-7} to t_{+4})

	Men			Women					Women with children		Childless women	
	Cumulated		Rate		Cumulated		Rate		Cumulated		Cumulate	
Foreign	1.46		0.000		2.39	***	0.001	**	4.76	***	−9.67	***
Age	−4.24	***	0.000		−2.96	***	−0.001	***	−4.69	***	0.51	
Age^2	0.08	***	0.000	*	0.04	***	0.000	***	0.05	***	0.00	
Year file opening	0.15		0.000	**	0.06		0.000	***	0.47	***	−0.87	***
Month file opening	0.07		0.000		−0.10		0.000		−0.01		−0.05	
# children < age 3					2.30	***	0.000		1.39	**		
# children age 3–6					2.64	***	0.000	*	2.41	***		
# children > age 6					2.75	***	0.001	***	4.38	***		
Parental leave					−0.01	***	0.000	***	−0.01	***		
Unemployment rate	0.49		−0.001	***	0.38		0.000	***	0.20		0.22	
Employment	0.02	***	0.000	***	0.01	***	0.000	***	0.01	***	0.02	***
$Employment^2$	0.00	***	0.000	***	0.00	***	0.000	***	0.00	***	0.00	***
Earnings employment	−3.59	***	−0.001	***	−1.33	***	0.000	***	0.27		−4.15	***
Earnings $employment^2$	−0.01	***	0.000	***	0.00		0.000		−0.03	***	0.06	***
Military service	−0.04	***	0.000	***								
Vocational training	0.01	***	0.000	*	−0.01	***	0.000	***	−0.01	***	−0.01	***
Constant	−255		0.366	**	−70		0.373	***	−854	***	1730	***
R^2	0.06		0.01		0.04		0.01		0.04		0.01	

Notes: *** $p < 0.001$, ** $p < 0.01$, * $p < 0.05$. Further control variables are time since separation (coefficients are displayed in Figs. 14.1, 14.2 and 14.3)

Table 14.5 Adjusted Wald test for the equality of two coefficients

	Men		Women		Women with children	Women without children
Year	Cumulated	Rate	Cumulated	Rate	Cumulated	Cumulated
−7	0.206	0.009	0.000	0.388	0.000	0.107
−6	0.192	0.050	0.000	0.119	0.000	0.188
−5	0.172	0.061	0.000	0.333	0.000	0.208
−4	0.091	0.001	0.000	0.911	0.000	0.197
−3	0.051	0.005	0.000	0.009	0.000	0.232
−2	0.020	0.001	0.000	0.001	0.000	0.257
−1	0.004	0.000	0.000	0.346	0.000	0.173
0	0.000	0.000	0.000	0.000	0.000	0.095
1	0.000	0.000	0.000	0.000	0.000	0.069
2	0.000	0.000	0.000	0.000	0.000	0.024
3	0.000	0.001	0.000	0.006	0.000	0.021
4	0.000	0.024	0.000	0.014	0.000	0.008

Notes: Displayed are p-values for the H0 hypothesis that two coefficients (control and divorced) are equal

References

Andreß, H. J., & Bröckel, M. (2007). Income and life satisfaction after marital disruption in Germany. *Journal of Marriage and Family, 69*(2), 500–512. https://doi.org/10.1111/j.1741-3737.2007.00379.x.

Benítez-Silva, H., Disney, R., & Jiménez-Martín, S. (2010). Disability, capacity for work and the business cycle: An international perspective. *Economic Policy, 25*(63), 483–536.

Booth, A., & Amato, P. (1991). Divorce and psychological stress. *Journal of Health and Social Behavior, 32*(4), 396–407. https://doi.org/10.2307/2137106.

Booth, A., & Johnson, D. R. (1994). Declining health and marital quality. *Journal of Marriage and Family, 56*(1), 218–223. https://doi.org/10.2307/352716.

Brockmann, H., & Klein, T. (2004). Love and death in Germany: The marital biography and its effect on mortality. *Journal of Marriage and Family, 66*(3), 567–581. https://doi.org/10.1111/j.0022-2445.2004.00038.x.

Couch, K. A., Tamborini, C. R., & Reznik, G. L. (2015). The long-term health implications of marital disruption: Divorce, work limit, and social security disability benefits among men. *Demography, 52*(5), 1487–1512. https://doi.org/10.1007/s13524-015-0424-z.

Dupre, M. E., Beck, A. N., & Meadows, S. O. (2009). Marital trajectories and mortality among US adults. *American Journal of Epidemiology, 170*(5), 546–555. https://doi.org/10.1093/aje/kwp194.

Dykstra, P. A., & Fokkema, T. (2007). Social and emotional loneliness among divorced and married men and women: Comparing the deficit and cognitive perspective. *Basic and Applied Social Psychology, 29*(1), 1–12. https://doi.org/10.1080/01973530701330843.

Fu, H., & Goldman, N. (2000). The association between health-related behaviour and the risk of divorce in the USA. *Journal of Biosocial Science, 32*(1), 63–88. https://doi.org/10.1017/S0021932000000638.

Gerstel, N., Kohler Riessman, C., & Rosenfield, S. (1985). Explaining the symptomatology of separated and divorced women and men: The role of material conditions and social networks. *Social Forces, 64*(1), 84–101. https://doi.org/10.1093/sf/64.1.84.

Goldman, N. (1993). Marriage selection and mortality pattern: Inferences and fallacies. *Demography, 30*(2), 189–208. https://doi.org/10.2307/2061837.

Hannighofer, J., Foran, H., Hahlweg, K., & Zimmermann, T. (2017). Impact of relationship status and quality (family type) on the mental health of mothers and their children: A 10-year longitudinal study. *Frontiers in Psychiatry, 8*, 266. https://doi.org/10.3389/fpsyt.2017.00266.

Johnson, W., & Skinner, J. (1986). Labor supply and marital separation. *American Economic Review, 76*(3), 455–469.

Kalmijn, M., & Poortman, A. R. (2006). His or her divorce? The gendered nature of divorce and its determinants. *European Sociological Review, 22*(2), 201–214. https://doi.org/10.1093/esr/jci052.

Keck, W., & Mika, T. (2016, September 22–23). *Versorgungsausgleichsstatistik – Ein neuer Analysedatensatz des FDZ-RV*. Jahrestagung des FDZ der Rentenversicherung, Erkner. [The statistics of the equalization of pension points – A new data set of the FDZ-RV]. Annual Meeting of the Research Data Centers of the German Pension Fund]. Berlin.

Keck, W., Mika, T., & Sezgin, H. (2017). 40 Jahre Versorgungsausgleich: Wie wirkt er sich aus? [40 years of equalization of pension points: How does it matter?]. *RVaktuell (Fachzeitschrift und amtliche Mitteilungen der Deutschen Rentenversicherung), 64*, 181–188.

Keck, W., Mika, T., Kreyenfeld, M., & Radenacker, A. (forthcoming). *FDZ-RV scientific use file: Statutory pension insurance accounts and divorce*. Data documentation of the FDZ-RV.

Kruse, E. (2007). Empirische Ergebnisse zur Erwerbsbeteiligung älterer Versicherter anhand der Statistiken der gesetzlichen Rentenversicherung. [The employment of elderly insured persons based on the statistics of the German Pension Fund]. *DRV, 2007*(11–12), 716–749.

Leopold, T., & Kalmijn, M. (2016). Is divorce more painful when couples have children? Evidence from long-term panel data on multiple domains of well-being. *Demography, 53*(6), 1717–1742. https://doi.org/10.1007/s13524-016-0518-2.

Lillard, L. A., & Panis, W. A. (1996). Marital status and mortality: The role of health. *Demography, 33*(3), 313–327. https://doi.org/10.2307/2061764.

Rosenbaum, P. R., & Rubin, D. B. (1985). Constructing a control group using multivariate matched sampling methods that incorporate the propensity score. *The American Statistician, 39*(1), 33–38. https://doi.org/10.1080/00031305.1985.10479383.

Shor, E., Roelfs, D. J., Bugyi, P., & Schwartz, J. E. (2012). Meta-analysis of marital dissolution and mortality: Reevaluating the intersection of gender and age. *Social Science and Medicine, 75*(1), 46–59. https://doi.org/10.1016/j.socscimed.2012.03.010.

Sondergutachten. (2015). *Krankengeld – Entwicklung, Ursachen und Steuerungsmöglichkeiten*. [Sick benefits – Developments, causes and possibilities for intervention]. Bonn: Sachverständigenrat zur Begutachtung der Entwicklung im Gesundheitswesen.

Stegmann, M., & Himmelreicher, R. K. (2008). *Die Versicherungskontenstichprobe als scientific use file*. [The scientific use file of the Sample of Insurance Accounts]. DRV-Schriften Band, 79.

Syse, A., & Kravdal, Ø. (2007). Does cancer affect the divorce rate? *Demographic Research, 16*(15), 469–492. https://doi.org/10.4054/DemRes.2007.16.15.

Tamborini, C. R., Reznik, G. L., & Couch, K. A. (2016). Work disability among women: The role of divorce in a retrospective cohort study. *Journal of Health and Social Behavior, 57*(1), 98–117. https://doi.org/10.1177/0022146515627849.

Teachman, J. (2010). Work-related health limitations, education, and the risk of marital disruption. *Journal of Marriage and Family, 72*(4), 919–932. https://doi.org/10.1111/j.1741-3737.2010.00739.x.

Umberson, D. (1987). Family status and health behaviors: Social control as a dimension of social integration. *Journal of Health and Social Behavior, 28*(3), 306–319. https://doi.org/10.2307/2136848.

Umberson, D. (1992). Gender, marital status, and the social control of behaviour. *Social Science and Medicine, 34*(8), 907–917. https://doi.org/10.1016/0277-9536(92)90259-S.

Umberson, D., Williams, K., Powers, D. A., Hui, L., & Needham, B. (2006). You make me sick: Marital quality and health over the life course. *Journal of Health and Social Behavior, 47*(1), 1–16. https://doi.org/10.1177/002214650604700101.

Wade, T. J., & Pevalin, D. J. (2004). Marital transitions and mental health. *Journal of Health and Social Behavior, 45*(2), 155–170. https://doi.org/10.1177/002214650404500203.
Waite, L. J. (1995). Does marriage matter? *Demography, 32*(4), 483–507. https://doi.org/10.2307/2061670.
Williams, K., Sassler, S., & Nicholson, L. M. (2008). For better or for worse? The consequences of marriage and cohabitation for single mothers. *Social Forces, 86*(4), 1481–1511.
Wilmoth, J., & Koso, G. (2002). Does marital history matter? Marital status and wealth outcomes among preretirement adults. *Journal of Marriage and Family, 64*(1), 254–268. https://doi.org/10.1111/j.1741-3737.2002.00254.x.
Yorgason, J. B., Booth, A., & Johnson, D. (2008). Health, disability, and marital quality: Is the association different for younger versus older cohorts? *Research on Aging, 30*(6), 623–648. https://doi.org/10.1177/0164027508322570.
Zhang, Z., & Hayward, M. D. (2006). Gender, the marital life course, and cardiovascular disease in late midlife. *Journal of Marriage and Family, 68*(3), 639–657. https://doi.org/10.1111/j.1741-3737.2006.00280.x.

The manufacturer's authorised representative in the EU is Springer Nature Customer Service Centre GmbH, Europaplatz 3, 69115 Heidelberg, Germany. If you have any concerns regarding our products, please contact ProductSafety@springernature.com

Printed and bound by CPI Group (UK) Ltd, Croydon, CR0 4YY
05/10/2026
02228121-0016